The Schoolwide Enrichment Model:
A How-To Guide for Educational Excellence

Second Edition

The Schoolwide Enrichment Model:

A How-To Guide for Educational Excellence

by Joseph S. Renzulli
Sally M. Reis

Creative Learning Press, Inc.
P.O. Box 320, Mansfield Center, Connecticut 06250

Consulting Editors
Debra Briatico
Carol Moran

Book Layout & Design, Cover Design, and Graphics
Siamak Vahidi

Creative Learning Press, Inc.
P.O. Box 320
Mansfield Center, CT 06250
Phone: (860) 429-8118
Fax: (860) 429-7783

D edication

We dedicate this book, with gratitude and love, to Ray and Lynn Neag in appreciation for their generosity and their vision in the creation of the Neag Center for Gifted Education and Talent Development at the University of Connecticut.

Preface

Your **Contribution to This Book**

What's a Model?

Before beginning to read this book, it might be worthwhile to reflect for a moment about the meaning and purpose of this or any other plan that is designed to bring about selected changes in a school and the ways in which educators serve young people. The first consideration in answering the above question is the distinction between two categories of educational models. We will refer to one category as administrative models and the second as theoretical models.

Administrative models consist of patterns of school organization and procedures for dealing with such issues as how educators group students, develop schedules, and allocate time, money, and human resources. Administrative models focus mainly on how educators "move students around" and how they *arrange* for the delivery of services. Issues dealt with in administrative models might include homogeneous versus heterogeneous grouping, length of the school day or year, inclusion of special education students in regular classrooms, and whether or not educators should use a resource room or within-the-classroom program for the gifted.

Theoretical models, on the other hand, usually focus on the actual services that educators provide to students, regardless of the ways in which they organize their schools or school schedules. Theoretical models consist of principles that guide the learning process and give direction to the content of the curriculum, the assessment and instructional strategies that teachers use, and ways in which educators evaluate the extent and quality of what their students have learned. Theoretical models focus on the actual outcomes of learning experiences that might take place within any given administrative pattern of organization. Theoretical models are influential in determining the *quality* of school experiences, whereas administrative models are more concerned with the efficiency and "smoothness" of the school's operation.

Although the model presented in this book has certain implications for organizational patterns, we consider it a theoretical model because it is based on: (1) a series of assumptions about individual differences in learners, (2) principles of learning, and (3) recommended practices that logically follow from these assumptions and principals. A crucial consideration in selecting this or any other model is whether or not there is a consensus of agreement among teachers, parents, and administrators about the assumptions, principles, and recommended practices. We have found that when such a consensus exists, the relatively small organizational or administrative changes necessary for implementing the model are easily accomplished by most schools. Our experience has also shown that a theoretical model that infuses instructional practices into existing administrative patterns of organization has a higher probability of success than an approach that tries to completely reorganize the school.

All Roads Lead to Rome!

We believe that the selection and use of a program development model has two essential requirements. First, a model should consist of a shared mission and set of objectives. Everyone (or at the very least, almost everyone) involved in the selection and implementation of a model should agree that the mission and objectives represent a "destination" that they would like to reach. If an agreed upon goal is "to get to Rome," then there is no ambiguity, vagueness, or misunderstandings about where everyone is going.

This first requirement of a model means that a great deal of front end time should be spent exploring alternative models, discussing and debating the advantages and disadvantages of various approaches, and examining related factors such as underlying research, implementation in other schools, and the availability of supportive resources. Reaching consensus *before* embarking upon a journey will help ensure that everyone involved will get to Rome rather than to Venice or Moscow!

There Are Many Ways to Get to Rome

Although we believe that programs based on the Schoolwide Enrichment Model should strive to accomplish an agreed upon mission and set of objectives, we also believe that any plan for program development must allow for a great deal of flexibility in the achievement of its objectives. This flexibility is necessary because no written plan or set of procedures can take into account the variations that exist at the local school level. Differences in school populations, financial resources, the availability of persons from the community at large, and a host of other local variables must be considered in the implementation of this or any other approach to school improvement. A model that does not allow for such flexibility could easily become a straightjacket that simply will not work when one or more of the local considerations is not taken into account. Some schools will have supplementary resource teachers for advanced level students and others will not. Some school districts will have an abundance of community resources readily available and others, perhaps more geographically isolated, will have limited access to museums, planetariums, colleges and universities, etc. Some schools may serve larger proportions of culturally diverse students than others and certain districts may have such large numbers of high achieving students that it is conceivable that the entire school population might be considered a Talent Pool.

Another reason why we believe that a model for program development must maintain a large degree of flexibility is that educators tend to quickly lose interest in "canned" programs and models that do not allow for local initiative, creativity and teacher input.

New and better ways to provide enrichment experiences to students will be discouraged if program development does not encourage local adaptation and innovation to occur. This book provides a certain amount of general direction in both the development of program objectives and in the procedures for pursuing these objectives. At the same time, however, the specific types of activities that educators select and develop for their programs, and the ways in which they make these activities available to various populations of students will actually result in the creation of their own programming model. Educators will, in effect, be writing their own resource guide, because the actual content of the enrichment experiences will be developed locally by their own school personnel. We believe that if the Schoolwide Enrichment Model objectives are maintained, even if in a slightly modified form, a school's program will achieve the integrity that is sought in this total system approach. In this regard, the Schoolwide Enrichment Model that educators develop will attempt to achieve the best of two worlds! First, programs will benefit from the theoretical and research developments and the many years of field testing and practical application that have led to the advice put forth in this book. Second, the ideas, resources, innovations, and adaptations that emerge from local situations will contribute to the uniqueness and practicality of programs that are developed to meet local needs.

Throughout this book we have consistently recommended that educators should make whatever modifications and adaptations that are necessary to the particular procedures recommended for accomplishing various program tasks. We believe that there are many pathways and alternatives to reaching desired program outcomes. Once everyone in a school has agreed upon a destination, the uniqueness and excitement of the journey should involve the creation of an individualized plan for getting there. If all roads lead to Rome, what an unimaginative, and indeed, even boring world it would be.

Your contribution to this book is the way that you selectively adopt, adapt, and create the methods, materials, and organizational components that will make your school and program an *original* application of the Schoolwide Enrichment Model.

Table of Contents

Table of Contents

Table of Contents

Table of Contents

List of Figures

List of Figures

List of SIMSITS

SIMSITS (Simulation Situations) are teacher training activities that are designed to help educators better understand different aspects of the Schoolwide Enrichment Model. These simulated learning experiences provide lists of teacher training objectives; information about the number of persons involved, approximate time, and necessary materials and equipment; a facilitator's guide; detailed directions; and ideas for follow-up activities and discussion.

Chapter 1

The Schoolwide Enrichment Model and Educational Reform

- A Vision and a Plan
- A Bird's Eye View of the SEM
- A Brief History of the SEM
- The Three-Ring Conception of Giftedness
- An Overview of the Enrichment Triad Model
- Newest Directions for the SEM
- Framework of This Book

A Vision and a Plan

The Schoolwide Enrichment Model (SEM) has been developed around a shared vision that we have had for a number of years. This vision is also embraced by thousands of teachers and administrators with whom we have worked in academic programs and summer institutes that date back to the 1970's. Simply stated, this vision is that *schools are places for talent development* (Renzulli, 1994). Academic achievement is an important part of the vision and the model for school improvement described in this book. The things that have made our nation great and our society one of the most productive in the world are manifestations of talent development at all levels of human productivity. From the creators and inventors of new ideas, products, and art forms, to the vast array of people who manufacture, advertise, and market the creations that improve and enrich our lives, there are levels of excellence and quality that contribute to our standard of living and way of life.

This vision of schools for talent development is based on the belief that *everyone* has an important role to play in societal improvement and that everyone's role can be enhanced if educators provide all students with opportunities, resources, and encouragement to aspire to the highest levels of talent development. Rewarding lives are a function of ways people use individual potentials in productive ways. Accordingly, the SEM is a practical plan for making our vision of schools for talent development a reality. We are not naive about the politics, personalities, and financial issues that often supersede the pedagogical goals that are the focus of this book. At the same time, we have seen this vision manifested in schools ranging from hard core urban areas and frequently poor rural areas to affluent suburbs and combinations thereof. We believe that the strategies described in this book provide the guidance for making any school a place for talent development.

There are no quick fixes or easy formulas for transforming schools into places where talent development is valued and vigorously pursued. Our experience has shown that once the concept of talent development catches on, students, parents, teachers, and administrators begin to view their school in a different way. Students become more excited and engaged in what they are learning; parents find more opportunities to become involved in all aspects of their children's education; teachers begin to find and use a variety of resources that, until now, seldom found their way into classrooms; and administrators start to make decisions that affect learning rather than "tight ship" efficiency.

Everyone has a stake in schools that provide all of our young people with a high-quality education. Parents benefit when their children lead happy and successful lives. Employers and colleges benefit when they have access to people who are competent, creative, and effective in the work they do and in higher educational pursuits. Political leaders benefit when good citizens and a productive population contribute to a healthy economy, a high quality of life, and respect for the values and institutions of a democracy. Professional educators at all levels benefit when the quality of schools for which they are responsible is effective enough to create respect for their work and generous financial support for the educational enterprise.

Everyone has a stake in good schools because schools create and *re*create a successful modern society. Renewed and sustained economic growth and the well-being of all citizens means investing in high-quality learning the same way that previous generations invested in machines and raw materials. Our schools are already dumping millions of functionally illiterate young people into the workforce. More and more colleges are teaching remedial courses based on material formerly taught in high school and college graduates in almost all fields are experiencing difficulty entering career areas of choice.

Although everyone has a stake in good schools, America has been faced with a "school problem" that has resulted in declining confidence in schools and the people who work in them, drastic limitations in the amount of financial support for education, and general public apathy or dissatisfaction with the quality of education our young people are receiving. The parents of poor children have given up hope that education will enable their sons and daughters to break the bonds of poverty. The middle class, perhaps for the first time in our nation's history, is exploring government supported alternatives such as vouchers and tax credits for private schools, home schooling, charter schools, and summer and after-school programs that enhance admission to competitive colleges. A great deal has been written about America's "school problem" and studies, commissions, reports, and even a Governor's Summit Conference have been initiated to generate solutions to

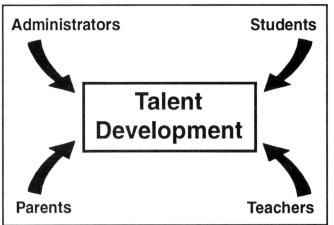

problems facing our schools. But the hundreds if not thousands of conferences, commissions, meetings, reports, proclamations, and lists of goals have yielded minimal results, because they generally focused on tinkering with traditional methods of schooling.

A Bird's Eye View of the SEM

The Schoolwide Enrichment Model (SEM) is a detailed blueprint for total school improvement that is flexible enough to allow each school to develop its own unique program based on local resources, student populations, school leadership dynamics, and faculty strengths and creativity. Although this research-supported model is based on highly successful practices that had their origins in special programs for gifted and talented students, its major goal is to promote both challenging and enjoyable high-end learning across the full range of school types, levels, and demographic differences. The model is not intended to replace or minimize existing services to high achieving students. Rather, its purpose is to integrate these services into "a-rising-tide-lifts-all-ships" approach to school improvement and expand the role of enrichment specialists by having these persons infuse specific practices for high-end learning into the total school program. The SEM provides educators with the means to:

- *Develop the talent potentials of young people by systematically assessing their strengths; providing enrichment opportunities, resources, and services to develop their strengths; and using a flexible approach to curricular differentiation and the use of school time.*
- *Improve the academic performance of all students in all areas of the regular curriculum and blend standard curriculum activities with meaningful enrichment learning.*
- *Promote continuous, reflective, growth-oriented professionalism of school personnel to such an extent that many faculty members emerge as leaders in curriculum and staff development, program planning, etc.*
- *Create a learning community that honors ethnic, gender, and cultural diversity and promotes mutual respect, democratic principles, and the preservation of the Earth's resources.*
- *Implement a collaborative school culture that includes appropriate decision making opportunities for students, parents, teachers, and administrators.*

Why Should Schools Focus on Talent Development?

Many people view America's public education system as a failed public monopoly. Policy makers, parents, educational leaders, and the corporate and business community are expressing the lowest level of confidence in public education in our nation's history. Parents of economically disadvantaged youth have all but given up on expectations that schools can improve their children's future and they have grown weary and suspicious of endless rhetoric and flavor-of-the-month reform initiatives that devour more and more of our limited dollars without producing any noticeable results. It doesn't take a rocket scientist or even a person who knows little more than elementary arithmetic to realize that the billions of federal and state dollars spent on remedial and compensatory education models have not produced achievement gains of any significance.

Lack of confidence in public education is also being expressed by middle class parents who have watched the slow but steady decline of SAT scores at the top-end of the achievement continuum. In an article entitled "The Other Crisis in Our Schools," Daniel Singal (1991) documented the effects of what happens when America's brightest students get a "dumbed-down" education. "The present generation of American parents has been failing in its obligation to provide its offspring with a high-quality education. . . . This failure will have specific consequences in a lower sense of professional fulfillment for these youngsters as they pursue their careers, and will hamper their ability to stay competitive with contemporaries in many European and Asian counties" (p. 74). The middle class has become so disenchanted with the quality of public education, that for the first time in history, they are asking for *public* funds to pursue private educational alternatives.

A Brief History of the SEM

The original Enrichment Triad Model (Renzulli, 1976) was developed in the mid-1970s and initially implemented by school districts primarily in New England. The model, which was initially field tested in several districts, proved to be quite popular and requests from all over the country for visitations to schools using the model and for information about how to implement the model increased. A book about the Enrichment Triad Model (Renzulli, 1977a) was published and more and more districts began asking for help in implementing this approach. It was at this point that a clear need was established for research about the effectiveness of the model and for other vehicles that could provide technical assistance for interested educators who wanted to develop programs in their schools. We had become fascinated by the different types of programs being developed by different types of teachers. In some programs, for example, Teacher A consistently elicited high levels of creative productivity in students while, Teacher B had *few* students who engaged in this type of work. In some districts, many enrichment opportunities were regularly offered to students not formally identified for the program, while in other districts only identified "gifted" students had any access to enrichment experiences. We wondered how we could replicate the success of one teacher or one district in implementing the model. For example, if Teacher A consistently produced high levels of creative productivity in students, how could we capture that skill and use it to provide professional development for other teachers? If certain resources proved to be consequential in promoting desirable results, how could we make those resources available to larger numbers of teachers and students? We became increasingly interested in why the model was working and how we could further expand the theoretical rationale underlying our work. Thus began almost twenty years of field testing, research, and dissemination.

In the almost two decades since the Enrichment Triad Model has been used as the basis for educational programs for high potential students, an unusually large number of examples of creative productivity have occurred on the parts of young people whose educational experiences have been guided by this plan. Perhaps, like others involved in the development of theories and generalizations, we did not fully understand at the onset of our work the full implications of the model for encouraging and developing creative productivity in young people. These implications relate most directly to teacher training, resource procurement and management, product evaluation, and other theoretical concerns (e.g., motivation, task commitment, self-efficacy) that probably would have gone unexamined, undeveloped, and unrefined without the favorable results that were reported to us by early implementers of the model. We became increasingly interested in how and why the model was working and how we could further expand the theoretical rationale underlying our work and the population to which services could be provided. Thus, almost two decades of research and field testing and an examination of the work of other theorists has resulted in the Schoolwide Enrichment Model described in this book.

The Three-Ring Conception of Giftedness

Research on creative/productive people has constantly shown that although no single criterion can be used to determine giftedness, persons who have achieved recognition because of their unique accomplishments and creative contributions possess a relatively well-defined set of three interlocking clusters of traits. These clusters consist of above average (not necessarily superior) ability, task commitment, and creativity (see Figure 1). It is important to point out that no single cluster "makes giftedness." Rather, it is interaction among the three clusters that research has shown to be the necessary ingredient for creative/productive accomplishment (Renzulli, 1978). This interaction is represented by the shaded portion of Figure 1. It is also important to point out that each cluster plays an important role in contributing to the display of gifted behaviors. This point is emphasized because one of the major errors that continues to be made in identification procedures is to over-emphasize superior cognitive abilities at the expense of the other two clusters of traits.

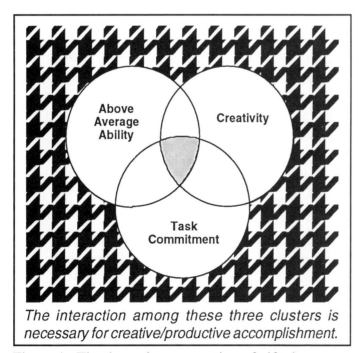

The interaction among these three clusters is necessary for creative/productive accomplishment.

Figure 1. The three-ring conception of giftedness.

Above Average Ability

Above average ability can be defined in two ways, general ability and specific ability.

1. General Ability consists of the capacity to process information, integrate experiences that result in appropriate and adaptive responses in new situations, and engage in abstract thinking. Examples of general ability are verbal and numerical reasoning, spatial relations, memory, and word fluency. These abilities are usually measured by tests of general aptitude or intelligence and are broadly applicable to a variety of traditional learning situations.

2. Specific Ability consists of the capacity to acquire knowledge and skill or the ability to perform in one or more activities of a specialized kind and within a restricted range. These abilities are defined in a manner that represents the ways in which human beings express themselves in real life (i.e., non-test) situations. Examples of specific abilities include chemistry, ballet, mathematics, musical composition, sculpture, and photography. Each specific ability can be further subdivided into even more specific areas (e.g., portrait photography, astrophotography, photo journalism, etc.). Specific abilities in certain areas such as mathematics and chemistry have a strong relationship with general ability and, therefore, some indication of potential in these areas can be determined from tests of general aptitude and intelligence. They can also be measured by achievement tests and tests of specific aptitude. Many specific abilities, however, cannot be easily measured by tests and must be evaluated through one or more performance-based assessment techniques.

Within this model the term *above average ability* will be used to describe both general and specific abilities. Above average should also be interpreted to mean the upper range of potential within any given area. Although it is difficult to assign numerical values to many specific areas of ability, we believe that people with well above average ability are individuals who are capable of performance or the potential for performance that is representative of the top 15 to 20 percent of any given area of human endeavor.

Task Commitment

The second cluster of traits that consistently has been found in creative/productive persons is a refined or focused form of motivation, known as task commitment. Whereas motivation is usually defined in terms of a general energizing process that triggers responses in organisms, task commitment represents energy that is brought to bear upon a particular problem (task) or specific performance area. The terms that are most frequently used to describe task commitment are perseverance, endurance, hard work, dedicated practice, self-confidence, and a belief in one's ability to carry out important work. In addition to perceptiveness (Albert, 1975) and a better sense for identifying significant problems (Zuckerman, 1979), research on persons of unusual accomplishment has consistently shown that a special fascination for and involvement with the subject matter of one's chosen field "are the almost invariable precursors of original and distinctive work" (Barron, 1969, p. 3). Even in young people who Bloom and Sosniak (1981) identified as extreme cases of talent development, early evidence of task commitment was present. Bloom and Sosniak report that ". . . after age 12 our talented individuals spent as much time on their talent field each week as their average peer spent watching television" (p. 94).

The argument for including this non-intellective cluster of traits in a definition of giftedness is nothing short of overwhelming. From popular maxims and autobiographical accounts to hard core research findings, one of the key ingredients that has characterized the work of gifted persons is their ability to involve themselves totally in a specific problem or area for an extended period of time.

Research on persons with high levels of creative productive behavior display a striking similarity in its major conclusions. First, academic ability (as traditionally measured by tests or grade point averages) shows limited relationships to creative/productive accomplishments. Second, non-intellectual factors, and especially those that are related to task commitment, consistently play an important part in the cluster of traits that characterize highly productive people. Although this second cluster of traits is not as easily and objectively identifiable as general cognitive abilities, these traits are, nevertheless, a major component of giftedness and should be reflected in our definition.

Creativity

The third cluster of traits that characterizes gifted persons consists of factors that usually have been lumped together under the general heading of "creativity." As one reviews the literature in this area, it becomes readily apparent that the words gifted, genius, and eminent creators or highly creative persons are used synonymously. In much of the research reviewed in previous publications about the three-ring conception of giftedness, the persons ultimately selected for intensive study were in fact recognized because of their creative accomplishments.

When discussing creativity, it is important to consider the problems researchers have encountered in establishing relationships between creativity tests and other more substantial accomplishments. A major issue that has been raised by several investigators deals with whether or not tests of divergent thinking actually measure "true" creativity. Although some validation studies have reported limited relationships between measures of divergent thinking and creative performance criteria (Torrance, 1969; Shapiro, 1968; Dellas & Gaier, 1970; Guilford, 1967), the research evidence for the predictive validity of such tests has been limited. Unfortunately, very few tests have been validated against real-life criteria of creative accomplishment; however, future longitudinal studies using these relatively new instruments might show promise of establishing higher levels of predictive validity. Although divergent thinking is indeed a characteristic of highly creative persons, caution should be exercised in the use and interpretation of tests designed to measure this capacity.

Given the inherent limitations of creativity tests, a number of writers have focused their attention on alternative methods for assessing creativity. Among others, Nicholls (1972) suggests that an analysis of creative products is preferable to the trait-based approach in making predictions about creative potential and Wallach (1976) proposes that student self-reports about creative accomplishment are sufficiently accurate to provide a usable source of data.

Although few persons would argue against the importance of including creativity in a definition of giftedness, the conclusions and recommendations discussed above raise the haunting issue of subjectivity in measurement. In view of what the research suggests about the questionable value of more objective measures of divergent thinking, perhaps the time has come for persons in all areas of endeavor to develop more careful procedures for evaluating the products of candidates for special programs.

A Definition of Gifted Behavior

Although no single statement can effectively integrate the many ramifications of the research studies described above, the following definition of gifted behavior attempts to summarize the major conclusions and generalizations resulting from this review of research:

> *Gifted behavior consists of behaviors that reflect an interaction among three basic clusters of human traits—above average ability, high levels of task commitment, and high levels of creativity. Individuals capable of developing gifted behavior are those possessing or capable of developing this composite set of traits and applying them to any potentially valuable area of human performance. Persons who manifest or are capable of developing an interaction among the three clusters require a wide variety of educational opportunities and services that are not ordinarily provided through regular instructional programs.*

The three-ring representation of this definition (see Figure 1) and the taxonomy of behavioral manifestations for each cluster (see Figure 2) represent a summary of the major concepts and conclusions emanating from the work of the theorists and researchers discussed above. As is always the case with lists of traits that indicate gifted behavior, there is an overlap among individual items and an interaction between and among the general categories and the specific traits. It is also important to point out that all of the traits need not be present in any given individual or situation to produce a display of gifted behaviors. It is for this reason the three-ring conception of giftedness emphasizes the interaction among the clusters rather than any single cluster. It is also for this reason that we believe gifted behaviors take place in certain people (not all people), at certain times (not all the time), and under certain circumstances (not all circumstances).

Discussion About the Three Rings

Since the original publication of the three-ring conception of giftedness (Renzulli, 1978), a number of questions have been raised about the overall model and the interrelationships between and among the three rings. In this section we will use the most frequently asked questions as an outline for a discussion that hopefully will clarify some of the concerns raised by persons who have expressed interest (both positive and negative) in this particular approach to the conception of giftedness.

? **Are There Additional Clusters of Abilities That Should Be Added to the Three-Ring Conception of Giftedness?**

One of the most frequent reactions to this work has been the suggestion that the three clusters of traits portrayed in the model do not adequately account for the development of gifted behaviors. An extensive examination of the research on human abilities has led to an interesting conclusion about this question and has resulted in a modification of the original model. This modification is represented graphically by the houndstooth background in which the three rings are now imbedded (see Figure 1).

The major conclusion is that the interaction among the original three rings is still the most important feature leading to the display of gifted behaviors. There are, however, a host of other factors that must be taken into account in our efforts to explain what causes some persons to display gifted behaviors at certain times and under certain circumstances. These factors have been grouped into the two traditional dimensions of studies about

Taxonomy of Behavioral Manifestations of Giftedness

Above Average Ability

General Ability

High levels of abstract thinking, verbal and numerical reasoning, spatial relations, memory and word fluency.

Adaptation to and the shaping of novel situations encountered in the external environment.

The automatization of information processing. Rapid, accurate and selective retrieval of information.

Specific Ability

The application of various combinations of the above general abilities to one or more specialized areas of knowledge or areas of human performance (e.g., the arts, leadership, administration).

The capacity for acquiring and making appropriate use of advanced amounts of formal knowledge, tacit knowledge, technique, logistics, and strategy in the pursuit of particular problems or the manifestation of specialized areas of performance.

The capacity to sort out relevant and irrelevant information associated with a particular problem or area of study or performance.

Task Commitment

The capacity for high levels of interest, enthusiasm, fascination and involvement in a particular problem, area of study or form of human expression.

The capacity for perseverance, endurance, determination, hard work and dedicated practice.

Self-confidence, a strong ego and a belief in one's ability to carry out important work, freedom from inferiority feelings and drive to achieve.

The ability to identify significant problems within specialized areas. The ability to tune into major channels of communication and new developments within given fields.

Setting high standards for one's work, maintaining an openness to self and external criticism, developing an aesthetic sense of taste, quality and excellence about one's own work and the work of others.

Creativity

Fluency, flexibility and originality of thought.

Openness to experience; receptive to that which is new and different (even irrational) in the thoughts, actions, and products of oneself and others.

Curious, speculative, adventurous and "mentally playful." Willing to take risks in thought and action, even to the point of being uninhibited.

Sensitive to detail, aesthetic characteristics of ideas and things. Willing to act upon and react to external stimulation and one's own ideas and feelings.

Figure 2. Taxonomy of behavioral manifestations of giftedness.

human beings commonly referred to as personality and environment. The research[1] clearly shows that the factors that influence gifted behavior each play varying roles in the manifestation of gifted behaviors. What is even more important is the interaction between the two categories and among the numerous factors listed in Figure 3. [Note: A houndstooth pattern was selected (over an earlier checkerboard design) in an effort to convey this interaction.] When we consider the almost limitless number of combinations between and among the factors listed, it is easy to realize why so much confusion has existed about the definition of giftedness.

An analysis of the role that personality and environment play in the development of gifted behaviors is beyond the scope of this book. In many ways for school persons who are charged with the responsibility of identifying and developing gifted behaviors, personality and environment are beyond the realm of their direct influence. Each of the factors in Figure 3 shares one or a combination of two characteristics. First, most of the personality factors are long-term developmental traits or traits that in some cases are genetically determined. Although educators can play an important role in developing things like courage and need for achievement, it is highly unrealistic to believe that educators can shoulder the major responsibility for overall personality formation. Second, many factors such as socioeconomic status, parental personalities, and family position are chance factors that are given at birth and must be dealt with as such by educators. They can't tell a child to be first born or to have parents who stress achievement. It is for these reasons that our efforts have been concentrated on the three sets of clusters set forth in the original model. Of course, certain aspects of the original three clusters are also chance factors, but a large amount of research clearly has shown that creativity and task commitment are in fact modifiable and can be influenced in a highly positive fashion by purposeful kinds of educational experiences (Reis & Renzulli, 1982). Although the jury is still out on the issue of how much of one's ability is influenced by heredity and environment, it seems safe to conclude that abilities (both general and specific) can be influenced to varying degrees by the best kinds of learning experiences.

? **Are the Three Rings Constant?**

Most educators and psychologists would agree that the above average ability ring represents a generally stable or constant set of characteristics. In other words, if an individual shows high ability in a certain area such as mathematics, it is almost undeniable the mathematical ability was present in the months and years preceding a "judgment day" (i.e., a day when identification procedures took place) and that these abilities will also tend to remain high in the months and years following any given identification event. In view of the types of assessment procedures that are most readily available and economically viable, it is easy to see why this type of giftedness has been so popular in making decisions about entrance into special programs. Educators always feel more comfortable and confident with traits that can be reliably and objectively measured, and the "comfort" engendered by the use of such tests often causes them to ignore or only pay lip service to the other two clusters of traits.

---

[1] Literally hundreds of research studies have been carried out on the factors listed in Figure 3.

Factors Influencing Gifted Behavior

Personality Factors	**Environmental Factors**
Perception of Self/Self Efficacy	SES
Courage	Parental Personalities
Character	Education of Parents
Intuition	Stimulation of Childhood Interests
Charm or Charisma	Family Position
Need for Achievement	Formal Education
Ego Strength	Role Model Availability
Energy	Physical Illness and/or Well Being
Sense of Destiny	Chance Factors
Personal Attractiveness*	Zeitgeist

* Although personal attractiveness is undoubtedly a physical characteristic, the ways in which others react to one's physical being are quite obviously important determinants in the development of personality.

Figure 3. Factors influencing gifted behavior.

In our identification model discussed in Chapter 4, we use above average ability as the major criterion for identifying a group of students who are referred to as the Talent Pool. This group generally consists of the top 10 to 15 percent of the general school population. Test scores, teacher ratings, and other forms of "status information" (i.e., information that can be gathered and analyzed at fixed point in time) are of practical value in making certain kinds of first-level decisions about accessibility to some of the general services that should be provided by a special program. This procedure guarantees admission to those students who earn the highest scores on cognitive ability tests. Primary among the services provided to Talent Pool students are procedures for making appropriate modifications in the regular curriculum in areas where advanced levels of ability can be clearly documented. It is nothing short of common sense to adjust the curriculum in those areas where high levels of proficiency are shown. Indeed, advanced coverage of traditional material and accelerated courses should be the "regular curriculum" for those students who demonstrate high ability in one or more school subjects.

The task commitment and creativity clusters are a different story! These traits are not either present or absent in the same permanent fashion as pointed out in our mathematics example above. Equally important is the fact that educators cannot assess them in the highly objective and quantifiable means that characterize test score assessment of traditional cognitive abilities. Educators simply cannot put a percentile on the value of a creative idea nor can they assign a standard score to the amount of effort and energy that a student might be willing to devote to a highly demanding task. Creativity and task commitment "come and go" as a function of the various types of situations in which certain individuals become involved.

There are three things that we know for certain about the creativity and task commitment clusters. First, *creativity and task commitment are variable rather than permanent.* Although there may be a tendency for some individuals to "hatch" more creative ideas than others and have greater reservoirs of energy that promote more frequent and intensive involvement in situations, a person is not either creative or not creative in the same way that one has high ability in mathematics or musical composition. Almost all studies of highly accomplished individuals clearly indicate that their work is characterized by peaks and valleys of both creativity and task commitment. One simply cannot (and probably should not) operate at maximum levels of output in these two areas on a constant basis. Even Thomas Edison, who is still acknowledged to be the world's record holder of original patents, did not have a creative idea for a new invention every waking moment of his life. The most productive persons have consistently reported "fallow" periods and even experiences of "burn out" following long and sustained encounters with the manifestation of their talents.

Creativity and Task Commitment Clusters

1. **They are variable rather than permanent.**

2. **They can be developed through appropriate stimulation and training.**

3. **Both clusters almost always stimulate one another.**

Second, *task commitment and creativity can be developed through appropriate stimulation and training.* We also know that because of variations in interests and receptivity, some people are more influenced by certain situations than others. The important point, however, is that educators cannot predetermine which individuals will respond most favorably to a particular type of stimulation experience. Through general interest assessment techniques and a wide variety of stimulus variation, educators can increase the probability of generating a greater number of creative ideas and increased manifestations of task commitment in Talent Pool students. In our identification model, the ways in which students react to planned and unplanned stimulation experiences has been termed "action information." This type of information constitutes the second level of identification and can be used to make decisions about which students might revolve into more individualized and advanced kinds of learning activities. The important distinction between status and action information is that the latter type cannot be gathered before students have been selected for entrance into a special program. Giftedness, or at least the beginnings of situations in which gifted behaviors might be displayed and developed, is in the responses of individuals rather than in the stimulus events. This second level identification procedure is part of the general enrichment experiences that are provided for Talent Pool students and is based on the concept of *situational testing* that has been described in the theoretical literature on tests and measurements (Freeman, 1962, p. 538).

Third, *creativity and task commitment clusters almost always stimulate one another.* When a person gets a creative idea, the idea is encouraged and reinforced by oneself and/or others. The person decides to "do something" with the idea and, as a result, his or her commitment to the task begins to emerge. Similarly, a large commitment to solving a particular problem will frequently trigger the process of creative problem solving.

Students participating in a SEM should be patently aware of opportunities involving creative ideas and commitments that have been stimulated in areas of particular interest. Similarly, persons responsible for special programming should be knowledgeable about strategies for reinforcing, nurturing, and providing appropriate resources to students at those times when creativity and/or task commitment are displayed.

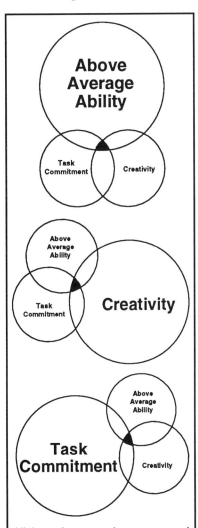

All three rings must be present and interacting to some degree for creative/productive behavior to emerge, though they need not be of equal size.

? Are the Rings of Equal Size?

In the original publication of the three-ring conception of giftedness, it was stated that the clusters must be viewed as "equal partners" in contributing to the display of gifted behaviors. This position should be modified slightly (see margin), but first let us set forth an obvious conclusion about lesson-learning giftedness. We do not doubt that the higher a person's traditionally measured cognitive ability, the better equipped the person will be to perform in most traditional (lesson) learning situations. As was indicated earlier, the abilities that enable individuals to perform well on intelligence and achievement tests are the same kinds of thinking processes called for in most traditional learning situations. The above average ability cluster is a predominant influence in lesson-learning giftedness.

When it comes to creative/productive giftedness, however, we believe that an interaction among all three clusters is necessary for high level performance. This is not to say that all clusters must be of equal size and that the size of the clusters must remain constant throughout the pursuit of creative/productive endeavors. For example, task commitment may be minimal or even absent at the inception of a very large and robust creative idea and the energy and enthusiasm for pursuing the idea may never be as large as the idea itself. Similarly, there are undoubtedly cases in which an extremely creative idea and a large amount of task commitment will overcome somewhat lesser amounts of traditionally measured ability. Such a combination may even cause a person to increase her or his ability by gaining the technical proficiency needed to see an idea through to fruition. Because we cannot assign numerical values to the creativity and task commitment clusters, empirical verification of this interpretation of the three rings is impossible. But case studies based on the experience of creative/ productive individuals and research that has been carried out on programs using this model (Reis, 1981) clearly indicate that larger clusters do in fact compensate for somewhat decreased size on one or both of the other two areas. The important point, however, is that *all three rings must be present and interacting to some degree in order for high levels of productivity to emerge.*

An Overview of the Enrichment Triad Model

The Triad Model was designed to encourage creative productivity on the part of young people by exposing them to various topics, areas of interest, and fields of study and to further train them to apply advanced content, process-training skills, and methodology training to self-selected areas of interest. Accordingly, three types of enrichment are included in the Enrichment Triad Model (see Figure 4).

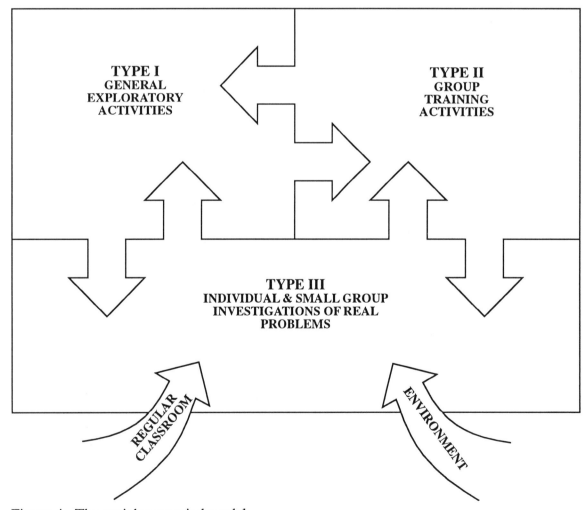

Figure 4. The enrichment triad model.

Type I Enrichment (see Chapter 7) is designed to expose students to a wide variety of disciplines, topics, occupations, hobbies, persons, places, and events that would not ordinarily be covered in the regular curriculum. In schools that use this model, an Enrichment Team consisting of parents, teachers, and students often organizes and plans Type I experiences by contacting speakers, arranging demonstrations or performances, or by ordering and distributing films, slides, videotapes, or other print or non-print media.

Type II Enrichment (see Chapter 8) consists of materials and methods designed to promote the development of thinking and feeling processes. Some Type II Enrichment is general and includes training in areas such as creative thinking and problem solving, learning how-to-learn skills such as classifying and analyzing data, and advanced reference and communication skills. Type II training, usually carried out in classrooms and enrichment programs, includes the development of:

1. Creative thinking and problem solving, critical thinking, and affective processes.
2. A wide variety of specific learning how-to-learn skills.
3. Skills in the appropriate use of advanced-level reference materials.
4. Written, oral, and visual communication skills.

Other Type II Enrichment is specific and cannot be planned in advance. In this case, it usually involves advanced instruction in an interest area selected by the student.

Type III Enrichment (see Chapter 9) involves students who become interested in pursuing a self-selected area and are willing to commit the time necessary for advanced content acquisition and process training in which they assume the role of a first-hand inquirer. The goals of Type III Enrichment include:

- *Providing opportunities for applying interests, knowledge, creative ideas, and task commitment to a self-selected problem or area of study.*
- *Acquiring advanced-level understanding of the knowledge (content) and methodology (process) that are used within particular disciplines, artistic areas of expression, and interdisciplinary studies.*
- *Developing authentic products that are primarily directed toward bringing about a desired impact upon a specified audience.*
- *Developing self-directed learning skills in the areas of planning, organization, resource utilization, time management, decision making, and self-evaluation.*
- *Developing task commitment, self-confidence, and feelings of creative accomplishment.*

The Revolving Door Identification Model (RDIM)

As our experience with Triad programs grew, our concern about students identified to participate in these programs also grew. We became increasingly concerned about students who were not able to participate in enrichment programs because they did not score in the top 1-3 percent of the population in achievement or intelligence tests.

Research conducted by Torrance (1962) had demonstrated that students who were rated highly on creativity measures did well in school and on achievement tests, but were often not selected for gifted programs because their scores fell below the cutoff for admission. Other research (Reis, 1981) indicated that when a broader population of students (15-20% of the general population) were able to participate in Types I and II Enrichment, they produced equally good Type III products as the traditional "gifted" students (the top 3-5%). This research produced the rationale for the Revolving Door Identification Model (RDIM) (Renzulli, Reis, & Smith, 1981) in which a Talent Pool of students received regular enrichment experiences and the opportunity to "revolve into" Type III creative productive experiences. In RDIM, we recommend that students be selected for participation in the Talent Pool on the basis of multiple criteria, including indices of creativity, because we believe that one of the major purposes of gifted education is to develop creative thinking and creative productivity in all students. Once identified and placed in the Talent Pool through the use of test scores, nominations (teacher, parent, or self), and examples of creative potential or productivity, students are observed in classrooms and enrichment experiences for signs of advanced interests, creativity, or task commitment. We have called this part of the process "action information" and have found it to be an instrumental part of the identification process in assessing students' interest and motivation to become involved in Type III creative productivity. Further support for this approach has been offered by Kirschenbaum (1983) and Kirschenbaum and Siegle (1993). The development of the RDIM led to the need for a guide that covered all the components of the previous Triad and the new RDIM. The resulting work was entitled *The Schoolwide Enrichment Model* (Renzulli & Reis, 1985).

The Schoolwide Enrichment Model

In the Schoolwide Enrichment Model (SEM), a Talent Pool of 10-15% of above average ability/high potential students can be identified through a variety of measures including: achievement tests, teacher nominations, assessment of potential for creativity and task commitment, and alternative pathways of entrance (self-nomination, parent nomination, etc.). High achievement test and IQ test scores automatically include a student in the Talent Pool, enabling those students who are underachieving in their academic school work to be included.

Once students are identified for the Talent Pool, they are eligible for several kinds of services. First, interest and learning styles assessments are used with Talent Pool students. Informal and formal methods help create and identify students' interests and encourage them to further develop and pursue their interests in various ways. Learning style preferences are also assessed and include: projects, independent study, teaching games, simulations, peer teaching, programmed instruction, lecture, drill and recitation, and discussion. Second, curriculum compacting (see Chapter 6) is provided to all eligible students for whom the regular curriculum is modified by eliminating portions of previously mastered content. This elimination or streamlining of curriculum enables above average students to avoid repetition of previously mastered work and guarantees mastery, while simultaneously finding time for more appropriately challenging activities (Reis, Burns, & Renzulli, 1992; Renzulli, Smith, & Reis, 1982). A form, entitled the Compactor, (Renzulli & Smith, 1978a) is used to document which content areas have been compacted and what alternative work has been substituted. Third, the Enrichment Triad Model offers three types of enrichment experiences to all students—Type I, II, and III Enrichment. However, Type III Enrichment is usually more appropriate for students with higher levels of ability, interest, and task commitment.

Separate studies on the SEM demonstrated its effectiveness in schools with widely differing socioeconomic levels and program organization patterns (Olenchak, 1988; Olenchak & Renzulli, 1989; Renzulli & Reis, 1994). The SEM has been implemented in several more school districts across the country (Burns, 1992b) and interest in this approach continues to grow.

Newest Directions for the SEM

Current school reform initiatives have resulted in heightened awareness on the part of administrators and policy makers about the expanded role of enrichment specialists and the role that enrichment programs can play in school reform. These programs have been the true laboratories of our nation's schools, because they have presented ideal opportunities for testing new ideas and experimenting with potential solutions to long standing educational problems. Programs for high potential students have been an especially fertile place for experimentation because such programs are usually not encumbered by prescribed curriculum guides or traditional methods of instruction. It was within the context of these programs that the thinking skills movement first took hold in American education and the pioneering work of notable theorists such as Benjamin Bloom, Howard Gardner, and Robert Sternberg first gained the attention of the education community. Other developments that had their origins in special programs are currently being examined for general practice. These developments include: a focus on concept rather than skill learning; the use of interdisciplinary curriculum and theme-based studies, student portfolios, performance assessment, cross-grade grouping, and alternative scheduling patterns; and opportunities for students to exchange traditional roles as lesson-learners and doers-of-exercises for more challenging and demanding roles that require hands-on learning, first-hand investigations, and the application of knowledge and thinking skills to complex problems.

The present reform initiatives in general education have created a more receptive atmosphere for more flexible approaches that challenge all students, and accordingly, the SEM has evolved based on the previous experiences and current changes in general education. The title of a new book describing the SEM is *Schools for Talent Development: A Practical Plan for Total School Improvement* (Renzulli, 1994). Chapter 2 describes the school structures upon which the model is targeted and the major components of the new SEM.

Framework of This Book

This book provides a practical plan for transforming schools into places where all students are encouraged to develop their talents and offers a step-by-step method for implementing the SEM in any school or district. It is intended to replace the previous edition, *The Schoolwide Enrichment Model* (Renzulli & Reis, 1985), and it infuses experience from more than ten intervening years of research. Chapter 2 provides an overview of the components that are new to the SEM and the remaining chapters describe the components and practical techniques for implementing the SEM. Chapter 3 discusses the importance of careful planning and development of an Enrichment Team for the success of the program. Chapter 4 details a flexible system for identifying students with potential and demonstrated talents. In chapters 5 and 6, the *Total Talent Portfolio* and curriculum modification techniques are presented. Chapters 7-10 offer various types of enrichment teaching and learning that are presented in the model including Type I, Type II, and Type III Enrichment and enrichment clusters. Appendices A and B contain a collection of Action Forms that educators can use to plan, organize, and evaluate different aspects of the SEM. The intent of this book is to present a practical step-by-step procedure for implementing components of the SEM in any school or district.

Chapter 2

Using the SEM as a Plan for School Improvement

- • The Secret Laboratory of School Improvement
- • Developing Gifted Behaviors in All Students
- • The Schoolwide Enrichment Model
- • School Structures
- • Service Delivery Components
- • The Enrichment Triad Model
- • Three Key Ingredients of School Improvement

Two afternoons a week, 12 year-old Kevin goes to an enrichment cluster at the Noah Webster School in Hartford, Connecticut. When he was selected for the program, Kevin said, "It feels good, but I was amazed. I was about to faint! I was super, super surprised." The reason for Kevin's amazement is that he never considered himself to be a good student, at least not in the traditional way educators usually view students. The program was not exactly the place where you found kids like Kevin, who lived in subsidized housing and whose family managed to survive on a monthly welfare check and food stamps.

But the program Kevin is enrolled in looks at talent development in a different way. Based on the Schoolwide Enrichment Model (SEM), the program seeks to identify a broad range of talent potentials in all students through the use of a strength assessment guide called the Total Talent Portfolio. This guide helps to focus attention on student interests and learning style preferences, as well as strengths in traditional subjects. These strengths serve as building blocks for advanced achievement. Kevin's strongest academic area is mathematics, and through a process called curriculum compacting, he is now being provided with mathematics material that is two grade levels above the level of math being covered in his classroom.

Kevin, who once described himself as a "mental dropout," now finds school a much more inviting place. He is hoping to enter the research he is doing on airplane wing design in his enrichment cluster into a state science fair competition. He is also thinking about a career in engineering. The enrichment specialist at his school has helped him apply for a special summer program at the University of Connecticut that is designed to recruit and assist minorities in mathematical and engineering-related professions. "School," says Kevin, "is a place where you have must-dos and can-dos. I work harder on my must-dos so I can spend more time working on my can-dos."

The Secret Laboratory of School Improvement

Kevin represents one example of the ways in which numerous students are given opportunities to develop talent potentials that too many schools have ignored for many years. The type of program in which Kevin is enrolled is not a radical departure from present school structures, but is based on assumptions about learners and learning that are different from those that have guided public education for many years. The factory model of schooling that gave rise to the clear and present danger facing our schools cannot be used to overcome the very problems that this model of schooling has created. And yet, as educators examine reform initiatives, it is difficult to find plans and policies that are qualitatively different from the established top-down patterns of school organization or the traditional linear/sequential models of learning that have dominated almost all of the curriculum used in their schools. Transcending these previous levels of consciousness will not be an easy task. If there is any single, unifying characteristic of present day schools, that characteristic is surely a resistance, if not an immunity, to change. The ponderous rhetoric about school improvement and the endless lists of noble goals need to be tempered with a gentle and evolutionary approach to change that school personnel can live and grow with rather than be threatened by. If the traditional methods of schooling have failed to bring about substantial changes, educators must look at different models that have shown promise of achieving the types of school improvement they have so desperately sought.

The SEM has demonstrated its effectiveness in bringing about significant changes in schooling. It is a systematic set of specific strategies for increasing student effort, enjoyment, and performance, and for integrating a broad range of advanced level learning experiences and higher order thinking skills into any curricular area, course of study, or pattern of school organization. The general approach of the SEM is one of infusing more effective practices into existing school structures rather than layering on additional tasks for schools to perform. This research-supported plan is designed for general education, but it is based on a large number of instructional methods and curricular practices that have their origins in special programs for high ability students.

Developing Gifted Behaviors in All Students

Research opportunities in a variety of special programs allowed us to develop instructional procedures and programming alternatives that emphasize the need to: (1) provide a broad range of advanced level enrichment experiences for *all* students and (2) use the many and varied ways that students respond to these experiences as stepping stones for relevant follow-up on the parts of individuals or small groups. This approach is not viewed as a new way to identify who is or is not "gifted!" Rather, the process simply identifies how subsequent *opportunities, resources,* and *encouragement* can be provided to support continuous escalations of student involvement in both required and self-selected activities. This approach to the development of high levels of multiple potentials in young people is purposefully designed to sidestep the traditional practice of labeling some students "gifted" (and by implication, relegating all others to the category of "non-gifted"). The term, "gifted," is used in our lexicon only as an adjective, and even then, it is used in a developmental perspective. We prefer to speak and write about the development of *gifted behaviors* in specific areas of learning and human expression instead of giftedness as a state of being. This orientation has allowed many students opportunities to develop high levels of creative and productive accomplishments that otherwise would have been denied through traditional special program models.

Practices that have been a mainstay of many special programs for the "gifted" are being absorbed into general education by reform models designed to upgrade the performance of all students. This integration of gifted program know-how is viewed as a favorable development for two reasons. First, the adoption of many special program practices is indicative of the viability and usefulness of both the know-how of special programs and the role enrichment specialists can and should play in total school improvement. It is no secret that compensatory education in the U.S. has largely been a failure! An overemphasis on remedial and mastery models has lowered the challenge level of materials for the very population that these programs attempt to serve. Second, *all* students should have opportunities to develop higher order thinking skills and pursue more rigorous content and first-hand investigative activities than those typically found in today's "dumbed down" textbooks. The ways in which students respond to enriched learning experiences should be used as a rationale for providing all students with advanced level follow-up opportunities. This approach reflects a democratic ideal that accommodates the full range of individual differences in the entire student population and it opens the door to programming models that develop the talent potentials of many at-risk students who traditionally have been excluded from anything but the most basic types of curricular experiences. In order to operationalize this ideal, educators need to "get serious" about the things they have learned during the past several years about programming models and human potential.

The application of gifted program know-how into general education is supported by a wide variety of research on human abilities (Bloom, 1985; Gardner, 1983; Renzulli, 1986; Sternberg, 1985). This research clearly and unequivocally provides a justification for much broader conceptions of talent development. These conceptions argue against the restrictive student selection practices that guided identification procedures in the past. Lay persons and professionals at all levels have begun to question the efficacy of programs that rely on narrow definitions, IQ scores, and other cognitive ability measures as the primary method for identifying students who can benefit from differentiated services. Traditional identification procedures have restricted services to small numbers of high scoring students and excluded large numbers of at-risk students whose potentials are manifested in other ways. This will be discussed in a later section that describes an SEM component called the Total Talent Portfolio.

Special services should be viewed as opportunities to develop "gifted behaviors" rather than merely finding and certifying them. In this regard, educators should judiciously avoid saying that a young person is either "gifted" or "not gifted." It is difficult to gain support for talent development when educators use statements such as "Elaine is a gifted third grader" as a rationale. These kinds of statements offend many people and raise the accusations of elitism that have plagued special programs. Note the difference in orientation when educators focus on the behavioral characteristics that brought this student to their attention in the first place: "Elaine is a third grader who reads at the ninth grade level and has a fascination for biographies about women of scientific accomplishment." The logical and justifiable services provided for Elaine include:

1. Under the guidance of her classroom teacher, Elaine was allowed to substitute more challenging books in her interest area for the third grade reader. The enrichment specialist helped the classroom teacher locate these books, which were purchased with funds from the enrichment program budget.
2. Elaine was allowed to leave the school two afternoons a month (usually on early dismissal days) to meet with a mentor who was a local journalist specializing in gender issues. The enrichment specialist arranged transportation with the help of the school's parent volunteer group.
3. During time made available through curriculum compacting in her strength areas (reading, language arts and spelling), the enrichment specialist helped Elaine prepare a questionnaire and interview schedule for use with local women scientists and female science faculty members at a nearby university.

Could even the staunchest anti-gifted proponent argue against the logic or the appropriateness of these services? When programs focus on developing the behavioral potential of individuals or small groups who share a common interest, it is no longer necessary to organize groups merely because they all happen to be "gifted third graders."

The Schoolwide Enrichment Model

The programming model that we have advocated since the early 1970's has always argued for a behavioral definition of giftedness and a greater emphasis on applying gifted program know-how to larger segments of the school population. The model is currently being used in hundreds of school districts across the country including major urban areas such as New York City, Detroit, St. Paul, San Antonio, and Fort Worth. The present reform initiatives in general education have created a more receptive atmosphere for more flexible approaches that challenge all students. We have organized the SEM so that it blends into school improvement activities that are currently taking place throughout the country. The following sections will present an overview of the school structures upon which the model is targeted and the three service delivery components. A graphic representation of the model is presented in Figure 5.

School Structures

The Regular Curriculum

The regular curriculum consists of everything that is a part of the predetermined goals, schedules, learning outcomes, and delivery systems of the school. The regular curriculum might be traditional, innovative, or in the process of transition, but its predominant feature is that authoritative forces (i.e., policy makers, school councils, textbook adoption committees, state regulators) have determined that the regular curriculum should be the "centerpiece" of student learning.

Application of the SEM influences the regular curriculum in three ways. First, the challenge level of required material is differentiated through processes such as curriculum compacting, textbook content modification procedures, and group jumping strategies. Second, the systematic content intensification procedures used to replace eliminated content with selected, in-depth learning experiences increases the challenge level by introducing the broad underlying principles of a discipline. Third, types of enrichment recommended in the SEM (described below) are integrated selectively into regular curriculum activities. Although our goal is to influence, rather than replace the regular curriculum, application of certain SEM components and related staff development activities have resulted in substantial changes in both the content and instructional processes of the entire regular curriculum.

Enrichment Clusters

Enrichment clusters are non-graded groups of students and adults who share common interests and come together during specially designated time blocks to pursue these interests (see Chapter 10). Like extra-curricular activities and programs such as 4-H and Junior Achievement, the main rationale for participation in one or more clusters is that *students and teachers want to be there.* All teachers (including music, art, physical

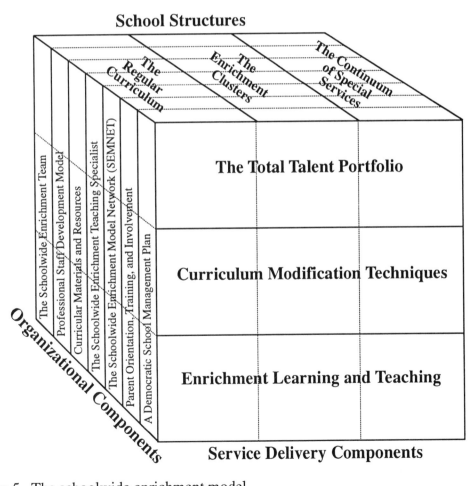

Figure 5. The schoolwide enrichment model.

education, instructional assistants, etc.) are involved in facilitating the clusters and teacher involvement in any particular cluster is based on the same type of interest assessment used for students. Community resource persons, parents, and other students are also invited to organize enrichment clusters.

The model for learning used with enrichment clusters is based on an inductive approach to the pursuit of real-world problems rather than traditional, didactic modes of teaching. This approach, called "enrichment learning and teaching," is purposefully designed to create a learning environment that places a premium on the development of higher order thinking skills and the authentic application of these skills in creative and productive situations. The theory underlying this approach is based on the work of constructivist theorists such as Jean Piaget, Jerome Bruner, and John Dewey and applications of constructivist theory to classroom practice. Enrichment clusters are excellent vehicles for promoting cooperativeness within the context of real-world problem solving and providing superlative opportunities for promoting self-concept. A major assumption underlying the use of enrichment clusters is that *every child is special if educators create conditions in which that child can be a specialist within a speciality group.*

Enrichment clusters are organized around major disciplines, interdisciplinary themes, or cross-disciplinary topics (e.g., a theatrical/television production group that includes actors, writers, technical specialists, costume designers, etc.). The clusters are modeled after the ways in which knowledge utilization, thinking skills, and interpersonal relations take place in the real world. Thus, all work is directed toward the production of a product or service. There are no lesson plans or unit plans. Direction is provided by the following key questions:

1. What do people with an interest in this area do?
2. What products or services do they provide?
   a. What are the different roles that are necessary to produce the product or service?
   b. What are the methods and resources used by professionals to produce high-quality products?
3. How and with whom do they communicate the results of their work?
4. Who are the people in our community interested in the product or service we will produce/provide?
5. What steps need to be taken to ensure that our product or service will have an impact on our audience?

The enrichment clusters are not intended to be the total program for talent development in a school, but they are a major vehicle for stimulating interests and developing talent potentials across the entire school population. They are also vehicles for staff development since they provide teachers an opportunity to participate in enrichment teaching. In this regard, the model promotes a spill-over effect by encouraging teachers to become better talent scouts and talent developers and apply enrichment techniques to regular classroom situations.

Schedules for and organization of clusters vary according to the needs of the school. Enrichment clusters are used by some schools on a half-day per week basis and in other schools as a daily occurrence. At one elementary school in St. Paul, Minnesota, a broad array of interdisciplinary clusters are offered daily. At another elementary school in Mansfield, Connecticut, enrichment clusters are offered two afternoons a month and taught jointly by teachers, administrators, and parent volunteers.

The Continuum of Special Services

A broad range of special services is the third school structure that is targeted by the model. A diagram representing these services is presented in Figure 6. Although the enrichment clusters and the SEM-based modifications of the regular curriculum provide a broad range of services to meet individual needs, a program for total talent development still requires supplementary services that challenge young people who are capable of working at the highest levels of their special interest areas. These services, which cannot ordinarily be provided in enrichment clusters or the regular curriculum, typically include: individual or small group counseling, direct assistance in the facilitation of advanced level work, arrangements involving mentorships with faculty members or community persons, and connections between students, their families, and out-of-school persons, resources, and agencies. For example, the schoolwide enrichment coordinator in one school district developed a Parent-Teacher Enrichment Guide of the city and surrounding area that included information about a wide variety of enrichment opportunities for parents and teachers.

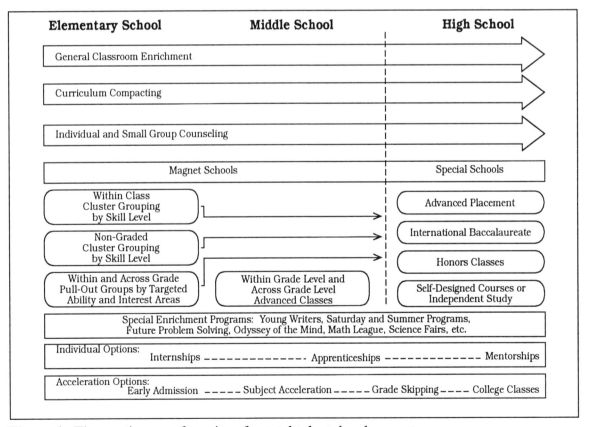

Figure 6. The continuum of services for total talent development.

Direct assistance involves setting up and promoting student, faculty, and parental involvement in special programs such as Future Problem Solving, Odyssey of the Mind, the Model United Nations program, and state and national essay, mathematics, and history contests. Another type of direct assistance consists of arranging out-of-school involvement for individual students in summer programs, on-campus courses, special schools, theatrical groups, scientific expeditions, and apprenticeships at places where advanced level learning opportunities are available. Provision of these services is one of the responsibilities of the schoolwide enrichment specialist or an Enrichment Team of teachers and parents who work together to provide options for advanced learning. A schoolwide enrichment specialist in Barrington, Rhode Island estimates she spends two days a week in a resource capacity to the faculties of two schools and three days providing direct services to students.

Cluster Grouping (An Example of One Service on the Continuum)

Cluster grouping is a popular and often recommended strategy for meeting the needs of high achieving students in the regular classroom. It has gained popularity in recent years due to heterogeneous grouping policies and financial cutbacks that have eliminated special programs for gifted and talented students (Purcell, 1993). Cluster grouping has been defined as the intentional placement of a group of high achieving or gifted students in an otherwise heterogeneous classroom with a teacher who has both the background and willingness to provide appropriate challenges for these students (McInerney, 1983).

Current research indicates that there are several major benefits of cluster grouping. First, gifted students interact with their intellectual peers, as well as their age peers on a regular basis. Second, cluster grouping provides services for gifted students without additional cost to the school district (Hoover, Sayler, & Feldhusen, 1993; LaRose, 1986; Rogers, 1991; Winebrenner & Devlin, 1994). Third, cluster grouping facilitates continuous programming for gifted or high achieving students in the regular classroom (Gentry, 1996; Hoover et al., 1993). Finally, recent research has shown the effective implementation of cluster grouping may have benefits that reach beyond the high achievers and the "cluster classroom" to students of all achievement levels and to other classroom teachers as well (Gentry, 1996). The following points provide a rationale upon which any thoughtful implementation of cluster grouping might be based (Gentry, 1996):

- *The program is cost effective.*
- *Students are clustered with their intellectual peers, as well as with age peers.*
- *The highest achieving students are placed with teachers who have had training and are interested in meeting their special needs.*
- *More efficient use of special education and chapter personnel is achieved by creating clusters of these students in one or two rooms instead of spreading them across several rooms.*
- *The highest achieving students are removed from other classrooms, thereby allowing new leaders and achievers to emerge.*
- *Some heterogeneous grouping is maintained while there is a deliberate reduction in the number and diversity of achievement groups that each teacher must teach.*

- *A high achieving or above average group of students exists in all classrooms.*
- *High expectations for all students are maintained across all classrooms.*

The use of cluster grouping allows an elementary school to:

1. Reduce the number of achievement groups that each teacher has in his/her classroom, while maintaining somewhat heterogeneous classes.
2. Place a group of above average students in every teacher's classroom.
3. Cluster the high achieving students in one classroom.
4. Cluster the students needing special services in classrooms with resource personnel assistance.
5. Honor parental requests for specific teachers.
6. Evenly distribute behavior problems among all classrooms.
7. Involve the teachers in developing the class lists.

Cluster grouping, when used in conjunction with challenging instruction and high teacher expectations, may improve how teachers view their students with respect to ability and achievement. With the highest achieving students grouped in one classroom, teachers in the other classrooms may have opportunities to recognize the talents and achievement of other students. Additionally, students who may not have been regarded as achievers may be recognized when the traditional high achievers are removed from the classroom and placed together in another classroom. These findings are contrary to popular views in the reform movement that believe grouping somehow damages the low achieving students (George, 1993; Oakes, 1985; Slavin, 1987; Wheelock, 1992), and should be considered together with analyses of ability grouping (Kulik & Kulik, 1992; Rogers, 1991) when decisions are made regarding how children will be placed in elementary classrooms. Cluster grouping may provide students with opportunities for academic growth as well as recognition by their teachers, and should be seriously considered by elementary school teachers and administrators.

Steps to Successful Cluster Grouping

1. Provide staff inservice.
2. Provide parent education on the program.
3. Identify student need—divide students into groups based on teacher input, parent input, and achievement test scores.
4. Adapt instruction to meet those needs.
5. Maintain ongoing communication and collaboration among teachers, administration, and parents.
6. Assess student achievement.

Service Delivery Components

The Total Talent Portfolio

The case study of Elaine presented earlier is an example of the ways in which the SEM targets specific learning characteristics that can serve as a basis for talent development. Our approach to targeting learning characteristics uses both traditional and performance-based assessment to compile information about three dimensions of the learner—abilities, interests, and learning styles. This information, which focuses on strengths rather than deficits, is compiled in a folder called the *Total Talent Portfolio* (*TTP*) and used to make decisions about talent development opportunities in regular classes, enrichment clusters, and in the continuum of special services.

Two questions summarize the intent of the *TTP*: (1) What are the very best things we know and can record about a student's best work? and (2) What are the best ways we can utilize this information to nurture a student's talents? This expanded approach to identifying talent potential is essential if educators are to make genuine efforts to include more underrepresented students in a plan for total talent development. This approach is also consistent with a more flexible plan for developing gifts and talents in all students. Chapter 5 presents the *TTP* in depth and discusses details for its implementation.

Curriculum Modification Techniques

The second service delivery component of the SEM is a series of curriculum modification techniques that are designed to: (1) adjust levels of required learning so that all students are challenged, (2) increase the number of in-depth learning experiences, and (3) introduce various types of enrichment into regular curricular experiences. The procedures used to carry out curriculum modification are numerous, including: curriculum compacting, textbook analysis and surgical removal of repetitious material from textbooks, and a planned approach for introducing greater depth into regular curricular material (see Figure 7).

Curriculum compacting (Reis, Burns, & Renzulli, 1992), described in Chapter 6, is a systematic procedure for modifying or streamlining the regular curriculum in order to eliminate repetition of previously mastered material, upgrading the challenge level of the regular curriculum, and providing time for appropriate enrichment and/or acceleration activities. This process includes: (1) defining the goals and outcomes of a particular unit or segment of instruction, (2) determining and documenting which students have already mastered most or all of a specified set of learning outcomes or students who are capable of mastering them in less time than their peers, and (3) providing replacement activities for material already mastered through the use of instructional options that enable a more challenging and productive use of a student's time. These options include content acceleration, individual or group research projects, peer teaching, and involvement in non-classroom activities discussed in the section on the continuum of services. A key feature of these options is that students have some freedom to make decisions about the topic and the methods through which the topic will be pursued. Curriculum compacting might best be thought of as organized common sense, because it simply recommends the natural pattern that teachers ordinarily follow when

Recommended Practices for Curriculum Modification and Differentiation

1. Administer interest inventories, learning styles questionnaires, and surveys regarding prior experiences or use teacher observations to identify student preferences, strengths, out-of-school accomplishments and talents.
2. Analyze and modify existing curriculum units to eliminate redundancy and increase authenticity, challenge, and the alignment between objectives, assessment, and teaching and learning activities.
3. Give students an overview of the curriculum unit or an initial learning activity that explains major goals and activities, demonstrates relevance, and enhances student motivation for learning.
4. Develop differentiated, open-ended, or product-oriented assignments to address individual differences.
5. Allow students the opportunity to communicate prior knowledge or experience with learning activities or objectives and indicate strengths, needs, and preferences for learning activities, products or extension activities.
6. Organize flexible, small group instruction to address individual differences with respect to unit objectives.
7. Implement some form of pretesting or preassessment prior to the beginning of an instructional unit, as a technique for identifying the extent to which individual students understand or can apply specific curriculum objectives.
8. Use a variety of large group teaching strategies (lecture, media, demonstration, hands-on activities, discussion, simulation, etc.) to ensure student engagement and learning.
9. Incorporate community resources or the services of districtwide curriculum specialists to increase student attention and content authenticity and promote talent development.
10. Provide explicit, strategy-based instruction to promote skills (e.g., cognitive, research, data collection, affective, communication and methodological) as necessary to promote independent inquiry.
11. Construct interest centers, discovery centers, contracts or optional assignments to strengthen independent learning skills and address individual needs, strengths and interests.
12. Offer problem solving simulations and activities that ask students to transfer learning objectives to authentic and complex applications and scenarios that require creativity and the use of higher level thinking skills.
13. Encourage students to pursue the answers to their own questions by providing suggestions and the opportunity for individual projects and exploratory learning activities.
14. Involve parents in home-based enrichment activities, tutoring, and the completion of challenging homework assignments.

—Deborah E. Burns

Figure 7. Recommended practices for curriculum modification and differentiation.

individualizing instruction or teaching in the days before textbooks were invented. Compacting might also be thought of as the "mirror image" of remedial procedures that have always been used in diagnostic/prescriptive models of teaching.

The second procedure for making adjustments in regular curricular material is the examination of textbooks in order to determine which parts can be economized upon through textbook analysis and "surgical" removal of repetitious drill and practice. The textbook *is* the curriculum in the overwhelming majority of today's classrooms. Despite all of the rhetoric about school and curriculum reform, this situation is not likely to change in the near future. Until such time that high quality textbooks are universally available, it is essential to deal with the curriculum situation as it currently exists. Although curriculum compacting is one procedure that can be used to get an unchallenging curriculum "off the backs" of students who are in need of curriculum modifications, the procedure is a form of "damage control." Therefore, educators need to take a more proactive stance to overcome the well-documented low levels of American textbooks.

The procedures for carrying out the textbook analysis and surgical removal process are based on the argument that "less is better" when it comes to content selection, and it is necessary to make wise decisions when determining which material will be covered in greater depth. The first step in the process might best be described as "textbook triage." Each unit of instruction is examined by grade-level teams to determine which material is needless repetition of previously covered skills and concepts. When repetition is eliminated, teachers then decide which material is necessary for review and important enough to cover in either a survey or an in-depth manner. What teachers teach is at the very heart of professional competency. The textbook analysis and surgical removal process offers teachers an opportunity to come together as a group of professionals around specific tasks within and across grade levels and subject areas to perform these important operations.

Adding more in-depth learning experiences is the third curriculum modification procedure. This approach is based on the work of Phenix (1964), who recommends that a focus on representative concepts and ideas is the best way to capture the essence of a topic or area of study. Representative ideas or concepts consist of themes, patterns, main features, sequences, organizing principles and structures, and the logic that defines an area of study. Representative ideas and concepts can also be used as the basis for interdisciplinary or multidisciplinary studies.

While the use of representative concepts allows teachers to capture the essence of an area of study, it also allows them to introduce economy into content selection. The vast amount of material within any given discipline prevents unlimited coverage of content. Therefore, material must be selected so that it is both representative and maximally transferable. Excellent resources are available to assist in this process. Books such as the *Dictionary of the History of Ideas* (Weiner, 1973) contain essays that cover every major discipline and emphasize interdisciplinary and cross-cultural relationships. The essays are cross-referenced to direct the reader to other articles which contain similar ideas in other domains. Additional resources can be found in books such as the *Syntopicon: An Index to the Great Ideas* (Adler, 1990), which lists concepts, ideas, and themes around which curriculum can be developed.

In-depth teaching is also concerned with the level of advancement or complexity of the material. First and foremost, the material must take into consideration the age, maturity, previous study, and background experiences of students. Beyond these considerations, three principles of content selection are recommended. First, curricular material should be selected so that it escalates along the hierarchy of knowledge dimensions: facts, conventions, trends and sequences, classifications and categories, criteria, principles and generalizations, and theories and structures. Second, movement toward the highest level, theories and structures, should involve continuous recycling to lower levels so that facts, trends and sequences, etc., can be understood in relation to a more integrated whole rather than as isolated bits of irrelevant information. Third, the cluster of diverse procedures surrounding the acquisition of knowledge, that dimension of learning commonly referred to as "process" or thinking skills, should themselves be viewed as a form of content. These more enduring skills form the cognitive structures and problem solving strategies that have the greatest transfer value.

A final characteristic of in-depth learning is a focus on methodology. This focus is designed to promote an understanding of and appreciation for the *application* of methods to the kinds of problems that are the essence of fields of knowledge. The goal of this emphasis on methodology is to cast the young person in the role of a first-hand inquirer, rather than a mere learner-of-lessons, even if this role is carried out at a more junior level than that of the adult professional. This role encourages young learners to engage in the kinds of thinking, feeling, and doing that characterizes the work of the practicing professional, because it automatically creates confrontations with knowledge necessary for active rather than passive learning!

Enrichment Learning and Teaching

The third service delivery component of the SEM is enrichment learning and teaching. Enrichment learning and teaching is based on the ideas of a small but influential number of philosophers, theorists, and researchers.[2] The work of these theorists, coupled with our own research and program development activities, has given rise to the concept we call enrichment learning and teaching. The best way to define this concept is in terms of the following four principles:

1. Each learner is unique, and therefore, all learning experiences must be examined in ways that take into account the abilities, interests, and learning styles of the individual.
2. Learning is more effective when students enjoy what they are doing, and therefore, learning experiences should be constructed and assessed with as much concern for enjoyment as for other goals.
3. Learning is more meaningful and enjoyable when content (i.e., knowledge) and process (i.e., thinking skills, methods of inquiry) are learned within the

---

[2] Although it is beyond the scope of this chapter to review the work of these eminent thinkers, the group includes: William James, Alfred North Whitehead, John Dewey, Maria Montessori, Jean Piaget, Paul Torrance, Jerome Bruner, Philip Phenix, Howard Gardner, Robert Sternberg, and Albert Bandura.

context of a real and present problem. Attention should be given to opportunities that personalize student choice in problem selection, the relevance of the problem for individual students at the time the problem is being addressed, and authentic strategies for addressing the problem.

4. Some formal instruction may be used in enrichment learning and teaching, but a major goal of this approach to learning is to enhance knowledge and thinking skill acquisition that is gained through formal instruction with applications of knowledge and skills resulting from a student's own construction of meaning.

The ultimate goal of learning that is guided by these principles is to replace dependent and passive learning with independent and engaged learning. Although all but the most conservative educators will agree with these principles, much controversy exists about how these (or similar) principles might be applied in everyday school situations. A danger also exists that these principles might be viewed as yet another idealized list of glittering generalities that cannot be manifested easily in schools which are entrenched in the deductive model of learning. Developing a school program based on these principles is not an easy task. Over the years, however, we have achieved a fair amount of success by gaining faculty, administrative, and parental consensus on a small number of easy-to-understand concepts and related services and by providing resources and training related to each concept and service delivery procedure. Numerous research studies (summarized in Renzulli & Reis, 1994) and field tests in schools with widely varying demographics have been conducted. These studies and field tests have provided opportunities for the development of large amounts of practical know-how that are readily available for schools that would like to implement the SEM.

The Enrichment Triad Model

In order for enrichment learning and teaching to be systematically applied to the learning process, it must be organized in a way that makes sense to teachers and students. The Enrichment Triad Model (Type I, Type II, and Type III Enrichment), introduced in the previous chapter, is used for this purpose. The role and function of each type of enrichment was presented in Chapter 1 (see Figure 4) and is again explained in greater detail in Chapters 7, 8, and 9. Here, we discuss three considerations that relate to the model in general.

Learning in a Natural Way

The Enrichment Triad Model is based on the ways in which people learn in a natural environment rather than the artificially structured environment that characterizes most classrooms. Just as scientists "look to nature" when they attempt to solve particular types of problems, the process of learning is examined as it unfolds in the non-school world. This process is elegant in its simplicity! External stimulation, internal curiosity, necessity, or combinations of these three starting points cause people to develop an interest in a topic, problem, or area of study. Humans are, by nature, curious, problem solving beings. However, in order for them to act upon a problem or interest with some degree of commitment and enthusiasm, the interest must be sincere and one in which they see a personal reason for taking action. Once the problem or interest is personalized, a need is created to gather information, resources, and strategies for acting upon the problem.

Problem solving in nature almost always results in a product or service that has a functional, artistic, or humanitarian value. The learning that takes place in real-problem situations is *collateral learning* that results from attacking the problem in order to produce a product or service. It was precisely this kind of natural problem solving situation that gave rise to the Enrichment Triad Model. The only difference between the natural learning that takes place in real-life situations and the use of the Triad Model within the more structured world of the school is that we view products as vehicles through which a wide variety of more enduring and transferable processes can be developed. Learning that focuses on the interaction between product and process results in the kinds of learning experiences that enhance both the present and the future.

More Than a Sum of the Parts

A second general consideration about the Enrichment Triad Model is that the interaction between and among the three types of enrichment is as important as any type of

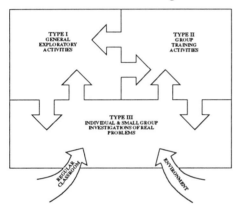

enrichment or the collective sum of all three types. In other words, the arrows in Figure 4 are as important as the individual cells, because they give the model dynamic properties that cannot be achieved if the three types of enrichment are pursued independently. A Type I experience, for example, may have value in and of itself, but it achieves maximum payoff if it leads to Type II or III experiences. In this regard, it is a good idea to view Type I and II Enrichment as "identification situations" that may lead to Type III experiences, which are the most advanced type of enrichment in the model.

As Figure 4 indicates, the regular curriculum and the environment in general (i.e., non-school experiences) can also serve as pathways of entry into Type III activities. An identification situation is simply an experience that allows students and teachers an opportunity to: (1) participate in an activity, (2) analyze their interest in and reaction to the topic covered in the activity and the processes through which the activity was pursued, and (3) make a purposeful decision about their interest in the topic and the diverse ways further involvement may be carried out. Type I and II Enrichment are general forms of enrichment that are usually pursued with larger groups of students. Type III Enrichment, on the other hand, is pursued only on a voluntary and self-selected basis.

All three types of enrichment occurred in an enrichment cluster entitled *Invention Convention* at an elementary school in Windham, Connecticut. In the cluster, students learned about inventors and became interested in their work (Type I), then learned about the process of inventing (Type II), and later transferred their knowledge into a creative product by developing their own inventions that offered a new solution to a problem (Type III). The inventions were then part of a local science fair and invention convention.

The interactiveness of the three types of enrichment also includes what are sometimes called the "backward arrows" in Figure 4 (e.g., the arrows leading back from Type III to

Type I). In many cases, the advanced work of students can be used as Type I and II experiences for other students. For example, the students who developed inventions (Type III's) in their enrichment cluster and presented their work at a science fair, promoted awareness about inventions and stimulated potential new interests (Type I's) in other students. In this regard, the model is designed to renew itself and bring students "inside" the pedagogy of the school enterprise, rather than viewing learning from a spectator's perspective.

Personal Knowledge/Metacognition

A third consideration about the Enrichment Triad Model in general is that it is designed to help students gain personal knowledge about their own abilities, interests, and learning styles. If, as Socrates said, "The unexamined life is not worth living," then educators should also consider a corollary to this axiom about life in school: "The unexamined lesson is not worth learning!" While it would be desirable to apply this corollary to all school experiences, the types of enrichment advocated in the Triad Model are excellent vehicles for examining preferences, tastes, and inclinations that will help students gain a greater understanding of themselves.

This corollary is operationalized in the model by recommending debriefings and post-learning analyses (sometimes called meta-learning) about both *what* has been learned and *how* a particular segment of learning has been pursued. Following exposure to a particular instructional style, a careful post-learning analysis should be conducted that focuses on the unique properties of the purposefully selected instructional technique. Students should be encouraged to discuss and record in personal journals their reactions to the instructional technique in terms of both efficiency in learning and the amount of pleasure they derive from the technique. The goal of the post-learning analysis is to help students understand more about themselves by understanding more about their preferences in a particular situation. Thus, the collective experiences in learning styles should provide: (1) exposure to many styles, (2) an understanding of which styles are the most personally applicable to particular subjects, and (3) experience in how to blend styles in order to maximize both the effectiveness and satisfaction of learning.

It is helpful to keep in mind that the Triad Model is part of the service delivery component that is targeted on three school structures: the regular curriculum, the enrichment clusters, and the continuum of special services. In many ways, enrichment learning and teaching can be thought of as an overlay which can be applied to these three school structures.

Three Key Ingredients of School Improvement

If the traditional methods of schooling have failed to bring about substantial changes, we must look to different models that show promise of achieving the types of school improvement we so desperately need. New models must focus their attention on three major dimensions of schooling—the act of learning, the use of time, and the change process itself.

The Act of Learning

School improvement must begin by placing the *act of learning* at the center of the change process. Organizational and administrative structures such as vouchers, site-based management, school choice, multi-aged classes, parent involvement, and extended school days are important considerations, but they do not *directly* address the crucial question of how educators can improve what happens in classrooms where teachers, students, and curriculum interact with one another. One of the things we have done in developing the SEM is to base all recommendations for school improvement on the learning process. It is beyond the scope of this summary to explain all components of the act of learning, but a figural representation of the learning process is depicted in Figure 8. The "Learner Circle" highlights important components that students bring to the act of learning. Thus, when examining the learner, educators must take into consideration: (1) present achievement levels in each area of study, (2) the learner's interest in particular topics and the ways in which they can enhance present interests or develop new interests, and (3) the preferred styles of learning that will improve the learner's motivation to pursue the material that is being studied. Likewise, the teacher and curriculum dimensions have subcomponents that must be considered when educators place the act of learning at the center of the school improvement process (Renzulli, 1992).

The Use of Time

Although it would be interesting to speculate about why schools have changed so little over the centuries, at least part of the reason has been our unwillingness to examine critically the issue of school time. If the ways we currently use school time were producing remarkably positive or even adequate results, there might be an argument for maintaining the traditional schedule and calendar. But such is not the case.

A universal pattern of school organization that has emerged over the years has contributed to our inability to make even the smallest changes in the overall process of learning. This universal pattern is well known to educators and lay persons alike. The "major" subject matter areas (Reading, Mathematics, Science, Language Arts, and Social Studies) are taught on a regular basis, five days per week. Other subjects, sometimes called "the specials," such as Music, Art, and Physical Education, are taught once or twice a week. So accustomed have educators become to the rigidity of this schedule that even the slightest hint about possible variations is met with a storm of protest. "We don't have time *now* to cover the regular curriculum." "How will we fit in the specials?" "They keep adding new things (Drug Education, Sex Education, etc.) for us to cover." The uncontested acceptance of the elementary and secondary school schedule causes educators to lose sight of the fact that at the college level, where material is ordinarily more advanced and demanding, they routinely drop from a five meetings per week schedule to a two-day or three-day per-week schedule of class meetings. The adherence to the more-time-is-better argument fails to take into account research that shows quite the opposite. For example, international comparison studies report that 8 of the 11 nations that surpass U.S. achievement levels in mathematics spend less time on math instruction than do American schools (Jaeger, 1992). In the SEM, a number of alternative scheduling patterns are based on selectively "borrowing" one or two class meetings per month from the major subject areas. This approach guarantees that a designated time will be available each week for advanced-level enrichment clusters.

The Process of Change: A Gentle and Evolutionary (But Realistic) Approach

The approach to school improvement being recommended in this model is realistic, because it focuses on those aspects of learning and development over which schools have the most influence, and, therefore, the highest probability of achieving success. Schools are being bombarded with proposals for change. These proposals range from total "systemic reform" to tinkering with bits and pieces of specific subjects and teaching methods. Oftentimes, the proposals are little more than lists of intended goals or outcomes. Even less information is provided about the effectiveness of recommended practices in a broad range of field test sites. Worse yet are the mixed messages that

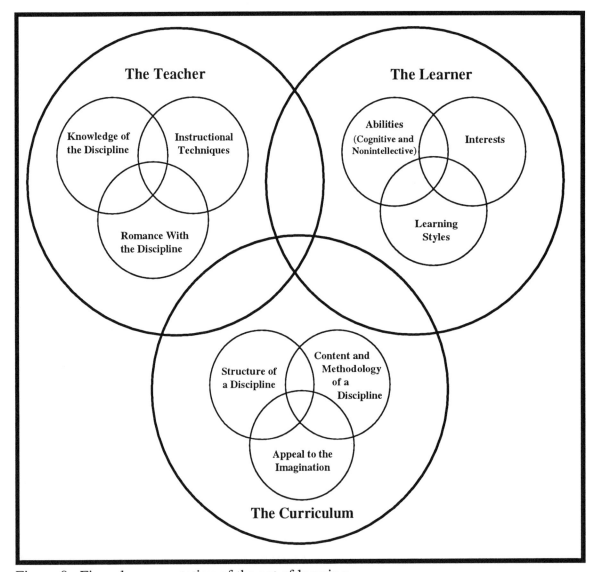

Figure 8. Figural representation of the act of learning.

policy makers and regulators are sending to schools at an unprecedented rate, messages that are often incompatible with one another. One state, for example, mandated a core curriculum for students, but then evaluated teachers on the basis of generic teaching skills that had nothing to do with the curriculum. Schools are encouraged to raise their standards and become more active in curriculum development. However, these same schools are rated on the basis of test scores tied to lists of state specified, outcome-based competencies. A recent study (Madaus, 1992) showed that the most widely used tests measure low level skills and knowledge and that teachers are under pressure to emphasize this kind of material, because it shows up on the tests. The study also reported that teachers and administrators believed the tests forced them to compromise their ideals about good teaching. In another study (Olson, 1992), researchers asked a group of teachers how they would evaluate school reform initiatives in their schools. They replied, "There's nothing but chaos. Our best strategy is to ignore them and close our doors and go about our business."

We believe that school improvement can be initiated and built upon through gentle and evolutionary strategies for change. These strategies must first and foremost concentrate on the act of learning as represented by the interactions that take place between and among learners, teachers, and the curriculum. In the early stages of the change process, these strategies should make minimal, but specific suggestions for change in existing schedules, textbook usage, and curricular conventions. These strategies should be based on practices that have already demonstrated favorable results in places where they have been used for reasonable periods of time and with groups from varying ethnic and economic backgrounds. We also believe that the individual school building is the unit-of-change for addressing school improvement and that effective and lasting change can only occur when it is initiated, nurtured, and monitored from within the school itself. Outside-of-school regulations and remedies have seldom changed the daily behaviors of students and teachers or dealt effectively with solutions to inside-of-school problems (Barth, 1990). A simple but sincere waiver of top-down regulations, a plan that involves consensus and shared decision making on the parts of administrators, parents, and teachers and incentives for specific contributions to the change process, is the starting point needed to initiate a gentle and evolutionary school improvement process.

Our goal in the SEM is not to replace existing school structures, but rather to apply the strategies and services that define the model to improve the structures to which schools have already made a commitment. Thus, for example, if a school has adopted national standards or outcomes, whole language learning models, or site-based management, the purpose of the SEM is to influence these structures in order to maximize their effectiveness. We view this process as an infusion rather than an add-on or replacement approach to school improvement. The main targets of the process are those factors that have a direct bearing on the act of learning. Evaluations of SEM programs (Olenchak & Renzulli, 1989; Renzulli & Reis, 1994) have indicated that the model is systematic, inexpensive to implement, and practical in a common-sense-sort-of-way that makes it appealing to both professionals and lay persons.

What's in It for Me?

Although everyone has a stake in good schools, it would be naive to assume that already overburdened professionals or parents who have had a limited impact on school change will make a commitment to a new initiative which requires time, energy, and participation in activities that are a departure from the *status quo*. Each person examining the SEM should ask himself or herself: What's in it for me? What will I have to do? What will I have to give or give up? What will I get out of it? Policy makers and administrators should examine these questions with an eye toward the kinds of public support necessary for adequate and perhaps even generous financial commitments to public education. The tide of criticism that is constantly being directed towards American schools has taken its toll and has resulted in low morale at all levels of the profession. Education is rapidly becoming a profession without an ego, because of this criticism. Hardly a month passes without someone writing yet another article or news story about the crisis in educational leadership. It would be nice to think that some magical force will "save us," but the reality is that leadership for better schools can come only from people who are responsible for schools at the local level.

More than any other group, teachers will have to ask themselves these hard questions. Almost every teacher has, or at one time had, an idea about what good teaching is all about. Yet, it is not an exaggeration to say that most teachers are dissatisfied with their work and with the regulations and regimentation imposed on their classrooms. A recent report (McLaughlin & Talbert, 1993) on teachers' response patterns to classroom practices indicated that teachers who adapt to traditional practices ". . . become cynical, frustrated, and burned out. So do their students, many of whom fail to meet expectations established for the classroom" (p. 6). We still, however, must raise the questions: Are there benefits for teachers who are willing to take on the challenge of variations in traditional practice? Can educators avoid the cynicism, frustration, and burnout that seems to be so pervasive in the profession? The SEM is designed to provide opportunities for a better "brand" of teaching through the application of more engaging teaching practices.

Parents must examine the above questions with an eye toward the kind of education they want for their sons and daughters. The SEM is not intended to replace the schools' focus on traditional academic achievement, but it does emphasize the development of a broader spectrum of the multiple potentials of young people. Schools do not need to be places to which so many young people dread going. In order to make schools more enjoyable places, parents must have an understanding of and commitment to an education that goes beyond the regimentation and drill that is designed only to "get the scores up." Schools should be viewed as places for developing the broadest and richest experiences imaginable for young people.

Chapter 3

Implementing the Schoolwide Enrichment Model:

A Six-Stage Planning Process for Consensus Building and the Development of a Mission Statement

- **The Importance of Building Trust and Consensus**
  - **Stage 1: Steering Committee**
  - **Stage 2: Discussion Groups**
  - **Stage 3: Steering Committee and Representatives of the Discussion Groups**
  - **Stage 4: Planning Groups**
  - **Stage 5: Program Proposal and Time Line**
  - **Stage 6: Establish an Enrichment Team to Guide the Implementation of the Model and Join SEMNET**
- **Adapting the SEM to Suit Your Needs**
- **Key Features of Successful SEM Programs**

This chapter presents a six-stage procedure for initiating the implementation of the Schoolwide Enrichment Model (SEM). The procedure involves the important preliminary work that leads to the actual adoption of the model and calls for ownership and involvement by staff, administration, and parents. Important steps include: team building, familiarization with the SEM by all involved, a decision to embrace or not to embrace the concepts of the SEM, the development of a mission statement, proposal and time line for the school, and the development of a Schoolwide Enrichment Team. The goals of each stage of the process described in this chapter include: (1) determining whether or not a school should proceed with the adoption of the SEM, (2) achieving consensus about a vision and mission statement that describes what educators want their school to be, and (3) developing an action plan and time line for implementing the model in a school.

The Importance of Building Trust and Consensus

The effectiveness of any group effort is based on the amount of trust that exists within the group. Forming groups without trust-building usually results in the creation of traditional barriers to problem solving such as criticism, blaming others for past problems, and attempts to seize power on the parts of individual or coalitions within the group. Because people *assume* that mutual trust is present in the pursuit of a common goal, they often overlook the important benefits of taking some time at the beginning of their work to build trusting relationships. As more schools move toward shared decision making and the use of teams to attack problems and initiate new programs, the tools and strategies of management science are being applied to the group decision making process.

We have examined a large number of research studies, theories of management science, and how-to books that can be used to promote effective team work. References to some of the most practical material discovered in our search are included at the end of this section. We recommend that a small group of persons who will be involved in the planning process review these materials and select a small number of activities that are designed to build trusting relationships and provide guidance in developing consensus about important decisions that each group will make. Our experience has shown that even eager and optimistic people, as well as those who are pessimists and nay-sayers, will think that engaging in group process training activities is a waste of time. Typical comments range from, "We don't need any of that group stuff" to "Let's get right down to business so we can get this job done." We urge you to consider the benefits of investing a small amount of front-end time to get ready for a very complex and demanding process. All educators have served on committees and task forces and they are aware of the kinds of personal dynamics and "power games" that often result in domination by a few individuals, acquiescence on the parts of others, and a general decline in enthusiasm that converts initial optimism into a "let's-get-it-over-with" attitude. When this attitude takes hold, the quality of the final product and the personal satisfaction that comes from contributing to the product are compromised. Building an effective Enrichment Team is discussed in detail in the last section of this chapter. The next section outlines the six-stage planning process for consensus building (see Figure 9).

Stage 1: Steering Committee

The unit of change upon which this planning process focuses is the individual school. If a districtwide plan to examine the SEM is being considered, one or more representatives of the school's steering committee should serve as representatives on a district committee. However, it is important to emphasize that decisions affecting individual schools should be made in those schools.

The first stage consists of forming a school steering committee that includes the building principal, three to five teachers, and three to five parents. Board of education members should be informed and invited to attend all meetings. It is also desirable to have a central office administrator (and upper-grade students) as members of the steering committee. Needless to say, persons invited to be on the steering committee should have a positive outlook, a can-do attitude, and a high energy level.

The responsibilities of the steering committee at this stage include:

- *To become familiar with the SEM through review of print material, videos, and related information about the model. Chapters 1 and 2 of this book provide an overview of the model, while later chapters provide greater detail. Steering committee members should have access to this book. Members may also wish to view key videotapes related to the model (Renzulli & Reis, 1987), available from Creative Learning Press (P.O. Box 320, Mansfield Center, CT 06250) and join*

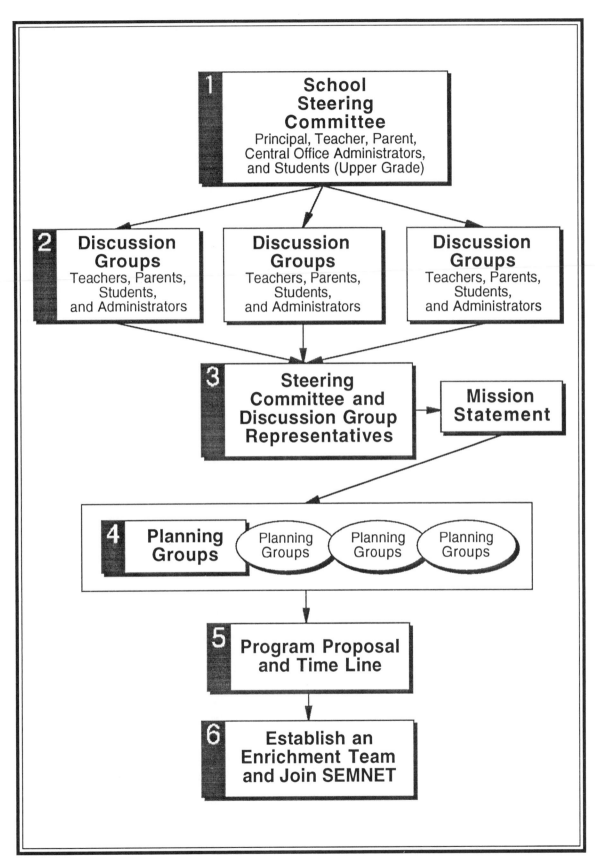

Figure 9. Six-stage planning process for the SEM.

SEMNET, described in stage six. Another excellent way to become familiar with the model is to view it first hand, if possible. School districts across the country have adopted the SEM and serve as great visitation sites.

- *To discuss the model among themselves and to prepare a list of questions that might be raised with consultants or persons who have had direct experience in implementing the model.*

- *To prepare a draft mission statement that reflects a shared system of beliefs among the committee members. This mission statement should address the question, "What do we want our school to be and how can we get where we want to be?" This mission statement should attempt to achieve a unity of purpose among committee members, but it should be viewed as working draft that reflects only the opinions of this committee. At subsequent stages of the process, input about the mission statement will be sought from constituent groups. At this stage, committee members do not want them to perceive the steering committee's statement as yet another top-down approach. The process followed by the steering committee will be replicated by other groups under the leadership of steering committee members. By going through the process themselves, members of the steering committee can "practice" facilitating the process with groups of their constituents.*

If a majority decision is reached to recommend further exploration of the SEM among the school community at large, the steering committee should initiate action leading to Stage 2.

Stage 2: Discussion Groups

Stage 2 is essentially a reiteration of the work of the steering committee. However, at this stage the goal is to expand the number of people involved in the planning process. Each member of the steering committee should serve as a facilitator for one or more discussion groups, but it is important for each discussion group to elect or appoint its own leader. The groups should be provided with a copy of this book and videotapes. The same goals should be pursued (i.e., to become familiar with the SEM, to discuss the model and raise questions, and to prepare a draft mission statement). The questions and draft mission statement should be submitted to the steering committee.

Stage 3: Steering Committee and Representatives of the Discussion Groups

The original steering committee and one representative from each discussion group should convene to examine all of the questions and draft mission statements prepared by the individual groups. An attempt should be made to reach consensus on a mission statement that reflects the majority of opinions expressed by the discussion groups. The statement should be circulated to all members of the school community and a "straw poll" should be taken to determine the extent of support for the mission statement. Although the steering committee (including representatives from the discussion groups) should set its own criteria for acceptance of the mission statement, we recommend that at least 80% of the persons responding to the straw poll should be in favor of the statement before steps are taken to proceed to the next planning stage. If support is strong, but not at a level that will ensure broad-based cooperation on the parts of teachers, parents, and administrators, another round of input should be sought and a second straw poll should be conducted. If an acceptable level of support is not achieved, it would be wise to examine another model! It is important to mention at this point that even when a go-ahead position is reached, the mission statement should still be viewed as a draft or working statement. If educators want the mission statement to eventually become "school policy," they should also keep in mind that policies are most successfully achieved when they are developed in conjunction with actual educational practices. As the practices begin to be implemented, it may be necessary to review the mission statement and make modifications that reflect an interaction between the mission statement and the practices that define the program.

Stage 4: Planning Groups

Interconnected planning groups should be formed so that there is vertical (across grade level by subject areas or departments) and horizontal (within grade level) representation. Thus, for example, in a K-4 school, all third grade teachers might meet as a group to deal with the respective subject areas (e.g., Reading and Language Arts, Math, etc.), and a third grade representative would then meet with a schoolwide (K-4) group that focuses exclusively on one subject area at a time. This approach will provide coordination and articulation within and across both subject areas and grade levels. In middle and secondary schools, which are usually organized by departments, existing subject matter teams should be supplemented with an across-subject matter group that includes one representative from each content area. Administrators and parents should be represented on each team and a master wall chart should be prepared to designate team names and membership.

A central planning group should coordinate the work of the respective groups. Each planning group should address questions based on the interaction between the school structures and the service delivery dimensions of the SEM. Thus, for example, the third grade team mentioned above should consider how the Total Talent Portfolio, curricular modification techniques, and enrichment learning and teaching can be infused into the regular curriculum, the enrichment clusters, and the continuum of special services. The teams should also examine roles and responsibilities and the needed resources for addressing the "slabs" designated by the organizational components of the model. For example, what types of training and resource materials are necessary in the Professional Staff Development slab to address curriculum modification training needs in individual subject areas?

Stage 5: Program Proposal and Time Line

The goal of the planning teams is to produce a comprehensive proposal and time line for implementing the SEM. Needless to say, it is not intended that all components of the model be implemented at once! Priorities should be set and target dates should be established that extend over a three to five-year period. Two of the easiest and most visible components to begin with are curriculum compacting and the enrichment clusters.

Practical guidance for organizing and implementing these components is provided in Chapters 6 and 10. Videotapes available from Creative Learning Press can provide additional direction and support.

Stage 6: Establish an Enrichment Team to Guide the Implementation of the Model and Join SEMNET

The formation of an Enrichment Team is vital to the success of a schoolwide enrichment program. We have found that with the organization of the an Enrichment Team, a sense of staff and community "ownership" in the enrichment program will develop. When classroom teachers are encouraged to become actively involved in the program, they eventually start to regard efforts for developing the talents of all students as a joint venture to be shared by all staff members. Through the active recruitment and utilization of staff talent by an Enrichment Team, staff members can become involved in curriculum development without the burdensome and often unwelcome task of "writing curriculum."

Over the last several years we have worked with many school districts which have implemented outstanding enrichment programs. In almost every case, the first step after the model was selected and administrative support sought was the organization of an inservice program to orient staff with the definition, identification and programming model and the establishment of an Enrichment Team. This team should work cooperatively to achieve the major objectives of Type I and Type II Enrichment, including enriching the lives of all students by expanding the scope of experiences provided by the school, giving teachers direction in making meaningful decisions about the kinds of process-oriented enrichment activities that should be organized for particular groups of students, and stimulating new interests that might lead to more intensive follow-up (Type III) activities by individuals or small groups of students.

Who Should Be on the Enrichment Team?

We have found that the most effective way to begin organizing an Enrichment Team is to recruit members from various segments of the school. The Enrichment Team should include parents, administrators, classroom teachers from various grades or departments, specials teachers, and the media specialist. It can be extremely effective to also include students. A reluctant community resource person told us that he could have easily refused an adult's invitation to present a workshop, but it was impossible for him to refuse the request when made by an excited fifth grader!

All staff should be invited to participate on the Enrichment Team, particularly those with an awareness of the SEM and the benefits of various types of enrichment experiences. The number of members on the team can vary depending on the size and needs of the school. We strongly advocate the inclusion of a building principal even if he or she only attends meetings on a periodic basis. By including a representative sample of parents, administrators, specialists, and teachers, the team will benefit from the additional contacts that each of these groups usually have at their disposal. Representation of these groups (such as parents) will vary according to availability, hence the make-up should remain flexible. No one, however, should ever be forced to serve on the Enrichment Team. We have found that once the benefits of the various types of enrichment experiences become obvious, more staff members become interested in joining the team in subsequent years. Negative energy from some outspoken staff members can often be channeled into a more positive direction by simply including this person on the team. <u>Note of caution:</u> one "negative" person may become more cooperative when included on the team; two or three negative teachers may very well become a coalition.

We recommend that the superintendent of schools write a letter of appointment to the individuals serving on the Enrichment Team commending them for volunteering and stressing the importance of their task. Also, whenever possible, the team should be given a budget. Although the great proportion of enrichment experiences can be organized at no cost.

Who Should Serve as the Chairperson of the Enrichment Team?

If an enrichment specialist is available in the school, we have found that especially in the first year of operation, that person should serve a chairperson of the team and organize regular meetings. The enrichment specialist often has a more flexible schedule to organize meetings or set up events. However, the role of the Enrichment Team is to subdivide these duties so that the responsibilities are shared as the year progresses. The key to successful functioning of the Enrichment Team is the division of labor among members. If an enrichment specialist is not present in the school, we recommend that group appoint someone who is organized, efficient, and personable to serve as the chairperson. Administrative support should allow this person additional time for team organization, even if it is just one hour per week.

How Often Should the Team Meet and What Should It Accomplish?

For teams that are just beginning, we recommend regular weekly meetings for the first two months then monthly meeting for rest of the school year. At these initial meetings, the logistical questions that face all Enrichment Teams should include:

1. The optimal time of the week to organize regular enrichment experiences.
There is no absolute time that is best for all teachers, but we have found that by discussing the plans for implementing regular Type I and Type II Enrichment and enrichment cluster experiences with the entire staff, problems can be avoided.

2. Location of enrichment activities.
The location depends upon the type of presentation and the needs of students. Enrichment activities in the regular classroom minimize disruption and are relatively easy to accomplish. However, if a presentation is special and will benefit a large number of students, it should be presented in a large group setting.

3. How to orient staff to the varied enrichment possibilities.
The Type I Planning Guide (see Chapter 7) should be handed out to staff members with a set of general guidelines about enrichment experiences and the roles and function of the Enrichment Team. If staff members begin to think about how different enrichment experiences can become a part of their classroom teaching, they have achieved a major goal of the model. By simply discussing the many

possible methods of delivery (on the left hand side of the Type I Planning Guide) at a staff meeting, teachers will develop an awareness of the different types of enrichment.

4. How many Type I and Type II experiences to organize per month.

This answer depends on the school's resources, parent and administrative support, and school size. There is no limit to the number of interest development centers, displays, articles, and books that can be shared by classroom teachers. What should be limited in the beginning of the year is the number of whole school or grade level Type I presentations. Teachers should be consulted about how many of these they would like to have scheduled. Some principals object to any changes in the schedule, while others are proud to provide a lot of flexibility. Team members should be very sensitive to the needs of administrators and staff when organizing enrichment events.

5. How to organize these activities with minimal disruption to the regular school day.

Minimum disruption to the school day can be accomplished by meeting with staff, as discussed earlier, to determine the most convenient time for all, with the least number of conflicts. If possible, this is best done prior to the school year when school schedules are determined. Enrichment activities may also be scheduled during times when specific students have compacted out of a particular area. A note from the classroom teacher will alert the enrichment specialist to a need for enrichment. There may be times throughout the year when a "break in the routine" may be helpful for classroom teachers and students (such as the week before the holiday recess in December). The general rule for minimizing disruption in the regular school day is to maintain communication with staff.

6. How to involve as many staff members as possible.

Creating ownership in the enrichment program often begins by asking staff members to volunteer conducting an enrichment cluster or share an interest, skill, or place they have visited. (This process is discussed further in Chapter 7). The team can then facilitate an exchange of talents by establishing a weekly hour or by contacting teachers with known talents and arranging "trade-offs." Care should be taken to locate a talent area for all faculty members. Even a superintendent can be encouraged to facilitate an enrichment cluster. Other staff members may follow suit. As understanding of and familiarity with the model increases, the staff will become more involved.

7. How to get started.

Let's begin at the beginning! First, the team must be formed and clear guidelines for what will occur throughout the year must be established. Second, roles and responsibilities must be clearly discussed and understood by all team members. Third, staff and parents should be oriented with the model and invited to facilitate an enrichment cluster or present a Type I or II experience. Recruiting methods are discussed in detail in Chapter 7.

These initial team functions will require additional time in the beginning of the year, and solutions will vary depending on the size of the school, space, staff flexibility, administrative support, and the team's available time. Team responsibilities are many and varied. The Enrichment Team should:

1. Serve as a planning agent and clearinghouse for visiting speakers, field trips, artistic performances, and other grade level, schoolwide, and interest group activities that are designed to expand the scope of the overall school experience.
2. Review a wide array of enrichment materials and determine where within the regular curriculum these materials might be most effectively integrated.
3. Recruit staff members and community resource persons who might present enrichment sessions or serve as mentors to individuals or small groups who are involved in advanced level research investigations or creative productions.
4. Review possible out-of-school enrichment opportunities for students (e.g., television programs, summer camps and programs, science fairs, literary competitions, local hobby and theater groups, etc.).
5. Organize enrichment clusters by helping to develop a schedule, recruiting volunteer facilitators, registering students, and providing an opportunity to share and celebrate products.

By having all requests for enrichment flow through a team, no one person will be called upon too often and become overwhelmed with evaluation concerns. These issues are discussed in more detail in Chapters 7-10.

SEMNET: The Schoolwide Enrichment Model Network

In order to facilitate better communication between educators who use the SEM, we have developed the Schoolwide Enrichment Model Network (SEMNET). This international network invites teachers and administrators to share a wide variety of SEM know-how such as instructional materials, effective teaching and learning strategies, program development and implementation ideas, and professional development resources.

This membership-based network disseminates information about outstanding educational programs, materials, and practices through bi-monthly newsletters, an electronic database system, a video library, a directory of resources, and an Internet site. In addition to these services, members also receive special discounts on materials published by Creative Learning Press, Inc.

Components of the SEMNET Membership

A one-year SEMNET membership includes the following materials and services:

Bi-Monthly Newsletters: These theme-based newsletters contain annotations of outstanding teacher and student resources, enrichment activity ideas, discussion questions, book and software reviews, and useful Internet connections. Past themes have included architecture, aviation, folk literature, math, nutrition, ocean, poetry, and trees. Teachers can reproduce these newsletters and use the information as springboards for Types I, II and III Enrichment in their classrooms.

Enrichment Materials Database: This electronic database contains the names and descriptions of hundreds of outstanding enrichment materials (books, videos, computer software, simulations, learning games, kits, and magazines) that can be used to enhance the regular curriculum. Each entry contains the following bibliographic information: title, author, publication date, publisher (address/phone number), ISBN, price, format, target audience, content area, age level, orientation, grouping, and description. This database contains materials designed for teachers, students, administrators, and parents.

Videotape Library: This library contains videos of recent speeches given by Joseph Renzulli, Sally Reis, Steven Caney, and other distinguished speakers. Some of the topics include curriculum compacting, new developments in SEM, and creativity. SEMNET members can borrow these videotapes and use them for staff development purposes.

SEMNET Directory: This directory contains the names, addresses, and phone numbers of SEMNET members who are currently using SEM in their schools. Interested teachers and administrators can use this list as a vehicle for communicating and sharing their SEM experiences with other schools around the United States and world.

Internet Site: The Internet presents a new and exciting way to share information about the SEM. A special SEMNET web site provides information about the model, shares curriculum ideas, and presents links to other educational sites. Teachers and students can use this site as a starting point for research projects and other learning experiences (*http://www.neca.com/~semnet*).

Special Discounts: Members receive special discounts on more than twenty-five books published by Creative Learning Press, Inc. This select group of materials focuses on different aspects of education and features titles by Joseph Renzulli, Sally Reis, Deborah Burns, Linda Smith, and other well-known educators.

For more information about newsletter subscriptions and a one-year membership to SEMNET, please contact Debra Briatico, SEMNET Director, P.O. Box 320, Mansfield Center, CT 06250.

Adapting the SEM to Suit Your Needs

This six-stage planning process and the resulting proposal should always be viewed as "experimental" and subject to revision based on actual implementation experiences. One of our chief concerns as the developers of the SEM is that each school develops its own unique application of the model that capitalizes on local creativity, resources, and initiative. It is only by encouraging local ownership and involvement and by advocating continuous modification and adaptation, that educators can ensure real and lasting change. As has been pointed out in *Schools for Talent Development,* top-down models that are imposed on schools by external forces seldom endure and are frequently viewed by teachers and others as another flavor-of-the-month "innovation" that will quickly fade from popularity. Similarly, "canned" programs that do not allow for maximum input and decision making on the parts of those persons who actually will implement the program, have been singularly unsuccessful in bringing about real and lasting change. All persons involved in this planning process should view themselves as inventors, architects, engineers, and artists! The SEM is based on a clear and reasonable set of common goals, but the many and varied ways that each school can reach these goals involves an untold amount of creativity on the parts of program developers.

Key Features of Successful SEM Programs

From our research and close interaction with various districts implementing our model, certain key practices made some programs more effective than others. All of the activities that will be identified can take place in any enrichment program through careful planning, staff development, and specific program monitoring activities. By concentrating on the practices described below, schools and districts interested in successfully replicating the SEM will be able to capitalize upon the many years of research and development that have been carried out in our field test districts.

Key Feature 1: The Golden Rule

In our experience with school districts that have implemented the SEM, we have discovered a simple and easily instituted feature of the most outstanding programs. The "golden rule," simply stated, is that the more thoroughly the instructional staff, students, parents, and administration understand the overall structure of the model, the easier it is to implement any particular identification procedure or learning activity. Orientation sessions, written materials, and visual displays are used to help each of the above groups understand the general and particular functions of all aspects of the model and each group's appropriate role in carrying out these functions.

A thorough understanding of the model provides everyone with a common language for effective communication. For example, it enables a teacher to inform a parent that his or her child "revolved into a Type III on film making as a result of a Type I presentation by a local cinematographer." Equally important in this example is that students know the purposes of a Type I. They are aware that the cinematography presentation is for purposes of informing and stimulating new interests and ideas. But they also know that if an individual or small group develops a high level interest in this topic and wants to pursue an advanced level follow-up that will emphasize creative and productive involvement, then the SEM provides a planned and purposeful connection between Type I and Type III Enrichment.

Understanding the language or major concepts of the model also helps to: (1) plan and organize activities according to their categorical function, (2) emphasize the purpose of particular staff development sessions, and (3) allocate time and money for each major type of enrichment. Evaluation reports are more easily prepared and understood when everyone involved has a common understanding of each component of the program and the interrelated role that the components play in the overall model. Thus, the golden rule is really a foundation for effective communication.

🗝 Key Feature 2: Planning Prior to Program Implementation

Our research studies showed that one of the most frequently cited reasons for the success of SEM programs was the careful planning that occurred prior to the implementation of the model. The planning groups discussed earlier perform a vital function by deciding how the model will be tailored to accommodate the unique characteristics and resources of a given school. This planning group should consist of both volunteers and persons selected by administrators. The planning team should also include a staff member who had been an outspoken critic of changes in the schedule. By appointing outspoken and negative faculty members to a planning team it is often possible to divert the negative energy into a more positive channel and thereby eliminate problems which may occur later.

🗝 Key Feature 3: Professional Development and Administrative Support

For any new program to be successful, carefully organized inservice training must be provided for all persons who will be involved. In our experience with research sites, the most successful programs involved the school administrators in the training. Principals, for example, need to be able to answer basic structural questions about the program. All administrative and instructional staff should be able to explain the main components of the program to parents and answer basic questions that may arise. Many complaints about special programs stem from the frustrations and feelings of downright foolishness that many teachers and administrators experience when they are asked a question that they are unable to answer.

Three types of inservice should be used to familiarize staff and administrators with SEM. The first type of inservice (which most teachers are familiar with and regularly attend) is formal inservice. Formal inservice should consist of short sessions focusing on specific topics and skills related to the implementation of the various components of the model. By beginning the formal inservice sessions with a structural overview of the major dimensions of the model, we have found it is easier for teachers to understand the nature and function of specific activities and the interrelatedness of each component that will be explained in later sessions.

The second type of inservice, called "informal inservice," refers to the regular interaction that enrichment specialists have with other staff members, parents, or community members. Informal inservice consists of the positive reinforcement that enrichment specialists can give to the program through conversations they have with other staff members. These conversations may occur in the hallway, the cafeteria, or the teacher's room. Positive but casual comments about individual student's work and/or planned enrichment experiences can sometimes do more to inform teachers about the special program than a multitude of formal inservice sessions.

Another type of informal inservice consists of having the persons responsible for program implementation (enrichment specialists, principals) always available for questions. At the risk of being assertive about this availability, enrichment specialists should continuously remind other staff members that they are ready, eager, and willing to answer any questions about the program.

The last type of inservice is easily accomplished, but has far-reaching effects on present and long-term program success. We advocate the distribution of brief but topic-specific materials that have been referred to in previous formal or informal inservice sessions. Theoretical or overly technical materials should not be used for inservice purposes. Instead, written material distributed to teachers should be directed toward a practical purpose that either enables teachers to do something specific with their students (e.g., enrichment clusters or the step-by-step procedures for curriculum compacting) or allows them to answer questions for themselves or parents who may express concerns about the program. Above all, these back-up materials should be brief, to-the-point, and practical.

Key Feature 4: The Schoolwide Enrichment Team

One of the most innovative and rewarding key features to emerge from our field studies was the development of Enrichment Teams in many of the schools implementing the model. As discussed earlier, these teams should include the principal, the enrichment specialist, three or four classroom teachers, some parents, and in some cases, a student. Efforts should be made to encourage principals to become working (peer) members of the teams, rather than persons who delegate responsibility to others.

In addition to participating in the planning and implementation of all key features described above, the Enrichment Team should help put into practice an essential part of the philosophy underlying the SEM. We believe that the total educational experience of all students should include varying amounts and levels of enrichment. It is nothing short of ridiculous to maintain that only identified "gifted" students should have access to all enrichment activities and that all of the other pupils should be denied any opportunity for a more challenging and rewarding school experience. It is precisely this attitude that has caused the gifted child movement to be viewed as elitist and has resulted in the irreconcilable separations that exist between regular and special programs and personnel.

Key Feature 5: Program Ownership and Involvement

A major concern of many teachers and administrators who are actively involved in SEM programs is the potential for the separation of that program from the rest of the school. An unfortunate reality is that in many schools, the enrichment and regular programs exist as two separate and unrelated entities. Program ownership involves strategies purposefully designed to make the entire school staff aware that everybody has a stake in developing the talents of the students. Many of the features already discussed are important in developing ownership, such as carefully organized program planning, inservice opportunities, and the creation of an Enrichment Team. In addition to inservice provided for everyone who will interact with the program before it is implemented, administrators should participate in a separate inservice in which their concerns and apprehensions about the enrichment program can be discussed honestly. It is essential that administrators understand their role in establishing and carrying out a successful SEM program. Administrative support is critical to many aspects of the program, such as curriculum compacting and enrichment clusters.

Other methods for promoting ownership may involve a variety of techniques. An exchange of talents and resources among teachers in various grades and subjects is effective for promoting teamwork and ownership. Ongoing communication between classroom teachers and the enrichment specialist is also vital. As audiences are an integral part of Type III investigations, students who complete products should be encouraged to share their work with their classmates and classroom teacher. The enrichment specialist and classroom teacher should also work together when assessing student work or arranging curriculum compacting. If classroom teachers are encouraged to actively participate in the enrichment program, they will come to regard efforts toward developing talents in all students as a shared responsibility.

In addition to tapping the talents of staff members, an active effort should be made to involve parents and community members. They can be encouraged to share their expertise or interest as speakers, mentors, resource persons, or enrichment cluster facilitators. By involving parents and community members, an awareness and appreciation of the enrichment program can be created and an advocacy for the program developed.

Key Feature 6: Student Orientation

All students should be given an unusually detailed orientation about opportunities that are available to them. This orientation should cover the following topics:

1. The Enrichment Triad Model, including the three types of enrichment experiences.
2. The rigor and demands of a Type III investigation (actual examples or slides of other students' Type III products should be shared with new Talent Pool students).
3. The *Total Talent Portfolio*, which serves as a record for a student's interests, strengths, and learning style preferences.
4. The procedure for completing an *Action Information Message* (see Chapter 9).
5. The process of curriculum compacting in its simplest form.
6. The philosophy behind enrichment clusters—students and adults who share a common interest come together to explore that interest in an authentic and meaningful way and develop a real-world product or service.
7. The responsibilities students have to both classroom and enrichment specialists for completing work and fulfilling obligations.

Key Feature 7: Communication With Prime Interest Groups

Another key feature which tended to be obvious in extremely successful field test districts was the communication devices that were used to keep various prime interest groups informed about any and all aspects of the program. The prime interest groups consisted of parents, classroom teachers, students, administrators, school board members, and the general public. This communication was achieved in several different ways including:

1. Initial parent, teacher, and student orientation sessions and posters about the programs' goals and procedures.
2. Follow-up inservice sessions whenever necessary.
3. Letters that informed parents about their child's membership in the Talent Pool.
4. Subsequent letters that informed parents that their child had revolved into and out of a Type III investigation.

5. Periodic evaluation forms that informed both parents and classroom teachers about student progress in the program.
6. Newsletters that described specific enrichment experiences and program happenings.
7. Evaluation forms for parents and classroom teachers.
8. Periodic invitations to visit the program events for parents, board members, and newspaper reporters.
9. Opportunities for parents and classroom teachers to interact while viewing the work that children had completed in the program. (This can be accomplished by a Type III Fair at the end of the school year.)
10. Requests for involvement (as a mentor, enrichment cluster facilitator, presenter).
11. Letters to parents describing upcoming enrichment clusters.

Key Feature 8: Flexibility

A further essential element in the success of the SEM is the flexibility of the model and the individuals involved in its implementation. In any new venture, certain realities emerge. One is that change is not only hard to effect, but that it is also difficult for some people to accept. SEM was purposefully developed to take into account the wide range of attitudes, resources, patterns of school organization, and other uniquenesses that exist in different schools. The attitudes of those involved in a given building must be constantly considered. Individual teachers must be dealt with according to their own styles. Each school serviced by the program should have its own "personality" and reflect the individual differences of its administration, staff, and students. Local adaptations of the model and the flexibility of resource teachers to adapt and mold the model to fit each situation will greatly influence the subsequent success of any program. SEM is a general organizational approach to programming rather than a prescription or "straight jacket" for delivering enrichment services to various segments of the school population. We firmly believe that any model that does not have this built-in flexibility is doomed in the long run to failure, because it will ignore the uniqueness of local schools and the initiative and creativity of persons at the local level. There is no such thing as a "pure" SEM, and because flexibility rather than prescription is emphasized, many exciting innovations in the model have been contributed by persons who have adapted it for use in their schools.

Key Feature 9: Evaluation and Program Monitoring

High quality programs do not happen by accident. In addition to careful planning and a commitment to carrying out specific responsibilities on the parts of all persons involved, a system for evaluation and monitoring must be built into the overall programming model. The schools that took part in our field studies agreed to participate in a wide variety of information gathering procedures. In addition to providing data necessary for research, these procedures enabled us to refine and develop a software package that is now being used for ongoing evaluation and program monitoring. The software package contains structured forms that are used to document major program activities, questionnaires for members of prime interest groups, and instruments designed to assess growth in cognitive and affective thinking processes. An instrument for evaluating fifteen specific dimensions of students' products is also included.

Each evaluation instrument is related to one or more of the major goals of the SEM. Regular use of the evaluation and monitoring system in and of itself helps to contribute to high levels of program quality. In other words, the items included in the monitoring system serve as a set of "friendly enforcers" in the pursuit of desirable program outcomes. It is one thing to know and to pursue the objectives of a given program, but it is quite another thing to show evidence of goal achievement. If educators are falling short of one or more major program objectives, the monitoring system will help them pinpoint areas of deficiency and take appropriate action.

The Significance of Key Features

In summary, what are the effects of considering these key features when implementing a SEM program? Our experience leads us to conclude that an outstanding enrichment program accomplishes many of the objectives discussed in our introduction. It opens its doors to all interested students when enrichment experiences are planned and reflects the excellence of students' hard work and intense interests. It displays that excellence, and in essence, challenges other students both within the program and in the regular classroom to emulate it. An outstanding enrichment program creates the opportunity for all students to participate in it without the constraints of predetermined intelligence or achievement cut-off scores. It further allows all teachers and students to share their interests and expertise with other interested students and teachers. It also provides the mechanism to relieve students of the burden of engaging each day in repetitious, uninspiring tasks and assignments of previously mastered material by responding to the individual needs of the students. Finally, an excellent enrichment program can be replicated in a manner which adapts to the individual needs of the district while simultaneously fulfilling the inherent principles and philosophies of the SEM.

Resources on Team Building

Carnegie, D. (1936). *How to win friends and influence people.* New York: Simon and Schuster.

Maddeux, R. B. (1992). *Team building: An exercise in leadership.* Menlo Park, CA: Crisp Publication.

Maeroff, G. I. (1993). *Team building for school change: Equipping teachers for new roles.* New York: Teacher's College Press.

Scearce, C. (1992). *100 ways to build teams.* Palatine, IL: IRI/Skylight Publishing.

Williams, R. B. (1993). *More than 50 ways to build team consensus.* Palatine, IL: IRI/Skylight Publishing.

Identifying Students for Participation in the SEM

- **What Makes Giftedness?**
    - **Step 1: Test Score Nominations**
    - **Step 2: Teacher Nominations**
    - **Step 3: Alternate Pathways**
    - **Step 4: Special Nominations (Safety Valve No. 1)**
    - **Step 5: Notification and Orientation of Parents**
    - **Step 6: Action Information Nominations (Safety Valve No. 2)**
- **The Importance of Using Multiple Identification Criteria**
- **A Change in Direction: From "Being Gifted" to the "Development of Gifted Behaviors"**

The need to identify and serve traditional populations of gifted students requires the development of a specific plan for identification. In many cases, such plans are specified by state regulations and include a variety of multiple criteria derived from test and non-test information sources. The system for identifying gifted and talented students described in this chapter was formulated with two goals in mind. First, an attempt was made to develop a system that is flexible enough to adapt to existing and emerging state regulations, which in most cases, specify either test cut-off scores or the percentage of students that can be served in special programs for the gifted. Second, an attempt was made to develop an identification system that takes into account the broad range of research that has accumulated over the years about the behavioral characteristics of highly creative and productive young people and adults. In the sections that follow, we will briefly review research that can be found in greater detail elsewhere (Renzulli, 1978, 1986), then provide a step-by-step description of an identification plan that accommodates both existing state regulations and the research findings.

What Makes Giftedness?

As was presented in Chapter 1, highly creative and productive people are characterized by three interlocking clusters of ability: above average ability, task commitment, and creativity. There is an interaction between and among the general categories and the specific traits of each cluster. It is important to reiterate that *all the traits do not need to be present in any given individual or situation to produce a display of gifted behaviors.* It is for this reason that the three-ring conception of giftedness emphasizes the interaction among the clusters, rather than any single cluster. It should also be emphasized that the above average ability cluster is a constant in the identification system described below. In other words, the above average ability group represents the target population and the starting point for the identification process. It will be students in this category that are selected through the use of test score and non-test criteria. Task commitment and creativity, on the other hand, are viewed as the developmental goals of special programs. By providing above average ability students with appropriate experiences, the programming model for which this identification system was designed, serves the purpose of promoting creativity, task commitment, and the development of gifted behaviors (Renzulli, 1977a).

The sections that follow outline the specific steps of an identification system that is designed to translate the three-ring conception of giftedness into a practical set of procedures for selecting students for special programs. The focal point of this identification system is a Talent Pool of students that will serve as the major (but not the only) target group for participation in a wide variety of supplementary services.

The goals of this identification system, as it relates to the three-ring conception of giftedness are threefold:

1. To develop creativity and/or task commitment in Talent Pool students and other students who may come to an educator's attention through alternate means of identification.
2. To provide learning experiences and support systems that promote the interaction of creativity, task commitment, and above average ability (i.e., bring the "rings" together).
3. To provide opportunities, resources, and encouragement for the development and application of gifted behaviors.

Before listing the steps involved in this identification system, three important considerations must be discussed. First, Talent Pools will vary in any given school depending upon the general nature of the total student body. In schools with unusually large numbers of high achieving students, it is conceivable that the Talent Pool will extend beyond the 15 percent level that is ordinarily recommended for most schools. Even in schools where achievement levels are below national norms, there still exists an upper-level group of students who need services above and beyond those which are provided for the majority of the school population. Some of our most successful programs have been in inner-city schools that serve disadvantaged and bilingual youth. Even though these schools were below national norms, a Talent Pool of approximately 15 percent of higher achieving students needing supplementary services was still identified. Talent Pool size becomes a function of the availability of resources (both human and material) and the extent to which the general faculty is willing to: (1) make modifications in the regular curriculum for above average ability students, (2) participate in various kinds of enrichment and mentoring activities, and (3) work cooperatively with any and all personnel who may have special program assignments. Finally, Talent Pool size may be predetermined by state regulations, either through the specification of a percentage of students that can be served or the number of students who fall above a fixed cut-off score on a standardized test.

Since teacher nomination plays an important role in this identification system, a second consideration is the extent of orientation and training that teachers receive about the program and procedures for nominating students. We recommend the use of a training activity that is designed to orient teachers to the behavioral characteristics of superior students (Renzulli & Reis, 1985, pp. 203-210).

A third consideration is, of course, the type of program for which students are being identified. The identification system that follows is based on models that combine both enrichment and acceleration, whether or not they are carried out in self-contained or pull-out programs. Regardless of the type of organizational model used, it is also recommended that a strong component of curriculum compacting (Renzulli, Smith, & Reis, 1982; Reis, Burns, & Renzulli, 1992) become an integral part of the services offered to Talent Pool students.

For purposes of demonstration, the examples that follow will be based on the formation of a 10-15 percent Talent Pool. Larger or smaller Talent Pools can be formed by simply adjusting the figures used in this example. Regardless of the specified size of the Talent Pool, the guiding principle of this identification system states that one half of the Talent Pool should be filled by test score nominees and the other half should be filled by students gaining entrance through non-test criteria.

Step 1: Test Score Nominations

If we were using nothing but test scores to identify a 15 percent Talent Pool, the task would be ever so simple! Any child who scores above the 85th percentile (using local norms) would be a candidate. In this identification system, however, we have made a commitment to leave some room in the Talent Pool for students whose potentials may not be reflected in standardized tests. Therefore, we will begin by dividing our Talent Pool in half (see Figure 10) and place all students who score at or above the 92nd percentile (again, using local norms) in the Talent Pool. This approach guarantees that all traditionally bright youngsters will automatically be selected and account for approximately 50 percent of the Talent Pool. This process guarantees admission to bright underachievers. The Class Survey Sheet (Figure 11) offers a practical system for documenting the criteria for which students are selected.

Any regularly administered standardized test (e.g., intelligence, achievement, aptitude) can be used for this purpose, however, we recommend that admission to the Talent Pool be granted on the basis of any single test or subtest score. This approach will enable students who are high in verbal or non-verbal ability (but not necessarily both) to gain admission, as well as students who may excel in one aptitude (e.g., spatial, mechanical). Programs that focus on special areas such as the arts, leadership, and athletics should use non-test criteria as major indicators of above average ability in a particular talent area. In a similar fashion, whenever test scores are not available or validity questions exist, the non-test criteria recommended in the following steps should be used. This approach (i.e., the elimination or minimization of Step 1) is especially important when considering primary age students, disadvantaged populations, or culturally different groups.

Talent Pool Composition
(15% of General Population)

Approximately 50% of the Talent Pool				Total Talent Pool Consists of Approximately 15% of the General Population
Approximately 50% of the Talent Pool	Step 1	99th %ile ↑ 92nd %ile	**Test Score Nominations** (Automatic and Based on Local Norms)	
Approximately 50% of the Talent Pool	Step 2		**Teacher Nominations** (Automatic Except in Cases of Teachers Who Are Over-Nominators or Under-Nominators)	
	Step 3		Alternate Pathways-- Case Study	
	Step 4		Special Nominations-- Case Study	
	Step 5		Notification of Parents	
	Step 6		Action Information Nominations	

Talent Pool Composition
(10% of General Population)

Approximately 50% of the Talent Pool				Total Talent Pool Consists of Approximately 10% of the General Population
Approximately 50% of the Talent Pool	Step 1	99th %ile ↑ 94th %ile	**Test Score Nominations** (Automatic and Based on Local Norms)	
Approximately 50% of the Talent Pool	Step 2		**Teacher Nominations** (Automatic Except in Cases of Teachers Who Are Over-Nominators or Under-Nominators)	
	Step 3		Alternate Pathways-- Case Study	
	Step 4		Special Nominations-- Case Study	
	Step 5		Notification of Parents	
	Step 6		Action Information Nominations	

Figure 10. Talent pool composition (10-15% of general population).

Class Survey Sheet

School _____ Grade _____ Teacher _____ Date _____

Check (√) if placed in Talent Pool	Name or Student Identification Numbers	BASIC CRITERIA							ALTERNATIVE PATHWAYS OF ENTRANCE TO THE TALENT POOL						COMMENTS
		Ability Test Scores		Teacher Nomination					Parent Nomination	Peer Nomination	Self-Nomination	Tests of Special Aptitude	Product Ratings	Other	If special reason for placement in Talent Pool. If further explanation of supplemental information (i.e., other categories are needed, etc.)
		(1)	(2)	Learning	Motivation	Creativity	Leadership	Other							

Figure 11. Class survey sheet.

Step 2: Teacher Nominations

The teachers should be informed about all students who have gained entrance through test score nominations so that they will not have to engage in needless paperwork for students who have already been admitted. Step 2 allows teachers to nominate students who display characteristics that are not easily determined by tests (e.g., high levels of creativity and/or task commitment, unusual interests and/or talents, or special areas of superior performance and/or potential). With the exception of teachers who are over-nominators or under-nominators, nominations from teachers who have received training in this process are accepted into the Talent Pool on an equal value with test score nominations. In other words, we do not refer to students nominated by test scores as the truly gifted and the students nominated by teachers as the moderately or potentially gifted. Nor do we make any distinctions in the opportunities, resources, or services provided, other than the normal individualization that should be a part of any program that attempts to meet unique needs and potentials. Thus, for example, if a student gains entrance on the basis of teacher nomination because he or she has shown advanced potential for creative writing, we would not expect this student to compete on an equal basis in mathematics with a student who scored at or above the 92nd percentile on a math test. Nor should we arrange program experiences that would place the student with talents in creative writing in an advanced math cluster group. Special programs should first and foremost respect and reflect the individual characteristics that brought students to our attention in the first place.

A teacher nomination form (see Figure 12) and rating scales (Renzulli, Smith, White, Callahan, & Hartman, 1976) are used for this procedure. The rating scales are not used to eliminate students with lower ratings. Instead, the scales are used to provide a composite profile of the nominated students. In cases of teachers who are over-nominators, a request is made that they rank order their nominations for review by a schoolwide committee. Procedures for dealing with under-nominators or non-nominators will be described in Step 4.

Step 3: Alternate Pathways

Although all schools using this identification system make use of test score and teacher nominations, alternate pathways are considered to be local options and are pursued in varying degrees by individual school districts. Decisions about which alternate pathways might be used should be made by a local planning committee and some consideration should be given to variations in grade level. For example, self-nomination is more appropriate for students who may be considering advanced classes at the secondary level.

Alternate pathways generally consist of parent nominations, peer nominations, tests of creativity, self-nominations, product evaluations, and virtually any other procedure that might lead to initial consideration by a screening committee. Samples of several alternative identification forms are shown on the following pages (see Figures 13-15). The major difference between alternate pathways on the one hand, and test scores and teacher nominations on the other, is that alternate pathways are not automatic. In other words, students nominated through one or more alternate pathways must first be reviewed

Teacher Nomination Form for SEM Programs

1. Student _____ 2. Teacher _____

3. Date of Referral _____ 4. School _____

5. Grade _____ 6. Date of Birth _____

7. Average Grades for Current School Year:

                Language Arts _____

                Social Studies _____

                Math _____

                Science _____

8. Parent Nomination (Check if appropriate): _____

9. SRBCSS Scale Total _____ 1. _____ 2. _____ 3. _____ 4. _____

10. Why do you think this student should be included in the Talent Pool? (You may wish to list examples of ideas, projects, creative endeavors, etc.)

_____

_____

_____

_____

_____

INTERESTS
Please indicate the areas of interest that the student has displayed in your class this year. If you've noticed other specific topics (computers, dinosaurs, etc.), please note this in the column entitled "Other."

	HIGH	AVERAGE	LOW		HIGH	AVERAGE	LOW
Fine Arts/Crafts				Music			
Science				Drama			
Creative Writing				Math			
Social Studies				Language Arts			
Psychomotor				Other			

CURRICULAR STRENGTH AREAS
Please indicate the curricular areas in which the student has demonstrated proficiency and could possibly be considered for curriculum compacting.

         Language Arts _____   Math _____

         Science _____   Social Studies _____

Figure 12. Teacher nomination form for SEM programs.

Things My Child Likes to Do

Cover Letter

TO: Parents of All Students

FROM: Carol Moran, Enrichment Specialist

DATE: October 1, 1996

One of the major goals of our Schoolwide Enrichment Program is to provide each student with an opportunity to develop his or her strengths and talents. We would also like to supplement our basic curriculum to offer your child experiences that are challenging, enjoyable, and of personal interest.

Although the work your child does in school provides a lot of information on his or her strengths and interests, activities your child pursues at home will help us develop ways to further enrich his or her school program. For this reason, we are asking you to complete the attached questionnaire.

Each of the items on the questionnaire deals with a general type of interest or activity you may or may not have seen in your child. These might be the result of school assignments, extra-curricular activities such as Girl Scouts or 4-H projects, or home activities. To help clarify the items, we have included an example. You should rate your child on the general item, not on the example. If possible, also include specific examples of your child's interests or activities.

If you have any questions, please feel free to contact me. I appreciate your help in providing the best possible educational program for your child.

Sincerely,

Carol Moran

Figure 13. Sample parent nomination form.

"Things My Child Likes to Do"

Your Name _____

Child's School _____

Your Child's Name _____

Child's Age _____

Today's Date _____

	Seldom or Never	Sometimes	Quite Often*	Almost Always*	Examples From Your Own Child's Life
1. My child will spend more time and energy than his/her agemates on a topic of his/her interest. (For example: Joan is learning to sew and spends every free minute designing new dress patterns and trying to sew them herself.)					
2. My child is a "self-starter" who works well alone, needing few directions and little supervision. (For example: After watching a film about musical instruments, Gary began to make his own guitar from materials he found around the garage.)					
3. My child sets high personal goals and expects to see results from his/her work. (For example: Marcy insisted on building a robot from spare machine parts even though she knew nothing about engines or construction.)					
4. My child gets so involved with a project that he/she gives up other pleasures in order to work on it. (For example: Don is writing a book about his town's history and spends each night examining historical records and documents— even when he knows he's missing his favorite TV show.)					
5. My child continues to work on a project even when faced with temporary defeats and slow results. (For example: After building a model rocket, Sally continued to try to launch it, despite several failures and "crash landings.")					

Jim Delisle, 1979

Figure 13. Sample parent nomination form (continued).

"Things My Child Likes to Do"

	Seldom or Never	Sometimes	Quite Often*	Almost Always*	Examples From Your Own Child's Life
6. While working on a project (and when it's finished) my child knows which parts are good and which parts need improvement. (For example: After building a scale model of a lunar city, Kenny realized that there weren't enough solar collectors to heat all the homes he had built.)					
7. My child is a "doer" who begins a project and shows finished products of his/her work. (For example: Mary began working on a puppet show four months ago, and has since built a stage and puppets and has written a script. Tomorrow she's presenting her play to the PTA!)					
8. My child suggests imaginative ways of doing things, even if the suggestions are sometimes impractical. (For example: "If you really want to clean the refrigerator, why don't we move it outside and I'll hose it down— that will defrost it, too.")					
9. When my child tells about something that is very unusual, he/she expresses him/herself by elaborate gestures, pictures, or words. (For example: "The only way I can show you how the ballet dancer spun around is if I stand on my tiptoes on the record player and put the speed up to 78.")					
10. My child uses common materials in ways not typically expected. (For example: "I'll bring a deck of cards when we go camping. If it rains, we can use them to start a fire and if it's dry, we can play *Go Fish* around the campfire.")					

Jim Delisle, 1979

Figure 13. Sample parent nomination form (continued).

"Things My Child Likes to Do"

	Seldom or Never	Sometimes	Quite Often*	Almost Always*	Examples From Your Own Child's Life
11. My child avoids typical ways of doing things, choosing instead to find new ways to approach a problem or topic. (For example: "I had trouble moving this box to the other side of the garage so I used these four broom handles as rollers and just pushed it along.")					
12. My child likes to "play with ideas," often making up situations which probably will not occur. (For example: "I wonder what would happen if a scientist found a way to kill all insects, then went ahead and did it.")					
13. My child often finds humor in situations or events that are not obviously funny to most children his/her age. (For example: "It was really funny that after our coach showed us a movie on playground safety, he sprained his ankle while lining us up to go back to class.")					
14. My child prefers working or playing alone rather than doing something "just to go along with the gang." (For example: "I always misspell the first word in a spelling bee; then I get to sit down and do something I like.")					

Jim Delisle, 1979

* If your child scores in either of these two columns, it would be helpful if you would write a specific example in the last column, using the reverse side of this page if necessary.

Figure 13. Sample parent nomination form (continued).

Peer Nomination Form

Name _____

School _____ Grade _____

Room Number _____

1. In your class, who would you like to help you with your homework in the following areas:

    Math _____

    Language Arts _____

    Reading _____

    Social Studies _____

    Science _____

2. In your class, who do you think is the best:

    Artist _____

    Singer _____

    Gymnast _____

    Instrumentalist _____ What instrument? _____

    Other _____

3. In your class, who has the:

    Best sense of humor _____

    The most original ideas _____

    Most respect for fellow students _____

4. In your class, who would you like to have as your group leader when you are doing group projects?

    _____

5. In your class, who is the best student?

    _____

Adapted from Charlottesville, VA Public Schools

Figure 14. Sample peer nomination form.

Self-Nomination Form

Name_____   Grade _____

School _____   Birthdate _____

In which areas do you have a special talent or ability?

_____	General Intellectual Ability	_____	Music
_____	Math	_____	Drama
_____	Science	_____	Dance
_____	Social Studies	_____	Creativity
_____	Language Arts	_____	Leadership
_____	Reading	_____	Other _____
_____	Art		

Why are you good at the areas you checked? Describe projects you have done, books you have read, or other activities that may explain why you are good at those areas.

Figure 15. Sample self-nomination form.

by a screening committee that makes a decision about inclusion in the Talent Pool. In most cases the screening committee carries out a case study that includes examination of all previous school records; interviews with students, teachers, and parents; and the administration of individual assessments recommended by the committee. In some cases, students that are recommended on the basis of one or more alternate pathways are placed in the program on a trial basis.

Step 4: Special Nominations (Safety Valve No. 1)

Special nominations represent the first of two "safety valves" in this identification system. This procedure involves circulating a list of all students who have been nominated through one of the procedures in Steps 1 through 3 to all teachers within the school and in previous schools if students have matriculated from another building. This procedure allows previous year teachers to nominate students who have not been recommended by their present teacher and it also allows resource teachers to make recommendations based on their own previous experiences with students who have already been in the Talent Pool or students they have encountered as part of enrichment experiences that were offered in regular classrooms. This step allows for a final review of the total school population and is designed to circumvent the opinions of present year teachers who may not have an appreciation for the abilities, style, or even the personality of a particular student. One last "sweep" through the population also helps to pick up students that may have "turned-off" to school or developed patterns of underachievement as a result of personal or family problems. This step also helps to overcome the general biases of an under-nominator or a non-nominator. As with the case of alternate pathways, special nominations are not automatic. Instead, a case study is carried out and the final decision rests with the screening committee.

Step 5: Notification and Orientation of Parents

A letter of notification and a comprehensive description of the program is forwarded to the parents of all Talent Pool students indicating that their child has been placed in the Talent Pool for the year (see Figure 16). The letter does not indicate that a child has been certified "as gifted," but rather explains the nature of the program and extends an invitation to parents for an orientation meeting. At this meeting a description of the three-ring conception of giftedness is provided, as well as an explanation of all program policies, procedures, and activities. Parents are informed about how admission to the Talent Pool is determined, that it is carried out on an annual basis, and that additions to Talent Pool membership might take place during the year as a result of evaluations of student participation and progress. Parents are also invited to make individual appointments whenever they feel that additional information about the program or their own child is required. A similar orientation session is provided for students, with emphasis once again being placed on the services and activities being provided. Students are not told that they are "the gifted," but through a discussion of the three-ring conception and the procedures for developing general and specific potentials, they come to understand that the development of gifted behaviors is a program goal, as well as part of their own responsibility.

Dear Parents:

We are pleased to inform you that your child, _____,
has been selected to participate in the Talent Pool of our Schoolwide Enrichment Program for this school year. This selection was based on your child's above average ability or potential for achievement. This information comes from several criteria, including teacher nominations, grades, achievement test scores, classroom performance, creativity, task commitment, interests, peer nominations, and self-nominations.

The Schoolwide Enrichment Model (SEM) program was developed to provide necessary challenge both within the regular classroom and in an enrichment room setting to ensure that all our students are motivated, interested, and encouraged to work at a challenging level. The program strives to develop critical and creative thinking skills and methodological skills for independent study so that students might become more productive adults. We are also committed to the pursuit of excellence. We strive to provide students with experiences in which they may excel by learning the value of work and commitment.

Approximately 15% of students in this district are selected for the Talent Pool. This program services all students with general exploratory experiences (Type I's), skill training (Type II's), and enrichment clusters. In addition, students who choose and demonstrate the ability to do so may pursue independent investigations (Type III's). Because your child has been included in the Talent Pool for this year, we would like to describe in more detail the ways students may be involved in the SEM.

• **Type I's.** Students are regularly exposed to a wide variety of topics, issues, and disciplines that are not normally covered in the regular curriculum. These Type I experiences are provided for general enrichment, as well as to "spark interests" in students who may want to pursue an advanced level of study (Type III investigation).

• **Type II's.** Students in the Talent Pool meet regularly with the enrichment specialist in the enrichment room. These students will spend at least one hour per week involved in Type II skill training activities. These include creative and critical thinking skills, advanced research and reference skills, and creative problem solving activities.

• **Enrichment Clusters.** Students are able to participate in a variety of enrichment clusters. Enrichment clusters are groups of students who meet regularly to pursue a common interest and the investigation of a real-world topic. These groups are interest-based, multi-age, and use real-world methodologies and resources to develop an authentic product or service.

• **Type III's.** Through increased involvement with other types of enrichment experiences, students in the Talent Pool may become interested in pursuing a Type III investigation. One of the major purposes of Type I and Type II Enrichment is to develop advanced level thinking skills and stimulate new interests in students. In this case, a student can spend up to five additional hours per week in the enrichment room. Students may work individually or in small groups based on interest. Projects may range in length from several weeks to several months.

(continued)

Figure 16. Notification letter for parents of talent pool students.

• **Curriculum Compacting**. Time spent in the enrichment room will not result in your child missing essential work in the regular classroom. A careful assessment of academic strengths has resulted in "compacting" the curriculum in those areas. This will allow your child to cover regular curricular material at a pace that is appropriate for his/her ability level and will avoid repetition of already mastered material. Curriculum compacting also helps avoid the boredom and frustration that many above-average students may experience. The time that is saved through curriculum compacting will be spent in the enrichment room.

• **Total Talent Portfolio**. A portfolio that highlights your child's interests, strengths and preferred learning styles is kept on file in the enrichment room. The portfolio includes an interest assessment filled out by the student, a learning styles inventory, plus a collection of representative work from the classroom, enrichment clusters, and special projects or Type III investigations. It is passed from grade to grade to show your child's progress and growth.

We hope this is helpful in clarifying the SEM Program. Your child will be given an overview at school. We have arranged an orientation meeting for parents to explain the SEM, distribute a parent handbook, and answer questions. The meeting will be held at _____ on _____ at _____.

We are delighted to be able to work with your child and provide these enrichment services. In addition, we welcome and encourage parent participation in the program, whether it is for a Type I workshop, an enrichment cluster, help with transportation, typing, or a mentorship. If you think you can donate an hour or more throughout the year, please complete the form below and bring it to the meeting.

Thank you for supporting our program. We hope to see you at the orientation meeting!

Sincerely,

- -

Schoolwide Enrichment Model Program

Please sign this form to indicate that you have received this notification and return it to your child's school as soon as possible.

Student's Name: _____

School: _____

Parent or Guardian: _____

Profession(s): _____

Phone: (hm) _____ (wk) _____

I am willing to donate one hour as a parent volunteer in the enrichment program in the following way:

_____ Share an interest, hobby or occupation with a small group of children
_____ Help locate and schedule Type I experiences
_____ Work as a mentor
_____ Facilitate an enrichment cluster
_____ Computer work _____ Driving _____ Other _____

Figure 16. Notification letter for parents of talent pool students (continued).

Step 6: Action Information Nominations (Safety Valve No. 2)

In spite of our best efforts, this system will occasionally overlook students, who, for one reason or another, are not selected for Talent Pool membership. To help overcome this problem, orientation related to spotting unusually favorable "turn-ons" in the regular curriculum is provided for all teachers. In programs following the SEM, we also provide a wide variety of in-class enrichment experiences that might result in recommendations for special services. This process is facilitated through the use of a teacher training activity and an instrument called an *Action Information Message* (Renzulli & Reis, 1985, pp. 41-42, 398-403).

Action information can best be defined as the dynamic interactions that occur when a student becomes extremely interested in or excited about a particular topic, area of study, issue, idea, or event that takes place in school or the non-school environment. It is derived from the concept of performance-based assessment and serves as the second safety valve in this identification system. The transmission of an *Action Information Message* (see Figure 17) does not mean that a student will automatically revolve into advanced level services, however, it serves as the basis for a careful review of the situation to determine if such services are warranted. *Action Information Messages* are also used within Talent Pool settings (i.e., pull-out groups, advanced classes, cluster groups) to make determinations about the pursuit of individual or small group investigations (Type III Enrichment in the Triad Model).

The Importance of Using Multiple Identification Criteria

In most identification systems that follow the traditional screening-plus selection approach, the "throw aways" have invariably been those students who qualified for screening on the basis of non-test criteria. Thus, for example, a teacher nomination is only used as a ticket to take an individual or group ability test, but in most cases the test score is always the deciding factor. The many and various "good things" that led to nominations by teachers are totally ignored when it comes to the final (selection) decision and the "multiple criteria approach" ends up being a smoke screen for the same old test-based approach.

The implementation of the identification system described in steps 1-6 has helped to overcome this problem, as well as a wide array of other problems traditionally associated with selecting students for special programs. Generally, students, parents, teachers, and administrators have expressed high degrees of satisfaction with this approach (Renzulli, 1988) and the reason for this satisfaction is plainly evident. By "picking up" that layer of students below the top few percentile levels usually selected for special programs and by leaving some room in the program for students to gain entrance on the basis of non-test criteria, we have eliminated the justifiable criticisms of those persons who know that these students are in need of special opportunities, resources, and encouragement. The research underlying the three-ring conception of giftedness clearly tells us that such an approach is justified in terms of what we know about human potential. By eliminating the endless number of "headaches" traditionally associated with

ACTION INFORMATION MESSAGE

GENERAL
CURRICULUM AREA _____
_____

ACTIVITY OR TOPIC_____
_____

IN THE SPACE BELOW, PROVIDE A BRIEF DESCRIPTION OF
THE INCIDENT OR SITUATION IN WHICH YOU OBSERVED HIGH
LEVELS OF INTEREST, TASK COMMITMENT OR CREATIVITY ON THE
PART OF A STUDENT OR SMALL GROUP OF STUDENTS. INDICATE
ANY IDEAS YOU MAY HAVE FOR ADVANCED LEVEL FOLLOW-UP ACTIVITIES,
SUGGESTED RESOURCES OR WAYS TO FOCUS THE INTEREST INTO A FIRST-
HAND INVESTIGATIVE EXPERIENCE.

TO:

FROM:

Date Received_____

DATE:

Date of Interview
with Child_____

☐ PLEASE CONTACT ME

☐ I WILL CONTACT YOU TO

Date When
Services Were
Implemented _____

ARRANGE A MEETING

J. S. R. '81

These forms are prepared on 3-part NCR paper and can be purchased in sets of 100 from Creative Learning Press.
Actual size 81/2" x 11".

Figure 17. Action information message.

identification, we have gained an unprecedented amount of support from teachers and administrators, many of whom, formerly resented the very existence of special programs.

A Change in Direction: From "Being Gifted" to the "Development of Gifted Behaviors"

Most of the confusion and controversy surrounding the definitions of giftedness that have been offered can be placed into proper perspective if we examine a few key questions. Is giftedness an absolute or relative concept? That is, is a person either "gifted" or "not gifted" (the absolute view) or can varying degrees of gifted behaviors be developed in certain people, at certain times, and under certain circumstances (the relative view)? Is gifted a static concept (i.e., you have it or you don't have it) or is it a dynamic concept (i.e., it varies within persons and learning/performance situations)? Research shows that labeling students as "gifted" is counter productive to educational efforts aimed at providing supplementary educational experiences for certain students in the general school population.

Even modest changes in the *status quo* inevitably raise concerns and questions on the parts of practitioners who might be affected by the proposed changes. One of the most frequently asked questions about the changes in identification procedures described earlier in this chapter is: "How will this approach 'square' with state guidelines?" Before answering this question, it should be pointed out that there seem to be very few people currently working in special programs who have not expressed dissatisfaction with the restrictiveness of identification guidelines. The research cited above, and the contributions of leaders in the field such as Bloom (1985), Gardner (1983), Guilford (1977), Sternberg (1985), Torrance (1979), and Treffinger (1982) clearly point the need for a re-examination of the regulations under which most programs are forced to operate. This research is so supportive of a more flexible approach to identification that the rationale for change no longer needs to be argued. Guidelines should be our servants, not our masters! If educators are to gain more control over their own destiny, they must take concrete steps to bring existing guidelines into line with present day theory and research.

Fortunately, change is in the wind and a bold new breed of leadership in gifted education is emerging in many state departments of education. These persons have been willing to re-examine present guidelines, and even in the absence of immediate changes, they have allowed for much more flexibility in the interpretation of existing regulations. Proposals that only a few years ago were being rejected, because they did not meet strict cut-off score requirements, are now being accepted and even encouraged.

To be certain, there will be a little less tidiness in the identification process, but the trade-off for tidiness and administrative expediency will result in many more flexible approaches to both identification and programming. With this flexibility will come new models for identifying and serving young people with great potential. From a research perspective, new data will be yielded, and thus, new dialogue and controversy will emerge. This is indeed how science goes on forever, how new ideas and insights are realized, and how a field of study continues to improve and revitalize itself.

Chapter 5

The Total Talent Portfolio:
Assessing Strengths, Interests, and Talents of All Students

- **Status Information: What We Already Know About Young People**
- **Action Information: New Things We Learn About Young People**
- **Student Goals and Co-Curricular Activities**
- **Talent Development Action Record**

The *Total Talent Portfolio* (*TTP*) acts as a systematic way to gather, record, and use information about each young person's strengths and abilities. The *TTP* is purposefully designed to assist teachers, students, and parents to:

1. **Collect** several different types of information that illustrate a student's strength areas and update this information regularly.
2. **Classify** the information into general categories including abilities, interests, learning style preferences, highly illustrative student products, and other related talent indicators.
3. **Review** the information contained in the *TTP* on a regular basis.
4. **Analyze** each young person's unique talent profile and his/her educational, personal, and career goals.
5. **Decide** which activities will most likely develop each young person's talents and abilities. Decisions about the most appropriate enrichment and acceleration options should emerge through a shared decision making process among the teacher, student, and parents.

Two questions guide the use of this new kind of school document: (1) What can educators learn about each student's interests and talents? and (2) How can educators use this information to develop students' interests and talents?

To use the *TTP*, educators must learn about students. What are their interests? What ideas motivate them? What are their preferred learning styles? With whom do they work best? Educators can record this information in the *TTP* and use it to design educational opportunities that nurture students' talents and interests.

This chapter reviews the steps needed to help teachers and students use the *TTP*, identify and record student talents and interests, and plan meaningful, high-level learning opportunities. The four sections—Status Information, Action Information, Student Goals

& Co-Curricular Activities, and Talent Development Action Record—provide techniques for collecting information about talent indicators.

Status Information: What We Already Know About Young People

The purpose of status information in the *Total Talent Portfolio* is to document students' talents. Learning strengths are talent indicators and manifest themselves in several ways. Three of the most revealing sources of data about young people's learning strengths include: abilities, interests and learning style preferences (Dunn & Dunn, 1992, 1993; Renzulli & Smith, 1978b; Sternberg, 1986, 1988) (see Figure 18).

Abilities

Abilities refer to a student's natural talent or aptitude for particular content areas. Traditionally, educators think of the four major content areas–Language Arts/Literature, Social Studies/History, Mathematics, and Science. Student strengths can also be displayed in less traditional areas such as Vocational Arts, Visual and Performing Arts, Computer Science, and others.

Standardized tests are a reality in today's schools, and in those cases where the tests meet the criteria of reliability, validity, objectivity, and audience appropriateness, they can provide educators with useful information if used properly within the context of the SEM. Although standardized test scores are gathered and recorded in the *Total Talent Portfolio*, it is important to emphasize that these scores are only one source of information about students' abilities. The most important use of standardized test scores is simply to identify which general area or areas are a student's greatest strengths.

Teacher-made assessments are usually designed to assess the degree of mastery of a specific unit that has been taught and to evaluate competence in an entire course or segment thereof. Objective teacher-made tests (e.g. multiple choice, matching, short answer) provide information about knowledge

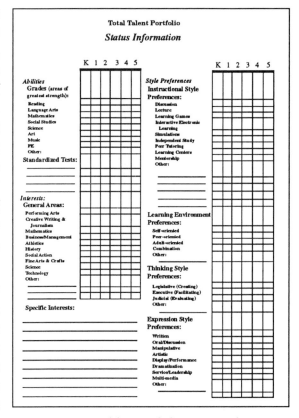

acquisition, the mastery of basic skills, and in some cases, problem solving strategies. This information is valuable for determining general levels of proficiency, but the most valuable kind of teacher-made assessments are those that elicit open-ended or extended responses. Responses of this type enable teachers to gain insight into complex student abilities such as constructing convincing arguments, using expressive written or oral

Joseph S. Renzulli

Abilities	Interests	Style Preferences			
Maximum Performance Indicators	Interest Areas	Instructional Styles Preferences	Learning Environment Preferences	Thinking Styles Preferences	Expression Style Preferences
Tests • Standardized • Teacher-Made Course Grades Teacher Ratings Product Evaluation • Written • Oral • Visual • Musical • Constructed (Note differences between assigned and self-selected products) Level of Participation in Learning Activities Degree of Interaction With Others	Fine Arts Crafts Literary Historical Mathematical/Logical Physical Sciences Life Sciences Political/Judicial Athletic/Recreation Marketing/Business Drama/Dance Musical Performance Musical Composition Managerial/Business Photography Film/Video Computers Other (Specify)	Recitation & Drill Peer Tutoring Lecture Lecture/Discussion Discussion Guided Independent Study * Learning /Interest Center Simulation, Role Playing, Dramatization, Guided Fantasy Learning Games Replicative Reports or Projects* Investigative Reports or Projects* Unguided Independent Study* Internship* Apprenticeship* *With or without a mentor	Inter/Intra Personal • Self-Oriented • Peer-Oriented • Adult-Oriented • Combined Physical • Sound • Heat • Light • Design • Mobility • Time of Day • Food Intake • Seating	Analytic (School Smart) Synthetic/Creative (Creative, Inventive) Practical/Contextual (Street Smart) Legislative Executive Judicial	Written Oral Manipulative Discussion Display Dramatization Artistic Graphic Commercial Service
Ref: General Tests and Measurements Literature	Ref: Renzulli, 1977b	Ref: Renzulli & Smith, 1978b	Ref: Amabile, 1983; Dunn, Dunn, & Price, 1975; Gardner, 1983	Ref: Sternberg, 1984, 1988, in press	Ref: Renzulli & Reis, 1985

Figure 18. Talent indicators.

language, generating relevant hypotheses, applying creative solutions to complex problems, and demonstrating deep levels of understanding.

The grades students have received in previously completed courses can also provide information about particular strength areas. When grades reflect both performance on teacher-made assessments and other accomplishments in less-structured situations, they provide a more comprehensive picture of student abilities than can be derived from test scores alone.

In addition to tests and grades, educators can also use rating scales to determine student strengths. One of the instruments that has played an important part in the SEM is a series of rating scales used to identify behavioral characteristics reflecting superior learning potentials. The *Scales for Rating the Behavioral Characteristics of Superior Students (SRBCSS)* (Renzulli, Smith, White, Callahan, & Hartman, 1976) have been widely used for special program assessment. However, their use in the *Total Talent Portfolio* is not intended to "label" students. Rather, the purpose of the *Scales* is to contribute information that will result in a comprehensive picture of a student's strengths. The *Scales* focus on the following areas: Learning, Motivation, Creativity, Leadership, Art, Music, Dramatics, Communication (Precision), Communication (Expressiveness), and Planning. Each scale is composed of a series of items derived from the research literature dealing with specific manifestations of superior abilities within the ten areas. (See margin for a sample scale from *SRBCSS*).

Interests

The heart of the Schoolwide Enrichment Model is the identification and nurturance of student interests, since talent flows from interest development. While we recognize that all of education cannot be centered around students' interests, we do believe that some classroom

---

SAMPLE ITEMS FROM *SRBCSS* CREATIVITY CHARACTERISTICS

1. Display a great deal of curiosity about many things; is constantly asking questions about anything and everything.

2. Generates a large number of ideas or solutions to problems and questions; often offers unusual "way out," unique, clever responses.

3. Is uninhibited in expressions of opinion; is sometimes radical and spirited in disagreement; is tenacious.

4. Is a high risk-taker; is adventurous and speculative.

5. Displays a good deal of intellectual playfulness; fantasizes; imagines "I wonder what would happen if . . .;" manipulates ideas (i.e., changes, elaborates upon them); is often concerned with adapting, improving, and modifying institutions, objects, and systems.

6. Displays a keen sense of humor and sees humor in situations that may not appear to be humorous to others.

7. Is usually aware of his/her impulses and more open to the irrational in himself/herself (freer expression of feminine interest for boys, greater than usual amount of independence for girls); shows emotional sensitivity.

8. Is sensitive to beauty; attends to aesthetic characteristics of things.

9. Is nonconforming; accepts disorder; is not interested in details; is individualistic; does not fear being different.

10. Criticizes constructively; is unwilling to accept authoritarian pronouncements without critical examination.

learning opportunities can be based on the varied interests of young people. In fact, the development of interest areas can encourage real-world creative productivity. Chapter 10 describes instruments and methods that can be used to identify these interests in students. Some of the instruments include the *Interest-A-Lyzer* (Renzulli, 1977b) and subsequent briefer adaptations (Burns, 1990; McGreevy, 1990; and Purcell & Siegle, 1995). Teachers are encouraged to use an interest assessment at the beginning of each school year to discover new interests and identify trends in their students' interests. Teachers should meet briefly with their students to discuss their responses on interest instruments. This oral review of the questions provides students with time to think and reflect about their answers, thereby ensuring more complete and accurate information for the interview. During these conversations, teachers should also prompt additional information from students related to specific areas of interest.

From student responses on interest surveys and discussions, patterns or general areas of interests will emerge. Two issues are important with respect to the general and specific areas of interest. First, young people will most likely have several areas of interest. Second, children's interests change over time. It is important that teachers and/or students periodically assess and document emerging interests on the *TTP*.

Style Preferences

The style preferences section of the *TTP* asks teachers to consider their students' instructional style preferences, learning environment preferences, thinking style preferences, and expression or product preferences. A brief explanation of each preference is provided below.

1. Instructional Style Preferences

Instructional styles are teacher strategies used for instruction. Although many instructional styles already exist, rapidly changing technology, especially in the computer and communications fields, is causing the number of instructional strategies to increase. Some common instructional strategies include:

- *Discussion*
- *Lecture*
- *Learning Games*
- *Interactive Electronic Learning*
- *Simulations*
- *Independent Studies*
- *Peer Tutoring*
- *Learning/Interest Centers*
- *Mentorships*

Student involvement in these teaching strategies ranges on a continuum from low to high (see Figure 19). Lecture, for example, is placed on the end of the continuum under low student involvement, whereas independent study is placed at the other end of the scale. By arranging the instructional strategies on this continuum, teachers will be able to notice that some students react positively to some instructional styles and less favorably to others.

Instructional Styles & Student Involvement

Independent Study

Mentorships

Projects

Simulations/Role Playing

Electronic Learning

Learning Games

Learning Centers

Field Trips

Cooperative Learning

Peer Tutoring

Small Group Discussions

Demonstration

Discussion

Lecture

Low Involvement ▬▬▬▬▬▬▬▬▬▬▬▬▬ High Involvement

Figure 19. Instructional style preferences.

Information about these preferred instructional strategies can be used by teachers to construct learning opportunities. By matching individual students or small groups of students' instructional style preferences with the instructional strategies used in learning activities, teachers can maximize learning and enhance students' enjoyment of learning.

Of course, students' preferred instructional strategies cannot always be addressed in the classroom. Some instructional time can be structured to address individual and small group style preferences. As with interests, it is also important to document students' preferences on an on-going basis, since these preferences may evolve.

One of the approaches used to gain information about student preferences for instructional techniques is an instrument called the *Learning Styles Inventory* (Renzulli & Smith, 1978b). This research-based instrument was developed to guide teachers in planning learning experiences that take into account the style preferences of students within their classrooms. The *Learning Styles Inventory* (*LSI*) is an instrument that seeks to identify the ways in which individual young people would like to pursue various types of educational experiences. (See next page for sample items from the *LSI*).

2. Learning Environment Preferences

Grouping pattern preferences, another talent indicator included on the status information section of the *TTP*, reflects students' preferences for working alone, in pairs, in teams, or with adults. When students are given freedom of choice, the extent to which they pursue group affiliation is almost always an indicator of social style preferences. Some students thrive in small or large peer group situations, others prefer to work with a single partner, and still others prefer to work alone or with an adult. Environmental preferences may vary as a function of the material being taught, the nature of the task to be accomplished, and the social relationships that exist within any given group of students.

Teachers should bring an image of each student to mind and ask the following question: *"When given a choice of grouping arrangements in the academic setting (individual, peer group, adult interaction, combination), which does the young person prefer?"*

3. Thinking Style Preferences

Robert Sternberg defines thinking styles as the manner in which "one directs one's intelligence" (1988). He identifies three distinct thinking styles: legislative, executive, and judicial (see Figure 20).

Teachers can observe the ways in which these thinking styles emerge in young people on a daily basis. Students with a legislative thinking style are the planners and creators. They design and invent both within the classroom and at home. Legislative thinkers prefer to plan, choreograph, design, create, compose, invent, animate, devise, develop, and write. Students with an executive thinking style are facilitators who like to fill in the content or details of existing structures. Executive thinkers prefer to facilitate, help, specify, simplify, interpret, clarify, support, sustain, assist, and explain. Students with a judicial thinking style are evaluators. They prefer to judge designs, structures or content and like to appraise, weigh, value, consider, assess, determine, and review.

Teachers are encouraged to ask the following question when considering a student's thinking style preference(s): *"Which set of verbs most clearly characterizes the actions and work of this young person over time?"* Teachers should emphasize that all thinking styles are good; one style is not better than another. While individual thinking style preferences can be addressed through choices of learning activities, it is equally important to remember that teachers should present students with opportunities to learn and work in all styles, since real-world learning situations require the use of all thinking styles. Teachers should also remember that students' preferred thinking styles may vary over time, so they should assess thinking styles periodically to determine continuing trends and variations.

SAMPLE ITEMS FROM THE LEARNING STYLES INVENTORY

A MEASURE OF STUDENT PREFERENCE FOR INSTRUCTIONAL TECHNIQUES

by
JOSEPH S. RENZULLI
LINDA H. SMITH

- Having other students who are experts on a topic present their ideas to the class.

- Going to the library with a committee to look up information.

- Having a friend help you learn material you are finding difficult to understand.

- Studying on your own to learn new information.

- Planning a project you will work on by yourself.

- Working on assignment where the questions are arranged in an order that helps you get them right.

- Playing a board game that helps you practice one of your school subjects. (An example of a "board game" is Scrabble or Monopoly.)

Sternberg's Thinking Styles

LEGISLATIVE	EXECUTIVE	JUDICIAL
design	facilitate	evaluate
create	simplify	appraise
choreograph	interpret	weigh
compose	help	assess
invent	specify	determine
animate	clarify	consider
develop	assist	review
write	explain	judge
film	support	critique
devise	sustain	value

Figure 20. Sternberg's thinking styles.

4. Expression Style Preferences

The final style preference on the *TTP* concerns young people's favored expression formats or products. Teachers can identify a student's expression style preferences by thinking about the student's favorite projects/products—e.g. written material, art projects, dramatic performances, etc. A knowledge of expression style preferences can help teachers expand the range of learning options for individuals and small groups by "legitimizing" a broader variety of the ways in which students express themselves.

Some styles of expression are more participative and leader-oriented than product-oriented. Organizations, management, and service activities such as starting a club or business, serving as a project or team leader, or participating in community service activities should be explored as alternatives to the traditional written or oral formats that characterize most formal learning activities. These alternatives are especially valuable for students with limited English proficiency or students who have had difficulty with standard writing or formal speaking skills. A knowledge of the ways in which young people prefer to express themselves can be a valuable tool for organizing cooperative learning and project groups.

Action Information: New Things We Learn About Young People

The previous section dealt with status information, what teachers *already know* about students. This section concerns action information, *new* information teachers learn about students. Teachers have many opportunities to observe action information when students express themselves and interact with others in the regular curriculum. Enrichment activities provide important contexts for students' interests and allow creative ideas to emerge. Student work and products offer special information on student strengths and talents. Information from action information forms (see Chapter 9) can be used in the *TTP*.

The Regular Curriculum and Enrichment Learning Situations

The regular curriculum consists of everything that is part of the pre-determined goals, schedules, learning outcomes, and delivery systems of the school. The heart of enrichment learning and teaching includes Type I, Type II, and Type III Enrichment. These activities are purposefully embedded into the regular curriculum to identify and nurture student interests and talents. Type I activities (see Chapter 7) are general exploratory activities that invite students to pursue a topic in more depth. Type II activities (see chapter 8) consist of skill training activities that focus on cognitive or methodological skills. These skills provide students with the "know-how" to complete Type III (see Chapter 9) independent investigations of real-world problems. These are the self-selected, independent studies of real-world problems which, in many cases, arise from students' previous exposures to Type I and Type II activities. By observing students' interests and responses to these types of activities and encouraging follow-up, teachers can find and promote new student interests and strengths and document these on the *TTP*.

Action Information Messages

Students who display a heightened interest in a topic will exhibit a variety of behaviors including: prolific questioning or constant discussion about a topic; hanging around experts in a topic; giving up free time to pursue a topic; and/or spending their own money on resources related to a topic. *Action Information Messages* (Renzulli, 1981) are

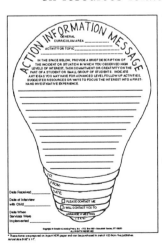

observations by educators that a child has demonstrated heightened interest in an area and/or commitment to a particular topic. These observations are important because they alert school personnel to the need for important follow-up by the observer, classroom teacher, enrichment specialist, parents, and others. Appropriate and timely follow-up ensures the likelihood that a student or small group of students will engage successfully in the independent investigation.

Action Information Messages can be completed by a student or teacher who recognizes a specific interest. Once an action information form has been completed, the classroom teacher or enrichment specialist should set up an interview with the student to try to assess his/her interest and commitment level and help him/her develop a *Management Plan* if commitment and interest are clear. The *Action Information Message* should then be included in the *TTP*. This will alert teachers and other school personnel to the interest area(s) of the student and provide important information for decision making. For information about the *Management Plan* and information about initiating a Type III investigation, see Chapter 9.

Student Work and Products: A Special Kind of Action Information

Student work and products are special kinds of action information. Like the student behaviors discussed earlier, they can illustrate the very best things educators know about young people and represent another important talent indicator for the *TTP*. Three things are important when considering student products and work for the *TTP* (Purcell & Renzulli, in press). First, the diversity of student products should be respected. Written work is probably the most common type of product, but teachers should examine other diverse ways that students can express their abilities and creativity.

Second, students should have autonomy with respect to the folder and its contents. While teachers need to provide students with broad guidelines such as the number of pieces they should include and specify different types of possible products, students should be the ones to decide which pieces of work or products are included in the folder. Equally important, students should be the ones to formulate and refine many of the criteria used to place pieces in the folder. Given the opportunity, students can identify rich, affective descriptors such as "I used commas correctly in this essay," "I really tried my hardest on this persuasive essay and revised it three times," and "I used lots of descriptive words to express my feelings in this paragraph." Young people who are provided with regular opportunities to share assessment descriptors and decide upon pieces to include in a their *TTP* reap a range of educational benefits, including becoming actively involved in their learning, creating personally meaningful criteria, developing an understanding of exceptional work, using high-level thinking skills, and taking responsibility for their learning (Purcell & Renzulli, in press).

The third issue deals with product storage in the *TTP*. Physically large products such as science projects, bulletin board displays, and mobiles can be documented with photographs (such as Polaroid shots) or sketches. If video cameras are available, it is important to capture presentations, debates, and other demonstrations on tape.

If there is a "golden rule" about the use of portfolios, it is that the products should not be skill and drill activities such as worksheets or routine assignments. If a student has produced a superior response to something like an essay question or a complicated mathematics problem, it should be considered and possibly included in the portfolio. It is important, however, to avoid turning the portfolio into a routine collection of seatwork and homework assignments.

Student Goals and Co-Curricular Activities

Teachers can discuss appropriate goals for the *TTP* by explaining the strong connection between goals and accomplishments. Achievable goals should be important, challenging, specific, realistic, and have a beginning and end point in time (Purcell & Renzulli, in press). Teachers can provide students with examples of important goals that will help students to select similar goals (see Figure 21). Goals can then be documented on the *TTP*.

"Co-curricular activities" is an inclusive term encompassing things that children do outside the school setting. These activities include lessons (ballet, piano, and gymnastics), products that children create at home (models of volcanoes, maps of Civil War battlefields, and replicas of the human body), important activities (leadership projects within the neighborhood and church, exemplary participation in scouting, significant contributions to 4-H Club, or devotion to a particular organization such as the Audubon Society), and performances that children give (city and town talent shows, home and neighborhood magic or puppet shows, and county fairs) (see Figure 21). The talent demonstrated out of school is important information for the *TTP*. Students should be encouraged to think about their outside-of-school activities.

Talent Development Action Record

The information collected by teachers and parents for the *TTP* can be used to create meaningful and appropriate high-level learning experiences to develop children's talents. This can involve enrichment clusters, curriculum compacting, and the action plan developed from the Talent Development Action Record.

High-Level Learning Options: Enrichment Clusters

Enrichment clusters (Chapter 10) are non-graded groups of students who come together during specially designated time blocks to pursue common interests. Clusters differ from traditional learning and teaching in several ways.

1. They cut across ability levels and grade levels.
2. They involve choice by students and are interest-based.
3. They are orchestrated around the production of a product or service.
4. They allow cluster participants to take on the roles of real-world practicing professionals.
5. They provide students with opportunities to develop higher order thinking skills and apply these skills in creative and productive situations.

High-Level Learning Options: Curriculum Compacting

Curriculum compacting (Reis, Burns, & Renzulli, 1992) (Chapter 6) is an easy-to-use instructional strategy in which teachers assess students' knowledge before they teach a curriculum unit to discover the proportion of material students already know. Already mastered material can be eliminated for some students and replaced with more challenging enrichment and acceleration learning options. Thus, compacting ensures mastery of the basic curriculum, helps students avoid spending endless class and homework time repeating material they already know, and provides time for students who demonstrate mastery to pursue high-level learning activities.

Samples of Student Goals

1. Write and publish an anthology of poetry in the next six months.
2. Start a recycling center for school trash this year.
3. Enter the spring science fair with a project about air pressure.
4. Develop a board game about insects.
5. Initiate a newspaper club for students interested in publishing a monthly student newspaper.
6. Create an interactive display about local history.
7. Work with a professional in a field that interests me.
8. Start a rock collection from local specimens to exhibit in the school display case.
9. Create a travel brochure for people traveling to Australia.
10. Choreograph a dance piece and present it at the student talent show.

Samples of Student Co-Curricular Activities

1. Member of a Youth Choir.
2. Guitar Lessons Weekly.
3. Member of Boy Scouts/Girl Scouts.
4. Captain of Saturday Basketball.
5. Ballet Lessons Bi-Weekly.
6. Chairperson of Kids' Crime Watch Unit.
7. Participant in Town Talent Show.
8. Creator of a Working Volcano Model.
9. Campaign Volunteer for Local Politician.
10. Member of Local 4-H Club.

Figure 21. Samples of student goals and co-curricular activities.

Creating the Talent Development Action Record

The Talent Development Action Record (Figure 22) provides a profile of a student's high-level learning experiences (enrichment clusters, curriculum compacting, Type I Enrichment, Type II Enrichment, and Type III Enrichment). This form, which can be completed by teachers or support personnel, contains brief statements about a student's talent development activities.

Recommendations

Teachers and parents must focus on children's abilities, interests, and learning style preferences as they prepare annual recommendations to escalate each student's creative productivity and academic achievement. Readers will quickly see that the high-level learning options (enrichment clusters, curriculum compacting, enrichment activities) overlap with these abilities, interests, and learning style preferences. It is important to note that a wide variety of high-level learning options exist. Practitioners in each building should develop their own unique combination of enrichment and acceleration options.

Type II Activities

Type I Activities

Type III Activities

Total Talent Portfolio Recommendations

Enrichment Clusters

Curriculum Modifications

Recommendations for the *TTP* are usually generated at the end of each academic year. At this time, teachers, parents, and students should carefully review all the information contained within the young person's *TTP* and discuss the notations and documents so that important information and a variety of perspectives can be brought to bear upon future plans.

Concluding Thoughts

This chapter is based on what we've learned about developing talent in young people. The *TTP* is a qualitatively different school document that teachers, students, and parents can use to facilitate individual student growth and, by doing so, facilitate the larger process of school change. The change process begins when teachers look at students in a new way—to see the best things in each student. "Best things" are talent indicators which manifest themselves through status information, action information, and students' goals and co-curricular activities.

The second phase of the school change process begins when teachers, parents, and students create action plans and recommendations around each young person's unique set of talent indicators. Action plans and recommendations are made up of high-level learning options that are provided by a school. Taken together, the high-level learning options form the school's continuum of special services. Student's opportunities to participate in escalating levels of enrichment and accelerative learning opportunities are the consummate criteria for determining the success of a school. (See Appendix B for a sample copy of the *Total Talent Portfolio*).

Talent Development Action Record

for:

Date	Grade	Teacher	Clusters	Curriculum Compacting	Exploratory Activities (Type I's)	Skill-Related Activities (Type II's)	Self-Selected Independent Investigations (Type III's)

Figure 22. Talent development action record.

Chapter 6

Curriculum Compacting:
A Systematic Procedure for Modifying the Curriculum for Above Average Ability Students

- **What is Curriculum Compacting?**
- **The Compacting Process**
- **The Compactor**
- **Enrichment and Acceleration Options**
- **Recommendations for Success**
- **Research on Curriculum Compacting**
- **Teacher Training**

The policy statements of almost every school district in the nation reflect a commitment to meet students' individual needs, yet many districts lack the capacity to put these policies into practice. An almost unlimited amount of remedial curricular material has helped teachers make necessary adjustments for lower achieving students. However, educators have lacked an orderly method to make comparable adjustments for students who are already achieving at well above average levels. This chapter describes curriculum compacting, an easy-to-implement instructional technique for modifying the curriculum for above average ability students. This technique can also be used for any student who displays strengths or high levels of interest in one or more content areas. The procedure has proven its effectiveness in a carefully controlled national research study, as well as through several years of classroom use in a variety of educational settings across the nation.

What Is Curriculum Compacting?

Curriculum compacting (Renzulli & Smith, 1978a) is an instructional technique that is specifically designed to make appropriate curricular adjustments for students in any curricular area and at any grade level (see Figure 23). Curriculum compacting has been developed and field tested over the last fifteen years (Imbeau, 1991; Renzulli, Smith, & Reis, 1982) as part of a total educational program for gifted and talented students. It can be used, however, as part of any educational program for more capable students and has been mentioned by several other developers of programming models as a method for modifying curriculum for high ability students (Betts, 1986; Clifford, Runions, & Smith,

Curriculum Compacting
Summary Sheet

DEFINITION: Modifying or "streamlining" the regular curriculum in order to eliminate repetition of previously mastered material, upgrade the challenge level of the regular curriculum, and provide time for appropriate enrichment and/or acceleration activities while ensuring mastery of basic skills.

TARGET AUDIENCES:

1. All Talent Pool students (according to individual strength areas), especially when involved in a Type III activity.

2. Any non-Talent Pool student who has previously mastered portions of the regular curriculum or is capable of mastering such material at an accelerated pace.

OBJECTIVES:

1. To create a challenging learning environment within the context of the regular curriculum.

2. To guarantee proficiency in basic curriculum.

3. To "buy" time for enrichment and acceleration.

KEY CONCEPTS: Modification of the Regular Curriculum Through an Assessment of Student Strengths.

Elimination or Acceleration of Skills Activities in Strength Areas Following Assessment.

Systematic Planning of Enrichment and/or Acceleration Activities to Replace Skills Students Have Already Mastered or Can Master at a Faster Pace.

ACTION FORMS: The Compactor

Figure 23. Curriculum compacting summary sheet.

1986; Feldhusen, & Kolloff, 1986; Treffinger, 1986). The procedure involves: (1) defining the goals and outcomes of a particular unit or segment of instruction, (2) determining and documenting which students have already mastered most or all of a specified set of learning outcomes, and (3) providing replacement strategies for material already mastered through the use of instructional options that enable a more challenging and productive use of the student's time. The specific steps for carrying out curriculum compacting in both basic skill and content areas will be described below.

The Compacting Process

This section takes a step-by-step look at the curriculum compacting process. For a more detailed look at this process, refer to the book entitled *Curriculum Compacting* (Reis, Burns, & Renzulli, 1992) which is a comprehensive guide for modifying the regular curriculum for high ability students (see Figure 24 for a brief overview of the curriculum compacting process).

Phase 1: Defining Goals and Outcomes

Step 1: Identify Objectives in a Given Subject or Grade

The first of three phases of the compacting process consists of defining the goals and outcomes of a given unit or segment of instruction. This information is readily available in most subjects because specific goals and outcomes usually can be found in teachers' manuals, curriculum guides, scope-and-sequence charts, and some of the new curricular frameworks that are emerging in connection with outcome-based education models. Teachers should examine these objectives to determine which objectives represent the acquisition of new content or thinking skills as opposed to reviews or practice of material that has been previously taught. The scope-and-sequence charts prepared by publishers or a simple comparison of the table of contents of a basal series will provide a quick overview of new versus repeated material. A major goal of this phase of the compacting process is to help teachers make individual programming decisions. A larger professional development goal involves helping teachers become better analysts of the material they are teaching and better consumers of textbooks and prescribed curricular material.

Phase 2: Identifying Candidates for Compacting

Step 2: Identify Students Who Should Be Pretested

The second phase of curriculum compacting is identifying students who have already mastered the objectives or outcomes of a unit or segment of instruction that is about to be taught. The first step of this phase consists of estimating which students have the potential to master new material at a faster than normal pace. Knowing one's students is, of course, the best way to begin the assessment process. Scores on previous tests, completed assignments, and classroom participation are the best ways of identifying likely candidates for compacting. Standardized achievement tests can serve as a good

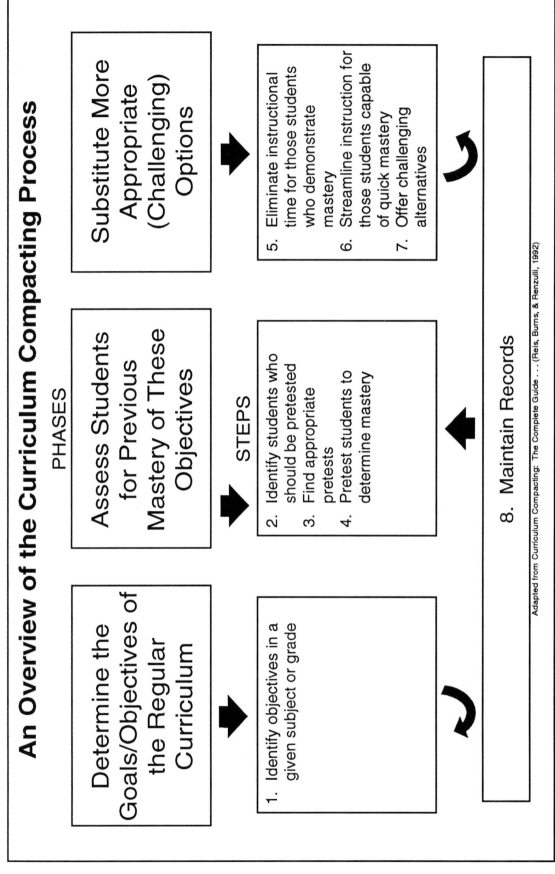

An Overview of the Curriculum Compacting Process

PHASES

Determine the Goals/Objectives of the Regular Curriculum

Assess Students for Previous Mastery of These Objectives

Substitute More Appropriate (Challenging) Options

STEPS

1. Identify objectives in a given subject or grade

2. Identify students who should be pretested
3. Find appropriate pretests
4. Pretest students to determine mastery

5. Eliminate instructional time for those students who demonstrate mastery
6. Streamline instruction for those students capable of quick mastery
7. Offer challenging alternatives

8. Maintain Records

Adapted from Curriculum Compacting: The Complete Guide . . . (Reis, Burns, & Renzulli, 1992)

Figure 24. An overview of the curriculum compacting process.

general screen for this step, because they allow teachers to list the names of all students who are scoring one or more years above grade level in particular subject areas.

Step 3: Find Appropriate Pretests

Being a candidate for compacting does not necessarily mean that a student knows the material under consideration. Therefore, the next step of identifying candidates consists of finding or developing appropriate tests or other assessment techniques that can be used to evaluate specific learning outcomes. Unit pretests or end-of-unit tests that can be administered as pretests are ready made for this task, especially when it comes to the assessment of basic skills. An analysis of pretest results enables the teacher to document proficiency in specific skills, and select instructional activities or practice material that can be used to help student master specific skills.

The process is slightly modified for compacting content areas that are not as easily assessed (Art) and for students who have not mastered the material, but are judged to be candidates for more rapid coverage. Students should have a thorough understanding of the goals and procedures of compacting, including the nature of the replacement process. A given segment of material should be discussed with the student (e.g., a unit that includes a series of chapters in a Social Studies text) and the procedures for verifying mastery at a high level should be specified. These procedures might consist of answering questions based on the chapters, writing an essay, or taking the standard end-of-unit test. The amount of time for completion of the unit should be specified and procedures such as periodic progress reports or log entries for teacher review should be agreed upon. An examination of potential acceleration and/or enrichment replacement activities should be a part of this discussion.

Another alternative is to assess or pretest all students in a class when a new unit or topic is introduced. Although this may seem like more work for the teacher, it provides the opportunity for all students to demonstrate their strengths or previous mastery in a given area. Using a matrix of learning objectives, teachers can fill in test results and establish small, flexible, and temporary groups for skill instruction and replacement activities. The important criterion to use when selecting a pretest is that it is aligned with the desired learning objectives.

Step 4: Pretest Students to Determine Mastery

All teachers within a given grade or subject need to first determine what constitutes "mastery" and how those students who are learning disabled or culturally different might be considered differently. If teachers choose to use an objective-referenced test, they should discuss the purpose of the test with students beforehand. This discussion should include pointing out that some students may be familiar with the material, asking students if they would like to skip some of the material covered in the unit if they can demonstrate partial mastery, and assuring students that they are not expected to know material that will be on the tests and will not be labeled or given a poor grade if they do not know it.

Performance-based tests are an alternative to objective-referenced tests, and though they may require more time, they provide a valid assessment of the process a student uses to arrive at an answer. They offer a valuable alternative for younger children or for those who may not test well.

Phase 3: Providing Acceleration and Enrichment Options

There are two options for compacting—basic skills compacting and content compacting. Basic skills compacting eliminates skills that students have already acquired. This type of compacting is appropriate for Math, Spelling, Grammar, and Language. Pretesting for basic skills is simpler and mastery can be demonstrated more precisely. Content compacting is more effective for general knowledge subjects, such as Social Studies, Science and Literature, where instruction and evaluation tends to be more flexible and less formal (see Figure 25).

Step 5: Eliminate Instructional Time for Those Students Who Demonstrated Mastery

Students who demonstrate mastery of the learning objectives should have the opportunity for acceleration or enrichment activities. Students should be allowed to miss those class sessions, activities, or reading that will cover those objectives, and previously mastered materials should be replaced with new and stimulating material that is more closely aligned with students' abilities and learning speed.

Step 6: Streamline Instruction for Those Students Capable of Quick Mastery

Some students may not demonstrate mastery of all objectives, but through mastery of some, show an ability to move through new content at a faster pace than their peers. These students who need less practice and require flexible instruction should be given an opportunity to progress at their own speed. Several criteria are important for this

Two Kinds of Curriculum Compacting

BASIC SKILL COMPACTING	CONTENT COMPACTING
1. Does the student already know the skills being covered in the classroom?	1. If the student already knows the content, will he/she have an opportunity to display competency of the subject or topic? (In English class, a teacher who has just distributed thirty copies of a novel to a sophomore class asks if anyone has already read the book.)
2. Can proficiency be documented?	
3. Can certain skills be eliminated?	
4. Will the student be allowed and encouraged to master missing skills at his/her own pace?	2. If students do not already know the content but have the ability to master the material at their own pace, will they be given that opportunity?
5. If skills can be mastered at a pace commensurate with a student's ability, will the student be able to help determine what he/she will do in the time earned by displaying mastery?	3. If content mastery can be demonstrated, will the student have the opportunity to select the work that will be substituted for previously mastered content?

Figure 25. Two kinds of curriculum compacting.

type of instruction to be effective: (1) the instruction must be high quality, (2) the instruction must be appropriate to students' levels, (3) students must be motivated to work on the tasks, and (4) student must have adequate time to learn (Reis, Burns, & Renzulli, 1992).

Step 7: Offer Challenging Alternatives

The next phase of the compacting process can be one of the most exciting aspects of teaching, because it is based on cooperative decision making and creativity on the parts of both teachers and students. Efforts can be made to gather enrichment materials and ideas from classroom teachers, librarians, media specialists, and content area or gifted education specialists. Materials and activities might include:

- *Self-directed learning activities.*
- *Instructional materials that focus on particular thinking skills.*
- *A variety of individual and group project oriented activities that are designed to promote hands-on research and investigative skills.*
- *Small group, special topic seminars that might be directed by students or community resource persons.*
- *Community-based apprenticeships or opportunities to work with a mentor.*
- *Peer tutoring situations.*
- *Involvement in community service activities.*
- *Opportunities to rotate through a series of self-selected mini-courses.*

The time saved through curriculum compacting can be used by the teacher to provide a variety of exciting enrichment or acceleration opportunities for the student. Enrichment strategies might include: self-selected independent investigations, mini-courses, advanced content, mentorships, and alternative reading assignments. Acceleration might include the use of material from the next unit or chapter, the use of the next chronological grade level textbook, or the completion of even more advanced work. Alternative activities listed in the third column of the *Compactor* (see Figure 26) should reflect an appropriate level of challenge and rigor that is commensurate with the student's abilities and interests.

Decisions about which replacement activities to use are always guided by factors such as time, space, and the availability of resource persons and materials. Although practical concerns must be considered, the ultimate criteria for replacement activities should be the degree to which they increase academic challenge and the extent to which they meet individual needs. Great care should be taken to select activities and experiences that represent individual strengths and interests rather than the assignment of more-of-the-same worksheets or randomly selected kits, games, and puzzles. This aspect of the compacting process should also be viewed as a creative opportunity for an entire staff to work cooperatively by organizing and instituting a broad array of enrichment experiences. Educators can teach a mini-course about a favorite topic or serve as a mentor to students who share a similar interest. Both teachers and students benefit from participating in the compacting process.

INDIVIDUAL EDUCATIONAL PROGRAMMING GUIDE
The Compactor

Prepared by: Joseph S. Renzulli
Linda M. Smith

NAME _____ AGE ____ TEACHER(S) _____

SCHOOL _____ GRADE ____ PARENT(S) _____

Individual Conference Dates And Persons
Participating in Planning Of IEP

CURRICULUM AREAS TO BE CONSIDERED FOR COMPACTING Provide a brief description of basic material to be covered during this marking period and the assessment information or evidence that suggests the need for compacting.	PROCEDURES FOR COMPACTING BASIC MATERIAL Describe activities that will be used to guarantee proficiency in basic curricular areas.	ACCELERATION AND/OR ENRICHMENT ACTIVITIES Describe activities that will be used to provide advanced level learning experiences in each area of the regular curriculum.

☐ Check here if additional information is recorded on the reverse side.

Figure 26. The compactor.

Step 8: Maintain Records

Documentation plays a critical part of any differentiated program, but can be time-consuming without proper planning. Staff and administrators should collectively decide on the best way to document the process. Records should include:

- *Student strength areas verified by test scores.*
- *Pretests used to determine mastery and learning objectives that were eliminated.*
- *Recommended enrichment and acceleration activities.*

The Compactor

The best way to get an overview of the curriculum compacting process is to examine the management form that guides this process. The *Compactor* (Renzulli & Smith, 1978a) is both an organizational and record keeping tool. Teachers should fill out one form per student or one form per group of students with similar curricular strengths (e.g., Reading or Math group). Completed *Compactors* should be kept in students' academic files and updated on a regular basis. The *Compactor* is divided into three sections: (1) curriculum areas to be considered for compacting, (2) procedures for compacting basic materials, and (3) acceleration and/or enrichment activities.

The first column should include information on learning objectives and student strengths in those areas. Teachers should list the objectives for a particular unit of study, followed by data on students' proficiency in those objectives, including test scores, behavioral profiles, and past academic records.

In the second column, teachers should detail the pretest vehicles they select, along with test results. The pretest instruments can be formal measures, such as pencil and paper tests or informal measures, such as performance assessments based on observations of class participation and written assignments. Specificity is extremely important. Recording an overall score of 85% on ten objectives, sheds little light on what portion of the material can be compacted, since students might show limited mastery of some objectives and high levels of mastery on others.

Column three is used to record information about acceleration or enrichment options. In determining these options, teachers must be fully aware of students' individual interests and learning styles. Teachers should never replace compacted regular curriculum work with harder, more advanced material that is solely determined by the teacher. Instead, students interests should be taken into account. If for example, a student loves working on science fair projects, that option may be used to replace material that has been compacted from the regular curriculum. Teachers should also be careful to help monitor the challenge level of the material that is being substituted. They want students to understand the nature of effort and challenge and they should ensure that students are not simply replacing the compacted material with simple reading or work that is not advanced.

Chapter 6

Sample Compactors

1. Alison: A Sample Compactor at the Elementary Level

Alison's *Compactor* (see Figure 27) reflects strengths in three areas. In Language Arts, she mastered most of the comprehension skills for the levels that were to be introduced in first grade and all of the Spelling levels. In Math she received almost a perfect score on the placement test and the follow-up individual tests for each level. She is a very precocious student in a small elementary school. She had few peers who were at a similar achievement level and she was very interested in Math and Science. It was clear that she could master all of the rest of her Language Arts objectives in one day each week.

Column two includes a listing of skills Alison had *not* mastered in the first grade Language Arts program. She met with her first grade group about one day each week or every other week to work on these areas. Her teacher also asked her to join the group whenever an enrichment lesson or an appropriate writing lesson was being taught. Because no other student in Alison's grade level was at a similar level, a decision was made to accelerate her to the second grade classroom for Mathematics. It must be pointed out that Alison's first grade teacher did not believe she could provide an individualized Math program because of time restraints and other demands. It should also be noted that a move into the second grade classroom was not

> **Enrichment Strategies Used in Column 3 of the Compactor**
>
> 1. Math Puzzles, Word Problems
> 2. Projects
> 3. Free Reading
> 4. Computer Time/Games
> 5. Creative Games
> 6. Critical Thinking Activities
> 7. Resource Room Time
> 8. Crossword Puzzles
> 9. Individualized Kits
> 10. Field Trips
> 11. More Challenging Words
> 12. Research
> 13. Utilization of Reference Materials
> 14. Creative Thinking Activities
> 15. Practice in Research Skills
> 16. Reports
> 17. Game Creation
> 18. Entering Games/Contests
> 19. Learning Centers
> 20. Public Speaking
> 21. Bulletin Boards
> 22. Journal Keeping
> 23. Science Experiments
> 24. Mentor-Guided Investigation

a panacea for meeting Alison's considerable strengths in Math. For students who are precocious in Mathematics, acceleration of only one grade is often not much more challenging than working on their own grade level material. In Alison's case, however, since she was so young, acceleration to grade two content did provide her with more challenge and an opportunity to complete more advanced work on something she loved—Mathematics. She was able to complete the regular second grade Math curriculum in half the time of other students, and the second grade teacher worked to provide challenging content in the remaining time Alison was in the classroom.

It should also be noted that Alison was well-suited to move into another classroom. Not only was she extremely intelligent, she was also quite mature for her age. She had already accepted her individual differences, often telling her teacher in the gifted program that she had realized from the time she was three or four years old that she was different from the children in her play group. Other very bright children are *not*

INDIVIDUAL EDUCATIONAL PROGRAMMING GUIDE
The Compactor

Prepared by: Joseph S. Renzulli
Linda M. Smith

NAME ___Alison___   AGE ___6___   TEACHER(S) _____   Individual Conference Dates And Persons Participating in Planning Of IEP

SCHOOL _____   GRADE ___1___   PARENT(S) _____

CURRICULUM AREAS TO BE CONSIDERED FOR COMPACTING Provide a brief description of basic material to be covered during this marking period and the assessment information or evidence that suggests the need for compacting.	PROCEDURES FOR COMPACTING BASIC MATERIAL Describe activities that will be used to guarantee proficiency in basic curricular areas.	ACCELERATION AND/OR ENRICHMENT ACTIVITIES Describe activities that will be used to provide advanced level learning experiences in each area of the regular curriculum.
Holt Basic Reading Series - Levels 3-6, as determined by Holt level tests. Alison has mastered most of the comprehension and phonetic objectives introduced in these levels.	Capital letters and periods. - Teacher made worksheets Continental Press. Alison will participate in classroom activities dealing with these skills. Check proficiency by Holt level 6 test. Capital letters and periods - pg 27. Contractions - Level 7 Teacher's Manual pages 81, 119, 175, 216, 217, and 255-256. Check proficiency by Holt Level 7 test (Contractions).	Classroom Alison's classroom teacher will use the language experience approach. Various reading and writing programs on the Apple computer will be used with Alison. Scholastic Individual Reading Kit will provide Alison with the opportunity to read independently and use instructional games and records. Alison will be provided time to work in her classroom on a Type III activity (independent study).
Individualized Spelling Program by Economy - Alison has mastered Levels 1-4. She will be placed in Level 5.	Change y to i and add es/and other plural forms: Level 9 Teacher's Manual pages 202 and 293-294. Level 8 Teacher's Manual pages 222-223, 246, 311. Check proficiency by Holt Level 9 test and reading consultant-made test for these plural forms not covered in the Level 9 test.	Talcott Mt. Science Center Alison will participate in Science programs presented in school—Crystals, weather, forest life, aerial photos and mountains, snow, planets and constellations.
Math - As determined by the first grade Math placement test, Alison has mastered most of this curriculum. She will begin her Math program in the 2nd grade classroom.	Compound Words - Level 9 Teacher's Manual pages 77, 267. Check for proficiency - Level 9 test page 9 (compound words).	TAC Resource Room Critical thinking skills, creative thinking skills, creative problem solving, critical problem solving, Type III independent study.
	Pronouns - Level 9 Teacher's Manual page 325. Check for proficiency - Level 9 test (language skills) page 9.	

☐ Check here if additional information is recorded on the reverse side.

Figure 27. Alison's compactor (elementary level).

always happy when they are singled out for curriculum compacting. In fact, with some students, the process of helping them accept services is a slow and careful one, because they consistently tell their teachers that they do not want to be different—they want to do the exact same work as their peers, *even if they have known the skills for years*. Their anxieties and the type of whole group instruction that has been standard in schools for so long must be recognized. If they had been taught to do work that was tailored to their needs, this particular problem would not exist. When it does, students must be helped to understand that requiring different assignments and work is appropriate. However, this process often takes time.

Alison's options in column three were many and varied. She worked on an Apple computer in her classroom that provided advanced reading and writing options. She was offered independent, advanced reading opportunities and a regular opportunity to discuss these books with her teacher. She spent up to five hours each week in a resource room in her school. Time in the gifted program resulted from specific instances of curriculum compacting in the classroom. During this time, she worked on a variety of experiences including an independent study with close monitoring and guidance from her resource teacher, units designed to provide advanced content and critical and creative thinking skills, and other alternatives based on Alison's curricular strengths and interests. She also participated in Science enrichment units taught by scientists from the regional science center. These units were designed for interested students and had optional follow-ups. Working with older students, Alison pursued two topics in which she was interested.

2. *Bill: A Sample Compactor at the Secondary Level*

Bill's area of strength and interest was History. His sophomore U.S. History teacher knew Bill before he entered his class, because Bill had often approached him asking to borrow textbooks or primary source books about the Civil War. His love for U.S. History in general, and his knowledge and fascination for the Civil War period, were well known to the entire History department. His History teacher had never requested help in the compacting process before, but Bill provided a good opportunity to field test it.

As indicated in column one in Figure 28, Bill was an excellent student. Besides having high achievement test scores, he also had read numerous texts and nonfiction books on American History, received top grades, and collected Civil War memorabilia as a hobby.

Bill took a mid-term exam in September—usually given in January—to determine his knowledge of American History. He scored an A+. He was excused from most discussions and class assignments (such as answering the questions at the end of every chapter, outlining each chapter, and doing group work related to concepts he already knew). Instead, he did independent reading, continued his research on Civil War memorabilia, worked in the Congressional campaign of a local candidate, and conducted intensive research on the Kennedy/Nixon debates during the 1960 election. All of these alternative experiences were made possible because Bill's teacher was willing to assess his knowledge in September.

INDIVIDUAL EDUCATIONAL PROGRAMMING GUIDE
The Compactor

Prepared by: Joseph S. Renzulli
Linda M. Smith

NAME ___Bill___   AGE __15__   TEACHER(S) ___Hébert___   Individual Conference Dates And Persons Participating in Planning Of IEP

SCHOOL ___Canton High School___   GRADE _10_   PARENT(S) ___Mr. Paul Jordan___   __9/31__ __10/25__ __11/30__ __12/10__

CURRICULUM AREAS TO BE CONSIDERED FOR COMPACTING Provide a brief description of basic material to be covered during this marking period and the assessment information or evidence that suggests the need for compacting.	PROCEDURES FOR COMPACTING BASIC MATERIAL Describe activities that will be used to guarantee proficiency in basic curricular areas.	ACCELERATION AND/OR ENRICHMENT ACTIVITIES Describe activities that will be used to provide advanced level learning experiences in each area of the regular curriculum.
U.S. History - Colonial History to Civil War 1. Reading 3 years above level (Achievement Test Results). 2. Bill's outside reading has allowed him to investigate many texts on history used in college courses. 3. Hobby—collecting Civil War memorabilia. 4. Straight A's in Social Studies.	1. Bill took an exam covering chapters 2-15 with a grade of A+. 2. Bill will write an interpretive paper on a self-selected topic. 3. Bill will not have to do regular curriculum work related to History.	1. Bill will develop skills in museum research (related to Civil War memorabilia). 2. Bill will develop poll-taking skills and work as a volunteer for a local Congressional candidate. 3. Bill has selected an interest area and will write a research paper on the political debates of 1960: Kennedy vs. Nixon.

☐ Check here if additional information is recorded on the reverse side.

Figure 28. Bill's compactor (secondary level).

3. Top Reading Group: A Sample Compactor at the Fourth Grade Level

Compacting a group of students is a practical alternative to the individual approach, if a teacher wants to pretest an entire class or group of students on units or skills to be covered. This enables teachers to group students by those skills they have yet to master (see Figure 29).

Enrichment and Acceleration Options

Enrichment and acceleration options can be divided into five general categories (Reis, Burns, & Renzulli, 1992):

- *Classroom Activities—Independent or small group study, escalated coverage of the curriculum, mini-courses, free reading, special interest groups, clubs, interest development centers, and special lessons for furthering cognitive and affective processes.*
- *Resource Room Activities—These can involve any of the classroom activities listed above, but take place in the resource room under the guidance of a special teacher.*
- *Accelerated Studies—Grade skipping, honors and advanced-placement courses, college classes, early admission to kindergarten, cross-grade grouping, continuous progress curricula, and special seminars.*
- *Out of School Experiences—Internships, mentorships, work study programs, and community programs.*
- *District, School, or Department Programs—Any of the options listed above plus correspondence courses, special counseling, career education, and library studies.*

Student interests should play a key role in choosing enrichment or acceleration options. Ideally, interest assessment should be done for all students at the beginning of the school year and results can help formulate plans for many components of an enrichment program. One effective form for determining present and potential student interests is the *Interest-A-Lyzer,* discussed in Chapter 10.

Independent study is an option that should be available to any student who displays the interest and task commitment to pursue the work. Independent study in the classroom or resource room can be divided into 12 general, flexible steps (Reis, Burns, & Renzulli, 1992):

1. Assess, find, or create student interests.
2. Determine interest commitment through student interviews.
3. Guide students toward a research question(s).
4. Develop a written plan.
5. Help students locate resources.
6. Provide methodological assistance.
7. Help students choose the question to investigate.
8. Offer managerial assistance.
9. Identify products and audiences.
10. Offer encouragement, praise, and constructive criticism.

INDIVIDUAL EDUCATIONAL PROGRAMMING GUIDE
The Compactor

Prepared by: Joseph S. Renzulli
Linda M. Smith

NAME _____ (Reading Group)   AGE _____ TEACHER(S) _____   Individual Conference Dates And Persons
Participating in Planning Of IEP

SCHOOL _____   GRADE __4__ PARENT(S) _____   S. K.   S. L.   T. H.

CURRICULUM AREAS TO BE CONSIDERED FOR COMPACTING Provide a brief description of basic material to be covered during this marking period and the assessment information or evidence that suggests the need for compacting.	PROCEDURES FOR COMPACTING BASIC MATERIAL Describe activities that will be used to guarantee proficiency in basic curricular areas.	ACCELERATION AND/OR ENRICHMENT ACTIVITIES Describe activities that will be used to provide advanced level learning experiences in each area of the regular curriculum.
I. Language Arts Test: Holt Level: 13 Unit: 5	1. No reinforcement on exercises in the Holt reading series showing mastery.	1. Reading for pleasure. 2. Creative writing (poetry, short stories, etc.). 3. Monthly book reports. 4. Participation in Talcott Mountain Science Center programs.
II. As determined by the Holt unit tests, these students consistently master over 85% in each skill area of the unit test.	2. No assignments in workbook pages of skills mastered. 3. Check proficiency by the Holt unit tests.	5. Great Books Program. 6. Reading Comprehension Library—Level D. 7. Research skills training in relation to Type III projects and classroom projects.
III. Spelling These students continue to achieve a grade of 100 on all Spelling tests.	Spelling The Economy Individualized Spelling Program will be utilized with this entire group.	8. Research courses with Library Media Specialist. 9. Letter writing--related to Type III projects. 10. Type II Training activities in resource room. 11. Mini-Course in Human Anatomy—with Mrs. Beck and Miss Towne.
		12. "Be a Better Reader." Alison--Level C Eric--Level B 13. Independent Study Projects in the resource room.

☐ Check here if additional information is recorded on the reverse side.

Figure 29. Group compactor.

Steps for guiding students through a Type III project are discussed in Chapter 9.

Recommendations for Success

- *Start Small.* Begin the compacting process by targeting a small group of students for whom it seems especially appropriate.

- *Select One Area.* Choose one content area in which the targeted student has demonstrated previous mastery or strengths and teachers have the most resources available to pretest for prior mastery and to enrich and accelerate the content.

- *Experiment With Pretesting.* Try different methods for assessment and solicit help from colleagues.

- *Compact by Topic.* Compact by unit, chapter, or topic rather than by marking period.

- *Decide How to Document.* Decide how to document compacted material and define proficiency based on staff consensus and district policy.

- *Find a Variety of Alternatives.* Solicit help from a variety of resources in order to create a range of opportunities to replace eliminated content.

- *Experiment.* Keep experimenting with new ideas and past successes.

- *Orient Parents and Students.* All students should be introduced to the compacting process in general and simple terms. Also, it is important that all students be given the opportunity to pursue various classroom enrichment activities, whether they have compacted out of an area or not. Maintain communication with parents (see Figure 30). Those who have a child involved in compacting should understand the process, since it will change the nature and amount of the child's paperwork coming home. Generally parents have been enthusiastic about the process.

Research on Curriculum Compacting

The University of Connecticut site of The National Research Center on the Gifted and Talented conducted a study to examine the effects of staff development on elementary teachers' ability and willingness to implement a technique entitled curriculum compacting (Reis, Westberg, Kulikowich, Caillard, Hébert, Plucker, Purcell, Rogers, & Smidst, 1993). This study addressed how much curriculum content could be eliminated for high ability students by teachers who had received high levels of staff development, investigated what would happen to students' achievement test scores, content area preference, and attitude towards learning if curriculum compacting was implemented. Teachers in twenty school districts throughout the country were randomly assigned by district to three treatment groups that received three different levels of staff development. Treatment Group 1 received 1 hour of videotaped training on compacting and a how-to book. Treatment Group 2 received the same as Treatment Group 1 and an additional staff development session on using a *Compactor*. Treatment Group 3 received all of the training that Groups 1 and 2 received and were also assigned to a peer coach for help

TO: Parents

FROM: Enrichment Specialist

RE: Your Child's Participation in the Enrichment Program

As you may know from previous correspondence and meetings, your child is involved in the enrichment program at school. Your child's classroom teacher and I have made a careful assessment of his/her strengths and agree that he/she would benefit from compacting the curriculum in his/her strength areas so that he/she will not be repeating work. This time saved will result in additional time in the resource room. This will not result in your child missing essential work in the regular classroom.

The form that accompanies this letter is the completed *Compactor*, agreed upon by the classroom teacher and me. Your child's academic strengths are listed in the first column and activities used to document proficiency are listed in the second column. Enrichment and/or acceleration activities that your child will pursue in the resource room are listed in the third column.

Please call me if you have any questions. I will be glad to meet and discuss your child's involvement in the enrichment program. Thank you for your continued interest and support.

_ _

Please sign this form to indicate that you have received the completed *Compactor* and return it to school as soon as possible.

Student's Name: _____

School: _____

Parent or Guardian Signature: _____

Date: _____

Figure 30. Parent letter explaining curriculum compacting.

with the compacting process. After receiving staff development services, teachers implemented curriculum compacting for one or two students in their classrooms. Seven districts were randomly assigned as control groups.

Three increasing levels of staff development (videotapes, books, peer coaching) were provided to the treatment groups that implemented curriculum compacting. The control group teachers identified one or two high ability students and continued normal teaching practices without implementing curriculum compacting. A battery of achievement tests (out-of-level *Iowa Tests of Basic Skills - ITBS*), content area preference scales, and a questionnaire regarding attitude towards learning were given to identified students in November, 1990 and at the completion of the school year.

The following statements represent some of the findings from the curriculum compacting study:

1. 95% of the teachers were able to **identify high ability students** in their classes and document students' strengths.
2. Approximately **40-50%** of traditional classroom material was compacted for selected students in one or more content areas (Mathematics, Language Arts, Science, and Social Studies).
3. The **most frequently compacted** subject was **Mathematics**, followed by Language Arts. Science and Social Studies were compacted when students demonstrated very high ability in those areas.
4. A **majority** of the teachers in all treatment groups said they would **compact curriculum again**; some said they would try again if they had additional information and assistance from a specialist.
5. A significant difference was found among treatment groups with respect to the overall quality of curriculum compacting, as documented on the *Compactor*. Treatment Group 3 had **significantly higher quality** *Compactors* than did Treatment Groups 1 or 2.
6. **80%** of the teachers were able to **document the curriculum** that high ability students had yet to master, **list appropriate instructional strategies** for students to demonstrate mastery, and **document an appropriate mastery standard**.
7. Replacement strategies consisted of **three broad instructional activities**: enrichment, acceleration, and other (e.g., peer tutoring, cooperative learning, correcting class papers).
8. Teachers in Treatment Group 3 used **significantly more replacement strategies** than did teachers in Treatment Groups 1 or 2.
9. While approximately **95%** of teachers used **enrichment** as a replacement strategy, 18% of teachers also used acceleration.
10. Replacement strategies did not often reflect the types of advanced content that would be appropriate for high ability students, indicating that **additional staff development**, as well as help from a specialist in the district, would be beneficial.
11. Approximately **60%** of the replacement strategies reflected **students' interests, needs**, and **preferences**.
12. Anecdotal records indicated that three different types of requests were made by teachers as they compacted curriculum:

- **Additional time** for students to work with the gifted specialist (if one was available).
- Assistance in locating additional **appropriate materials**.
- **Consultant assistance** as teachers worked through the compacting process.

13. When teachers **eliminated as much as 50% of the regular curriculum** for gifted students, no differences in the out-of-level post achievement test (*ITBS*) results between treatment and control groups were found in Math computation, Social Studies, Spelling and Reading.
14. In Science, Treatment Group 1 **scored significantly higher** on the out-of-level posttest (*ITBS*) than did the control group whose curriculum was not compacted.
15. Students whose curriculum was compacted in Mathematics **significantly outperformed** their control group counterparts in the Mathematical concepts subscale on the *ITBS*.
16. Students whose curriculum was compacted in Mathematics had **significantly better attitudes** toward learning than students in the control group.
17. Students whose curriculum was compacted in Mathematics had **significantly higher preferences for Mathematics** than students in the control group.

This study demonstrated the following:

- *Curriculum compacting can be implemented in the regular classroom to provide more appropriate educational experiences for gifted and talented students.*
- *Staff development and peer coaching can improve teachers' use of the compacting process.*
- *Teachers will need additional training and help to be able to substitute appropriately challenging content and work to students whose curriculum has been modified.*
- *Curriculum compacting can have positive effects on students.*

Teacher Training

Our experience in encouraging classroom teachers to implement the compacting process usually involves providing them with the specific three phases and eight steps described earlier. In addition, we have used SIMSIT 1, included on the following pages, to provide practice with the compacting process. This activity can be completed during a staff meeting or inservice session.

Summary

Curriculum compacting takes time and energy on the parts of both teachers and students. Yet, over the years, we've discovered that it saves teachers precious hours, once they're familiar with the process. Most educators who now compact regularly say that it takes no longer than normal teaching practices. More importantly, they tell us that the benefits to all students certainly make the effort worthwhile. One teacher's evaluative comments about the compacting process reflects the attitude of most teachers who participated in our research: "As soon as I saw how enthusiastic and receptive my students were about the compacting process, I began to become more committed to implementing this method in all my classes." Teachers also overwhelmingly indicated that although they had been asked to target one or two students, they were able to use the compacting process with a much broader segment of their students. Many teachers in our research studies have said that as the school year progressed, they extended compacting to as many as eight or ten students in their classes.

The many changes that are taking place in our schools require all educators to examine a broad range of techniques for providing equitably for *all* students. Curriculum compacting is one such process. It is not tied to a specific content area or grade level, nor is it aligned with a particular approach to school or curricular reform. Rather, the process is adaptable to any school configuration or curricular framework and is flexible enough to be used within the context of rapidly changing approaches to general education. Practical experience gained through several years of field testing and refining the compacting process have demonstrated that many positive benefits can result from this process for both students and teachers.

**SIMSIT 1
FACILITATOR'S GUIDE**

What Should We Do for Joanie?
A Simulation on Curriculum Compacting

Teacher Training Objectives
- *Major Objective.* To familiarize enrichment specialists with strategies to be used in helping classroom teachers to compact regular curricular material.
- To train classroom teachers in the methodology of compacting including: assessing strengths, documenting proficiency, and replacing previously mastered material with more challenging work (based on student interests if possible).

Number of People Involved
Two teams of two persons per team
The entire group, divided into pairs (strongly suggested)

Approximate Time
45 minutes to 1 hour

Materials and Equipment
Directions for the Classroom Teacher
Directions for the Enrichment Specialist
Blank *Compactor* Forms

Directions
Form two teams of two, an enrichment specialist and classroom teacher. Provide each member with directions and have them take a few minutes in another room alone to practice their respective roles. The enrichment specialist should also receive directions for the classroom teacher.

If there are people in the group that are acting as observers, review directions with them as the teams practice their roles and ask them to observe during the simulations and look for strategies. You may choose to tape the discussion.

Have the enrichment specialist and classroom teacher return. The enrichment specialist should begin the simulation by asking the classroom teacher how Joanie is doing with the compacting process. The role of the enrichment specialist is to provide advice, encouragement, and practical suggestions to aid the classroom teacher in completing the form. The goal of the simulation is to have each person complete the *Compactor*. Even though the subject area to be completed is Math, the enrichment specialist should be encouraging the classroom teacher to consider Joanie's entire curriculum and gently encourage her to consider compacting in other areas.

The discussion should be allowed to come to a natural resolution, but should not exceed 15 minutes. When the first team is done, the second team can follow the same format. After both are finished, observers should comment on styles and strategies used during the simulations.

At this point, you as facilitator, should guide the group in brainstorming a list of do's and don'ts about curriculum compacting. You might also brainstorm a list of suggestions for enrichment specialists and classroom teachers.

SIMSIT 1
Curriculum Compacting (continued)

Directions for the Classroom Teacher

Using considerable persuasion, the enrichment specialist has convinced you that Joanie could be compacted in Math in order to provide additional time to pursue work in the resource room. Since your Math group is about to begin a new unit on division, you have given her the unit test as a pretest. Her pretest and *Strength-A-Lyzer* have been provided. Using the pretest as a guide, complete a *Compactor* for Joanie. You have available the unit test, a parallel extra unit test, and practice masters for each skill. The following questions may serve as guidelines.

Column 1:
    What regular curricular material is to be compacted?
    What are Joanie's general indications of strength in this area?
    What specific material has been mastered? How do you know?

Column 2:
    What pages in Unit 4 might be eliminated for Joanie?
    What skills are still needed?
    What activities could be used to teach those skills?
    How will you assess mastery of needed skills?

Column 3:
    If Joanie was not already involved in a Type III project, what enrichment and/or acceleration activities might be planned?

Your goal is to begin the process of curriculum compacting with the help of the enrichment specialist. You are trying to find the time for Joanie to be in the resource room. You are also trying to increase the challenge level of her classroom experience by eliminating work that she has already mastered.

SIMSIT 1
Curriculum Compacting (continued)

Directions for the Enrichment Specialist

It has taken you two months to convince Joanie's teacher to try to compact her curriculum. You've let her know that you'll help her in any way possible. Now that she has agreed, your job is to help her complete the *Compactor*. Her teacher has said that Joanie is good in Math, but she has complained of boredom in other areas too. The task now is to also have Joanie's teacher consider other areas for possible compacting. Review the classroom teacher's directions and make sure that you understand the compacting process so that you can provide the necessary assistance.

SIMSIT 1
Curriculum Compacting (continued)

INDIVIDUAL EDUCATIONAL PROGRAMMING GUIDE
Strength - A - Lyzer

Prepared by: Joseph S. Renzulli
Linda M. Smith

NAME __Joan Sutton__   AGE __10__   TEACHER(S) _____

SCHOOL __Brookside__   GRADE __5__   PARENT(S) _____

Individual Conference Dates and Persons
Participating in Planning of IEP

ABILITIES

INTELLIGENCE - APTITUDE - CREATIVITY

In the spaces below, enter the results of standardized test scores and circle all scores above the _____ percentile.

Test	Area	Date	Raw Score	Grade Equiv.	%ile
	IQ		126		94
CTBS	Composite				97
	Reading				93
	Math				95

TEACHER RATINGS

In the spaces below, enter the scores from the Scale for Rating Behavioral Characteristics of Superior Students. Circle unusually high scores.

Scale	Score	Group Mean	Scale	Score	Group Mean
Learning	28		Musical		
Motivation	25		Dramatic		
Creativity	29		Comm.: Precision		
Leadership	24		Comm.: Expressive		
Artistic			Planning		

END OF YEAR GRADES

Enter final grades for the past two years.

Reading	A	A	Art	A	A
Mathematics	A	A	Foreign Language		
Language Arts	A	A	Other		
Social Studies	B+	A	Other		
Science	A	A			
Music	B	A			

INTERESTS

As a result of student responses to the Interest-A-Lyzer or other interest assessment procedures, indicate the general area(s) in which levels of interest seem to be High, Average, and Low.

	H	A	L		H	A	L
Fine Arts/Crafts	X			Managerial			X
Scientific/Technical		X		Business			X
Literary/Writing	X			Historical			X
Political/Judicial			X	Performing Arts			X
Mathematical	X			Other			
Athletic		X		Other			

SPECIFIC AREAS OF INTEREST

As a result of individual discussions with the student, indicate particular topics, issues, or areas of study in which the student would like to do advanced level work.

short story writing

poetry

mathematical puzzles and games

LEARNING STYLES

Enter the scores from the Learning Styles Inventory in the spaces below. Circle the highest area(s).

Learning Style	Score	Learning Style	Score
Projects	4.2	Teaching Games	3.5
Simulation	2.6	Independent Study	4.3
Drill and Recitation	3.0	Programmed Instruction	1.0
Peer Teaching	4.1	Lecture	2.0
Discussion	3.5		

Comments regarding informal observation about Learning Styles and relationships between areas of interest and learning styles.

Joanie is an excellent independent worker, but can also fit into group situations. She seems to adapt to the task at hand.

SUMMARY AND RECOMMENDED ACTION BASED ON ASSESSMENT INFORMATION

In this space below summarize (1) strengths, interests, and learning styles, (2) areas in which remedial work or additional skill building appears to be warranted, and (3) specific higher mental processes and advanced skills that should be developed.

Joanie is extremely strong in all basic skills areas and shows above average ability as an independent worker. She is an avid reader with a flair for creative writing and love of literature. Joanie interacts well with her peers and participates actively in group situations. At times this can be a problem for her, as she will "go along" with the group rather than pursue her own interests.

☐ Check here if additional information is recorded on the reverse side.

SIMSIT 1
Curriculum Compacting (continued)

Unit Test

26/30   **Joanie**

Divide. (pages 74-77)
1. 3 R2, 8)26
2. 3 R3, 9)30
3. 40, 7)280
4. 80 R3, 5)403

Divide. (pages 78-81)
5. 30 R1, 2)61
6. 23 R3, 6)141
7. 71 R2, 5)357
8. 68 R1, 4)273
9. 74 R4, 6)448
10. 74 R4, 8)596
11. 93 R2, 7)653
12. 84 R2, 9)758

Divide. (pages 82-87)
13. 243 R1, 3)730
14. 742 R4, 5)3714
15. 838 R1, 8)6705
16. 2367 R3, 4)9471
17. 6357 R1, 6)38143
18. 40 R4, 5)204
19. 705 R2, 7)4937
20. 640 R6, 8)5126

Divide. (pages 88-89)
21. 3 R5, 20)65
22. 9 R24, 40)384
23. 8 R5, 30)245
24. 9 R46, 80)766

Write the GCF of each pair of numbers. (pages 90-91)
✓ 25. 8 and 12?
✓ 26. 15 and 45?
✓ 27. 16 and 40?
✓ 28. 18 and 51?
What does GCF Mean?

Solve. (page 92)
29. What is the cost of 94 bottles of soda at 20¢ a bottle? **$18.80**
30. How many 20-cent bottles can be bought with 94¢? **4 bottles**

Extra Unit Test

This unit test parallels the unit test in the student's text. It may be used as a review for the unit test in the student's text or as the unit test itself. Also included in this Teacher's Edition (see Resource chart) is an extra unit test in multiple-choice format.

Divide. (pages 74-77)
1. 3 R2, 7)23
2. 3 R3, 6)21
3. 40R4, 5)204
4. 90 R1, 3)271

Divide. (pages 78-81)
5. 22 R2, 2)68
6. 23 R3, 9)210
7. 65 R2, 4)262
8. 68 R1, 2)137
9. 74 R4, 7)522
10. 74 R4, 5)374
11. 93 R2, 3)281
12. 84 R2, 6)506

Divide. (pages 82-87)
13. 276 R2, 3)830
14. 742 R4, 6)4456
15. 838, 4)3354
16. 2367, 5)11835
17. 6357 R1, 2)12715
18. 40 R4, 9)364
19. 705 R2, 8)5642
20. 640 R6, 7)4234

Divide. (pages 88-89)
21. 4 R2, 20)82
22. 9 R24, 70)654
23. 8 R5, 60)485
24. 9 R46, 90)856

Write the GCF of each pair of numbers. (pages 90-91)
25. 12 and 15? **3**
26. 15 and 30? **15**
27. 24 and 40? **8**
Solve. (page 92)
28. What is the cost of 83 tickets at 40¢ each? **$33.20**
29. How many 40-cent tickets can be bought with 83¢? **2 tickets**

Resources

Practice Master	4-10	Teacher's Edition
Review Lesson	4-10	Laboratory Activity p. 97a
Enrichment Activity	4-10	Math News p. 97c
Test 4—Problem Solving		Multiple-choice Test p. 97d

Type I Enrichment:
General Exploratory Experiences

- **Planning a Type I Enrichment Program**
- **Implementing Type I's in the Enrichment Program**

Where did you first get the inspiration for pursuing a hobby, an interest, or a career? At some point you were exposed to a topic that "sparked" some interest in you. It may have been an especially compelling course in college, someone you knew personally who shared his or her work, a place you visited as a child, or one of countless other experiences. It is often these types of childhood experiences that strongly influence our career decisions later in life. In the Schoolwide Enrichment Model, Type I Enrichment is designed to perform this function, by exposing students to a wide variety of disciplines, topics, ideas, concepts, issues, and events that are not ordinarily covered in the regular curriculum. Type I Enrichment serves as the "launching point" for many students to pursue further enrichment.

There are several goals for the Type I component of a program (see Figure 31). First, it serves to enrich the lives of all students by expanding the scope of experiences provided by the school. Second, it stimulates new interests that might lead to more intensive (Type III) follow-up activities. Third, it gives teachers direction in making meaningful decisions for process skill (Type II) activities. Type I Enrichment provides the foundation for a healthy enrichment program that serves all students.

Planning a Type I Enrichment Program

Getting Started

A stimulating Type I Enrichment program can be implemented in a school regardless of whether or not an enrichment specialist is available. In any case, it is essential that there is coordination among Enrichment Team members and staff, and the enrichment specialist (if one is available), in order to achieve the objectives of the SEM and to promote program ownership discussed in earlier chapters.

The kind of Type I planning that is done will depend upon whether an enrichment specialist is available, how his or her time is allocated among buildings, and what function he/she performs. For example, if the enrichment specialist covers several buildings and spends most of his/her time directly with students, then the major responsibility for

Type I Enrichment
Summary Sheet

DEFINITION: Experiences and activities that are purposefully designed to expose students to a wide variety of disciplines, topics, issues, occupations, hobbies, persons, places, and events not normally covered in the regular curriculum.

TARGET AUDIENCES:

1. All students.

2. Talent Pool students.

OBJECTIVES:

1. To enrich the lives of all students by expanding the scope of experiences not covered by the school.

2. To stimulate new interests that might lead to more intensive follow-up (Type III) activity on the parts of individuals or small groups of students.

3. To give teachers direction in making meaningful decisions about the kinds of Type II Enrichment activities that should be selected for particular groups of students.

KEY CONCEPTS: Exposure to New Topics that Differ from the Regular Curriculum.
Dynamic Activities that Will Stimulate New Interests.
Event-Oriented.

ACTION FORMS: Type I Planning & Documentation Form
Resource Directory Form
Type I Resources By Subject Area

Figure 31. Type I enrichment summary sheet.

planning will rest on the Enrichment Team. On the other hand, if the enrichment specialist's responsibilities are more administrative in nature, then he/she can be more involved in the planning. Regardless of the planning specifics, it is critical to the program goals that staff and parents be involved in the planning process right from the start. Starting an Enrichment Team (see Chapter 3) is a prerequisite to program planning.

In Figure 32, target audiences and group organizational patterns are listed for a school that has an enrichment specialist and regularly scheduled sessions for Talent Pool students. If an enrichment specialist is not available, then planning should be restricted to the left side of the diagram. However, it is important to remember that the activities could certainly be carried out with or without the presence of an enrichment specialist. The major responsibility for organizing the overall Type I effort belongs to the Enrichment Team. (This group can coordinate Type II experiences as well.) Team members should plan and organize meetings, coordinate Type I efforts among grades and schools, and research and contact new sources for Type I experiences. The success of topic and grade level planning, however, depends primarily upon the participation of teachers who will be affected.

If teachers are interested in planning a series of Type I's that supplement the writing curriculum and expose students to different types of writing used in today's world, they could plan presentations from local authors, editors, reporters, poets, public relations experts, advertising copywriters, etc. The Enrichment Team could set up a meeting to plan these events and invite the enrichment specialist, reading coordinator for the school or district, and any staff members and parents who have an interest in writing. This group could also research and select possibilities for Type I writing experiences, make contacts and schedule the events.

More specifically, a Type I effort can be planned for a particular grade level. For example, fourth grade teachers may want to supplement their Social Studies unit. The Enrichment Team should set up a planning meeting and invite those who have teaching responsibilities in fourth grade Social Studies. Participants can include the enrichment specialist, resource teachers, the program coordinator for the school, and the Social Studies or general

curriculum coordinator for the district. (Districtwide people can help make districtwide resources available and offer valuable suggestions. Their involvement will also help integrate the regular curriculum and Type I efforts.) This group is responsible for the selection of Type I topics. An important point to keep in mind is that selected topics should serve as extensions to the regular curriculum. Curriculum guides and textbook chapters often help identify related topics or interesting offshoots to traditional units of study.

Although these planning meetings are most effectively carried out school by school, there are advantages to joint planning meetings that

Target Audiences and Group Organizational Patterns for Type I Enrichment

General Population (Including Talent Pool Students)

Target Audience		
Major Planning Responsibility	Enrichment Team (with Consultation from Enrichment Specialist and Subject Area Coordinators)	

Group	Examples	Location
The Entire School	Mime Presentation Rocket Launch	Auditorium Playground
Grade Level Clusters	Puppet Show (K-3) Collecting Pond Water Samples (4-5)	Cafeteria Outdoor Education Center
Single Grade Level	Assigned Television Documentary (Related to 6th Grade Science Curriculum)	At Home (With Follow-up Discussions in Individual Classrooms)
Students Responding to an Invitation of Special Topic Presentations	A Lecture on Problems Associated With Acid Rain	Library

Talent Pool Students

Target Audience		
Major Planning Responsibility	Enrichment Specialist (with consultation from Enrichment Team)	

Group	Examples	Location
All Talent Pool Students at a Given Grade Level	Lecture on Chemical Food Additives by a Local College Professor	Enrichment Room
Talent Pool Students From 2 or 3 Grade Levels With a Common Interest, Plus Non-Talent Pool Students With the Same Interest	Procedures Involved in Newspaper Production	Local Newspaper Office and Plant
	Q & A Session With a Local Children's Author	Library (With Follow-up Discussions on a Voluntary Basis in the Enrichment Room)

Figure 32. Target audiences and group organizational patterns for type I enrichment.

involve several schools in a district. Type I's can be shared among schools and kept for future use by all. For instance, teachers can videotape visiting speakers and performances and keep them in a district library for use by all schools in the district.

Identifying Type I Topics

Some of the Type I planning may be carried out before the school year begins, but it is essential to add new topics and activities as they become known and as new student interests emerge throughout the year. The following section offers some ideas for identifying high priority topics from staff and students.

Completing the Type I Planning and Documentation Form

We have developed the Type I Planning and Documentation Form to help educators effectively organize their Type I Enrichment experiences (see Figures 33 and 34). One of the goals for using this form is to introduce various ways of bringing Type I experiences to students by setting some target objectives regarding the number and diversity of these experiences. By varying the topics and the methods of delivery, a wider number of students can benefit from the enrichment experiences and as a result, the number of Type III investigations may increase. The forms can also serve as summary sheets for evaluation purposes at the end of the year. There are three options for cataloging the Type I activities (on the top left side of the form)—General Matrix, Grade Level, or Subject Area.

The first alternative, the General Matrix, can be used by the Enrichment Team in each school to plan general Type I experiences over a wide variety of subject areas (listed horizontally across the top of the form) using several methods of delivery (listed down the left-hand side). This is key to providing ideas for the diverse ways in which Type I Enrichment can be offered. A well-rounded Type I program should accommodate the learning styles and needs of a variety of students and a wide variety of enrichment opportunities including speakers, field trips, artistic presentations, enrichment clusters, museum displays, learning centers, TV programs, and more.

A second option, which may be used by the Enrichment Team or classroom teachers, is the grade level category. This option may be used by all of the grade level teachers in a building or district. Inservice planning time might be devoted to having all fifth grade classroom teachers in a district meet together to plan certain topics for Type I Enrichment for that grade level. Forms completed by grade level teachers may be submitted to the Enrichment Team with requests to locate speakers or as a tally for Type I topics already organized within classrooms.

A third option invites educators to use the Planning and Documentation Form to set some target objectives regarding the number and diversity of Type I experiences for one particular subject area. This option is most appropriate for secondary school settings, where it can be used on a department-

Type I Planning and Documentation Form

Check all that apply: ____ General Matrix _____ ____ Grade Level _____ ____ Subject Area _____ Methods of Delivery	Content Areas				TOTAL
I. Resource Persons					
Speakers					
Enrichment Clusters					
Demonstrations					
Artistic Performances					
Panel Discussion/Debate					
E-Mail					
Other _____					
II. Media					
Films					
Filmstrips					
Slides					
Audio Tapes/CDs					
Videotapes					
Television Programs					
Newspaper/Magazine Articles					
Computer Programs					
Other _____					
III. Other Resources					
Interest Development Centers					
Displays					
Field Trips					
Museum Programs					
Learning Centers					
Internet					
Other _____					
TOTAL					

Figure 33. Type I planning and documentation form.

Type I Planning and Documentation Form

Check all that apply: General Matrix _____ x Grade Level _Grade 10_ x Subject Area _Social Studies_ Methods of Delivery	Content Areas				
	Economics	Local History	Anthropology	Geography	TOTAL
I. Resource Persons					
Speakers	1	2	1		4
Enrichment Clusters					
Demonstrations				1	1
Artistic Performances					
Panel Discussion/Debate		2			2
E-Mail					
Other _____					
II. Media					
Films	1		1		2
Filmstrips	1			2	3
Slides					
Audio Tapes/CDs					
Videotapes		2	1		3
Television Programs	1		2	1	4
Newspaper/Magazine Articles	1	3	1		5
Computer Programs					
Other _____					
III. Other Resources					
Interest Development Centers	1	1		1	3
Displays					
Field Trips					
Museum Programs			1		1
Learning Centers					
Internet					
Other _____					
TOTAL	6	10	7	5	28

Figure 34. Type I planning and documentation form (sample).

by-department basis. It should be forwarded periodically to the Enrichment Team. For example, a secondary Social Studies department might decide that they would like to schedule at least one Type I for each of several specific areas, such as Economics, local History, Geography, Political Science, and current events. Teachers might also decide to include at least six or eight methods of delivery in order to accommodate differences in student learning styles. This two-fold approach can work well, but the availability of resources usually dictates the methods of delivery for any given topic.

Planning Procedures by the Enrichment Team

Enrichment Team members may also initiate topic identification, which can have a general or specific focus. Members might begin by listing all topics and available resources that could enhance the Social Studies curriculum. They might also choose to focus on a specific topic such as the Civil War, Latin American geography, or aviation catastrophes. Members should brainstorm all ideas and record them whether or not they fit into the Type I Matrix. Some topics may not be relevant to the planning focus, but may be useful for other planning efforts and subjects. For example, a suggestion about a film dramatization of an aspect of the Civil War might end up being included as a suggested Type I experience in the Language Arts curriculum. Since members of the Enrichment Team will have an overview of all the planning in a particular school, they can share and coordinate these ideas, avoiding duplication of topics and providing for a integrated schoolwide Type I effort.

During Type I planning, the Enrichment Team needs to consider both topics and method of delivery. Often this occurs simultaneously, but planning can proceed by using either criterion independently. For example, the group described above might decide that the topic *airplane safety* would be an important enrichment topic for students studying aviation. Once they reach consensus on the specific enrichment topic, they can then explore different methods of delivery such as a speaker, movie, or display. An alternative approach to organizing Type I experiences is to begin with the method of delivery. Here, the topic *airplane safety* might emerge only after a review of film catalogs or a series of newspaper articles.

Generating Topic Lists From Students

When generating possible topics for Type I experiences, it is often useful to assess student interests by using interest surveys such as *If I Ran the School* (see Chapter 10).

Another approach for determining student interests is to ask students the following questions:

1. What's worth knowing?
2. What are some things you wonder about?

Students should have a few days to answer the questions and have the option of signing or not signing their names to their papers. The answers can be compiled into a list of topics. Through class discussion, the general interests of the group will emerge.

The interests generated through interest surveys or class questions should be discussed by members of the Enrichment Team. The selected topics should then be considered for

Type I experiences and enrichment clusters. The Enrichment Team can research methods of delivery and sources and make informed decisions about specific Type I experiences. This approach is especially valuable because it assures that Type I experiences will be well-received by many students. Student ideas should be saved! Individual responses of any given student can be used as a point of entry for what may later become a Type III experience.

Generating Topic Lists From Staff

As well as students, staff input for Type I topics is a valuable source for ideas. On the following pages we include a brainstorming activity for staff designed to generate lists for possible Type I topics (see Figures 35 and 36). This activity will help assess staff needs, involve all staff in the planning process of Type I's, encourage group interaction among regular teachers and resource teachers, and help promote valuable ownership of the program. It can be carried out at staff or grade level meetings.

Developing a list of Type I experiences should be an ongoing process that invites staff to keep their eyes open to potential Type I topic ideas. A good way to promote this process is to establish an "Idea Box" outside the enrichment room and solicit ongoing contributions from staff and students. A regular review of magazines, newspaper features, stage company brochures, museums, etc. will provide contemporary and especially stimulating ideas.

Identifying Type I Topic Sources

The Type I dimension of the SEM can be very exciting, because it brings various experiences into the school that are not ordinarily covered in the regular curriculum. It can also actively involve people outside the school and help spread information about and support for the enrichment program within the community. The number and variety of Type I resources that teachers can locate will become a major factor in the program's success.

An important factor to keep in mind as Type I sources are identified is that the process is developmental and should be accomplished over several years. A list of Type I resources cannot be built overnight. There is a large degree of networking that takes time. This work is most effectively accomplished by assigning specific tasks to Enrichment Team members and subgroups of interested teachers and by polling parents, staff and students to help identify sources of specific Type I experiences. For example, one teacher discovered a high degree of interest among students in several topics: exploring the Internet, Photography, and Structural Engineering. By requesting help in the enrichment newsletter, she was able to locate parents and community members who were interested in sharing their interests and skills in these areas.

School Staff

Survey the staff to discover special talents, hobbies, and interests. This can be done easily with adult interest surveys such as *Inspiration: Targeting My Ideal Teaching and Learning Situation* (see Chapter 10). Undoubtedly the staff will have inconspicuous

Tips for Brainstorming Type I Topics

1. Conduct Pre-Brainstorming.
Since the major purpose of Type I Enrichment is to identify topics that are not ordinarily covered in the regular curriculum, it is a good idea to have staff review textbooks, curriculum guides, and supplementary materials used in a particular subject before the actual brainstorming process begins. These materials may spark ideas related to the curriculum. For example, a group of middle grade Science teachers noted that their regular curriculum included an extensive unit on "heat," but nothing on "cold," and as a result "cryogenics" (the study of the effects of extreme low temperatures on matter) was added as a possible Type I experience. Familiarity with the regular curriculum will help avoid a mere downward extension of topics that ordinarily might be covered in subsequent years.

2. Focus on Topics.
Review what is meant by a Type I experience and its function in the Schoolwide Enrichment Model. The focus of Type I brainstorming should be on *topics* not ordinarily covered in the regular curriculum, not on *procedures*. Many teachers feel compelled to list activities (or ready-to-implement Type III projects) rather than topics. Type I exploratory experiences may ultimately *lead to* real-life Type III investigations.

3. Discuss Brainstorming Procedures.
Review general brainstorming procedures. The idea is to create as many ideas as possible. There should be no criticism.

4. Form Groups.
Divide into groups by subject area (or grade) and elect a chairperson. Each group can also divide into subgroups by grade level if the original group is too large. Ideally, the final group size should be 4-8.

5. Develop a List.
Each group should develop and record all ideas for possible Type I topics. *Topic Branching* is an activity that can be used to facilitate this process. The group can begin with one general topic and derive related areas or subtopics using available resources. For example, "Drama" can branch into costuming, set design, directing, script writing, etc. For any one topic area, there are vast resources available that can be used to explore different subtopics. Group members may need to break off to research a particular topic and reconvene later.

6. Review the List.
Once an extensive list is formed, the group should reexamine it and circle topics for which they would like to develop Type I activities.

Figure 35. Tips for brainstorming type I topics.

Brainstorming Type I Topics
Worksheet

General
Content Area _____

Grade
Range _____

Number of People
in this Group _____

1. Choose a chairperson to report back for the group.
2. Develop a list of ideas by using topic branching or another brainstorming method. These ideas should be topics (not specific activities) and areas not typically covered in the regular curriculum.
3. When your list is formed, go back and circle those topics for which you'd like to develop Type I experiences.
4. List possible sources for each topic circled.

Figure 36. Brainstorming type I topics worksheet.

interests that may provide the basis for valuable Type I experiences for students. Include any information on already organized Type I experiences that a staff member may have available, such as interest development centers, enrichment clusters, or in-class projects.

Parents

Parent talents are often overlooked, but parents can be a valuable and willing resource for Type I needs. They enjoy a variety of professions, hobbies, interests, skills, and travel expertise that can be shared for Type I experiences. A brief note in an enrichment newsletter or other forms of correspondence may uncover special skills and interests among parents or additional community contacts (see Figures 37-39). Parent involvement will also help build valuable support for the enrichment program.

Public Agencies, Professional Organizations, and Societies

The youth services division of local police department, fire department, or park are all excellent sources for Type I experiences. These agencies may already visit schools for presentations, but they are typically eager to do more and are accustomed to working with large groups of children.

Many professional organizations and societies can also be valuable resources and may provide assistance in identifying resource people in a specific area. Two great sources of information include: (1) *The Directory of American Youth Organizations: A Guide to 500 Clubs, Groups, Troops, Teams, Societies, Lodges, and More for Young People* (Published by Freespirit Publishing, 400 First Avenue, N., Suite 616, Minneapolis, MN 55401) and (2) *The Encyclopedia of Associations Index* (Published by Gale Research, Inc., 835 Penebscot Building, Detroit, MI 48226-4094). Some of the organizations in these books have prepared categorical lists of community resource opportunities. For example, The American Association for the Advancement of Science (1776 Massachusetts Ave., NW., Washington, D.C. 20036) has published a booklet called *Out of School Programs in Science*. This booklet is organized by state and lists Science museums, environmental educational organizations, Archaeological field sites, and Science organizations that have existing resources for young people. An introductory section describes how the book can be used in identifying local, national, and regional resources.

Similarly, many state historical societies, commissions on the Arts, and other special interest groups maintain directories of local organizations that can serve as an invaluable source of Type I experiences. Educators can begin by looking in the Yellow Pages of the phone book under "Associations." The Blue Pages also list a variety of government organizations that can provide possible speakers, films, field trips, and other resources for effective Type I experiences.

Colleges and Universities

College and university staff can be valuable sources of information for an enrichment program. University course catalogs are organized by department and present information about staff and the specialty areas they teach. The staff directory is another good source of information. Many universities maintain a public service speakers bureau. The university's office of public information houses information on these speakers, visitations, lecture series, artistic presentations, and other events and often maintain a mailing list for special events promotions. A university or college may offer services to local schools

An Open Letter to Parents and Community Members

Prepared by
Deborah E. Burns
University of Connecticut

Dear Interested Parents and Community Members:

This letter has been distributed to you as part of our efforts to locate adults within our community who might be willing to share their professional expertise, talents, and experiences with the students in our schools.

In designing programs to meet the needs of our children, it is important that we provide a wide variety of enrichment experiences. Classroom studies, independent research, and special classes already meet many of their learning needs. Yet the abilities of many of our students are often so unique that it becomes necessary to look beyond the boundaries of the traditional classroom in order to locate appropriate resources and role models.

It is our belief that advanced level interests can best be encouraged by bringing children in touch with adult professionals who share their interests and ambitions. In this way, children will have an opportunity for intense exploration of individual interests and a wide exposure to adults of varying lifestyles and ideologies. We firmly believe that children who have this prolonged contact with adult role models will gain an appreciation for task commitment, creativity, and problem-solving by observing the "practicing professional" in a realistic setting. Children who have this experience will be more likely to eventually develop positive attitudes toward independent learning, self-motivation, and in-depth investigation.

The community involvement we seek differs a great deal from traditional volunteer programs. We are not searching for chaperones, cookie bakers, or teachers' aides. Instead, we are asking you to share your professional expertise, your experiences, talents, and hobbies. Depending on student needs, this sharing and exploration might involve service as a classroom speaker or as a mentor for an individual child involved in a long-term project.

The survey that follows is our attempt to locate those community members who are willing to share their talents with our students. It will provide us with helpful information regarding your areas of expertise and interest in volunteering your services. If the idea intrigues you, please complete the survey and return it to your local coordinator of enrichment programs. We will contact you regarding future involvement in the program as soon as we have located students who share your interests.

Please accept, in advance, our gratitude for your cooperation.

Return to:

Sincerely,

Figure 37. An open letter to parents and community members.

Community Resources Survey

Directions: Please scan this list in search of subjects that reflect your personal interests, skills, talents, or experiences. Circle any subjects that you can discuss with interested students.

Social Sciences
1. Anthropology
2. Alcohol and Drugs
3. American Culture
4. History
5. Amish
6. Archaeology
7. Black History
8. Careers
9. Child Abuse
10. Cowboys
11. Crime/Criminology
12. Current Events
13. Death/Dying
14. Elections
15. Ethnic Heritage
16. Families
17. Famous People
18. Festivals/Holidays
19. Foreign Policy
20. Futures
21. Genealogy
22. Geography
23. Government
24. Handicapped People
25. Hypnosis
26. Indians
27. Law/Courts
28. Mental Illness
29. Military
30. Ohio History
31. Penology Prisons
32. Politics
33. Pollution
34. Population Control
35. Presidents
36. Psychology
37. Public Opinion
38. Pyramids
39. Religion
40. Senior Citizens
41. Social Problems
42. Unions
43. United States/ Specific State
44. Urban Development/City Planning
45. Wars
46. Women's Rights
47. Wild West
48. World Affairs
49. World Travels

Language Arts/ Communication
50. Advertising
51. Authors
52. Book-Making
53. Broadcasting
54. Comic Strips
55. Communication
56. Debate
57. Etymology
58. Foreign Languages
59. Game Design
60. Graphics/Printing
61. Handwriting/ Graphology
62. Interviewing
63. Journalism/ Newspaper
64. Legends
65. Letter Writing
66. Libraries
67. Linguistics
68. Literature
69. Mythology
70. Oral History
71. Play Writing
72. Poetry
73. Polling
74. Public Speaking
75. Publishing
76. Shakespeare
77. Sign Language/ Deafness
78. 20th Century Writers

Science
79. Agriculture/Farming
80. Anatomy
81. Animals
82. Astrology/Stars
83. Astronomy
84. Biology
85. Biorhythms/ Chronobiology
86. Birds
87. Botany
88. Chemistry
89. Conservation
90. Dinosaurs
91. Disasters
92. Ecology
93. Electronics
94. Energy
95. Engineering
96. Evolution
97. Fish
98. Fossils
99. Forestry
100. Genetics
101. Health/Medicine
102. Human Body
103. Insects
104. Inventions
105. Metals
106. Microscopes
107. Monsters
108. Natural Resources
109. Nature Study
110. Nutrition
111. Oceanography
112. Optics
113. Outdoor Education
114. Outer Space/ Aeronautics
115. Phobias/Fears
116. Physics
117. Pollution
118. Reptiles
119. Robots
120. Rocks and Minerals
121. Rockets
122. Scientific Method/ Scientists
123. Snakes
124. Weather
125. Wildlife

Mathematics
126. Accounting
127. Algebra
128. Banking
129. Business
130. Calculators
131. Chisanbop
132. Computers
133. Consumerism
134. Economics
135. Geometry
136. Inflation
137. Matrices
138. Money Management
139. Statistics/ Probability
140. Stock Market
141. Taxes

Visual/Performing Arts
142. Acting
143. Animation
144. Antiques
145. Architecture
146. Art History
147. Artists

(continued)

Figure 38. Community resources survey.

Community Resources Survey

(continued)

148. Ballet
149. Broadway
150. Calligraphy
151. Cartooning
152. Choreography/ Dancing
153. Cinematography/ Filmmaking
154. Clay
155. Clowns
156. Commercial Art
157. Costumes Design
158. Dramatics
159. Drawing
160. Folk Art/Music
161. Graphics
162. Make-Up Design
163. Modern Dance
164. Movies
165. Musical Instruments
166. Music Theory
167. Musicians
168. Opera
169. Origami
170. Painting
171. Pantomime
172. Photography
173. Play Production
174. Puppetry
175. Radio Shows
176. Television

177. Theater
178. Weaving

Thinking/Research/ Study Skills
179. Brain Games
180. Chess
181. College
182. Creativity
183. Decision-Making
184. Deductive/ Inductive Reasoning
185. Human Relations
186. Imagination
187. Leadership Training
188. Listening Skills
189. Logic
190. Memory Skills
191. Preparing AV Materials
192. Problem-Solving
193. Research
194. Simulations
195. Speed Reading
196. Typing
197. Values/Moral Education

Careers/Avocations
198. Advertising

199. Aviation/Airplanes
200. Construction
201. Cosmetology
202. Dentistry
203. Drafting
204. Fashion Design
205. Food Services
206. Industry
207. Insurance
208. Interior Decorating
209. Journalism
210. Landscaping
211. Law/Lawyers
212. Law Enforcement
213. Manufacturing
214. Medicine/Surgery
215. Merchandising
216. Nursing
217. Optometry
218. Psychiatry/ Psychology
219. Real Estate
220. Retailing
221. Secret Service
222. Transportation
223. Veterinarian
224. Ventriloquism

Recreation
225. Aerobics
226. Archery

227. Backpacking
228. Baton Twirling
229. Beekeeping
230. Boating
231. Bicycles
232. Camping
233. Cars
234. C. B. Radios
235. Cheerleading
236. Coins/Stamps
237. Crafts
238. Drag Racing
239. Gardening
240. Horses
241. Houseplants
242. Hunting
243. Kites
244. Magic
245. Martial Arts
246. Model Building
247. Motorcycles
248. Orienteering
249. Pets
250. Sailing
251. Scuba Diving
252. Snowmobiles
253. Sports
254. Toys
255. Treasure Hunting
256. War Games
257. Woodworking

Is there any other information about your career, travels, education, cultural experiences, hobbies, publications, collections, competitions, community activities, politics, research, pet projects, or special interests that you are willing to share with us?

(continued)

Figure 38. Community resources survey (continued).

Would you be willing to share your special talents and interests with the children in our enrichment program?
If yes, please indicate the format(s) you would prefer:

☐ I am willing to conduct a 45 minute lecture/discussion/demonstration with groups of interested students.

☐ I am willing to teach a short workshop for a small group of interested students.

☐ I am available for a phone conference with a student who shares my interests.

☐ I am willing to have a private conference with a student who shares my interests.

☐ I am willing to have interested student(s) visit me at my place of business/home.

☐ I am willing to answer written correspondence from a student who shares my interests.

☐ I am willing to commit ten or more hours to serve as a mentor for a student who shares my interests.

☐ I am willing to help serve as an evaluator of a student's project in a mutual interest area.

☐ I can suggest other resource people, organizations, and/or introductory books and magazines in my interest area(s).

If we are able to schedule a working session for students who share your interests, would you:

☐ Volunteer your time and expertise? Require payment? If so, what are your fees? Have any other special limitations? Please specify.

Your Name _____   Place of Business _____
Profession _____   Business Phone _____
Business Address _____   Home Phone _____
_____
Home Address_____
_____

Please accept, in advance, our appreciation for your time and cooperation in sharing information about your experiences and talents. Your expertise will certainly be a valuable addition to our enrichment program.

OFFICE USE ONLY

Resource Codes: Permission to reproduce this page granted by Creative Learning Press, Inc.

Figure 38. Community resources survey (continued).

Follow-Up Letter to Community Volunteers

Dear Volunteer:

Thank you so much for returning the community resources survey that was distributed by our office. The children who are participating in the enrichment programs in our local schools will benefit greatly from your experiences and talents. As you know, responding to the survey will allow us to put your name in our resource file that will make your topic available to area teachers who have students interested in your subject area. We truly appreciate your willingness to share your expertise with our students, especially in light of your busy schedule.

Since we have found that the best resource speakers are those who are familiar with the teacher's goals and who know what to expect, the following guidelines have been compiled to assist you in your preparation, so that you can be assured of maximum success.

1) Let the teacher know if there is anything that should be done to prepare the class for your visit. Perhaps there are experiments that could be performed or vocabulary that could be learned before you come.

2) Since the primary goal of our program is to encourage our students to become creative producers in their interest areas, our teachers and students will be looking for follow-up activities to do after you visit. Can you think of ways that our students can become active in your area at their level of achievement? What problems exist in your field that need meaningful solutions?

3) Feel free to discuss the age level or general knowledge of the group with the teacher ahead of time. Often the teacher will have specific wishes about the focus or scope of the program.

4) If you need any audiovisual equipment, please let the teacher know ahead of time.

5) Hands-on activities are great! Do you have something to demonstrate? Something with which the children could assist? Photos to share? If you have materials to examine or manipulate, plan to hand them out at the appropriate moment in order to enhance attention and to increase interest level.

6) Please allow time at the end of your presentation for students to ask questions. In most cases there will be specified time allotment, but don't hesitate to shorten presentations if students are becoming restless. It is convenient to conclude by indicating, for instance, that there is time for "one more question."

If it is acceptable with you, we will contact you in the near future regarding your future involvement with individuals or small groups of students who share your interests. If you have any questions, feel free to call our office for further assistance.

Again, thank you so much for your cooperation.

Sincerely yours,

Figure 39. Follow-up letter to community volunteers.

to fulfill community service requirements. This also provides them with an opportunity to familiarize future "recruits" with the university.

Another possible source for Type I experiences (and later mentorships, enrichment clusters, and internships) are college students. Check with the faculty chairperson of a specific department for referrals. If the university has an education department, a staff person there can recommend students who are interested in the field of education and eager to gain experience with groups of youngsters and develop ties with a local school. An enrichment program is an excellent opportunity for college or graduate students to fulfill a community service requirement or an internship.

Businesses

Local retailers and businesses can provide excellent authentic Type I experiences. For example, an educator might have the product development manager from a nearby manufacturer come in and show students how and why new products are developed for his/her company. A local engineering firm might share the fundamentals of engineering for a new property being developed. These types of opportunities can serve as inspirations to students for later career opportunities.

National businesses, such as game or toy companies, book or magazine publishers, and printing companies often have outreach programs and resources that would serve as excellent Type I experiences. If such a business exists near a school, contact their public relations department for possible ideas.

A good place to begin locating interested businesses is to ask staff and parents for suggestions. The phone book is also a comprehensive resource.

Senior Citizens

Senior citizens can share a wide variety of occupations, hobbies, talents, and interests, as well as serve as an audience for presentations and Type III products developed by students. Many seniors have time available during the day and are eager to develop relationships with children. Check the Blue Pages of the phone book for senior centers in the area and contact the center's recreation director for referrals.

Students

Peers at the school and older students at other local schools can offer very exciting Type I experiences to students. The experience can include presenting a Type III investigation, sharing an out-of-school interest, performing a special talent, or setting up a hobby display. Older students have also offered very successful enrichment clusters (this requires some adult monitoring). While the concept behind enrichment clusters is to pursue a Type III investigation, an enrichment cluster can also serve as a valuable Type I or II experience. At one local elementary school, several 3rd and 4th graders facilitated an enrichment cluster on ballet dancing because of their interest in it. Members of this cluster learned about ballet (Type I), practiced the skill (Type II), choreographed a piece on their own (Type III), then shared their new dance with the rest of the school (Type I).

Television

Although many people have characterized television as a "great waste land," it has remarkable potential for introducing students to topics that are not ordinarily covered in the curriculum. It is essential to preview the listings of upcoming programs and encourage students to view particular programs. A variety of exemplary shows are offered, such as *National Geographic* specials, *Bill Nye the Science Guy*, *World of Discovery* specials, *Nova*, and many others. A television guide or schedule from the newspaper should provide information on upcoming worthwhile shows.

Publicizing preselected television events to students, encouraging viewing of particular programs, and conducting follow-up discussions provides a ready-made source of extremely rich exploratory experiences. This procedure can take students into the world's best known theaters, laboratories, and places where history is made, while exposing them to people who are on the forefront of creative developments in a variety of fields. For many students, this experience may be the spark that ignites a sustained involvement in a particular field of study. Teachers can invite parents to tape special programs for classroom use. These taped programs can be kept in the library and used as classroom Type I experiences or for viewing during indoor recess.

Media

An almost endless supply of Type I experiences can be found in various catalogs for films, AV materials, computer supplies, and other forms of non-print media. Several good sources are listed below:

- *The National Directory of Addresses and Telephone Numbers.* (1994). Edited by Darren L. Smith. ISBN# 0-7808-0020-6. Also available in CD ROM: ISBN# 0-7807-0039-7. This book is an invaluable source of government offices, associations, cultural and recreation centers, newspapers, television stations, publishers, and a variety of public and private agencies.
- *Lesko's Info-Power, Vol. 2.* (1994). Written by Matthew Lesko. Published by Gale Research, Inc., 835 Penobscot Bldg., Detroit, MI 48226-4094. ISBN# 0-8103-9485-5.
- *State Department of Education Listings.* Many State Departments of Education publish an annual guide of instructional television programs and resources.

In additional to these sources, large corporations may offer display materials and resources valuable for a Type I display. Contact their public relations department for information.

Interest Development Centers

A major source of Type I experiences includes teacher developed interest centers that are specifically designed to stimulate new interests. Interest development centers provide teachers with an opportunity to pursue their own interests and exercise their own creativity. Although the SEM does not require teachers to be writers and developers of their own curriculum, this is one opportunity for interested teachers to use curriculum development to explore their interests and skills. The development of an interest center is discussed later in the chapter.

The Internet

The Internet provides a wide range of resources for Type I experiences. Learners can explore many facets of a topic by conducting electronic searches on the Internet. Some of the most popular Internet search engines include:

AltaVista (http://altavista.digital.com)
Excite (http://www.excite.com)
Infoseek (http://infoseek.com)
Lycos (http://www.lycos.com)
Magellan (http://www.mckinley.com)
Specs for Kids (http://www.newview.com/kidshome)
WebCrawler (http://webcrawler.com)
Yahoo (http://www.yahoo.com)
Yahooligans (http://www.yahooligans.com)

These search engines help learners find quick and easy ways to browse through the Internet's immense collection of web sites, newsgroups, e-mail addresses, and FAQs.

The Internet contains a wealth of information on almost every imaginable topic—from bats and electricity to Shakespeare and aviation. The best thing about the Internet is that it offers a little something for everyone. Whether it is a discussion group on birds of prey or a database that contains information on automobiles, learners of all ages can find facts, activities, and resources on a topic of their choice. (See below for a listing of useful Internet sites.)

As the Internet continues to expand, learners will be able to use this worldwide network as a comprehensive reference guide (dictionaries, encyclopedias, and digitized museums), electronic mentor, communication device (e-mail and chat groups with others who share similar interests), and resource tool (addresses and links). The Internet offers a great way for youngsters to explore different interest areas and learn about the exciting world around them.

Outstanding Internet Sites

AstroWeb (http://fits.cv.nrao.edu/www/astronomy.html)
The Butterfly Zone (http://www.butterflies.com)
Dinosauria Online (http://www.dinosauria.com)
Discovery Channel Online (http://www.discovery.com)
Exploratorium Homepage (http://www.exploratorium.edu)
Food and Nutrition Information Center (http://www.nalusda.gov/fnic)
Ion Science (http://www.injersey.com/Media/IonSci)
The Library of Congress (http://www.loc.gov)
Monarch Watch (http://monarch.bio.ukans.edu)
NASA (http://www.nasa.gov)
National Geographic (http://www.nationalgeographic.com)
National Weather Service (http://www.nws.noaa.gov)
Quest (http://quest.arc.nasa.gov)
Sea World's Animal Information Database (http://www.bev.net/education/SeaWorld/homepage.html)
The Shakespeare Web (http://www.shakespeare.com)
Steve and Ruth Bennett's Family Surfboard (http://www.familysurf.com)
The Smithsonian Institute (http://www.si.edu)
VolcanoWorld Home Page (http://volcano.und.nodak.edu/noframe_index.html)

The World of Benjamin Franklin (http://sln.fi.edu/franklin)
World Wide Web of Sports (http://www.tns.lcs.mit.edu/cgi-bin/sports)

Developing a Type I Source File

The Resource Directory Form

As community resources are surveyed and discovered, this information needs to be recorded and organized for future enrichment planning. The Resource Directory Form (see Figure 40) presents one approach for recording these resources. Information such as the contact person, organization, address, phone, availability, method of delivery, supporting resources, and cost can all be documented and later filed by subject. Depending on the contact, the resources and information on these forms can be extensive. For example, the director at a local planetarium might offer to present a slide show or a lecture, provide a field trip to the planetarium, or offer to loan a variety of NASA materials for display. The Resource Directory Form should reflect all these options and can be filed under an appropriate subject. If there is a need later for a Type I experience on rockets, this contact will be valuable. The important point is to develop a systematic procedure for keeping track of Type I sources so they can be easily disseminated to others or retrieved for later use.

As contacts are made, they should be noted on the Resource Directory Form. These forms can then be filed by subject and kept in a loose-leaf notebook so they can be easily updated. Teacher, student, and presenter evaluations can also be included behind the Resource Directory Forms. At some point, all sources for a particular subject should be recorded on one form (see Figure 41) and filed or circulated to staff so they may make selections. Teachers may want to meet periodically to update the forms and use a "Type I Idea Box" in the hall for ongoing submissions of ideas.

The Type I source file will build over the years and can be kept in the enrichment library for access to everyone in the school, as it will be a valuable tool later for Type II and Type III needs. Teachers may also choose to distribute it to all schools in their district.

Teacher Training

The *25¢ Type I Challenge* (see SIMSIT 2 at the end of the chapter) is an activity that will give teachers experience in arranging an exciting Type I activity or an enrichment cluster. It can be done during an inservice lunch hour, evening, or extended break and requires a later session for follow-up. There are several benefits to this type of activity. First, it shows teachers how easy (and fun) it is to arrange stimulating Type I experiences. Second, it emphasizes locating Type I topics and issues as extensions to the regular curriculum. Third, it shares involvement and ownership of the enrichment program with those who may not be directly involved in it.

Resource Directory Form

Name:

Topic:

Address:

Phone:

Materials Available: ☐ Film   ☐ Video
                      ☐ Display   ☐ Samples
                      ☐ Other _____

Mode of Delivery: ☐ Mentor   ☐ Field Trip
                   ☐ Presentation ☐ Enrichment Cluster
                   ☐ Other _____

Cost:

Contacts Made:

Figure 40. Resource directory form.

Type I Resources by Subject Area

TOPIC	AGENCY & CONTACT PERSON	PHONE	MATERIALS	MODE OF DELIVERY	NOTES

Figure 41. Type I resources by subject area.

Chapter 7

Implementing Type I's in the Enrichment Program

Scheduling

Since the SEM advocates a variety of enrichment experiences for all students, one of the primary responsibilities of the enrichment specialist is to help develop a schedule that allows schoolwide enrichment to occur regularly. The scheduling discussed here should not be confused with the Talent Pool or enrichment cluster schedules. The Type I schedule functions to accommodate large, schoolwide events. Further information for developing a comprehensive enrichment schedule is included in Chapters 8 and 9.

Once a district has adopted the model, any schoolwide scheduling is best done prior to the school year during the scheduling of specials, to limit the number of conflicts. If this has not been arranged, then the enrichment specialist, Enrichment Team, and principal should work together to develop a schedule that accommodates the different requirements of the staff. Finding time for regularly scheduled Type I Enrichment is always a challenge, but a general rule of thumb for scheduling is to provide time for one large Type I event each month. This time block can be used for schoolwide or all-grade events.

The first step should involve a brainstorming session with staff for possible scheduling ideas. This meeting can also focus on additional grade level enrichment activities, either for all students in a grade level or a group of interested students. For example, if teachers are interested in supplementing their Language Arts curriculum with a series of authors, they can invite various authors to visit the school once a month. By the end of the school year, students will have been exposed to a variety of writing styles and types of literature.

Interest Development Centers

The primary difference between interest development centers and the traditional kinds of "learning centers" found in many classrooms is that the interest development centers do not focus primarily on skill development, the completion of worksheets, or other activities designed to develop basic skills. The following pages include a procedure for using Type I experiences to create interest development centers (see Figures 42 and 43). These topics should emanate from classroom teachers, the Enrichment Team, or any other source discussed previously. Whenever possible, interested students should be included in the development of these centers. Parents can also provide valuable contributions, whether from their professional resources, hobbies and interests, or special contacts with community people. It is always worthwhile to circulate information about centers under development through a program newsletter or special announcement. This will increase the variety of material in the interest development centers and also generate greater program ownership.

Organizing these centers provides teachers with excellent opportunities for exercising their creativity and sharing their interests and excitement on a topic with children. It is through this "modeling" that an interest in a topic is likely to be passed from teacher to student. A good center can be shared among teachers and used year after year by implementing an exchange program among teachers in a school or district. Interest

Tips for Organizing
Interest Development Centers

1. Focus on a Topic
Select your topic and enter it in the box at the top of the worksheet. Consider whether or not the topic should be more specific. (For example, arthropods might be refined to arachnids or spiders specific to your area.) You may need to consult with a resource person or book to make this decision.

2. Decide on One or More Type I Activities
The first box on this worksheet lists some of the possible activities that may be used to convert this topic to a Type I experience. Activities checked at this stage are tentative because of the availability or prohibitive cost of some resources.

3. Explore Available Resources
The choice of activity depends in part on the kinds of resources available. Your librarian can help locate books, magazines, computer programs, film and media catalogs, and other materials for use in the development of interest development centers.

4. Explore Available Resource People
This process is especially important if an interest development activity is going to include a visiting speaker. Consider community people, museums, local colleges and universities, professional organizations, historical societies, local businesses, and hobby groups. These people can also suggest field trips, other contacts, and additional resources.

5. Brainstorm Specific Activities
Brainstorm specific activities that might stimulate student interest in your topic. This process consists of translating one or more of the items you checked off in the first box into an activity. For example, if you checked off "field trip" you may want to list specific field trip sites, a tentative date, contact person, and suggested follow-up activity (e.g., discussion, simulation, letter, etc.). If you decide upon an interest development center, organize an attractive display to draw children's attention to the materials. A center might include posters, charts, manipulatives, newspaper or magazine articles, a computer, or AV materials.

Figure 42. Tips for organizing interest development centers.

Organizing Interest Development Centers Worksheet

Content Area: _____ Grade Range: _____

TOPIC: [_____]

General Exploratory Activities
(Check all that apply. Star the most likely after reviewing resources.)

____ Visiting Speaker	____ Computer Software
____ Enrichment Cluster	____ Internet Sources
____ Demonstration	____ Newspaper/Magazine Articles
____ Discussion/Debate	____ Interest Development Center
____ Film/Filmstrip/Slides	____ Display
____ Tape/Videotape	____ Field Trip/Museum Program
____ Television	____ Other

Related Curricular Materials

Books

Visitations/Speakers

Magazines/Journals

Computer Software

Audio-Visuals

Internet Sources

Display Items

Specific Exploratory Activities

(Use the back of this sheet if you need additional space.)

Figure 43. Organizing interest development centers worksheet.

development centers can also provide opportunities for students to share their interests and talents with other students.

Advertising Type I Events

Read All About It...

The primary goal of Type I Enrichment is to spark student interest and pursue a Type II skill or a Type III investigation. For this reason, advertising upcoming Type I events is very important, as it will help attract as many interested students as possible. There are many ways to announce an upcoming event (See Figures 44-47):

- *Regular Enrichment Newsletters*
- *Calendar Announcements*
- *Intercom Announcements*
- *Bulletin Board Messages*
- *Personal Invitations to Students, Parents, Staff, and Board of Education Members*

These announcements will help ensure good attendance, and since Type I experiences are highly visible, they will help promote support from parents and decision makers for the enrichment program. Whenever an unusually dynamic Type I is planned (i.e., a well-known author, hot-air balloon launch, etc.), consider inviting a local newspaper or television reporter. These communications are all important for gaining and maintaining support for the program.

Maximizing Payoff of Type I Events

One of the primary goals of Type I Enrichment is to stimulate new interests that might lead to follow-up by students who share a common interest. Teachers can help maximize this type of payoff by conducting student discussions following each event. This is especially important for Talent Pool students in order to promote Type III exploration.

After successful Type I's have been conducted, teachers can share this information with parents through a summary letter (see Figure 48). These letters can provide information about the Type I topic and presenter, as well as suggestions for extensions that can be done at home.

Whenever possible, a Type I presenter should be invited to meet with students who may be interested in pursuing a Type III investigation. This type of mentor role can be extremely motivating and exciting for students. A letter (see Figure 49) may be sent to orient presenters with the procedures used to organize these more advanced sessions. If the presenter is not available, the follow-up discussions can be presented by classroom teachers and/or the enrichment specialist who attended the session. Discussions should be directed toward the initiation of *Action Information Messages* that might result in certain students revolving into Type III investigations (see Chapter 9). The discussions might also lead to more advanced Type I presentations on the same topic or result in the need for Type II training or an enrichment cluster. Type I's should be viewed as potential beginning points for any students who might want to pursue a new interest. During these discussions, presenters and teachers should watch for high levels of interest or

Type I Schedule for 1996-97

TO: Eastview Elementary Teachers & Parents
FROM: Eastview Enrichment Team
DATE: October 4, 1996
RE: Type I Schedule for 1996-97

Listed below is the tentative schedule of Type I activities which the Enrichment Team has planned for the 1996-97 school year. You will receive notice of each event as dates and times are finalized.

We want to schedule activities that address student interests and we will rely upon your input as these interests develop. Please let the enrichment specialist know of any particular student interests and we will do our best to accommodate these needs. Also, please see team members if you have questions or suggestions for future Type I activities. Thanks!

Date	Presenter	Topic	Grade
November:	The Chronicle	Photography	1-6
November:	The Chronicle	Reporting & Editing	1-6
November:	NE Associates	Advertising & Design	1-6
December:	UConn Geology Dept.	Archaeology	K-3
December:	Anne Joseph	Electronics	4-6
January:	Dinosaur State Park	Paleontology	K-3
January:	AV Associates	Computers	4-6
February:	EB Animal Hospital	Animals & Pets	K-3
February:	Eastview Historical Society	Genealogy	4-6
March:	SNET Phone Co.	Simulation	K-3
March:	Planetarium Field Trip	Astronomy	4-6
April:	Natural History Museum	Flowers & Birds	K-3
April:	Natural History Museum	Insects	4-6
May:	Art Geary	Ballooning	K-3
May:	Windham Airport	Aviation	4-6

These dates and topics are tentative and may change as the year progresses.

Figure 44. Sample type I schedule.

Enrichment Program Announcement

TO: Parents of Talent Pool Students
FROM: The Enrichment Specialist
DATE: February 4
RE: Type I Enrichment: TV

As part of our overall Enrichment Program, we have planned a year-long series of general exploratory experiences using outstanding programs from public and commercial television. As you may recall, Type I Enrichment is designed to expose students to disciplines, topics and ideas not covered in the regular curriculum.

Each month we will send home a calendar of selected PBS programs that might be valuable exploratory experiences for your child. Since commercial television programming is not available a month in advance, we will send home "TV Bulletins" on special upcoming commercial programs.

Please review these announcements with your children and choose shows that may be of interest. Programs that appear with a star (*) will have follow-up discussions and activities at the school.

If you have any questions or suggestions, please feel free to call me at the school.

Enrichment Program Announcement

TO: Grade 5 & 6 Teachers
FROM: Enrichment Specialist
DATE: February 4
RE: Type I Enrichment Activity on Architecture

Jim Foster, Jennifer's father, will be here on Friday at 2:00 PM to do a Type I lecture on Architecture. I can accommodate up to 35 students in my room. Please assess the interest of your students and let me know by Thursday, February 8 who will attend.

Thank you.

Figure 45. Sample enrichment program announcements.

March 1996—PBS Specials

Sun	Mon	Tue	Wed	Thu	Fri	Sat
					1	2 1:00 PM Mansion: The Great Houses of Europe
3 2:30 PM Scottish Fiddle Orchestra	4 6:30 PM The Internet	5 6:30 PM Nature: Ghost Bear	6	7	8	9 8:00 PM Over America
10 8:30 PM Backyard Birdwatcher	11	12 8:00 Nova: The Miracle of Life	13	14	15	16 7:00 PM Mystery of the Full Moon*
17	18 9:00 PM One Woman, One Vote*	19 8:00 PM Nova: Carbon Molecules	20	21 8:00 PM Wing and a Prayer/The Decline of Birds	22	23 12:00 PM Religion & Race in America
24 5:00 PM Creatures Great and Small	25	26 8:00 PM Nature: Man's Best Friend*	27	28	29	30 8:00 PM Apollo 13: To The Edge & Back*
31						

* These programs will have follow-up discussions and activities at school.

Figure 46. Sample television schedule.

Type I Scoop!

What: Coins & Stamps Presentation

When: Tuesday, December 8

Where: Art Room
Who may attend:
Up to 30 students, Grades 1-3

Mr. Martin Nagel is scheduled to give a presentation on coins and stamps to interested primary students. Martin is an attendance counselor with the Richland County Department of Education and is also an avid coin and stamp collector. He has given numerous talks to students in the past. In addition to giving students some facts and history on coins and stamps, he will share his valuable collection with the students.

It is our hope that some students who attend this Type I will be interested in pursuing a Type III project in this area and perhaps starting collections of their own.

Please discuss this opportunity with your class and submit up to five names to me by Friday, December 4.

If you are interested in having this session for your entire class let me know and we'll try and schedule it. Thanks!

Figure 47. Sample type I announcement.

<u>Figure 47.</u> Sample type I announcement (continued).

Type I Memo!

TOPIC: Coral Reefs
WHEN: November 2, 2 PM
WHERE: Room 202

Please discuss this invitation with your students and submit interested names to me by Oct. 21.

TV Bulletin!
From Your Enrichment Cluster

Tiger: Lord of the Wild
Saturday, March 16
ABC 8 PM

This program takes a close look at the magnificent Bengal Tiger and the international efforts to save it from extinction. Habitat destruction and a thriving black market for tiger parts threaten the remaining Bengal Tigers in the wild.

Figure 47. Sample type I announcement (continued).

This is What We Did Today!
Type I Summary

Date: _____

Dear _____,

    Today we had a Type I event: _____

_____

_____

_____

_____

_____

_____

_____

                                            Sincerely,

                                    _____

Comments from the Enrichment Teacher:

Mary Emick, a professor at the University of Connecticut, visited our school today to explain botany with interested primary students. She discussed the role of a botanist in Ecology, Biology and Wildlife Management. We learned to recognize a seed embryo by dissecting a corn seed and planting the embryo in agar. We used iodine to test for the presence of starch—the embryo's food—by seeing its absence near the embryo (it had been eaten) and its presence farther away from the seed. She brought several plants and discussed the need for sugar and oxygen consumption by these plants in order for photosynthesis to occur.

Several students expressed interest in the topic. I told them they can submit a "light bulb" for a Type III investigation if they are interested in pursuing an independent or small group research study. Good luck to our future botanists!

Suggestions for Extensions at Home:

• Visit a library and check out books or videos on plants.
• Visit the wildflower exhibit at the Natural History Museum, May 1 & 2.
• Have your child help with gardening, planning the garden, planting, etc.
• Experiment growing plants from avocados, carrots, potatoes, etc.

Figure 48. Sample type I enrichment activity summary.

February 26

Alan Porter
Wickware Planetarium
Willimantic, CT

Dear Alan:

We wish to confirm your visit to Southeast Elementary School on Monday, March 4th at 10:00 am. You will be meeting with the third and fourth grade students for approximately 1 hour. We are delighted that you have volunteered to share your expertise.

Our objectives for this experience are to:

1. Expose students to topics beyond the scope of the regular curriculum that might inspire interest in an independent investigation.
2. Go beyond the facts about a topic to understand how it is studied, why it is important, and what inspires people to get involved in the profession.

In order to facilitate the first objective, we would like you to visit for about 30 minutes with a small group immediately following your large group presentation. These students (about 10) will be those who have expressed a special interest in your topic. They may question you about your presentation, how you became interested in your profession, your training and background, and the problems, frustrations, and rewards you encounter. You may have ideas to share for future student projects.

Enclosed is some background information describing the rationale and components of our Schoolwide Enrichment Program. If you have any further questions, please feel free to contact me at Southeast School.

We look forward to your visit!

Sincerely,

Susan Lindsay
Enrichment Specialist

Figure 49. Sample letter to presenters of a type I session.

participation from individual students. Some students may be reluctant to show interest in front of others and may need a private meeting.

The importance of conducting debriefing or follow-up discussions cannot be overemphasized! Our experience has shown that many outstanding opportunities are lost because teachers fail to take a few minutes for follow-up time that might result in the initiation of related Type II or Type III activities.

Follow-Up Discussion Questions for

Type I Enrichment:

- What did you like best about this presentation?
- Of all the Type I's we have had so far, who feels that this was the most interesting?
- Did anyone get any good ideas for follow-up exploration?
- What questions did this presentation raise in your mind? What else might be explored?
- Did anyone think of any interesting projects, research, or creative writing to pursue on this topic (such as film making, photography, community action)? Whom might you share it with?
- Where could we learn more about this topic? Is there anyplace we could visit or anyone we could contact to get more information?
- Are there any careers that this presentation made you think of?
- Would anyone like to meet with me or the presenter to explore follow-ups on this topic?

Documentation and Evaluation of Type I Enrichment

Using the Type I Planning and Documentation Form as an Evaluation Device

At the end of the school year, the columns and rows of your Type I Planning and Documentation Form (discussed earlier in the chapter) can be added and the figures in each converted to percentages. This provides an overview of Type I scope and diversity. This information will be extremely valuable for subsequent year budgeting and planning. It is also helpful in documenting and reporting the systematic ways teachers provided enrichment to both the general school population and Talent Pool students. A blank matrix may also be distributed to individual classroom teachers as well, to record the number and variety of Type I experiences that they are arranging within their classroom, in addition to those arranged by the Enrichment Team. If this is done, the form can be used either as a gentle enforcer or an evaluation device to determine whether or not the objective has been accomplished.

A good method for developing a year-end evaluation report is to gather appropriate data on a regular basis throughout the year. A brief notation about each Type I recorded on the original Planning Form will serve as a ready reference for repeating successful Type

I's. These notations can be kept in the Type I file, and when preparing a final report, the Planning Form can serve as a cover sheet for the overall Type I effort. Evaluation forms can be attached as back-up information for those who need more information on a particular activity. A few minutes invested in the documentation of each Type I activity as it occurs, will not only save time, but will also provide an impressive picture of the Type I program.

It is also worthwhile to videotape Type I's (with permission) for use in presentations to parent groups, boards of education, and subsequent inservice training events. Photographs (and especially slides) are extremely effective in helping others understand the important role Type I's play in the overall enrichment program, particularly if a resulting Type II or Type III is captured on film as well. These "flow-through" examples help demonstrate the connection between different types of enrichment in the SEM. Finally, a good way to explain how a Type III can convert back into a Type I is to show a slide of a student presenting his or her Type III to other students.

Type I Evaluation Tools

On the following pages are sample forms that can be used to gather evaluation data for Type I's (see Figures 50-54). In order to prevent evaluation from becoming a burden on teachers and students, these forms should be used on a limited basis rather than for every Type I event. At least one evaluation should be made by a teacher or enrichment specialist for every Type I event in the file, in order to assess worthiness for the future. Student and additional teacher evaluations can be completed on a random basis. This information should be sufficient for reporting to administrators, boards of education, or funding agencies. In addition, all instances of student follow-up (Type II or III) should be documented. Such extensions represent the best examples of payoff for this component of the SEM program.

Type I Enrichment Evaluation Form
Student Form for Primary Grade Levels

Presentation: _____ Date: _____

To help us plan future programs, please circle the number under the sentence that tells how you feel about the presentation. If you feel in between two of the sentences, circle the number between them.

I enjoyed the experience.		It was O.K.		It was boring.
(circle one) 5	4	3	2	1
I liked the performers.		The performers were O.K.		I did not like the performers.
(circle one) 5	4	3	2	1
I learned a lot about the subject.		I learned something about the subject.		I learned nothing about the subject.
(circle one) 5	4	3	2	1
I would like to see more of this subject.		I am not sure if I want to see more of this subject.		I do not want to see any more of this subject.
(circle one) 5	4	3	2	1

Would you like to make any comments?

Please return this form to your enrichment specialist.

Figure 50. Type I enrichment evaluation form (student, primary grade levels).

Type I Enrichment Evaluation Form
Student Form for Elementary Grade Levels

Please help us plan future Type I's by filling out this form.

Speaker's Name _____ Your Grade _____

Topic of Talk _____

	Yes	No	Unsure
This Type I was really interesting.	☐	☐	☐
I enjoyed this Type I.	☐	☐	☐
I learned about things I did not know before.	☐	☐	☐
This presentation was interesting for students my age.	☐	☐	☐
This Type I helped me think of project ideas or ways to learn more about this topic.	☐	☐	☐

Was there something "super special" about this Type I? What was it?

What would you change about this Type I?

Please give this form to your teacher. Thank you.

Figure 51. Type I enrichment evaluation form (student, elementary grade levels).

Type I Enrichment Evaluation Form
Student Form for Intermediate and Secondary Grade Levels

Please help us plan future Type I's by filling out this form.

Speaker's Name _____ Your Grade _____

Topic of Talk _____

	Yes	No	Unsure
This Type I was interesting.	☐	☐	☐
I enjoyed this Type I.	☐	☐	☐
The speaker covered a topic not usually covered in my classes.	☐	☐	☐
This presentation was appropriate for my age and grade level.	☐	☐	☐
This presentation stimulated ideas for possible training I might need or follow-up studies I might conduct.	☐	☐	☐
The speaker gave me ideas for further exploration or possible projects.	☐	☐	☐

What did you like most about this Type I?

What would you change about this Type I?

Please give this form to your teacher. Thank you.

Figure 52. Type I enrichment evaluation form (student, intermediate and secondary grade levels).

Type I Enrichment Evaluation Form
Teacher's Form

Speaker's Name _____

Topic of Talk _____

Date _____ Your Grade _____

	Low		Medium		High
Speaker's knowledge of topic.	1	2	3	4	5
Organization of presentation.	1	2	3	4	5
Use of audiovisual aids.	1	2	3	4	5
Student interest or enthusiasm.	1	2	3	4	5
Appropriateness for this age group.	1	2	3	4	5
Suggestions for extension and further study.	1	2	3	4	5

Describe any extensions (Type II's or Type III's) that will result from this presentation.

Overall success: Would you want to repeat this Type I next year?

Comments:

Figure 53. Type I enrichment evaluation form (teacher).

Type I Enrichment Evaluation Form
Presenter's Form

Name_____

Topic _____ Grade Level(s) _____

Date_____ Audience Size (approx.) _____

	Yes	No
Did you feel the students' ages were appropriate for your presentation?	☐	☐
Were you comfortable with the group size?	☐	☐
Was the class prepared for your presentation?	☐	☐
Did they have adequate background knowledge?	☐	☐
Were the physical accommodations (room size, AV, etc.) satisfactory?	☐	☐
Were you able to give suggestions for further exploration in this area?	☐	☐
Would you be willing to repeat your presentation next year?	☐	☐

Do you have any suggestions to help make the experience of presenting a Type I a happy, successful one?

Thank you!

Figure 54. Type I enrichment evaluation form (presenter).

SIMSIT 2
FACILITATOR'S GUIDE

The 25¢ Type I Challenge
A Simulated Planning Activity

This SIMSIT can be used in a variety of ways and situations. It may be used by an enrichment specialist to recruit staff to serve on the Enrichment Team, encourage program ownership, or expose teachers to the many and varied ways Type I Enrichment may be provided. The key to the success of this SIMSIT is flexibility for whatever type of session has been arranged.

Teacher Training Objectives
- To demonstrate to teachers how easy it is to arrange exciting Type I Enrichment activities.
- To encourage teachers to locate Type I Enrichment sources which will expose students to topics and issues not normally covered in the regular curriculum.
- To share involvement and ownership in the enrichment program with staff members who may not be directly involved in it.

Number of People Involved
Any size group

Approximate Time
A lunch hour, an evening, or an extended break period
An additional 45 minutes for follow-up

Materials and Equipment
Directions for participants
Access to telephones and directories

Directions
Teachers are to break off individually or in pairs and arrange an actual Type I experience from the resources available to them (phones, directories, school resources). Unless there are multiple phones available, it is difficult to complete this activity in less than one hour. Stress to participants that the actual time, date, and location of their Type I need not be secured. The goal is to simply have a presenter agree to participate at a future date. The facilitator could challenge staff to arrange the most creative Type I for a later prize. Before teachers break off to arrange their Type I's, share a few past creative examples.

After teachers have had a chance to arrange their Type I, reconvene and provide a brief opportunity for sharing. This follow-up usually takes no more than 45 minutes. Past participants have been proud of the resources they've been able to locate in a limited amount of time, and the process often stimulates other ideas from the group. One of the participants could briefly record these ideas, and a compiled list could later be circulated, voted on by staff, and a bottle of champagne awarded to the owner of the top idea.

SIMSIT 2
Type I Enrichment (continued)

Directions for Participants

One of the most challenging tasks of any teacher in a Schoolwide Enrichment Program is organizing stimulating Type I Enrichment activities. One goal of a good enrichment specialist should be the formation of an Enrichment Team in each building. This team is responsible for organizing these activities for students in the Talent Pool and in the general student population. However, this may not be possible in the beginning of the program. The enrichment specialist may need to use his or her own creativity to develop exciting Type I experiences.

In this simulation, you are an enrichment specialist faced with that challenge! We invite you to use your own resourcefulness in the specified time period to organize the most exciting Type I activity that you can. You need not actually arrange a time and place; just try and have your presenter agree to some future date. You may use any resources available to you here. Contact friends, local agencies, businesses, etc. Your creativity is the limit! In the past, some of the best Type I's have been arranged by a single "cold call" to someone in the phone book. Good luck!

Chapter 8

Type II Enrichment:
Group Training Activities

- **Overview of Type II Enrichment**
- **Planning a Type II Enrichment Program**
- **Implementing a Type II Enrichment Program**

Overview of Type II Enrichment

Have you ever been really interested in something that you wanted to explore further? Before the "exploration," you first needed to learn the skill related to that topic. A Type II skill is that "knowledge how" component of enrichment, the process skill(s) needed to pursue independent investigations. Think of it as learning how to grow plants. You first may have knowledge about plants, but before you can actually germinate seeds and develop a garden, you need to learn how to take on the project. Type II Enrichment provides the instructional methods and materials designed to promote the development of thinking and feeling processes (see Figure 55). Type II Enrichment can be planned, include systematic skills instruction, develop from student interests generated from a Type I exposure, or develop from a need related to a Type III investigation.

Objectives and Strategies for Type II Training

Several objectives are related to Type II Enrichment. The first objective involves developing general cognitive skills such as creative problem solving, critical thinking, and decision making. The second objective involves developing affective skills such as sensing, appreciating, and valuing. The third objective involves developing and practicing a variety of how-to-learn skills, such as notetaking, interviewing, or analyzing data. The fourth objective involves developing advanced research skills, such as using on-line databases, researching directories, or reviewing abstracts. The final Type II objective involves developing written, oral, and visual communication skills, primarily directed toward maximizing the impact of students' products. Within each of these general skills is a range of related skills, each of which can be taught separately. A taxonomy of these process skills is summarized in Figure 56.

Type II Target Audiences

The range of skills makes Type II training valuable for both Talent Pool students and the general population. This approach to schoolwide enrichment offers many advantages.

Type II Enrichment
Summary Sheet

DEFINITION: Instructional methods and materials that are purposefully designed to promote the development of thinking and feeling processes.

TARGET AUDIENCES:
1. All students (basic training).
2. Talent Pool students (basic training, plus advanced level experiences according to individual abilities and interests).

OBJECTIVES:
1. To develop general skills in creative thinking and problem solving, and critical thinking.
2. To develop affective processes such as sensing, appreciating, and valuing.
3. To develop a wide variety of specific learning how to learn skills such as notetaking, interviewing, classifying and analyzing data, drawing conclusions, etc.
4. To develop skills in the appropriate use of advanced level reference materials such as readers guides, directories, abstracts, computer software, the Internet, etc.
5. To develop written, oral, and visual communication skills that are primarily directed towards maximizing the impact of students' products upon appropriate audiences.

KEY CONCEPTS: A Taxonomy of Process and Thinking Skills Development.
Group Interaction.
A "Scope & Sequence" Approach to Process Development.
Methods-Oriented and Materials-Oriented.

ACTION FORMS: Planning Matrix for Organizing and Teaching Type II Skills
Materials & Activities Selection Worksheet for Planning Type II Enrichment
Enrichment Materials Specification Form

Figure 55. Type II enrichment summary sheet.

Taxonomy of Type II Enrichment Processes

I. Cognitive Training

A. Creativity. Developing and Practicing the Use of:

Fluency	Modification Techniques:
Flexibility	Adaptation
Originality	Magnification
Elaboration	Minification
Brainstorming	Substitution
Forced Relationships	Multiple Uses
Attribute Listing	Rearrangement
Fantasy	Combination
Imagery	Reversal
Association	
Comparison	
Risk Taking	

B. Creative Problem Solving and Decision Making: Developing and Practicing the Use of:

Creative Problem Solving:	Decision Making:
Mess Finding	Stating Desired Goals and Conditions Related to a Decision That Needs to Be Made
Fact Finding	Stating the Obstacles to Realizing the Goals and Conditions
Problem Finding	Identifying the Alternatives Available for Overcoming Each Obstacle
Idea Finding	Examining Alternatives in Terms of Resources, Costs, Constraints and Time
Solution Finding	Ranking Alternatives in Terms of Probable Consequences
Acceptance Finding	Choosing the Best Alternative
	Evaluating the Actions Resulting from the Decision

Figure 56. Taxonomy of type II enrichment processes.

Taxonomy of Type II Enrichment Processes

I. Cognitive Training

C. Critical and Logical Thinking. Developing and Practicing the Use of:

Conditional Reasoning
Ambiguity
Fallacies
Emotive Words
Definition of Terms
Categorical Propositions
Classification
Validity Testing
Reliability Testing
Translation
Interpretation
Extrapolation
Patterning
Sequencing
Flow Charting
Computer Programming

Analogies
Inferences
Inductive Reasoning
Deductive Reasoning
Syllogisms
Probability
Dilemmas
Paradoxes
Analysis of:
    Content
    Elements
    Trends and Patterns
    Relationships
    Organizing Principles
    Propaganda and Bias

II. Affective Training

Understanding Yourself
Understanding Others
Working With Groups
Peer Relationships
Parent Relationships
Values Clarification
Moral Reasoning
Sex Role Stereotypes
Assertiveness Training
Self Reliance

Dealing With Conflict
Coping Behaviors
Analyzing Your Strengths
Planning Your Future
Interpersonal Communication
Developing Self Confidence
Developing a Sense of Humor
Showing an Understanding of Others
Dealing With Fear, Anxiety and Guilt
Dealing With the Unknown

Figure 56. Taxonomy of type II enrichment processes (continued).

Taxonomy of Type II Enrichment Processes

III. Learning How-To-Learn Skills

A. Listening, Observing, and Perceiving. Developing and Practicing the Use of:

Following Directions
Noting Specific Details
Understanding Main Points, Themes, and Sequences
Separating Relevant From Irrelevant Information
Paying Attention to Whole-Part Relationships
Scanning for the "Big Picture"
Focusing in on Particulars
Asking for Clarification
Asking Appropriate Questions
Making Inferences
Noting Subtleties
Predicting Outcomes
Evaluating a Speakers Point of View

B. Notetaking and Outlining. Developing and Practicing the Use of:

Notetaking:

Selecting Key Terms, Concepts, and Ideas
Disregarding Unimportant Information
Noting What Needs to Be Remembered
Recording Words, Dates, and Figures That Help You Recall Related
    Information
Reviewing Notes and Underlining or Highlighting the Most Important Items
Categorizing Notes in a Logical Order
Organizing Notes So That Information From Various Sources Can Be Added
    at a Later Time

Outlining:

Using Outlining Skills to Write Material That Has Unity and Coherence
Selecting and Using a System of Notation Such as Roman Numerals
Deciding Whether to Write Topic Outlines or Sentence Outlines
Stating Each Topic or Point Clearly
Using Parallel Structure
Remembering That Each Section Must Have at Least Two Parts

Figure 56. Taxonomy of type II enrichment processes (continued).

Taxonomy of Type II Enrichment Processes

III. Learning How-To-Learn Skills

C. Interviewing and Surveying. Developing and Practicing the Use of:

Identifying the Information Being Sought
Deciding on Appropriate Instrument(s)
Identifying Sources of Existing Instruments
Designing Instruments (e.g., Checklists, Rating Scales, Interview Schedules)
Developing Question Wording Skills (e.g., Factual, Attitudinal, Probing, Follow-up)
Sequencing Questions
Identifying Representative Samples
Field Testing and Revising Instruments
Developing Rapport With Subjects
Preparing a Data Gathering Matrix and Schedule
Using Follow-up Techniques

D. Analyzing and Organizing Data. Developing and Practicing the Use of:

Identifying Types and Sources of Data
Identifying and Developing Data Gathering Instruments and Techniques
Developing Data Recording and Coding Techniques
Classifying and Tabulating Data
Preparing Descriptive (Statistical) Summaries of Data (e.g., Percentages, Means, Modes, etc.)
Analyzing Data With Inferential Statistics
Preparing Tables, Graphs and Diagrams
Drawing Conclusions and Making Generalizations
Writing Up and Reporting Results

Figure 56. Taxonomy of type II enrichment processes (continued).

Taxonomy of Type II Enrichment Processes

IV. Using Advanced Research Skills and Reference Materials

A. Preparing for Type III Investigations

Developing Time Management Skills
Developing a Management Plan
Developing Problem Finding and Focusing Skills
Stating Hypotheses and Research Questions
Identifying Variables
Identifying Human and Material Resources
Selecting an Appropriate Format and Reporting Vehicle
Obtaining Feedback and Making Revisions
Identifying Appropriate Outlets and Audiences

B. Library Skills

Understanding Library Organizational Systems
Using Informational Retrieval Systems
Using Interlibrary Loan Procedures
Understanding the Specialized Types of Information In Reference Books
    Such As:

Bibliographies	Yearbooks	Periodicals
Encyclopedias	Manuals	Histories and Chronicles
Dictionaries and	Reviews	of Particular Fields
Glossaries	Readers Guides	Organizations
Annuals	Abstract	Concordances
Handbooks	Diaries	Data Tables
Directories and	Books of Quotations,	Digests
Registers	Proverbs, Maxims	Surveys
Indexes	and Familiar Phrases	Almanacs
Atlases	Source Books	Anthologies

Figure 56. Taxonomy of type II enrichment processes (continued).

Taxonomy of Type II Enrichment Processes

IV. Using Advanced Research Skills and Reference Materials

B. Library Skills (continued)

Understanding the Specific Types of Information in Non-Book Reference Materials Such as:

Art Prints	Globes	Films
Talking Books	Maps	Study Print
Videotapes	Film Loops	Models
Microfilms	Pictures	Filmstrips With Sound
Filmstrips	Records	Flashcards
Realia	Slides	Audio Tapes
Transparencies	Charts	Data Tapes

Using Electronic Media to Gather Information:

Commercial On-Line Services	E-mail/Mailing Lists	FTP
Internet	CD-ROMs	Gopher
World Wide Web	Chat Rooms	News Groups

C. Community Resources

Identifying Community Resources Such as:

Private Businesses and Individuals
Governmental and Social Service Agencies
College and University Services and Persons
Clubs, Hobby and Special Interest Groups
Professional Societies and Associations
Senior Citizens Groups
Art and Theater Groups
Service Clubs
Private Individuals
Museums, Galleries, Science Centers, Places of Special Interest or Function

Figure 56. Taxonomy of type II enrichment processes (continued).

Taxonomy of Type II Enrichment Processes

V. Developing Written, Oral, and Visual Communication Skills

A. Written Communication

Planning the Written Document (e.g., Subject, Audience, Purpose, Thesis, Tone, Outline, Title)
Choosing Appropriate and Imaginative Words
Developing Paragraphs With Unity, Coherence and Emphasis
Developing "Technique" (e.g., Metaphor, Comparison, Hyperbole, Personal Experience)
Writing Powerful Introductions and Conclusions
Practicing the Four Basic Forms of Writing (Exposition, Argumentation, Description, and Narration)
Applying the Basic Forms to a Variety of *Genre* (i.e., Short Stories, Book Reviews, Research Papers, etc.)
Developing Technical Skills (e.g., Proofreading, Editing, Revising, Footnoting, Preparing Bibliographies, Writing Summaries, and Abstracts)

B. Oral Communication. Developing and Practicing the Use of:

Organizing Material for an Oral Presentation
Vocal Delivery
Appropriate Gestures, Eye Movement, Facial Expression, and Body Movement
Acceptance of the Ideas and Feelings of Others
Appropriate Words, Quotations, Anecdotes, Personal Experiences, Illustrative Examples, and Relevant Information
Appropriate Use of Audiovisual Materials and Equipment
Obtaining and Evaluating Feedback

C. Visual Communication. Developing Skills in the Preparation of:

Photographic Print Series	Overhead Transparencies
Slide Series	Motion Pictures
Filmstrips	Videotape Recordings
Audiotape Recordings	Multimedia Images

Note: The Taxonomies displayed in Figure 56 are not intended to be a complete listing of every thinking and feeling process, nor are the processes listed here mutually exclusive. Rather, there are many instances in which the processes interact with one another and even duplicate items from various categories. Because of this interaction and the need to use several processes simultaneously in their application to real problems, it is important to teach them in various combinations rather than in an item-by-item fashion.

Whenever possible, we have attempted to list the process skills in a logical hierarchy, but it is important to point out that the appropriate use of thinking skills often proceeds in a cyclical rather than linear fashion. For this reason, it is not necessary to teach each set of skills in a rigidly sequential fashion, however, there may be instances when a sequence will facilitate comprehension and application.

Figure 56. Taxonomy of type II enrichment processes (continued).

First and foremost, it avoids the assertion that only those identified as "gifted" can and should develop their thinking and feeling processes. Second, time and energy need not be spent defending which activities are or are not good for high ability students. Since most process activities are open-ended and exist along a continuum of difficulty, these activities provide opportunities for a range of responses and therefore can be used with groups of varying abilities. A third advantage to this approach is that it represents a systematic and organized procedure for expanding the scope of the regular curriculum and enriching the learning experiences of all students.

Sharing of Staff Expertise

The major purpose of this chapter is to develop an organizational plan for providing Type II Enrichment to two target audiences—Talent Pool students and the general population. Figure 57 presents an organizational plan in which Type II Enrichment can be presented in both the regular classroom and with an enrichment specialist. Deciding which people will be responsible for presenting specific Type II skills will depend upon the specific strength areas of the staff. This approach to Type II Enrichment provides many opportunities for sharing talents and skills within a school or district and for sharing specialized areas of interest with exchanged groups of students.

Careful planning and administrative support are essential for a successful Schoolwide Enrichment Model (SEM) program and several approaches have been successful. One technique is to set aside a designated period each week for teacher-exchanged Type II training throughout the building. A more informal approach invites classroom and resource teachers to make arrangements among themselves for exchanging groups of students. Outside resource people will further extend the variety of enrichment experiences that are available to students and extend opportunities for schedule flexibility of all staff.

Varieties of Type II Enrichment

There are three different dimensions of Type II Enrichment. The first involves the type of planned, systematic enrichment that can be organized in advance for any given grade level, group or regularly scheduled part of an SEM program. This chapter concentrates mainly on this dimension, since that is what can be planned in advance.

The second dimension involves process skills that cannot be planned in advance. Experiences in this case usually result from student interests arising out of regular curricular experiences, planned Type I and Type II experiences, or interests outside of school. These process training experiences may result from previous training and therefore Type II planning must remain flexible. The materials described in the following sections should therefore be considered a reservoir upon which to draw as individual student interests emerge.

The third dimension includes processes needed for Type III investigations. As we will point out in the next chapter, a major focus of teacher guidance in Type III situations is to provide advanced level training in the methodological and process skills that are necessary for carrying out advanced level investigative and creative activities. The listing of Type II materials in this chapter will identify appropriate process and training

Target Audiences and Group Organizational Patterns for Type II Enrichment

General Population (Including Talent Pool Students)

Target Audience

Major Planning Responsibility: Type II Committee of the Enrichment Team (with Consultation from Enrichment Specialist and Subject Area Coordinators)

Group	Examples	Trainer
Entire Classroom	Process Training Related to a Regular Curricular Topic (e.g., Creativity Training in Language Arts)	Classroom Teacher
	Specialized Process Training (e.g., Data Gathering and Recording Using Community Survey Instruments)	Enrichment Specialist or Community Resource Person
Single Grade Level or Grade Level Cluster	Applied Process Training (e.g., Brainstorming for Ideas in Creative Stories and Poetry)	Classroom Teacher or Enrichment Specialist; Librarian; Outside Resource Person
Small Groups Within Classroom	Advanced Computer Programming Techniques for "Top" Math Group	Math Consultant or Computer Specialist; With Follow-up by Classroom Teacher
Individuals or Small Groups Who Self-Select Enrichment Materials	"Wff n' Proff"* "News Kit" *"Back-of-the-Room" Enrichment Materials	(No Teacher Direction Needed)

Talent Pool Students

Target Audience

Major Planning Responsibility: Enrichment Specialist (with Consultation from Type II Committee)

Group	Examples	Trainer
Talent Pool Groups Who Are Regularly Scheduled Into the Enrichment Room	Predetermined Process Training Sessions From Type II Scope & Sequence Plan	Enrichment Specialist
	Advanced Reference and Research Skills	School Librarian or Outside Reference Specialist
	Specialized Process Training (e.g., Astrophotography)	Outside Resource Person or Classroom Teacher* With Expertise in This Area
Talent Pool Students With a Common Interest Plus Non-Talent Pool Students With the Same Interest (by Invitation)	Type II Enrichment Cluster in Oral History Techniques (Four Sessions at 90 Minutes Per Session)	Community Volunteer or Classroom Teacher With Expertise in This Area

*When a classroom teacher is serving as a guest instructor in the enrichment room, the enrichment specialist may then provide process training in that teacher's classroom, thereby facilitating an exchange of talents among staff members.

Figure 57. Target audiences and group organizational patterns for type II enrichment.

skills for the SEM program. For example, if one or more students decide to research investigative reporting, teachers can quickly identify process training activities related to interviewing by examining the materials listed.

In this chapter, the process training can be planned using a scope and sequence approach. The five categories of Type II Enrichment (cognitive, affective, learning how-to-learn, research and reference procedures, and communication procedures) are subdivided into general categories of process skills. These skills are further divided into a "taxonomy" of specific process skills. This offers an organized approach to development of a wide array of process skills and helps to guarantee some diversity, while avoiding needless repetition. This approach also helps program planners to view a broad spectrum of training activities and subsequently make decisions about which activities are most appropriate for various age and grade levels and for logical supplements to the regular curriculum. Finally, this approach helps with budgeting, evaluating, and making inservice decisions.

Planning a Type II Enrichment Program

An educator's initial reaction to the plan presented in this chapter might be that the approach is overwhelming! Teachers should keep several important things in mind as they begin planning. The first factor is time. The total Type II effort should be viewed as a long-term developmental plan to be accomplished over several years. Modest and realistic goals should be set each year for adding new components to the SEM program and it is important that everyone involved take part in decision making about these goals. If teachers have input into this process, they are less likely to feel burdened.

The second factor that will help ensure a successful program is a division of labor. Every program development activity recommended in this chapter should be broken down by into component parts by grade, subject area, and/or areas of specialized interest within a school's staff. The Enrichment Team should serve as the coordinating and organizational body responsible for assigning specific tasks to individuals or small groups.

A third factor is the need for strong administrative support and commitment. From the board of education and superintendent down to each building principal, a clear policy statement and expectation should be in evidence. When these decision makers say, in effect, "these are the kinds of activities that we *expect* from our staff in order to improve education in our schools," then educators will have the kind of administrative "muscle" that make their efforts more than a voluntary frill.

Awareness and Needs Assessment

Before educators begin the step-by-step procedure for developing a Type II program, it is important to help the staff understand what is meant by Type II Enrichment. Many of the Type II processes and thinking skills are probably already a part of the staff's teaching repertoire. If this message is conveyed to them, this helps to demystify this aspect of the model and provides the basis for bringing some organization and coordination to the overall teaching of process skills within the school or district. A comprehensive approach will also help ensure that there are no areas being overlooked. Another purpose to this process is simply to create a vehicle for encouraging awareness, dialogue and interaction among staff. This helps to endorse the educational value of these activities.

The first step in developing awareness is to provide information on the concept of Type II skills, how a Type II program fits into the overall educational program, and the anticipated staff role in the planning, decision making and teaching of Type II skills. Educators can accomplish this by distributing copies of the Bird's Eye View of SEM (see Chapter 1), the Type II Summary Sheet, Target Audiences and Group Organizational Patterns for Type II Enrichment, and the Taxonomy of Type II Enrichment Processes. The Taxonomy is organized according to the major objectives of Type II Enrichment and can be used for awareness training, needs assessment, and program evaluation. It should be made clear that a review of these materials will precede a needs assessment activity to help staff analyze their present level of process teaching and develop plans for an expanded and coordinated approach to Type II instruction.

Figures 58 and 59 provide examples of how a subset of skills can be converted into a needs assessment form. Educators can adapt these forms to suit their needs by dealing with each objective separately or by adding or deleting specific process skills. Even if educators do not go through the formal process of filling out the forms, they can nevertheless be used as the basis for discussion. The major purpose of these forms is to develop a common understanding about what we mean by Type II Enrichment and to create an awareness about the need for systematic planning that will be described in the following sections.

The Enrichment Team is responsible for determining the extent and nature to which this needs assessment and awareness process will be used. It is important to keep requests for paperwork to a minimum and encourage staff participation in small easy steps so as not to burden them with additional work. Small group activities at regularly scheduled staff meetings or staff development sessions are effective substitutes to the typical "sitting and listening" activities. Whenever enrichment specialists and coordinators use program development activities such as this, they should emphasize to the staff that this is their opportunity to participate in curriculum decision making. Teachers will appreciate the opportunity to have a role in the reshaping of some aspects of the school curriculum rather than simply having a new teaching requirement imposed upon them!

Teacher Training

During the distribution of the needs assessment or during the introduction of the general concept of Type II training, some classroom teachers may not be familiar with process training activities used in enrichment programs, such as creativity, problem solving, and/ or critical thinking training. When the idea of Type II training is introduced to classroom teachers, they will need assurance that these skills have been more recently stressed by educators and were probably not covered in their teacher certification programs.

Some process training will be necessary for teachers to embrace the concept. The training may be conducted in a variety of ways. One approach is to have teachers select an objective (such as creativity training) and "go shopping" for corresponding materials. This method of simply reviewing the instructions will familiarize classroom teachers with how some process skills can be applied to classrooms. Educators need to stress the

Needs Assessment of Type II Enrichment Skills
(General Areas)

Date: _____

Person(s) Completing This Form: _____

Subject Areas/Grade Levels Being Considered: _____

Teachers
Thank you for your help with this survey. We will use this information to help us plan Type II training in the enrichment room and in the classrooms.

Directions
Please read the following list of skills and rank each on a 1-5 scale (5 being highest) according to the amount of time devoted to teaching students how to use this skill. Then, in the right hand columns, rate each of these skills in terms of their importance for all students and for Talent Pool students who are receiving additional instruction time in the enrichment room or regular classroom. Thank you.

Process Skills	Present Degree of Coverage in the Regular Curriculum	Degree to which it should be covered:		
		In the Regular Classroom for All Students	In the Regular Classroom for Talent Pool Students	In the Enrichment Room for Talent Pool Students
	Low . . . . High	Low . . . . High	Low . . . . High	Low . . . . High
1. Training to develop creativity.	1 2 3 4 5	1 2 3 4 5	1 2 3 4 5	1 2 3 4 5
2. Training to teach problem solving critical thinking skills.	1 2 3 4 5	1 2 3 4 5	1 2 3 4 5	1 2 3 4 5
3. Training students to use critical thinking skills.	1 2 3 4 5	1 2 3 4 5	1 2 3 4 5	1 2 3 4 5
4. Teaching to the affective domain.	1 2 3 4 5	1 2 3 4 5	1 2 3 4 5	1 2 3 4 5
5. Teaching listening, observing and perceptual skills.	1 2 3 4 5	1 2 3 4 5	1 2 3 4 5	1 2 3 4 5
6. Teaching reading, notetaking and outlining skills.	1 2 3 4 5	1 2 3 4 5	1 2 3 4 5	1 2 3 4 5
7. Training for interviewing and surveying skills.	1 2 3 4 5	1 2 3 4 5	1 2 3 4 5	1 2 3 4 5
8. Teaching students to analyze and organize data.	1 2 3 4 5	1 2 3 4 5	1 2 3 4 5	1 2 3 4 5
9. Teaching students how to prepare for Type III investigations.	1 2 3 4 5	1 2 3 4 5	1 2 3 4 5	1 2 3 4 5
10. Teaching basic and advanced library, research and reference skills.	1 2 3 4 5	1 2 3 4 5	1 2 3 4 5	1 2 3 4 5
11. Teaching students how to find and use community resources.	1 2 3 4 5	1 2 3 4 5	1 2 3 4 5	1 2 3 4 5
12. Teaching students how to prepare media projects.	1 2 3 4 5	1 2 3 4 5	1 2 3 4 5	1 2 3 4 5
13. Teaching students how to prepare oral projects.	1 2 3 4 5	1 2 3 4 5	1 2 3 4 5	1 2 3 4 5
14. Teaching students how to prepare written projects.	1 2 3 4 5	1 2 3 4 5	1 2 3 4 5	1 2 3 4 5

Figure 58. Needs assessment of type II enrichment skills (general areas).

Needs Assessment of Type II Enrichment Skills
(Specific Areas)

Date: _____

Person(s) Completing This Form: _____

Objective: ___*Interviewing*_____

Grade Levels Being Considered: _____

Directions
Listed below are a number of process skills related to the above objective. Review each skill and rate it according to the following four scales.

Process Skills	Present Degree of Coverage in the Regular Curriculum	Degree to which it should be covered:		
		In the Regular Classroom for All Students	In the Regular Classroom for Talent Pool Students	In the Enrichment Room for Talent Pool Students
	Low . . . . High	Low . . . . High	Low . . . . High	Low . . . . High
1. Identifying the information being sought.	1 2 3 4 5	1 2 3 4 5	1 2 3 4 5	1 2 3 4 5
2. Deciding on appropriate instruments.	1 2 3 4 5	1 2 3 4 5	1 2 3 4 5	1 2 3 4 5
3. Identifying sources of existing instruments.	1 2 3 4 5	1 2 3 4 5	1 2 3 4 5	1 2 3 4 5
4. Designing instruments (e.g., checklists, rating scales, interview schedules).	1 2 3 4 5	1 2 3 4 5	1 2 3 4 5	1 2 3 4 5
5. Developing question wording skills (e.g., factual, attitudinal, probing, follow-up).	1 2 3 4 5	1 2 3 4 5	1 2 3 4 5	1 2 3 4 5
6. Sequencing.	1 2 3 4 5	1 2 3 4 5	1 2 3 4 5	1 2 3 4 5
7. Identifying representative samples.	1 2 3 4 5	1 2 3 4 5	1 2 3 4 5	1 2 3 4 5
8. Field testing and reviewing instruments.	1 2 3 4 5	1 2 3 4 5	1 2 3 4 5	1 2 3 4 5
9. Developing rapport with subjects.	1 2 3 4 5	1 2 3 4 5	1 2 3 4 5	1 2 3 4 5
10. Preparing a data gathering matrix and schedule.	1 2 3 4 5	1 2 3 4 5	1 2 3 4 5	1 2 3 4 5
11. Using follow-up techniques.	1 2 3 4 5	1 2 3 4 5	1 2 3 4 5	1 2 3 4 5

Figure 59. Needs assessment of type II enrichment skills (specific areas).

value of these skills in the regular curriculum, not just enrichment programs. A second approach is to arrange demonstration lessons by a staff member who thoroughly understands the specific skill in the classroom setting. It is helpful to have each classroom teacher in the school learn one of the thinking skills in the taxonomy and share his/her knowledge with other classrooms. A third approach is to have the enrichment teacher demonstrate Type II skills in classrooms while teachers observe. Many enrichment teachers in the SEM currently reserve two to three hours per week for these classroom Type II sessions. Formal inservice is another approach for process skills training.

SIMSIT 3 (see the end of this chapter) is a good activity to complete with teachers who may feel reluctant about the need for Type II training in their classrooms. It offers a way to introduce a variety of benefits to students and teachers.

The Organizational Plan for Developing a Type II Enrichment Component

A major part of our efforts to develop a comprehensive Type II Enrichment program has been to analyze and categorize hundreds of available materials that can be used for Type II training. These materials are listed on the completed Planning Matrix for Organizing and Teaching Type II Skills with Commercial Enrichment Materials (see Figure 60), followed by a selection of publishers (see Figure 61). The identification, review and selection of Type II materials should be an ongoing process that potentially involves everyone on the staff. As new materials are discovered and developed, entries should be made on the planning matrices and periodically circulated among teachers in the district. Descriptive literature should be left for review at a central location. The Enrichment Team should then review those recommendations and decide which items should be ordered. In addition to providing a comprehensive approach to the identification of enrichment materials, this process also assists in program budgeting. Each year, a portion of the school's total budget should be allocated to new Type II materials, with a "Needs List" for subsequent years.

One goal in accumulating Type II materials is to establish a library or materials center for classroom and enrichment room use. The procedure for making selections is described in the next section. Again, this approach is part of a continuous effort and should be carried out over several years of program development. Realistic and modest goals should be set each year and these updated forms should also be used as part of the program's annual evaluation report.

Developing a Type II Source File

Ideas for Type II Enrichment can come from a variety of sources, including publishers' catalogs, existing school resources, inservice programs, professional journals, and display materials from professional conferences. An excellent source of books and resources is SEMNET (The Schoolwide Enrichment Model Network), discussed in Chapter 3. As good source books are identified, they should be placed in a special "Source Book" in the materials center (or library) of the school or school district. They should also be reviewed by members of the Enrichment Team in order to identify new materials for inclusion on the Planning Matrix.

Planning Matrix for Organizing and Teaching Type II Skills With Commercial Enrichment Materials

I. Cognitive Training

	K-3	4-8	9-12
A. Creative Thinking Skills	Be An Inventor * Brainstorming: The Book of Topics Creativity 1, 2, 3 New Directions in Creativity: A New Directions in Creativity: B On The Nose Steven Caney's Kids' America Steven Caney's Play Book Steven Caney's Toy Book Think About It! Wondering	Be An Inventor Brainstorming: The Book of Topics Challenge Boxes Creativity 1, 2, 3 Imagining New Directions in Creativity: Mark 1 New Directions in Creativity: Mark 2 New Directions in Creativity: Mark 3 On The Nose Steve Caney's Invention Book Steven Caney's Kids' America Steven Caney's Play Book Steven Caney's Toy Book Think About It! Untrapping Your Inventiveness	Brainstorming: The Book of Topics Challenge Boxes On The Nose Steve Caney's Invention Book Steven Caney's Kids' America Steven Caney's Play Book Untrapping Your Inventiveness
B. Creative Problem Solving and Decision Making	Be An Inventor Creativity 1, 2, 3 On The Nose Think About It! Wondering	Be An Inventor Challenge Boxes Creativity 1, 2, 3 Gee, Whiz! Imagining On the Nose Steven Caney's Invention Book Think About It! Untrapping Your Inventiveness	Challenge Boxes Gee, Whiz! Steven Caney's Invention Book Untrapping Your Inventiveness

* All the books listed in Figure 60 are available from Creative Learning Press, Inc., P.O. Box 320, Mansfield Center, CT 06250.

Figure 60. Planning matrix for organizing and teaching type II skills with commercial enrichment materials.

Planning Matrix for Organizing and Teaching Type II Skills With Commercial Enrichment Materials

I. Cognitive Training (continued)

	K-3	4-8	9-12
C. Critical and Logical Thinking	Hands-On Equations How to Think Like a Scientist Organizing Thinking: Books 1 and 2 The Private Eye Think About It! Used Numbers	Chi Square, Pie Charts and Me Critical Thinking in United States History Gee, Whiz! Hands-On Equations How to Think Like a Scientist Leadership for Students Organizing Thinking: Books 1 and 2 Save the Earth The Private Eye Students and Research Take Ten . . . Steps to Successful Research Think About It! Used Numbers You Decide!	Chi Square, Pie Charts and Me Critical Thinking in United States History Gee, Whiz! How to Analyze Data Leadership for Students Organizing Thinking: Books 1 and 2 Save the Earth Students and Research The Private Eye You Decide!

II. Affective Training

A. Affective Skills	How To Encourage Girls in Math and Science Project Funny Bone	A Student's Guide to Volunteering Famous People How To Encourage Girls in Math and Science The Kid's Guide to Service Projects The Kid's Guide to Social Action Kids with Courage Leadership for Students Project Funny Bone Save the Earth Values Are Forever	A Student's Guide to Volunteering Famous People How To Encourage Girls in Math and Science The Kid's Guide to Service Projects The Kid's Guide to Social Action Kids with Courage Leadership for Students Save the Earth Values Are Forever

Figure 60. Planning matrix for organizing and teaching type II skills with commercial enrichment materials (continued).

Planning Matrix for Organizing and Teaching Type II Skills With Commercial Enrichment Materials

III. Learning How-To-Learn Skills

A. Listening, Observing, and Perceiving	K-3	4-8	9-12
	Birdwise Bugwise Entomology Foodworks Genealogy The Kids' Nature Book The Private Eye Ready, Set, Grow!	A Student's Guide to Conducting Social Science Research Acting and Directing The Amateur Geologist The Amateur Meteorologist The Amateur Naturalist Blood and Guts Birdwise Bones, Bodies and Bellies Bugwise Ecology Entomology Experimenting with a Microscope Exploring the Sky Foodworks Gee, Whiz! Genealogy How to Make a Chemical Volcano and Other Mysterious Experiments How to Tape Instant Oral Biographies Kids Are Consumers, Too! Kids Gardening The Kids' Nature Book Like It Was Look to the Night Sky Microscope The Private Eye Project Earth Science: Astronomy Project Earth Science: Meteorology Ready, Set, Grow! The Reasons for Seasons Scienceworks Science Wizardry for Kids Take Ten . . . Steps to Successful Research Tell Me About Yourself Tom Brown's Field Guide to Nature Observation and Tracking Understanding and Collecting Rocks and Fossils The Usborne Book of Science Fun Usborne Guide: The Young Astronomer Usborne Guide: The Young Naturalist Weatherwatch The Whole Cosmos Catalog The World of the Microscope Writing Family Histories and Memoirs	A Student's Guide to Conducting Social Science Research Acting and Directing The Amateur Geologist The Amateur Meteorologist The Amateur Naturalist The Craft of Interviewing Experimenting with a Microscope Exploring the Sky Gee, Whiz! Genealogy Getting Started in Debate How to Make a Chemical Volcano and Other Mysterious Experiments How to Tape Instant Oral Biographies Kids Are Consumers, Too! Like It Was Look to the Night Sky Microscope Oral History The Private Eye Project Earth Science: Astronomy Project Earth Science: Meteorology Tell Me About Yourself Tom Brown's Field Guide to Nature Observation and Tracking The Whole Cosmos Catalog The World of the Microscope Writing Family Histories and Memoirs

Figure 60. Planning matrix for organizing and teaching type II skills with commercial enrichment materials (continued).

Planning Matrix for Organizing and Teaching Type II Skills With Commercial Enrichment Materials

III. Learning How-To-Learn Skills (continued)

	K-3	4-8	9-12
B. Reading, Notetaking, and Outlining	Classroom Publishing Lives of Promise Super Kids Publishing Company	A Student's Guide to Conducting Social Science Research Beginner's Guide to Getting Published Classroom Publishing Creating Short Fiction Extra! Extra! Getting Started in Journalism Getting the Words Right How to Tape Instant Oral Biographies How to Trace Your Family Tree How to Write and Give a Speech Kids Are Consumers, Too! Market Guide for Young Writers Painting the Sky Pursuing the Past Roots for Kids Super Kids Publishing Company Take Ten . . . Steps to Successful Research Tell Me About Yourself Tom Brown's Field Guide to Nature Observation and Tracking The Writing Book Writing Family Histories and Memoirs	A Student's Guide to Conducting Social Science Research Beginner's Guide to Getting Published Classroom Publishing The Craft of Interviewing Creating Short Fiction Getting Started in Journalism Getting the Words Right How to Tape Instant Oral Biographies How to Trace Your Family Tree How to Write and Give a Speech Kids Are Consumers, Too! Like It Was Market Guide for Young Writers Oral History Pursuing the Past Roots for Kids Tell Me About Yourself Tom Brown's Field Guide to Nature Observation and Tracking Writing Family Histories and Memoirs

Figure 60. Planning matrix for organizing and teaching type II skills with commercial enrichment materials (continued).

Planning Matrix for Organizing and Teaching Type II Skills With Commercial Enrichment Materials

III. Learning How-To-Learn Skills (continued)

	K-3	4-8	9-12
C. Interviewing and Surveying	Genealogy Lunchroom Waste Lives of Promise	A Student's Guide to Conducting Social Science Research The Craft of Interviewing Genealogy How to Tape Instant Oral Biographies How to Trace Your Family Tree Lives of Promise Oral History Pursuing the Past Roots for Kids Writing Family Histories and Memoirs	A Student's Guide to Conducting Social Science Research Genealogy How to Tape Instant Oral Biographies How to Trace Your Family Tree Lunchroom Waste Lives of Promise Pursuing the Past Roots for Kids Tell Me About Yourself Writing Family Histories and Memoirs

Figure 60. Planning matrix for organizing and teaching type II skills with commercial enrichment materials (continued).

Planning Matrix for Organizing and Teaching Type II Skills With Commercial Enrichment Materials

III. Learning How-To-Learn Skills (continued)

D. Analyzing and Organizing Data	K-3	4-8	9-12
	Birdwise Bugwise Digging Through Archaeology Entomology Foodworks How to Think Like a Scientist The Kids' Nature Book Lives of Promise Lunchroom Waste Organizing Thinking: Books 1 and 2 The Private Eye **4-8** A Student's Guide to Conducting Social Science Research The Amateur Geologist The Amateur Meteorologist The Amateur Naturalist Blood and Guts Birdwise Bones, Bodies and Bellies Bugwise Chi Square, Pie Charts and Me Critical Thinking in United States History (Books 1-4) Digging Through Archaeology Ecology Entomology	Experimenting with a Microscope Exploring the Sky Foodworks Gee, Whiz! How to Make a Chemical Volcano and Other Mysterious Experiments Kids Are Consumers, Too! Look to the Night Sky Microscope The Private Eye Project Earth Science: Astronomy Project Earth Science: Meteorology The Reasons for Seasons Scienceworks Science Wizardry for Kids The Scientist Within You (Volume I and II) Students and Research Take Ten . . . Steps to Successful Research Tom Brown's Field Guide to Nature Observation and Tracking Understanding and Collecting Rocks and Fossils The Usborne Book of Science Fun Usborne Guide: The Young Astronomer Usborne Guide: The Young Naturalist Weatherwatch The Whole Cosmos Catalog The World of the Microscope You Decide!	A Student's Guide to Conducting Social Science Research The Amateur Geologist The Amateur Meteorologist The Amateur Naturalist Chi Square, Pie Charts and Me Critical Thinking in United States History (Books 1-4) Digging Through Archaeology Exploring the Sky Gee, Whiz! How to Analyze Data How to Make a Chemical Volcano and Other Mysterious Experiments Kids Are Consumers, Too! Look to the Night Sky The Private Eye Project Earth Science: Astronomy Project Earth Science: Meteorology Students and Research Tom Brown's Field Guide to Nature Observation and Tracking Understanding and Collecting Rocks and Fossils The Whole Cosmos Catalog The World of the Microscope You Decide!

Figure 60. Planning matrix for organizing and teaching type II skills with commercial enrichment materials (continued).

Planning Matrix for Organizing and Teaching Type II Skills With Commercial Enrichment Materials

IV. Using Advanced Research Skills and Reference Materials

	K-3	4-8	9-12
A. Preparing for Type III Investigations	Cartoon Art Classroom Computers Digging Through Archaeology Entomology Gaming It Up With Shakespeare Genealogy Go For It! Lights! Camera! Action! Lives of Promise Lunchroom Waste M.A.G.I.C. Kits More M.A.G.I.C. Kits My Backyard History Book Not Just Another Science Fair Storytelling Tales As Tools Victorian Housekeeping	The Animation Book Cartoon Art Classroom Computers The Complete Science Fair Handbook Creating Short Fiction Digging Through Archaeology Entomology Experimenting with Inventions Gaming It Up With Shakespeare Genealogy Getting the Words Right Go For It! Great Science Fair Projects How to Become an Expert How to Make Pop-Ups How to Make Super Pop-Ups How to Make Visual Presentations How to Tape Instant Oral Biographies How to Trace Your Family Tree How to Write and Give a Speech KidVid Lights! Camera! Action! Like It Was Lives of Promise	The Animation Book Classroom Computers The Craft of Interviewing Creating Short Fiction Digging Through Archaeology Entomology Gaming It Up With Shakespeare Genealogy Getting the Words Right Great Science Fair Projects How to Make Pop-Ups How to Make Super Pop-Ups How to Make Visual Presentations How to Tape Instant Oral Biographies How to Trace Your Family Tree How to Write and Give a Speech KidVid Lights! Camera! Action! Like It Was Lives of Promise Lunchroom Waste M.A.G.I.C. Kits More M.A.G.I.C. Kits My Backyard History Book

Figure 60. Planning matrix for organizing and teaching type II skills with commercial enrichment materials (continued).

Planning Matrix for Organizing and Teaching Type II Skills With Commercial Enrichment Materials

IV. Using Advanced Research Skills & Reference Materials (continued)

	K-3	4-8	9-12
A. Preparing for Type III Investigations (continued)		Lunchroom Waste M.A.G.I.C. Kits More M.A.G.I.C. Kits My Backyard History Book Not Just Another Science Fair Public Speaking Pursuing the Past Roots for Kids Stamp Collecting Start Collecting Stamps Storytelling Student Projects: Ideas and Plans Students and Research Take Ten . . . Steps to Successful Research Tales As Tools Tell Me About Yourself The Usborne Complete Book of Drawing Usborne Guide to Drawing Usborne Guide to Pottery The Usborne Guide to Technical Drawing The Usborne Young Cartoonist Victorian Housekeeping Writing Fiction The Young Cartoonist	Not Just Another Science Fair Oral History Public Speaking Pursuing the Past Roots for Kids So You've Got a Great Idea Speak for Yourself Start Collecting Stamps Storytelling Student Projects: Ideas and Plans Students and Research Tales As Tools Tell Me About Yourself Unpuzzling Your Past The Usborne Complete Book of Drawing Usborne Guide to Drawing Usborne Guide to Pottery The Usborne Guide to Technical Drawing The Usborne Young Cartoonist Victorian Housekeeping Writing Fiction

Figure 60. Planning matrix for organizing and teaching type II skills with commercial enrichment materials (continued).

Planning Matrix for Organizing and Teaching Type II Skills With Commercial Enrichment Materials

IV. Using Advanced Research Skills & Reference Materials (continued)

	K-3	4-8	9-12
B. Library Skills	Classroom Computers Kids On-Line	Classroom Computers How to Become an Expert How to Tape Instant Oral Biographies How to Trace Your Family Tree How to Make Visual Presentations How to Prepare Your Portfolio Kids On-Line KidVid Like It Was Lives of Promise My Backyard History Book Oral History Pursuing the Past Roots for Kids Take Ten . . . Steps to Successful Research Tell Me About Yourself Unpuzzling Your Past Writing Family Histories	How to Tape Instant Oral Biographies How to Trace Your Family Tree How to Make Visual Presentations How to Prepare Your Portfolio Kids On-Line KidVid Like It Was Lives of Promise Oral History Pursuing the Past Roots for Kids Unpuzzling Your Past Writing Family Histories
C. Community Resources	Career Awareness Day Digging Through Archaeology Community Talent Miner	A Student's Guide to Volunteering Career Awareness Day Digging Through Archaeology Community Talent Miner The Kid's Guide to Service Projects The Kid's Guide to Social Action Kids with Courage Save the Earth	A Student's Guide to Volunteering Digging Through Archaeology Community Talent Miner The Kid's Guide to Service Projects The Kid's Guide to Social Action Kids with Courage Save the Earth

Figure 60. Planning matrix for organizing and teaching type II skills with commercial enrichment materials (continued).

Planning Matrix for Organizing and Teaching Type II Skills With Commercial Enrichment Materials

V. Written, Oral, and Visual Communication Skills

	K-3	4-8	9-12
A. Written Communication	Creating a Page-Turner: A Helpbook for Young Writers Genealogy Lives of Promise Lunchroom Waste My Backyard History Book Project Funny Bone	The Adventures of Dr. Alphabet Beginner's Guide to Getting Published The Craft of Interviewing Creating a Page-Turner: A Helpbook for Young Writers Creating Short Fiction Extra! Extra! Genealogy Getting the Words Right Getting Started in Journalism How to Write and Give a Speech Kids Are Consumers, Too! Leadership Like It Was Lives of Promise Lunchroom Waste Market Guide for Young Writers My Backyard History Book Painting the Sky Project Funny Bone Pursuing the Past Roots for Kids Super Sentences Take Ten . . . Steps to Successful Research Tell Me About Yourself The Writing Book Writing Family Histories and Memoirs Writing Fiction	The Adventures of Dr. Alphabet Beginner's Guide to Getting Published The Craft of Interviewing Creating Short Fiction Genealogy Getting the Words Right Getting Started in Journalism How to Write and Give a Speech Kids Are Consumers, Too! Leadership Like It Was Lives of Promise Lunchroom Waste Market Guide for Young Writers Oral History Pursuing the Past Roots for Kids Super Sentences Writing Family Histories and Memoirs Writing Fiction

Figure 60. Planning matrix for organizing and teaching type II skills with commercial enrichment materials (continued).

Planning Matrix for Organizing and Teaching Type II Skills With Commercial Enrichment Materials

V. Written, Oral, and Visual Communication Skills (continued)

	K-3	4-8	9-12
B. Oral Communication	Gaming It Up With Shakespeare Genealogy Kids Make Music Project Funny Bone Storytelling Tales as Tools	Acting and Directing Gaming It Up With Shakespeare Genealogy Getting Started in Debate How to Tape Instant Oral Biographies How to Write and Give a Speech Joining In Kids Make Music Leadership Like It Was Make Mine Music Project Funny Bone Public Speaking Pursuing the Past Storytelling Tales as Tools Tell Me About Yourself The Theater Props Handbook	Acting and Directing The Craft of Interviewing Gaming It Up With Shakespeare Genealogy Getting Started in Debate How to Tape Instant Oral Biographies How to Write and Give a Speech Joining In Leadership Like It Was Make Mine Music Oral History Public Speaking Pursuing the Past Storytelling Tales as Tools The Theater Props Handbook

Figure 60. Planning matrix for organizing and teaching type II skills with commercial enrichment materials (continued).

Planning Matrix for Organizing and Teaching Type II Skills With Commercial Enrichment Materials

V. Written, Oral, and Visual Communication Skills (continued)

	K-3	4-8	9-12
C. Visual Communication	Cartoon Art Classroom Publishing Eco-Art Hands Around the World The Kids' Multicultural Art Book The Kids' Nature Book Lights! Camera! Action! Project Funny Bone Victorian Housekeeping	The Animation Book The Art of Construction Cartoon Art Classroom Publishing Eco-Art Frank Lloyd Wright for Kids Hands Around the World How to Make Pop-Ups How to Make Super Pop-Ups How to Make Visual Presentations How to Tape Instant Oral Biographies The Kids' Multicultural Art Book The Kids' Nature Book KidVid Lights! Camera! Action! Make Mine Music Project Funny Bone Usborne Guide to Calligraphy The Usborne Book of Calligraphy Projects The Usborne Complete Book of Drawing Usborne Guide to Drawing Usborne Guide to Lettering and Typography Usborne Guide to Painting Usborne Guide to Photography Usborne Guide to Pottery Usborne Guide to Technical Drawing The Usborne Young Cartoonist Victorian Housekeeping The Young Cartoonist	The Animation Book The Art of Construction Classroom Publishing Frank Lloyd Wright for Kids How to Make Pop-Ups How to Make Super Pop-Ups How to Make Visual Presentations How to Tape Instant Oral Biographies KidVid Lights! Camera! Action! Make Mine Music Usborne Guide to Calligraphy The Usborne Book of Calligraphy Projects The Usborne Complete Book of Drawing Usborne Guide to Drawing Usborne Guide to Lettering and Typography Usborne Guide to Painting Usborne Guide to Photography Usborne Guide to Pottery Usborne Guide to Technical Drawing The Usborne Young Cartoonist Victorian Housekeeping

Figure 60. Planning matrix for organizing and teaching type II skills with commercial enrichment materials (continued).

Sample Publishers of Commercial Enrichment Materials

ACI Publishing
PO Box 40398
Eugene, OR 97404-0064
Phone: 800-935-7323
Fax: 503-689-2154

Acorn Naturalists
17300 East 17th Street, #J-236
Tustin, CA 92680
Phone: 800-422-8886
Fax: 800-452-2802

Addison-Wesley Publishing Company
2725 Sand Hill Road
Menlo Park, CA 94025
Phone: 800-552-2259
Fax: 800-333-3328

Alarion Press
PO Box 1882
Boulder, CO 80306-1882
Phone: 800-523-9177
Fax: 303-443-9098

American Library Association
50 East Huron Street
Chicago, IL 60611
Phone: 312-944-6780

Avon Books
1350 Avenue of the Americas
New York, NY 10019
Phone: 800-223-0690

Barron's Educational Series, Inc.
Hauppage, NY 11788
1250 Wireless Boulevard
Phone: 516-434-3311
Fax: 516-434-3723

Berkley Putnam Books
200 Madison Avenue
New York, NY 10016
Phone: 800-223-0510
Fax: 212-951-8793

Blue Heron
24450 NW Hansen Road
Hillsboro, OR 97124
Phone: 503-621-3911
Fax: 503-621-9826

Broderbund
PO Box 6125
Novato, CA 94948-6125
Phone: 800-521-6263

Career Press
3 Tice Road
PO Box 687
Franklin Lakes, NJ 07417
Phone: 800-227-3371
Fax: 201-848-1727

Chicago Review Press
814 North Franklin Street
Chicago, IL 60610
Phone: 800-888-4741
Fax: 312-337-5985

Consumer Information Catalog
Consumer Info. Center-5C
PO Box 100
Pueblo, CO 81002
Fax: 719-948-9724

Crabtree
350 Fifth Avenue, Suite 3308
New York, NY 10118
Phone: 800-387-7650
Fax: 800-355-7166

Creative Learning Press
PO Box 320
Mansfield Center, CT 06250
Phone: 860-429-8118
Fax: 860-429-7783

Creative Publications
5623 West 115th Street
Worth, IL 60482
Phone: 800-624-0822
Fax: 800-624-0821

Creative Teaching Press
10701 Holden Street
Cypress, CA 90630
Phone: 800-287-8879
Fax: 800-229-9929

Critical Thinking Press and Software
PO Box 448
Pacific Grove, CA 93950
Phone: 800-458-4894
Fax: 408-372-3230

Cuisenaire Company of America, Inc.
PO Box 5026
White Plains, NY 10602-5026
Phone: 800-237-0338
Fax: 800-551-RODS

D.O.K. Publishers
PO Box 1099
Buffalo, NY 14224-8099
Phone: 800-458-7900
Fax: 716-853-1289

Dale Seymour
PO Box 10888
Palo Alto, CA 94303
Phone: 800-872-1100
Fax: 415-324-3424

Dandy Lion
3563 Sueldo, Suite L
San Luis Obispo, CA 93401
Phone: 800-776-8032
Fax: 805-544-2823

Davidson & Associates, Inc.
PO Box 2961
Torrance, CA 90509
Phone: 800-545-7677
Fax: 310-793-0601

Dearborn Financial Publishing
520 North Dearborn
Chicago, IL 60610
Phone: 800-533-2665
Fax: 312-836-1146

Delta Education
PO Box 3000
Nashua, NH 03061-3000
Phone: 800-442-5444
Fax: 800-282-9560

Discovery Enterprises, Ltd.
31 Laurelwood Drive
Carlisle, MA 01741
Phone: 800-729-1720
Fax: 508-287-5402

DK Multimedia, Inc.
95 Madison Avenue
New York, NY 10016
Phone: 800-DKMM575
Fax: 212-213-5240

Figure 61. Sample publishers of commercial enrichment materials.

Sample Publishers of Commercial Enrichment Materials

Doubleday Dell Publishing, Inc.
1540 Broadway
New York, NY 10036
Phone: 212-354-6500

EDC Publishing Company
Division of Educational
Development Corporation
PO Box 470663
Tulsa, OK 74147-0663
Phone: 800-475-4522
Fax: 800-665-7919

Edmark
PO Box 97021
Redmond, WA 98073-9721
Phone: 800-362-2890
Fax: 206-556-8430

ETA
620 Lakeview Parkway
Vernon Hills, IL 60061
Phone: 800-445-5985
Fax: 800-ETA-9326

F&W Publications
1507 Dana Avenue
Cincinnati, OH 45207
Phone: 800-289-0963
Fax: 513-531-4082

Falmer Press
1900 Frost Road, Suite 101
Bristol, PA 19007-8312
Phone: 800-821-8312
Fax: 215-785-5515

Franklin Watts
95 Madison Avenue
New York, NY 10016
Phone: 800-672-6672

Free Spirit Publishing, Inc.
400-1st Avenue North,
Suite 616
Minneapolis, MN 55401-1730
Phone: 800-735-7323
Fax: 612-337-5050

Good Apple
4350 Equity Drive
PO Box 2649
Columbus, OH 43216
Phone: 800-321-316
Fax: 614-771-7362

Good Year Books/Scott Foresman
1900 East Lake Avenue
Glenview, IL 60025
Phone: 800-628-4480 x3038
Fax: 800-353-1560

Grolier Education Corporation
Sherman Turnpike
Danbury, CT 06816
Phone: 800-243-7256
Fax: 860-797-3285

Guarionex Press, Ltd.
201 West 77th Street
New York, NY 10024
Phone: 212-724-5259

Harcourt Brace and Company
525 B Street, Suite 1900
San Diego, CA 92101
Phone: 800-543-1918
Fax: 800-874-6418

Harper Collins Publishers
10 East 53rd Street
New York, NY 10022
Phone: 800-242-7737
Fax: 800-822-4090

Health Communications, Inc.
3201 SW 15th Street
Deerfield Beach, FL 33442-8190
Phone: 954-360-0909

Houghton Mifflin
222 Berkeley Street
Boston, MA 02116
Phone: 800-225-3362

Human Sciences Press
72-5th Avenue
New York, NY 10011
Phone: 800-221-9369

Incentive Publication
3855 Cleghorn Avenue
Nashville, TN 37215-2532
Phone: 800-421-2830
Fax: 615-385-2967

Independent Publishers Group
814 North Franklin Street
Chicago, IL 60610
Phone: 800-888-4741
Fax: 312-337-5985

Insect Lore
PO Box 1535
Shafter, CA 93263
Phone: 800-LIVE BUG
Fax: 805-746-0334

Interact
1825 Gillespie Way, #101
El Cajon, CA 92020-1095
Phone: 800-359-0961
Fax: 619-448-6722

International Reading Association
800 Barksdale Road
PO Box 8139
Newark, DE 19714-8139
Phone: 800-336-READ
Fax: 302-737-0878

John Muir Publications
PO Box 613
Santa Fe, NM 87504
Phone: 800-888-7504
Fax: 505-988-1680

John Wiley & Sons, Inc.
605-3rd Avenue
New York, NY 10158-0012
Phone: 212-850-8800

Kendall/Hunt Publishing Company
2460 Kerper Boulevard
PO Box 539
Dubuque, IA 52004-0539
Phone: 800-228-0810

Figure 61. Sample publishers of commercial enrichment materials (continued).

Sample Publishers of Commercial Enrichment Materials

Kerry Ruef & Associates Educational Consulting
7710-31st Street NW
Seattle, WA 98117
Phone: 206-784-8813

Klutz Press
2121 Staunton Court
Palo Alto, CA 94306
Phone: 800-558-8944
Fax: 800-524-4075

Knowledge Adventure
1311 Grand Central Avenue
Glendale, CA 91201
Phone: 800-542-4240
Fax: 818-246-5604

Knowledge Unlimited
PO Box 52
Madison, WI 53701-0052
Phone: 800-356-2303
Fax: 608-831-1570

Leadership Publishers Group
PO Box 8358
Des Moines, IA 50310
Phone: 515-278-4765
Fax: 515-270-8303

Learning Works
PO Box 1370
Goleta, CA 93116
Phone: 800-235-5767

Lerner Publications Group
241-1st Avenue North
Minneapolis, MN 55401
Phone: 800-328-4929
Fax: 800-332-1132

Little, Brown & Company
Time & Life Building
1271 Avenue of the Americas
New York, NY 10020
Phone: 800-343-9204
Fax: 617-890-0875 (MA)

Macmillan/Simon & Schuster
866-3rd Avenue
New York, NY 10022
Phone: 800-223-2336

Maxis
2121 North California
Boulevard, Suite 600
Walnut Creek, CA 94596-9854
Phone: 800-33-MAXIS
Fax: 510-927-3581

McGraw-Hill Company
Princeton Road
Hightstown, NJ 08520
Phone: 800-722-4726

MECC
6160 Summit Drive North
Minneapolis, MN 55430-4003
Phone: 800-215-0368 x788
Fax: 612-569-1551

Millbrook Press, Inc.
Box 335
2 Old New Milford Road
Brookfield, CT 06804-0335
Phone: 800-462-4703

NASCO
901 Janesville Avenue
PO Box 901
Fort Atkinson, WI 53538-0901
Phone: 800-558-9595

National Council for Social Studies
3501 Newark Street, NW
Washington, DC 20016
Phone: 800-683-0812

National Geographic Society
Educational Services
PO Box 98018
Washington, DC 20090-8018
Phone: 800-368-2728
Fax: 301-921-1575

National Science Teachers Association
1840 Wilson Boulevard
Arlington, VA 22201-3000
Phone: 800-722-NSTA
Fax: 703-243-7177

National Storytelling Association
PO Box 309
Jonesborough, TN 37659
Phone: 800-525-4514
Fax: 423-753-9331

National Textbook Company
4255 West Touhy Avenue
Lincolnwood, IL 60646-1975
Phone: 800-323-4900

National Women's History Project
7738 Bell Road
Windsor, CA 95492
Phone: 707-838-6000
Fax: 707-838-0478

Ohio Psychology Press
PO Box 90095
Dayton, OH 45490
Phone: 513-890-7312
Fax: 513-454-1033

Overlook Press
Lewis Hollow Road
Woodstock, NY 12498
Phone: 914-679-6838

Penguin USA
375 Hudson Street
New York, NY 10014
Phone: 800-526-0275
Fax: 800-227-9604

Prufrock Press
PO Box 8813
Waco, TX 76714-8813
Phone: 800-998-2208
Fax: 800-240-0333

Random House
201 East 50th Street,
31st Floor
New York, NY 10022
Phone: 800-733-3000
Fax: 800-659-2436

Running Press Book Publishers
124 South 22nd Street
Philadelphia, PA 19103
Phone: 800-345-5359
Fax: 800-453-2884

Figure 61. Sample publishers of commercial enrichment materials (continued).

Sample Publishers of Commercial Enrichment Materials

Sage Publications
2455 Teller Road
Newburry Park, CA 91320
Phone: 805-499-0721
Fax: 805-499-0871

Scholastic, Inc.
730 Broadway
New York, NY 10014-3657
Phone: 800-807-2466
Fax: 800-325-6149

Silver Burdett/J. Messner
4350 Equity Drive
PO Box 2649
Columbus, OH 43216
Phone: 800-848-9500
Fax: 614-771-7361

St. Martin's Press
175 5th Avenue
New York, NY 10010
Phone: 800-221-7945
Fax: 212-995-2584

Stravon Educational Press
324 North Broadway, Suite 2
Yonkers, NY 10701
Phone: 914-969-2251

Sunburst
101 Castleton Street
PO Box 100
Pleasantville, NY 10570
Phone: 800-321-7511
Fax: 914-747-4109

Synergetics
PO Box 84
East Windsor Hill, CT 06028-0084
Phone: 860-291-9499
Fax: 860-282-9040

Teacher Ideas Press
PO Box 6633
Englewood, CO 80155-6633
Phone: 800-237-6124
Fax: 303-220-8843

Teachers & Writers Collaborative
5 Union Square West
New York, NY 10003-3306
Phone: 212-691-6590
Fax: 212-675-0171

Ten Speed Press/Tricycle Press
PO Box 7123
Berkeley, CA 94707
Phone: 800-841-2665
Fax: 510-559-1629

Tom Snyder Publications
800 Coolidge Hill Road
Watertown, MA 02172-2817
Phone: 800-342-0236
Fax: 617-926-6222

Trillium Press/Royal Fireworks Press
First Avenue
Unionville, NY 10988
Phone: 914-726-4444
Fax: 914-726-3424

University of Texas Press
PO Box 7819
Austin, TX 78713-7819
Phone: 800-252-3206

William Morrow & Company
1350 Avenue of the Americas
New York, NY 10019
Phone: 800-843-9389
Fax: 201-227-6849

Williamson Publishing
Box 185
Church Hill Road
Charlotte, VT 05445
Phone: 802-425-2102
Fax: 802-425-2199

Workman Publishing
708 Broadway
New York, NY 10003
Phone: 800-722-7202
Fax: 800-521-1832

Yellow Moon Press
PO Box 1316
Cambridge, MA 02238
Phone: 800-497-4385
Fax: 617-776-8246

Zephyr Press
3316 North Chapel Road
PO Box 66006-C
Tucson, AZ 85728-6006
Phone: 520-323-5090
Fax: 520-323-9402

Figure 61. Sample publishers of commercial enrichment materials (continued).

Another source of Type II materials is, of course, the recommendations of staff members who have had previous experience with various types of enrichment activities and materials. A brief survey of staff members will help SEM coordinators integrate materials that are already being used. This source is especially valuable because teachers familiar with materials can be encouraged to provide workshops and demonstration lessons based on effective reasoning.

A final source of Type II materials consists of state, regional, or local resource centers. Often, area or county service agencies maintain excellent collections of supplementary materials, and in many cases, these resources are already classified or categorized. These materials are usually available to schools on a lending basis, which provides an opportunity for trying out materials before purchasing them.

Maintaining an up-to-date resource file is an ongoing process and individuals should be assigned specific subject areas for reviewing materials. Once a name has been entered into the publishers' mailing lists, that person will continue to receive catalogs from each company. A quick review of each catalog by that person will help identify new materials.

Implementing a Type II Enrichment Program

Materials and Activities Selection Worksheets

Schools implementing a Type II Enrichment program should use the Materials and Activities Selection Worksheet (see Figure 62), which is designed to assist program planners in making decisions about Type II activities that will be used in the enrichment room and/or regular classroom. These forms are coordinated with the five major objectives of Type II Enrichment and the specific subcategories. The major objective is printed at the top of each worksheet and the subcategories are listed in the boxes on the left side. Educators may want to modify the worksheet by adding or deleting subcategories or by modifying them to fit Type II objectives specific to their program.

These worksheets, sometimes referred to as "Shopping Guides," are designed to help make selections from the vast amount of available enrichment activities. The forms are divided into two major areas. The first deals with enrichment activities for Talent Pool students in the enrichment room and the second deals with enrichment activities for the regular classroom. These forms are designed to be completed over a period of several years. Educators should not be concerned with comprehensive coverage of any given cell in the matrix at the beginning of their planning effort. The activities recorded in the cells will grow in number and diversity during the first few years of the program and will eventually result in a comprehensive "Scope and Sequence Guide" for Type II Enrichment activities. These forms will facilitate cooperative planning between the enrichment specialist and classroom teachers and will involve input from subject and curriculum specialists in the school district. Initial efforts to complete the forms might begin on a grade level and building-by-building basis, but the forms can also be used for districtwide planning of Type II Enrichment for various grades and subjects.

Materials and Activities Selection Worksheet for Planning Type II Enrichment

Grade: _____ _____

Subject(s): _____ _____

I. Cognitive Training

	Enrichment Room	Regular Classroom	
		Group Activities	Self-Selected Activities
A. Creative Thinking Skills			
B. Creative Problem Solving and Decision Making			
C. Critical and Logical Thinking			

II. Affective Training

A. Affective Skills			

Figure 62. Materials and activities selection worksheet for planning type II enrichment.

Materials and Activities Selection Worksheet for Planning Type II Enrichment

Grade: _____

Subject(s): _____

III. Learning How-To-Learn Skills

	Enrichment Room	Regular Classroom	
		Group Activities	Self-Selected Activities
A. Listening, Observing and Perceiving			
B. Reading, Notetaking and Outlining			
C. Interviewing and Surveying			
D. Analyzing and Organizing Data			

Figure 62. Materials and activities selection worksheet for planning type II enrichment (continued).

Materials and Activities Selection Worksheet
for Planning Type II Enrichment

IV. Using Advanced Research Skills & Reference Materials

Grade: _____

Subject(s): _____

	Enrichment Room	Regular Classroom	
		Group Activities	Self-Selected Activities
A. Preparing for Type III Investigations			
B. Library Skills			
C. Community Resources			

Figure 62. Materials and activities selection worksheet for planning type II enrichment (continued).

Materials and Activities Selection Worksheet for Planning Type II Enrichment

V. Written, Oral, and Visual Communication Skills

Grade: _____

Subject(s): _____

	Enrichment Room	Regular Classroom	
		Group Activities	Self-Selected Activities
A. Visual Communication			
B. Oral Communication			
C. Written Communication			

Figure 62. Materials and activities selection worksheet for planning type II enrichment (continued).

An important principle to keep in mind when completing these forms is that they are designed to promote a coordinated enrichment program. Since many enrichment materials are not assigned rigid grade level designations, there is a great amount of flexibility that can enter into the selection process. A coordinated plan will avoid duplications of an enrichment activity among grade levels and within classrooms. As educators begin making plans to select materials for various cells in the matrix, they should keep in mind that there is some "logic" about the placement of certain activities, but there is no inherent "right or wrong" about material selection and placement. All such planning activities should be approached on an experimental basis. Materials can be added, deleted, or "moved around" as a result of the experiences of any given teacher. Similarly, the forms should be considered developmental in nature. As new materials are discovered and changes take place in overall curriculum planning, teachers will undoubtedly want to make additions, deletions, and modifications to these worksheets.

Enrichment Room Selections

The main criterion for selecting enrichment room materials should be the level or complexity of the activities. Since Talent Pool students generally exhibit higher abilities, the levels of challenge should be greater than those offered in the regular classroom. Some activities are unquestionably good for all students, but there are also materials that require higher levels of involvement and response. There is no "hard core" science in making these decisions, but familiarity with materials will help make appropriate selections for the enrichment room. For example, learning how-to-learn skills are certainly worthwhile for all students. Some of these skills such as notetaking, outlining, etc. benefit all learners, but more advanced skills such as selecting appropriate research designs, analyzing data, and using college library facilities might be more appropriate for Talent Pool students. Similarly, activities that require more complex responses, such as debating or advanced creative writing might also be more appropriate in an enrichment room setting. Since "giftedness is in the response," it is also safe to say that the way in which students are encouraged to respond to activities probably helps to set the level more effectively than the activities themselves. Many of the commercially developed activities often require short responses (circling, matching, etc.). These activities have value in skill development, but if teachers are to capitalize on the advanced abilities of Talent Pool students, they need to select activities that involve more complex thinking and writing skills.

A second consideration when selecting enrichment materials is the regular curriculum. The busy schedules of classroom teachers and the large amount of material they need to cover often preclude the use of additional enrichment activities in the required subject areas. Enrichment materials and activities which support/enhance the regular curriculum objectives should be considered for use in the regular classroom before the enrichment room.

A third consideration for selection relates to special equipment needs. Skills that require hands-on learning and practice (e.g., computers, microscopes, cameras, telescopes, etc.) are easier facilitated in the smaller enrichment room groups. Similarly, activities that involve out-of-school follow-up, such as interviewing, data gathering, visitation, etc. might also be more appropriately used in the enrichment room. Enrichment specialists often enjoy greater flexibility in scheduling and/or accessing outside facilities and equipment (darkroom, planetarium, computer center, etc.). In addition, there are certain activities that might require special experience or training. Other activities may be "favorites" of enrichment specialists because of their social value for the Talent Pool group or because they facilitate objectives within the enrichment program.

Once again, a great amount of flexibility exists for selecting the processes and subsequent materials for an enrichment program. Nevertheless, giving some thought to these guidelines will help educators avoid random decisions.

Regular Classroom Selections

Group Activities. Two areas are designated for selecting enrichment materials for use in the regular classroom. The first consists of group activities that are ordinarily accomplished with teacher direction. These activities usually involve group interaction and require group teaching skills, such as brainstorming ideas for a class newspaper. As mentioned above, the major guideline in making decisions about these activities should be the degree to which these activities support and enhance regular curricular topics. Although it is not necessary to always show a direct relationship between regular curriculum topics and enrichment activities, an integrated approach should be pursued whenever possible. Some of the enrichment material produced by major textbook companies have already been coordinated with regular curriculum topics in the scope and sequence charts that accompany such material. Although the overall approach should be one of selecting group activities that are extensions of regular curricular topics and objectives, any activity or set of materials might be selected if it shows promise for developing one or more of the goals set forth for Type II Enrichment.

Self-Selected Activities. The column entitled "Self-Selected Activities" should be reserved for those types of materials that ordinarily can be pursued individually and do not require teacher direction. Kits, puzzles, challenge cards, etc. placed in learning centers can be used by all students, but are especially valuable for those Talent Pool students who have additional time available because of curriculum compacting or early completion of work. Each student should keep a record of his or her use of these activities. This approach is especially important for Talent Pool students, because it will create opportunities that might lead to other interests.

The self-selected materials can be rotated among classrooms and signed out from the school's materials center or library. Whenever new materials are brought into a classroom, it is important for teachers to introduce the materials and highlight ones that may be especially exciting or motivating. Student suggestions about materials they have experienced elsewhere might provide good ideas for self-selected activities. They can bring in materials from home, such as science kits, computer software, and manuals that teach a certain skill and might be of interest to other students.

General Approach for Completing the Materials and Activities Selection Worksheets

There are a number of ways these guides can be completed, but the best approach is through a team effort that involves the enrichment specialist and specific groups of classroom teachers. These groups can be organized by grade levels and/or subject areas in order to improve the selection of activities that best fit the existing curriculum. The enrichment specialist can help make appropriate decisions about materials that will: (1) result in the greatest integration with the regular curriculum and (2) lead to a coordinated (rather than overlapping) relationship with enrichment room activities.

A well-stocked materials center or library is, of course, the best way to make effective use of the Materials and Activities Selection Worksheets. Catalogs or lists such as the ones included in this book can give some direction to materials selection. It is important that teachers keep a comprehensive list of catalogs, highlighting those that carry quality enrichment materials. We also recommend that teachers use these worksheets while visiting other programs and districts.

Again, the Type II planning process is developmental. Teachers should not be expected to produce a comprehensive scope and sequence plan "overnight!" Rather, specific subjects within grade levels should be attacked one worksheet at a time, with only one or two entries per cell. Over time, additional entries can be made and more worksheets completed. By setting modest but regular goals, a comprehensive plan will emerge and the process will not become overburdening to teachers.

Materials Review, Evaluation, and Selection

Decisions about which materials should be purchased are dependent upon many things, not the least of which are budget concerns. It may take several years to build up a diversified collection of Type II materials, and opinions will vary on which materials to select. The following recommendations are offered as general guidelines in early efforts of the selection process.

- *Include at least one set of materials per cell for each of the "boxes" on the Materials and Activities Selection Worksheets.*
- *Because of the important role creativity plays in the overall development of gifted behaviors, strive to acquire at least one set of creativity training materials for each grade level. (Whenever possible, attempts should be made to identify creativity training material for various subjects.)*
- *Focus on finding materials that encourage Type III follow-up.*
- *Seek materials that require a range of student responses (writing, drama, art, debates, media products, etc.) This approach respects the diversity in learning styles and modes of expression, as well as the diversity in topics.*
- *Identify materials that provide different levels of difficulty or complexity in their response options. Materials with open-ended response options can be used with groups of varying abilities and interests and will permit more able students to escalate their responses to higher levels.*
- *Consider the teacher training that may be required for new materials. The need for inservice training should not discourage educators from selecting quality activities, but the training needed, its costs, and trainer availability should all be considered beforehand. In this regard, the overall Type II planning effort can serve as a guide for decision making about long-range staff development. If there is a separate budget for staff development, the enrichment specialist should*

work closely with the person responsible for inservice training. Since Type II Enrichment is targeted to all students, at least some financial support for staff development should be devoted to Type II Enrichment.

Commercial Evaluation Guide

The evaluation of curricular materials is a time-consuming and complex process, but when financial resources are limited, it is important to provide some structure to the decision making process for Type II materials. Even more important is to guarantee that materials chosen are the very best available from the vast and increasing number of options in the market today.

One of the first ways to decide about materials is from informal and subjective teacher evaluations. Teacher satisfaction based on actual experience should always be highly valued because ultimately, it will be the teachers using these materials. Also, very few commercial and non-commercial materials have been validated through formal research, therefore, teacher judgments and "face validity" should become major influences when selecting curricular materials.

Another option for materials evaluation is the use of materials evaluation forms, like the one presented in Figure 63. The forms should act as guides to help focus on particular aspects of the enrichment materials, add some objectivity to the process, and serve as a vehicle for gathering and quantifying the opinions of several people. Whenever a new set of materials is being considered for inclusion in the Planning Matrix, members of the Enrichment Team should appoint two or three people to make independent evaluations by using one of these forms. The evaluators should then meet as a group and arrive at a consensus about the quality of the materials.

This evaluation dimension adds an extra measure of work to the overall Type II effort, but it can have valuable payoff in a number of ways. First, it provides a vehicle for systematic rather than random efforts for materials evaluation. Second, the results of these evaluations can be included in the annual program evaluation reports, which will make decision makers aware of the careful planning and effort that goes into the enrichment program. Finally, this procedure provides yet another vehicle for involving staff in decision making, thus helping to further develop program ownership.

Once materials are selected for the classroom as well as the enrichment room, members of the Enrichment Team are responsible for ordering materials. Those materials that are chosen, but not available, can be used to prepare a "Needs List" for subsequent years.

Enrichment Materials Specification Form

The Enrichment Materials Specification Form (see Figure 63) is designed to provide a quick overview of the major features of any given set of enrichment materials available to a school's staff. The form should be placed in a loose leaf notebook in the school's materials center or library, and as it expands over the years, its index can be updated periodically and separated into categories by tabs for quick access.

Each set of materials can be described twice—as it relates to a process skill (Type II focus) and a content area. (Much of the information for the forms can be taken directly from the material's publisher.) In addition to formal information on the form, teachers

Enrichment Materials Specification Form

_____ Major Process Area(s) _____

_____ Major Content Area(s) _____

Planning Matrix Classification _____

Title: _____   Cost: _____

_____   Order No.: _____

                                          Grade/Age Level(s): _____

Author: _____

Publisher (Address): _____

_____

Brief Description:

(For a more complete description see):

Format (Workbook, Flash Cards, Video, etc.):

Topics or Units of Study in the Regular Curriculum Related to These Materials:

Thinking and/or Feeling Processes Developed:

Local Resource Person(s) Familiar With Materials (Please check the names of persons who are willing to conduct workshops or demonstration lessons):

Comments:

Figure 63. Enrichment materials specification form.

should be encouraged to add their own anecdotal notes, useful techniques, variations, and follow-up activities.

Those teachers who show a special interest in a given set of materials may also volunteer as trainers for local demonstrations of materials. This not only saves the cost and hassle of external consultants, but provides an opportunity to recognize and value staff expertise. This type of involvement should be purely voluntary, since some staff members may not be comfortable carrying out inservice training in front of large groups. These teachers instead may prefer working with small groups, videotaping their demonstration, or demonstrating with another teacher. It is important for the enrichment specialist to be present at initial training sessions to help ensure that the atmosphere remains friendly and non-threatening. Staff involvement will help promote program ownership and help teachers develop their own creative potential and hidden talents. Any professional contributions should be formally recognized with a thank you letter that has been sent to the principal, department chair, and superintendent.

Disseminating Information on Type II Enrichment

The information that is reviewed, evaluated, selected, and described through the above process using the Materials and Activities Selection Worksheets and the Enrichment Materials Specification Form will have minimal impact unless there is an effective way to share this information throughout the school or district. This information should be provided to teachers at their schools, rather than expecting them to travel across town to a district materials center or library. This can be facilitated in several ways:

- *Announcements about new materials in an enrichment newsletter.*
- *Announcements at staff meetings.*
- *Individual notes to teachers who have relevant curriculum needs or interests (this may be a good way to interest reluctant teachers in process skill activities).*
- *Memo to be routed, with a Materials Specification Form attached. A copy can then be included in the loose leaf notebook created for the materials center.*

A regular enrichment newsletter can be a particularly valuable tool for disseminating information on Type II Enrichment, while also generating support for an enrichment program (see Figure 64). Not only does a newsletter provide a vehicle for advertising new Type II materials, but it's a great vehicle for discussing upcoming Type I events, exemplary Type II products, enrichment clusters, Enrichment Team meetings, and inservice opportunities. This type of tool publicly documents a school's efforts and alerts decision makers to the various ways enrichment is provided to all students in the school.

Spotting Talent in Type II Activities

Type II Enrichment can be used as a pathway for revolving interested or talented students into Type III investigations. This is suggested by the arrow in the Triad Model connecting Type II to Type III Enrichment.

For this reason, it is extremely important for teachers to be sensitive to possible interests or abilities of students during Type II training. We have found this type of follow-up

SOUTHEAST SCHOOL
Enrichment Program **Newsletter**

Developing Talents in All Students • June 1996

Developing Talents With Total Talent Portfolios

Every student in kindergarten through fourth grade now has a Total Talent Portfolio. This portfolio stores samples of each student's strengths and interests and allows the teacher and student to select that student's best pieces of work from the year. The portfolio will follow the student through his or her years at Southeast. It is a valuable tool that enables teachers to design individualized instruction to best meet each student's needs.

Southeast School Store...

is open for business! Six fourth grade students have organized a school store at Southeast and it is a great success so far. Items were sold out on the first day! Items included: Pencils, erasers, stencils, bookmarks, and student-made cards and posters.

Store Hours:
Mon. & Wed. 8:50-9:00; 12:00-1:00

Type III Projects

May 22nd was a busy day at Southeast School. It was Young Authors' Day and students had the opportunity to read and share the books they authored with other students and parents. They also discussed the writing process with local author, Mark Shasha, who shared his inspirations and techniques with excited groups of students.

At the end of the day, students and teachers gathered for the evening's Type III Project Night. The enrichment room and regular classrooms were packed with a variety of student displays and projects from grades 1-4. We were glad that so many families could come share in the event!

We are already thinking of Type III project ideas for next year!

A Sneak Preview . . .

The Schoolwide Enrichment Team is planning the following events for next year:

- **Enrichment clusters** will be on Thursdays during the fall. This will allow all of our specials teachers to participate. The spring session will be scheduled after school begins.
- **Family Science Night** - October
- **Family Math Night** - March
- **Science Fair & Invention Convention** - February
- **Artist in Residence** - Douglas Day, a local singer/songwriter, will help students compose and perform their own songs for one week in April. His visit will culminate in a student performance.
- **What a Bummer, Here Comes Summer** - June

What an exciting year! We hope you can join us for many of these events.

Figure 64. Enrichment program newsletter.

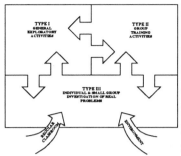

especially frequent when students are taught new research methods or ways to investigate particular types of problems or when students learn skills in connection with the fifth objective of Type II training (developing written, oral and visual communication skills). As with maximizing Type I payoff, this follow-up is most likely to occur when teachers and students are familiar with opportunities for follow-up and there is opportunity for questions and discussions of Type II experiences after they occur. Teachers should be encouraged to conclude each segment of Type II training with questions and should always be on the lookout for students who show advanced ability or interest in Type II activities.

Procedures for Evaluating Type II Enrichment

There are several different approaches that can be used to evaluate Type II Enrichment and this section examines a variety of them. Before describing the instruments however, it is important to point out that the evaluation of programs for advanced level students requires a special technology that is somewhat different from typical skill evaluation procedures used in standardized achievement tests. *A Guidebook for Evaluating Programs for the Gifted and Talented* (Renzulli, 1975) is a book that deals with many of the theoretical and practical issues involved in program evaluation and contains examples of evaluation instruments used throughout the United States. This book is available from Creative Learning Press (P.O. Box 320, Mansfield Center, CT 06250. Phone: (860) 428-8118. Fax: (860) 429-7783.) It is a valuable resource for anyone planning a comprehensive evaluation and will provide information on procedural techniques and the availability of already developed instruments.

Follow-Up Discussion Questions for Type II Experiences

- What did you like best about this activity?
- Of all the Type II's we have had so far, who feels that this was the most interesting?
- Did anyone get any good ideas for follow-up exploration?
- What questions did this skill raise in your mind? What else might be explored?
- Did anyone think of interesting projects, research, or creative writing that can be pursued on this topic (such as film making, photography, community action)? Whom might you share it with?
- Where could we learn more about this topic? Is there anyplace we could visit or anyone we could contact to get more information?
- Are there any careers that this presentation made you think of?
- Would anyone like to meet with me or the presenter to explore follow-ups on this topic?

Chapter 8

The Class Activities Questionnaire

The *Class Activities Questionnaire (CAQ)* was originally developed in connection with the statewide evaluation of the Illinois Gifted and Talented Program (Steele, 1982). It is one of the best instruments available for evaluating thinking skills and factors related to the instructional climate that should characterize Type II Enrichment. The instrument, which is based on Bloom's *Taxonomy of Educational Objectives* (1956), obtains feedback from both teachers and students. It can be used to assess the dimensions and factors related to thinking processes and classroom climate. The five major dimensions include: lower thought processes, higher thought processes, classroom focus, classroom climate, and student opinion. Each of these dimensions is composed of a number of factors, each represented by several items in the questionnaire.

One successful method for using the *CAQ* is to administer it as a pre and post tool for goal setting. In this case, it can be given to teachers and students approximately six weeks into the school year. After teachers study their results, they may meet with the enrichment specialist or principal to review their individual profiles. Feedback can be used as a basis for goal setting and decision making about specific inservice training that teachers feel will help them achieve their desired teaching goals. The *CAQ* can then be administered again at the end of the school year. Our experience with this approach shows an improvement in the achievement of teaching goals and an increase in the number of positive evaluations by students.

The instrument is prepared on optical scanning sheets for computer scoring and analysis. A manual includes reliability and validity data, as well as directions for administration and interpretation. Information on the *CAQ* is available from Creative Learning Press.

Tests of Process Skills

A primary approach for Type II evaluation consists of tests that assess general and specific process skills. Most available tests focus on the cognitive domain, but there are also a small number of instruments that evaluate factors such as self-concept, locus of control, and various attitudinal measures. Before making decisions about the use of such instruments, teachers should review the first chapter of *A Guidebook for Evaluating Programs for the Gifted and Talented*. Much of the discussion in this chapter focuses on the use of standardized achievement tests for evaluating programs for advanced ability students. However, the same concepts and cautions apply to tests of general cognitive ability, like the examples described below.

Three measures of cognitive ability and additional Type II evaluation instruments are described in the following sections. It is the task of the Enrichment Team to examine the descriptions of these instruments and select evaluation tools for review and possible use. Obviously, the most important consideration is the extent to which the test accurately reflects the desired objectives. Additional statistical and practical considerations are described in *A Guidebook for Evaluating Programs for the Gifted and Talented*.

Developing Cognitive Abilities Tests (COGAT)

This instrument is a measure of learning characteristics and abilities that contribute to academic performance in grades 2 through 12. The tests measure verbal, quantitative, and spatial abilities, and also provide information dealing with five levels of Bloom's

Taxonomy: knowledge, comprehension, application, analysis, and synthesis. The tests measure flexible, non-stable traits important for school success and they can be used to evaluate those aspects of Type II Enrichment that focus on general cognitive development. The tests require approximately 50 minutes to administer. Machine scoring is available and provides national and local percentiles for the three content levels and five *Taxonomy* levels.

The Ross Test of Higher Cognitive Processes

This test assesses abstract and critical thinking skills among Talent Pool students and the general population in grades 4 through 6. The test consists of 105 items divided into 8 sections and involves three levels of Bloom's *Taxonomy*: analysis, synthesis, and evaluation. It can be administered individually or in groups and is timed in two sittings of 50 and 55 minutes respectively.

The Synthesis, Evaluation, and Analysis Test (SEA)

This instrument was designed specifically for higher ability students. Questions are based on twenty-one objectives from the three upper levels of Bloom's *Taxonomy* and cover a broad range of instructional content areas. Two forms of the test are available. The twenty-one objectives are equally represented in the questions on each form, so that either form may be used as a pretest or posttest.

Each form is divided into three parts. Questions from each of the three cognitive areas are distributed across each of the test parts and each part contains both multiple choice and short answer questions. The parts may be given on separate days or at an individual session. Each part takes about 20-30 minutes and comes with a detailed manual for administration. Reliability and validity studies are reported for sample populations in grades 5 through 8.

Additional Approaches to Evaluating Type II Enrichment

There are several additional approaches for evaluating Type II Enrichment. In some cases, these instruments cover a cross-section of skills from several different objectives. The first approach follows a pattern similar to that used in obtaining feedback from students on Type I experiences and can be administered following any given segment of Type II training. This consists of modified versions of Type I evaluation forms that determine student attitudes toward specific segments of the training, the degree to which students feel they have developed specific skills, and whether or not they would like to pursue additional related activities (i.e., Type III Enrichment).

A second approach to the evaluation of Type II Enrichment consists of developing behavioral checklists of Type II skills and abilities. Items can be selected from the Type II Taxonomy presented earlier in this chapter. These checklists are similar to those developed for needs assessment and can be completed as a self-assessment by students or by the teacher as an estimation of the degree of proficiency of any given skill by the student. Although we have found this approach to evaluation useful, it is important to point out that many of the materials educators select for Type II Enrichment will cut across several of the general and specific categories of the Taxonomy. For this reason teachers need to carefully analyze the nature of training materials and include in any behavioral checklists specific process skills that may not be included on the Taxonomy or that may cut across several categories of the Taxonomy.

A third approach for evaluating Type II Enrichment consists of preparing rating scales related to the specific content areas covered during the Type II training. This approach is similar to teacher-made unit tests, and in fact, can be combined with test items that assess content mastery. These items can be prepared with the help of the person who designed the instructional unit. They reflect an advanced level of content mastery, as well as the specific process objectives that were the focus of the unit.

As is always the case in any evaluation effort, enrichment specialists want to avoid placing unreasonable burdens upon both teachers and students. A carefully developed evaluation plan that helps enrichment specialists sample various types of data is more practical then efforts that demand more time. The best approach is to review several options and select those that they feel will provide an accurate and comprehensive picture of the Type II program.

SIMSIT 3
FACILITATOR'S GUIDE

Type II Training in the Classroom
A Simulated Planning Activity

Teacher Training Objectives
- To prepare enrichment specialists and resource teachers for persuading classroom teachers to become involved in regular Type II training in their classrooms.
- To develop skills at analyzing the content versus process philosophy that may occur in this simulation.

Number of People Involved
Two teams of two people per team.
The entire group may participate in teams of two people.

Approximate Time
Forty-five minutes to one hour

Materials and Equipment
Directions for the Classroom Teacher
Directions for the Enrichment Specialist

Directions
Form two teams consisting of an enrichment specialist and a classroom teacher and hand out directions to each. (Participants should not see each other's directions.) Send participants out of the room to practice their roles, and in the meantime, review both sets of directions with the rest of the group. Ask the group to observe and take notes on strategies used by the enrichment specialist in trying to convince the classroom teacher to tackle more work.

In a few minutes, bring the teams back to the room one at a time. The team discussion should be allowed to come to a natural resolution, but should not exceed 15 minutes. (You may wish to tape it for later review.) After the first team is done, bring the second team in to discuss. When both teams are finished, discuss the good strategies and styles used by each teacher.

SIMSIT 3
Type II Training in the Classroom (continued)

Directions for the Enrichment Specialist

Mr. Staid has been teaching 5th grade in your district for the past 28 years. You've been working with Mr. Staid for two years and in many ways, you believe he is a fine teacher. He is organized, thorough and works very hard at preparing lessons and providing individualized instruction. Although he was initially apprehensive about compacting, he has done a good job on the compacting process for his five Talent Pool students.

Now you are ready to approach him with another challenge. You'd like him to consider doing some Type II training in his classroom for all students and have made an appointment with him to discuss this. You have some outstanding materials for critical thinking that would be great for his class. You know perfectly well that Mr. Staid has no idea what critical thinking is all about. He also is not familiar with the movement to teach thinking skills in the classroom. You have done some demonstration lessons on creative problem solving in his class and although he liked the lessons, he indicated to you that he just didn't know how he would ever find the time to do Type II training in his classroom with all he had to cover.

Your goal is to convince Mr. Staid of the importance of process training and the need to infuse it into the regular curriculum. You win this simulation if Mr. Staid agrees to implement a weekly lesson of Type II training activities. He may focus on the skill in a separate lesson or work it into his regular curriculum.

SIMSIT 3
Type II Training in the Classroom (continued)

Directions for the Classroom Teacher

You are a fifth grade classroom teacher who has been teaching in your district for the past 28 years. In that time you've seen a lot of change occur and you feel pretty good that you've been able to "roll with the punches." You like this new enrichment specialist, Ms. Enna Vator, who has been helpful to you in providing services for your bright students. She's brought you materials, arranged speakers to come into your classroom, and really helped you in a new process called curriculum compacting. Since you've done that, you've received a lot of positive reinforcement from parents and your principal.

Initially you were apprehensive about this new program. In some ways, you've seen them come and you've seen them go!! Career Ed, Environmental Ed, and a host of other programs that just seemed to bring you MORE WORK! But now this new program seems to have resulted in you getting some help. Ms. Vator has asked you to drop by her enrichment room during your free period. You're curious about what she wants and hope it doesn't involve more work. You've got a busy schedule and a lot more to cover with your fifth graders this year. You simply don't think you can take on any new work at this time of year. You walk down the hall and enter her room.

Type III Enrichment:
Individual and Small Group Investigations of Real Problems

- **Targeting Type III Enrichment**
- **Initiating Type III Enrichment**
- **Problem Finding and Focusing**
- **Focusing on Methodology**
- **The Editorial and Feedback Process**
- **Finding Outlets and Audiences for Student Products**
- **Not All Ideas Are Type III's**
- **Enrichment Clusters as Type III Experiences**
- **Examples of Type III Enrichment**
- **Implementing Type III Enrichment**
- **Completing the Type III Mentor Matrix**
- **Suggestions for Conducting a Type III Fair**
- **Establishing a "Research Foundation"**
- **Procedures for Evaluating Type III Enrichment**
- **Teacher Training Activities**

Targeting Type III Enrichment

In the Enrichment Triad Model, Type III Enrichment is the highest level of experience that can be offered in special programs utilizing this particular approach. In this chapter, we will attempt to describe the responsibilities of teachers in initiating, planning, and carrying out Type III Enrichment experiences. Although there is a great deal of "technology" in the planning and facilitation of Type III Enrichment, the information presented in this chapter is designed to provide step-by-step guidance in achieving the objectives set forth on the summary sheet of this chapter (see Figure 65). We will also describe in detail the guidelines for completing various action forms and provide examples of forms that have been completed by persons in programs where the Schoolwide Enrichment Model (SEM) has been field tested.

Initiating Type III Enrichment

Action Information Forms

The *Action Information Messages* (see Figures 66 and 67) were designed to help classroom teachers, students, enrichment specialists, or parents document and

Type III Enrichment
Summary Sheet

DEFINITION: Investigative activities and artistic productions in which the learner assumes the role of a first-hand inquirer; the student thinking, feeling and acting like a practicing professional.

TARGET AUDIENCES: Individuals and small groups of students who demonstrate sincere interests in particular topics or problems and who show a willingness to pursue these topics at advanced levels of involvement.

OBJECTIVES:

1. To provide opportunities in which students can apply their interests, knowledge, creative ideas, and task commitment to a self-selected problem or area of study.
2. To acquire advanced level understanding of the knowledge (content) and methodology (process) that are used within particular disciplines, artistic areas of expression, and interdisciplinary studies.
3. To develop authentic products that are primarily directed toward bringing about a desired impact upon a specified audience.
4. To develop self-directed learning skills in the areas of planning, organization, resource utilization, time management, decision making, and self-evaluation.
5. To develop task commitment, self-confidence, feelings of creative accomplishment, and the ability to interact effectively with other students, teachers, and persons with advanced levels of interest and expertise in a common area of involvement.

KEY CONCEPTS: Personalized Learning by Doing.
Real Purpose Applied to the Production of a Real Product for a Real Audience.
Student's Role is Transformed from Lesson Learner to First-Hand Inquirer.
A Synthesis and Application of Content, Process and Personal Involvement.

ACTION FORMS: Action Information Message
Management Plan for Individual and Small Group Investigations
Specification Form for Methodological Resource Books
Type III Mentor Matrix

Figure 65. Type III enrichment summary sheet.

ACTION INFORMATION MESSAGE

GENERAL
CURRICULUM AREA _____

ACTIVITY OR TOPIC_____
_____

IN THE SPACE BELOW, PROVIDE A BRIEF DESCRIPTION OF
THE INCIDENT OR SITUATION IN WHICH YOU OBSERVED HIGH
LEVELS OF INTEREST, TASK COMMITMENT OR CREATIVITY ON THE
PART OF A STUDENT OR SMALL GROUP OF STUDENTS. INDICATE
ANY IDEAS YOU MAY HAVE FOR ADVANCED LEVEL FOLLOW-UP ACTIVITIES,
SUGGESTED RESOURCES OR WAYS TO FOCUS THE INTEREST INTO A FIRST-
HAND INVESTIGATIVE EXPERIENCE.

TO:

FROM:

DATE:

☐ PLEASE CONTACT ME

☐ I WILL CONTACT YOU TO
ARRANGE A MEETING
J. S. R. '81

Date Received_____

Date of Interview
with Child_____

Date When
Services Were
Implemented _____

These forms are prepared on 3-part NCR paper and can be purchased in sets of 100 from Creative Learning Press.
Actual size 81/2" x 11".

Figure 66. Action information message (elementary version).

TO: _____ Talent Pool Class Teacher
_____ Program Coordinator
_____ Other

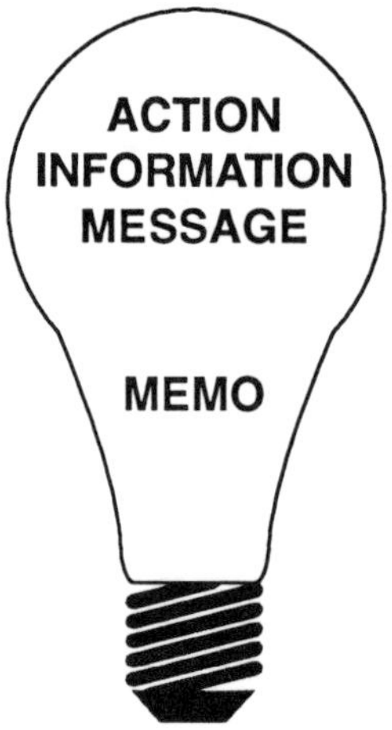

**ACTION
INFORMATION
MESSAGE**

MEMO

FROM: Student (print name) _____

Teacher (print name) _____

Other _____

General Curriculum Area: _____

_____

Idea for Investigation of Study: _____

_____

_____

In the space below, provide a brief description of evidence of high levels of task commitment or creativity on the part of a student or small group of students. Indicate any ideas you may have for advanced level follow-up activities, suggested resources or ways to focus the interest into a first-hand investigative experience.

Date Received _____

Date of Interview _____

Mentor Located _____ Yes _____ No

Name of person who will be responsible for facilitating this Type III

These forms are prepared on 3-part NCR paper and can be purchased in sets of 100 from Creative Learning Press. Actual size 81/2" x 11".

Figure 67. Action information message (secondary version).

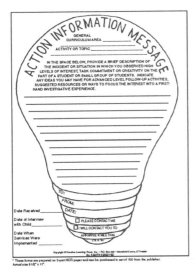

communicate information about student interests to those responsible for guiding advanced level research studies. On the elementary version, this form has been prepared in the shape of a light bulb in order to highlight its overall role in the SEM. On the secondary version, the light bulb concept is maintained through the illustration provided in the upper right-hand corner of the form. The information requested on each of these forms is essentially the same and includes the general subject area of a student's study, the specific idea for the study, and a brief description of possible directions and resources to be pursued.

Before discussing the procedures to follow after receiving an *Action Information Message*, there are certain other "hints" that can help to determine signs of heightened interest or commitment on the parts of students. The list provided in Figure 68 was derived from discussions with classroom teachers, who were asked to record personal experiences relating to the expression of action information.

Student Interviews

When the enrichment specialist receives an *Action Information Message*, certain steps should be immediately followed if vacant slots or spaces exist in the enrichment room. First, the enrichment specialist should either contact the classroom teacher and gather as much information as possible about the student or group of students. Interest in the topic, task commitment, and curricular strength areas should be analyzed by both teachers. If the individual student or group of students show particular strengths in certain subject areas, the enrichment specialist may also want to begin discussing possible strategies for curriculum compacting at this time.

The next step involves the actual interview with the student(s) who have been recommended for enrichment room or independent study time. The enrichment specialist may want to invite the classroom teacher to a very brief and informal pre-interview meeting in order to gain background information about the student(s). At this time, the two teachers can decide if the classroom teacher should be involved in the student interview. Whenever possible such involvement should be encouraged, because this participation will result in a greater interest and understanding in the student's project and the overall nature of what is actually happening in the enrichment room.

Several important topics should be dealt with at the time of the student interview. The enrichment specialist should try to assess how much interest is really present for further pursuit of the topics. Several questions may be asked that will lead the teacher to determine whether or not a true interest is being pursued. For example, if the investigation or interest involves journalism and the student wants to produce a monthly elementary school newspaper, the following questions might be asked at the initial student interview:

- *How long have you been interested in journalism?*
- *What sources have you contacted to learn more about this subject?*
- *Have you ever tried to publish a class or neighborhood newspaper? If not, why?*

Examples of Action Information

A student who shows exceptional ability in a specific area: one who goes above and beyond the call of duty in completing an assignment that calls for creative expression; whose product quality literally "pops out of the deck" because of superlative quality; who is sought for advice and help by classmates because he/she is an "expert" in the area; or who is labeled by peers (not always in a complimentary fashion) according to a particular interest.

A student who displays an "obsession" with or excitement for a particular topic: one who often selects the same book or type of book from the library; who almost always deals with the same theme, issue or topic when given free choice to write; who always talks about (indeed, even bores people with) an interest outside of school; who "hangs around" or seeks out a particular adult because of that adult's special interest, talent, hobby, or commitment to a particular cause (e.g., women's rights, environmental protection, etc.); who "forgets" to return to class or is always late when coming from a special interest area such as the "computer room;" who is typically the "class clown," but suddenly becomes very serious and immersed in a particular topic; who requests help getting books not available in the school library; or who is eager to share projects with peers and voluntarily brings things on a particular theme to class.

A student who displays unusual emotion about a particular topic: one who is ordinarily quiet and reserved but suddenly becomes excited about a certain topic; who shows unusual amount of emotion about a perceived injustice or social problem; or who goes out of his or her way to make a point, prove someone wrong, or present a serious disagreement with an authority figure.

A student who shows creativity with a specific topic: one who extends a topic under discussion to another (e.g., in a lesson on simple machines, the student quickly makes connections with solar energy, modern technology, etc.); who is a clever humorist and can "see" sometimes zany or whimsical connections with what are otherwise considered to be serious situations; or who makes exceptional creative products.

A student who shows persistence and task commitment: one who continues to work on a project despite frustration from a lack of progress; who spends an inordinate amount of time on projects because of enjoyment and the pursuit of perfection; who feels "compelled" to work on a certain topic; who voluntarily asks to do additional work on a project, story, etc. even though it has been accepted as complete; who is persistent in questioning on a particular topic; or who avoids doing certain kinds of "fun things" in order to concentrate on the one thing that excites him/her (e.g., the student who stays indoors at recess in order to make sure the class newspaper deadline is met.)

A student who pursues an interest independently: one who contacts an outside resource person on his or her own; who sets up and purchases materials for a special interest area at home (e.g., laboratory, darkroom, etc.); who voluntarily visits places of interest (museums, power plants, etc.); who starts a club, interest group or project independently; who initiates independent activities (e.g., "Let's petition the Prime Minister of Canada to stop the slaughter of baby seals"); who has extra-curricular activities far more important to him/her than the regular curriculum; or who develops a particular interest through participation in an enrichment cluster.

Figure 68. Examples of action information.

- *Have you ever tried to visit our local newspaper?*
- *Do you know any other students or adults that are interested in this topic?*
- *Have you looked at any books or talked with anyone who might help you get started on a monthly newspaper? If I can help you find a couple of books or someone to talk to about this project, do you think this might give you some ideas?*
- *How did you become interested in this topic?*

Questions such as these will help to assess interest and commitment to the topic in mind. The last question is especially important because educators want to be certain that the interest is in fact the student's. In one case at our field test sites, the enrichment specialist asked this question and listened in surprise as the student honestly responded that she really wasn't interested in the subject, but her mother was!

To further analyze the student's desire to complete the task, questions about procedures should also be asked at this time. If the idea for the monthly newspaper is being discussed, the enrichment specialist should, at this point, ask questions that will reveal whether or not the student has thought about the task commitment that will be required to complete the project or product.

- *How do you think you should get started?*
- *How many hours do you think it will take you to completely organize a monthly school newspaper?*
- *How many other students do you think you will need to involve?*
- *How will you recruit reporters?*
- *How can you reproduce your newspaper?*
- *Do you have any ideas that might help you develop a newspaper that is somewhat different from others you have seen?*

Questions such as these will help the enrichment specialist to determine if the student has really considered the amount of work involved in the actual completion of the product. In a few cases, a student may even change his or her mind about undertaking a project because of the amount of time and actual work that may be involved. The interview should not "frighten" away individuals or small groups of students from beginning an investigation or product-oriented study in the enrichment room. Instead, it should help an enrichment specialist reserve his/her time and energy for students who have a genuine interest in their subject and a sincere desire to work. Very few *Action Information Messages* result in the students not "ever" revolving into advanced level work. Instead, some students realize that pursuing Type III projects involves work and it is not just a "fun" thing to do.

Several important points must be considered regarding this initial interview. The first deals with student products. Many classroom teachers will complete *Action Information Messages* which detail an interest that they have noticed in a particular student, but include no actual idea for a product or an investigation. The interview should then center on the interest and possible outlets or products for that interest. It would be unfair to deny any individual or group of students admission to the enrichment room because a final product had not been indicated on the *Action Information Message*.

That is often the responsibility of the enrichment specialist and ideas for final products sometimes change or become modified after initial research has been completed. In fact, some students will have an intense interest and desire to study and research a particular area and will need much assistance from the enrichment specialist to focus on a way to synthesize their research into an idea. As will be discussed in the next section, problem focusing will often result in a narrower topic being chosen for the final product or investigation.

Another important point that should be remembered about the initial student interview is that the experience will be radically different for a sixth grader than it is for a first grade student. In our field test sites, all kindergarten through second grade Talent Pool students spent at least an hour a week in the resource room either browsing, working on Type II activities (creativity training, math enrichment activities, mind bending exercises, etc.) or participating in Type I activities (seeing films and filmstrips, hearing speakers, attending workshops by guest presenters, etc.). By including the entire Talent Pool of these primary grades in weekly scheduled activities in the enrichment room, the enrichment specialist was able to suggest many products or Type III investigations from enrichment experiences that were scheduled in the weekly sessions. In that way, both the enrichment specialist and the student's classroom teacher closely watched as interests developed and suggested possible extensions of the interests. These students also benefited from a weekly exposure in the resource room. When an interest developed, the classroom teacher sent an *Action Information Message* to the enrichment specialist. In some cases, an enrichment specialist initiated an *Action Information Message*.

The Intake Interview Checklist for Type III Investigations (see Figure 69) highlights and organizes the main ideas that have been presented about Type III interviews. We recommend that this checklist be used to summarize the results of discussions with students rather than as a format to follow during the actual interview process. It is counter-productive to "quiz" students about their interests, creativity and task commitment as they relate to intended projects or research questions. Students will tend to become uncomfortable and rigid in their responses if they feel they have to "get the right answers" on a predetermined set of questions. It is our hope that the interview situation will be a positive one in which students learn something new about themselves and their potential interest areas. This goal can only be accomplished if teachers engage students in an open-ended dialogue that evolves naturally.

Selecting Students to Pursue Type III Investigations

Some *Action Information Messages* sent to the enrichment specialist from a classroom teacher may indicate ideas for products or investigations which, at first, seem to be inappropriate for advanced level work. Examples of these types of "light bulbs" may be students who want to write a report or write a short story. It should be noted that writing a report or a simple short story is not an activity which necessarily requires time and space in the enrichment room. Indeed, if these types of projects were to be accepted as long term assignments in the enrichment room, the enrichment specialist might be in some way saying to the classroom teacher that he/she does not feel that this activity can be completed in the classroom. And this, of course, is not the case. It should also be

The Intake Interview Checklist for Type III Investigations

Deborah E. Burns
University of Connecticut

Name _____   Grade _____
Date _____   Teacher _____
Topic _____

Directions:
Based on the information and responses solicited from the student, how would you evaluate his/her readiness to initiate and complete an independent research project? Using a five-point rating scale, please respond to the following questions:

A. Interest
  1. To what extent did this project idea come directly from the child's personal interests (as opposed to teacher/parent pressure)?

5	4	3	2	1
	to a great extent		to a limited extent	

  2. How long has the student had an interest in this topic?

5	4	3	2	1
	a long time		a short time	

  3. What is the student's general attitude toward the proposed project?

5	4	3	2	1
	eager		cautious	

  4. To what extent is this interest faddish and likely to be short-lived?

5	4	3	2	1
	unlikely		likely	

B. Above Average Ability
  1. How much preliminary reading and research has the child already completed?

5	4	3	2	1
	a great deal		very little	

  2. What is this child's current level of knowledge about this topic?

5	4	3	2	1
	advanced		basic	

  3. How broad or general is the topic proposed for investigation?

5	4	3	2	1
	focused		nonspecific	

  4. How well stated is the research question to be investigated?

5	4	3	2	1
	concise		formless	

Figure 69. The intake interview checklist for type III investigations.

C. Creativity

1. How original is the project under investigation?

5	4	3	2	1
	unique		replication	

2. To what extent does the child hope to make a change, improvement or a creative contribution to the subject under investigation?

5	4	3	2	1
	comprehensive		minimal	

3. How elaborate is the idea or plan for this project?

5	4	3	2	1
	detailed		sketchy	

4. How action-oriented is the project under consideration?

5	4	3	2	1
	active		passive	

D. Task Commitment

1. How does the child feel about the time and energy this project will entail?

5	4	3	2	1
	accepting		uneasy	

2. How does the child feel about revising, rewriting and polishing his/her product?

5	4	3	2	1
	favorable		resistant	

3. Is the child capable of concentrating on a project for an extended length of time?

5	4	3	2	1
	able		unable	

4. How many other demands does the child have on his/her time and energy?

5	4	3	2	1
	multiple		few	

E. Methodology

1. Describe the reference materials/resources the student plans to use.

5	4	3	2	1
	diverse		standard	

2. How able is the child to use advanced methodology in the chosen field of study?

5	4	3	2	1
	with ease		with difficulty	

3. What provisions have been made for raw data gathering as a step toward answering the research question?

5	4	3	2	1
	lengthy		minimal	

4. How willing is the child to research the topic, take notes, interview mentors, etc.?

5	4	3	2	1
	enthusiastic		unsure	

Figure 69. The intake interview checklist for type III investigations (continued).

Summary of Interview

Topic: _____

Problem to Be Investigated: _____

Product: _____

Audience: _____

Time Line (in weeks): _____

   (in hrs./wk): _____

Best Possible Compacted Time: _____

Provisions for Data Gathering: _____

Provisions for Preliminary Research: _____

Comments: In order to begin this Type III, the following things must first happen:

Figure 69. The intake interview checklist for type III investigations (continued).

noted, however, that some classroom teachers who are not trained in problem focusing procedures may use the term "report" when the student can delve much further and complete much more than an actual report in the traditional sense.

Enrichment specialists should also remember that what might not be a bona fide Type III investigation for a student in a sixth grade classroom may be a legitimate point of entry for a first or second grade student. Many examples of this differing set of acceptable standards for entry into the enrichment room were found in our field test sites. In one case, a first grade student expressed an interest in writing a short story and developing a pop-up book. At least four or five different drafts of the story were written by the student before the illustrations were started and plans for the pop-ups were designed. This, obviously, was a legitimate point of entry into scheduled enrichment room time beyond the weekly period allotted to all kindergarten through second graders. Writing a short story might not, however, guarantee entrance into the enrichment room for a fifth or sixth grade student, since writing and revising short stories are standard tasks for that age group. The enrichment specialist must then either try to expand the idea with the student, give the student some tips and advice on writing, or schedule some Type II training in creative writing or creativity for that student and other interested students.

If the enrichment specialist decides not to accept an *Action Information Message* and not to admit the student to the enrichment room for one of the reasons already listed, that decision must be diplomatically explained to the classroom teacher who has sent the *Action Information Message*. We found that in most cases in our field test sites, the classroom teachers reacted well to the decision, particularly when they had been involved in the interview. Some teachers indicated that they had been unsure about even sending the *Action Information Message*, but they had noticed an interest and thought that the enrichment specialist should be notified. This is exactly how the procedure should work. The classroom teacher should be a part of the decision and should not consider an *Action Information Message* that was not accepted, a "failure."

Scheduling Details and Curriculum Compacting

If a successful interview results in the enrichment specialist and the classroom teacher agreeing that the student or group of students should begin working in the enrichment room, certain scheduling details must be followed. If an enrichment room does not exist in the school, the classroom teacher must make his or her own decision about the student's product and try to revolve the student into a particular place in the room or school where the student can begin work. If a space exists in the enrichment room, schedules should be devised that will allow the student or group of students to be out of the classroom during a time when the teacher is covering material that the student has already mastered. At this time, the student's regular curriculum should be compacted so that time may be made available to begin the investigation or Type III project (see Chapter 6). In addition, a contract or planning guide should be completed which documents the nature and scope of the student's proposed investigation. The *Management Plan for Individual and Small Group Investigations* (Renzulli & Smith, 1977) is one such device that has served to help students formulate their objectives, locate and organize appropriate resources and identify relevant outlets and audiences for their creative work (see Figure 70).

MANAGEMENT PLAN FOR INDIVIDUAL AND SMALL GROUP INVESTIGATIONS
(Actual Size: 11" x 17")

Prepared by: Joseph S. Renzulli
Linda H. Smith

NAME _____ GRADE _____

TEACHER _____ SCHOOL _____

Beginning Date _____ Estimated Ending Date _____

Progress Reports Due on Following Dates _____

GENERAL AREA(S) OF STUDY (Check all that apply)

___ Language Arts/Humanities   ___ Science   ___ Personal and Social Development

___ Social Studies   ___ Music   ___ Other (Specify) _____

___ Mathematics   ___ Art   ___ Other (Specify) _____

SPECIFY AREA OF STUDY
Write a brief description of the problem that you plan to investigate. What are the objectives of your investigation? What do you hope to find out?

METHODOLOGICAL RESOURCES AND ACTIVITIES
List the names & addresses of persons who might provide assistance in attacking this problem. List the how-to-do-it books that are available in this area of study. List other resources (films, collections, exhibits, etc.) and special equipment (e.g., camera, tape recorder, questionnaire, etc.). Keep continuous record of all activities that are part of this investigation.

INTENDED AUDIENCES
Which individuals or groups would be most interested in the findings? List the organized groups (clubs, societies, teams) at the local, regional, state, and national levels. What are the names and addresses of contact persons in these groups? When and where do they meet?

1. _____
2. _____
3. _____
4. _____
5. _____

INTENDED PRODUCT(S) AND OUTLETS
What form(s) will the final product take? How, when, and where will you communicate the results of your investigation to an appropriate audience(s)? What outlet vehicle (journals, conferences, art shows, etc.) are typically used by professionals in this field?

GETTING STARTED
What are the first steps you should take to begin this investigation? What types of information or data will be needed to solve the problem? If "raw data," how can it be gathered, classified, and presented? If you plan to use already categorized information or data, where is it located and how can you obtain what you need?

A complete description of the model utilizing this form can be found in: *The Enrichment Triad Model: A Guide For Developing Defensible Programs For The Gifted And Talented.* Creative Learning Press, Inc., P.O. Box 320, Mansfield Center, CT 06250.

Figure 70. Management plan for individual and small group investigations.

Problem Finding and Focusing

The process of problem finding and focusing should begin by first determining the student's general area(s) of interest. This determination can be made through the formal submission of an *Action Information Message* or it might result by simply observing the way in which a student responds to experiences in the regular curriculum, Type I and/or Type II Enrichment activities, or informal interests that may stem from out-of-school experiences. There are two important considerations that must be taken into account if teachers are going to promote maximum amounts of Type III involvement on the parts of their students. First, teachers must have a thorough understanding of the model in general and specific training and orientation about how to spot advanced level interests in particular topics or areas of study. Suggestions for spotting these kinds of interests are described in Chapters 4 and 5.

A second consideration relates to the awareness of students with regard to the model in general and the opportunities to take self-initiated steps toward revolving into Type III Enrichment. It is absolutely essential for students to view the special program as a place where they can bring their interests and ideas and gain some assistance in determining whether or not an idea might subsequently result in the development of a Type III project. In order to achieve appropriate levels of awareness from both teachers and students, it will be necessary to conduct several orientation and inservice training sessions with both groups, especially during the early years of a program. An effective method for carrying out these sessions is to provide both groups with examples of *Action Information Messages* that have been received in previous years or those presented in this book and describe the types of follow-up that took place as a result of the submission of these forms. This dimension of training related to the SEM cannot be overemphasized. It is suggested that during the early years of a program, teachers should consider doing somewhat of an "overkill" in this area of orientation and training.

Most teachers have little difficulty recognizing general families of interest—scientific, historical, literary, mathematical, musical, athletic. However, problems arise when they attempt to capitalize upon these general interests and use them as the starting point for focusing in on a specific manifestation of general interests and structuring specific interests into researchable problems. How teachers deal with interests, both general and specific, is crucial and if handled improperly will undoubtedly get students off on the wrong track.

We know of one student who expressed an unusual interest in sharks. The teacher appreciated the student's enthusiasm and reacted in what he thought was an appropriate fashion: "I'm glad that you have such a great interest in sharks—why don't you do a report about sharks?" Those awful words, "do a report . . ." lead to an inevitable end result—yet another summary of facts and drawings based entirely on information copied from encyclopedias and "all-about books." While the student prepared a very neat and accurate report, her major investigative activity was "looking up" and summarizing already existing information. Although previous (background) information is always an important starting point for any investigative endeavor, one of our goals in Type III

Type III Enrichment: Individual and Small Group Investigations

Enrichment is to help students extend their work beyond the usual kinds of reporting that often results when teachers and students view the Type III process as merely looking up information. Some training in reporting is a necessary part of good education for all students. Indeed, the pursuit of new knowledge should always begin with a review of what is already known about a given topic. The end result of a Type III investigation, however, should be a creative contribution that goes beyond the already existing information typically found in encyclopedias and general reference books.

How can teachers help students learn to focus problems and become more involved in advanced types of creative and productive projects? The first step is to help students ask the right kinds of questions routinely raised by persons who do investigative research within particular fields of knowledge. At this point, however, educators are faced with a practical problem. Because most teachers are not well-versed in asking the right questions about specific fields of study, they must assist students in obtaining the methodological books (or resource persons, if available) that routinely list these important questions. In other words, if educators want to ask the right questions about problem focusing in anthropology, then they must begin by looking at techniques used by anthropologists. Every field of organized knowledge can be defined, in part, by its methodology. In every case this methodology can be found in certain kinds of guidebooks or manuals. These how-to books are the key to escalating studies beyond the traditional report writing approach. We will devote a later section of this chapter to procedures for identifying and making the best use of how-to books. Unfortunately, many of these books are not ordinarily included in elementary or high school libraries, but the fact that they are not easily available, does not mean that able students cannot make appropriate use of at least selected parts of advanced materials.

A few years ago we worked with a small group of high ability sixth graders who had a strong interest in history. We obtained a book for them entitled *Understanding History: A Primer of Historical Method* (Gottschalk, 1969) from a college library. This book contained a wealth of practical information about how to actually become a historian rather than merely learning more about the accumulated facts of history. One section of the book neatly listed the kinds of questions that historians tend to raise during the process of problem finding and focusing. These questions are reproduced below:

1. **Geographical Questions.** These questions center around the interrogative (Where?). What areas of the world do I wish to investigate? The Far East? Brazil? My Country? My City? My Neighborhood?
2. **Biographical Questions.** These questions center around the interrogative (Who?). What persons am I interested in? The Chinese? The Greeks? My Ancestors? My Neighbors? A Famous Individual?
3. **Chronological Questions.** These questions center around the interrogative (When?). What period of the past do I wish to study? From the Beginning of Time Until Now? The 5th Century B.C.? The Middle Ages? The 1780's? Last Year?
4. **Occupational Questions.** These questions center around the interrogative (What?). What spheres of human interest concern me most? What kinds of human activity? Economics? Literature? Athletics? Politics?

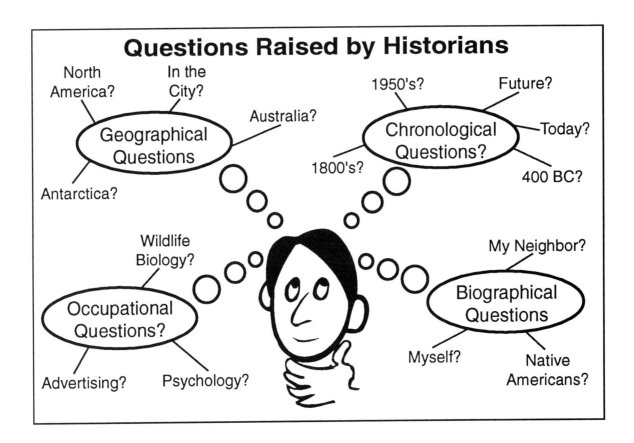

Several brainstorming and individual discussion sessions were conducted using these questions as guides. Within a short time almost every student converted his or her historical interest into a specific topic or problem. The questions were reproduced on a form with ample space for students to record their responses and ideas. The students were fascinated by the almost limitless number of opportunities for original historical investigations that could be conducted right in their own communities and the vast array of primary source documents that were available locally.

Educators can avoid the error of confusing traditional reporting with Type III investigations by keeping the concept of raw data in mind. Raw data can be thought of as relatively unorganized bits and pieces of information that can be gathered and analyzed in order to reach a conclusion, discover a principle, support an argument, or create a unique product or presentation. (In a certain sense, even a poet uses new combinations of words, ideas, and feelings as "raw data" to create an original poem.) The ways in which researchers use data and the purposes toward which data are directed are important considerations in defining a Type III experience. In the following example we will try to highlight important steps and key concepts in problem focusing by noting these concerns in brackets.

> *Jason's teacher was aware of his special interest in anything and everything having to do with science. [Keep in mind that science is an area rather than a problem.] She provided him with several copies of **Popular Science** and asked him to review and pick out the articles he liked best. [This is a good example of an exploratory activity (Type I), because these magazines include many topics that are not ordinarily covered in the regular science curriculum.]*

*When the teacher asked Jason if there was any article he would like to follow-up by doing some research of his own, he selected the area of hydroponics gardening. [The general area of science has now been narrowed down somewhat, but hydroponics gardening is a topic rather than a problem.] The teacher obtained a copy of **Hydroponics Gardening** by Raymond Birdwell from the county library and Jason practically devoured it in one night.*

Through discussion with his teacher, Jason got an idea to grow corn under varying conditions. [Now we have an "investigatable" problem.] He constructed several growing trays using paper milk cartons and obtained the necessary nutrients from his chemistry set, a high school chemistry teacher, and a university extension agent with whom he made contact through assistance from his teacher. By varying the amounts of certain macronutrients (nitrogen, phosphorus, potassium) and keeping other conditions constant [good research procedures] he was able to observe different rates of growth. He kept meticulous records and recorded weekly measurements [data] of growth rates and plant "health" [more data]. He also photographed plants grown under varying conditions by placing a standard growth-grid chart behind each plant [visual data]. He prepared graphics and statistical summaries [data summary and analysis] and developed a written report [communication of results]. Jason also organized an audiovisual presentation of his work [another mode of communication].

One of the most important points that we want to convey at this time is that it is not necessary for teachers to become "experts" in all of the methodological techniques of different fields of study. This is indeed an impossible task, but it does not mean that they will be unable to provide very sophisticated levels of methodological technique to students who develop interests in specialized fields of knowledge. A teacher's primary responsibilities in problem focusing and facilitating Type III Enrichment include: (1) knowing about the existence of methodological resource books in the various fields of knowledge; (2) knowing where such books are located and how he/she can obtain them for students; (3) Taking the time and effort necessary to help students obtain these materials which will frequently be located in other places than the school; and (4) providing or obtaining the assistance that might be necessary for interpreting advanced-level material that might be difficult for younger students to understand.

Focusing on Methodology

The second major responsibility of teachers in facilitating Type III Enrichment is to give students methodological and managerial assistance. Methodological assistance means helping students acquire and make appropriate use of the specific data gathering tools and investigative techniques that are the standard and necessary methods for authentic research in particular fields of study. If a problem is well-defined and focused, the correct guidance by teachers during this phase of a study can almost guarantee that students will be first-hand investigators rather than reporters. This step of the process involves shifting emphasis from learning about topics to learning how one gathers, categorizes, analyzes, and evaluates information in particular fields.

Every field of knowledge is characterized, in part, by certain kinds of raw data. New contributions are made in a field when investigators apply well-defined methods to the process of "making sense" out of previously random bits and pieces of information.

Although some investigations require levels of sophistication and equipment that are far beyond the reach of younger students, almost every field of knowledge has entry level and junior level data gathering opportunities.

We have seen scientifically respectable questionnaire studies on food and television preferences carried out by primary grade students. A group of middle grade students gathered and analyzed water samples as part of a large Northeast area study on the extent and effects of acid rain. Their work had been so thoroughly and carefully done that their findings have been requested for use by a state environmental agency. Another group of elementary students used very professional techniques when producing a weekly television show broadcast by a local cable television company. A fifth grade student has written a guidebook that was adopted by the city council as the official historical walking tour of his city. A group of high school students engaged in a very sophisticated community research and citizens' action project that resulted in the appropriation of $200,000 for a citywide system of bikeways. The success and high level of product development reflected in these examples can be traced to the proper use of authentic methods and techniques, even if those techniques were carried out at a somewhat junior level.

At this stage of Type III activity, the teacher's role is to help students identify, locate and obtain resource materials and/or persons that can provide assistance in the appropriate use of investigative techniques. In some cases, teachers may have to consult with librarians or professionals within fields for advice about where and how to find resource materials. Teachers may also need professional assistance in translating complex concepts into levels students can understand. Although methodological assistance is a major part of the teacher's responsibility, it is not necessary nor realistic to expect teachers to have mastered a large number of investigative techniques. A good general background and orientation toward the overall nature of research is necessary, but the most important skill is the ability to know where and how to help a student obtain the right kind of material and the willingness to reach beyond the usual school resources for specialized kinds of materials and resource persons.

In a later section of this chapter we will recommend specific procedures through which teachers can obtain a general background about the overall nature of research methodology. At this point, however, it is important to emphasize that our approach is to draw upon the descriptions of methodological procedures that can easily be found in the books written by subject-matter specialists.

Managerial assistance consists of helping students to "make arrangements" for obtaining the types of data and resources necessary for Type III investigations. Setting up an interview with a public official, arranging for the distribution of a questionnaire to students or parents, and providing transportation to a place where data can be gathered are all examples of managerial functions fulfilled by teachers in Type III situations. Additional activities might include gaining access to laboratories or computer centers, arranging for the use of a college library, helping students gain access to a telephone or photocopying machine, and driving downtown to pick up some photographic materials or electronic parts. The teacher's responsibilities in this regard are similar to the combined roles of research assistant, advocate, ombudsman, campaign strategist, and enthusiastic friend.

At this stage of product development the student should be the leader and emerging expert, while the teacher assumes a supportive rather than authoritative posture. The teacher's typical comments should be: "What can I do to help you? Are you having any problems? Do you need to get a book from the university library? Would you like to bounce a few ideas off of me? Are there some ways that we might explore raising the money you need for solar cells?"

The major purpose of the managerial role is to help the student stay on track and move toward each intermediate goal and accomplishment. A planned strategy for bringing the teacher up to date on progress between meetings will create a vehicle for fulfilling the managerial role. A log, notebook or annotated time line are good examples of such vehicles. This procedure should involve a review and analysis of the *Management Plan* (see Figure 70).

The Editorial and Feedback Process

Even the most experienced researchers, writers and creative producers need feedback from individuals who can reflect objectively upon a given piece of work. For young scholars who are having initial experiences in the often frustrating task of first-hand inquiry, this feedback must be given in a firm, but sensitive manner. The major theme or idea underlying the feedback process is that almost everything can be improved upon in varying degrees through revisions, rewriting, and attention to details, both large and small. This message must be conveyed to students without harsh criticism or discouraging comments. Each student must be made to feel that the teacher's most important concern is to help the aspiring artist or scholar reach the highest possible level of excellence. Just as a champion athlete or dancer knows that a rigorous coach has the performer's best interests at heart, so also must students learn that critical feedback is a major service that good teachers must offer.

There are several ways students can learn about the relationship between high quality products and the feedback process. Books, such as Gottschalk's, describe the functions of succeeding drafts of historical manuscripts. The text provides examples of first draft and edited copies of the same manuscript. A similar strategy is to locate well-written journal articles in the student's area of research and other products that profoundly illustrate how a particular method was described or results were reported. Outstanding examples of work completed by other students of the same age will also provide prototypes, as well as motivation to pursue revisions that might be necessary.

The teacher should view his or her role in the feedback process as that of a "resident escalator." Sensitive and specific recommendations about how particular aspects of the work can be improved will help the aspiring scholar to move slowly but surely toward higher and higher levels of product excellence. Every effort should be made to pinpoint specific areas where suggested changes should be made. This approach will help avoid student discouragement and reconfirm a belief in the overall value of his/her endeavors. The following poem will help reinforce the idea that just about everything can be improved upon:

Good better best,
Never let it rest,
Until the good is better,
Until the better is best.

Finding Outlets and Audiences for Student Products

In many ways we believe that the magic key which has unlocked the success of so many Type III projects is the "sense of audience" that students have developed in connection with their creative efforts. It is the real-life audience which helps give students a reason for wanting to improve the quality of their products and develop effective ways of communicating their results with interested individuals. We also believe that audience is a primary contributor to the creation of task commitment and the concern for excellence and quality that we have witnessed in so many Type III investigations.

If the Type III dimension of our model is to have maximum value in the overall development of young scholars and creative producers, major attention must be given to helping them find appropriate outlets and audiences for their most creative efforts. This concern is once again modeled after the modus operandi of creative and productive individuals. If we could sum up in as few words as possible the raison d'être of highly creative artists and scholars, it would certainly be "impact upon audience." Creativity is a source of personal satisfaction and self-expression, but a good deal of the rewards come from bringing about desired changes in the human condition. The writer hopes to influence thoughts and emotions, the scientist carries out research to find better ways to contribute to the knowledge of his or her field, and the artist creates products to enrich the lives of those who view his/her work. Teachers can help young people acquire this orientation by encouraging them to develop a sense of audience from the earliest stages of a Type III investigation.

The teacher's role regarding outlets and audiences requires helping students take one small, but often neglected step, in the overall process of product development. The first step is to consider how people typically communicate results or products within given fields of the arts and sciences. Once again, teachers can examine the activities of practicing professionals and the how-to books for guidance. In most cases, young artists and scholars will be restricted to local outlets and audiences, but there will be occasions when products of unusual excellence can be shared with larger audiences. Some examples of vehicles that have been used regularly in programs organized around the SEM are presented in Figure 71. We have also included a list of publishing opportunities for students in Figure 72.

Although school and local audiences are an obvious starting point in the search for outlet vehicles, teachers should always help students gain a perspective for more comprehensive outlet vehicles and audiences beyond local opportunities (see Figure 73). Many organizations, for example, prepare newsletters and journals at state and national levels and are usually receptive to high quality contributions by young people. Similarly, state and national magazines often carry outstanding work by young people. Whenever student products achieve unusually high levels of excellence, encourage them

Vehicles & Products for Type III Investigations

Literary
- An enrichment cluster on poetry
- Magazine
- School/class newspaper
- Book reviews
- Storytelling
- Puppeteers
- Student editorials
- Kid's page in local newspaper
- Classbook
- Calendar book
- Greeting cards with original poetry
- Script for a play
- Poetry reading
- Organizer of story hour in library
- Comic book or series
- Organizer of debate society
- Monologue or sound track
- Production of home page on Internet
- Literary collections (i.e. folklore)

Artistic
- Displays, exhibits
- Greeting cards
- Sculpture
- Graphic/computer design for school newspaper
- Illustrated books
- Cartoons
- Mural
- Bulletin display
- Set design for school play
- Costume design

Musical, Dance
- An enrichment cluster on dance
- Musical instrument construction
- Original music or lyrics
- Books about the life of a famous composer
- History of dance, costumes
- Electronic music

Media
- Children's TV show
- Children's radio show
- Photo essay
- Children's reviews (books, movies) on local news shows
- Photo exhibit (talking)
- Slide show
- Video of school events
- Video production
- Design ads

Scientific
- Science journal
- Meteorologist posting daily weather
- Science fair
- Science column in newspaper
- Organizer of natural museum
- Creation of a nature walk
- Book on pond life
- Working model of a solar home
- Acid rain study
- Working model of a windmill
- Prolonged experimentation using manipulation of variables

Math
- Original puzzles, quizzes, etc. for children's section of a newspaper and/or magazine
- Editor of computer newsletter
- Math or computer consultant for school
- Organizer of metric conversion
- Original computer programming
- A how-to book about computer programming
- Creation of a business/school store
- Involvement in the Stock Market

Historical & Social Sciences
- Historical series in newspaper
- Establishment of oral history tape library
- Local folklore collection
- Published history—written, taped, pictorial
- Video on historical topic
- Historical play
- Historical board game
- Archaeological dig

Figure 71. Vehicles and products for type III investigations.

Publishers of Children's Work

The Acorn
1530 Seventh Street
Rock Island, IL 61201
(309) 788-3980
All ages

AIM Magazine
7308 South Eberhart Avenue
Chicago, IL 60619
(312) 874-6184
Ages 14-18

Boodle, By Kids for Kids
P.O. Box 1049
Portland, IN 47371
(219) 726-8141
Ages 6-12

Calliope: World History for Young People
Cobblestone Publishing, Inc.
7 School Street
Peterborough, NH 03458
(603) 924-7209
Ages 8-12

Chickadee Magazine
Young Naturalist Foundation
56 The Esplanade, Suite 306
Toronto, Ontario
Canada M5E 1A7
(416) 868-6001
Ages 3-9

Child Life
Children's Better Health Institute
P.O. Box 567
Indianapolis, IN 46206
(317) 636-8881
Ages 7-9

Children's Digest
Children's Better Health Institute
P.O. Box 567
Indianapolis, IN 46206
(317) 636-8881
Ages 8-12

Children's Playmate
Children's Better Health Institute
P.O. Box 567
Indianapolis, IN 46206
(317) 636-8881
Ages 6-8

Cobblestone
Cobblestone Publishing Inc.
7 School Street
Peterborough, NH 03458
(603) 924-7209
Ages 8-15

Creative Kids
Prufrock Press
P.O. Box 8813
Waco, TX 76714
(800) 998-2208
Ages 8-15

Creative With Words
CWW Publications
P.O. Box 223226
Carmel, CA 93922
All ages

Cricket Magazine
Carus Publishing
P.O. Box 300
Peru, IL 61354
(815) 223-1500
Ages 7-14

Figure 72. Publishers of children's work.

Publishers of Children's Work

Dolphin Log
The Cousteau Society
870 Greenbriar Circle
Suite 402
Chesapeake, VA 23320
(804) 523-9335
Ages 7-15

Highlights for Children
803 Church Street
Honesdale, PA 18431
(717) 253-1080
Ages 3-12

Junior Scholastic
Scholastic, Inc.
555 Broadway
New York, NY 10012
(212) 505-3071
All ages

McGruffy Writer
400-A McGruffy Hall
Miami University
Oxford, OH 45156
Ages 5-17

Merlyn's Pen
Merlyn's Pen, Inc.
98 Main Street
P.O. Box 1058
East Greenwich, RI 02818
(800) 247-2027
Ages 13-18

Read Magazine
Weekly Reader Corp.
245 Long Hill Road
P.O. Box 2791
Middletown, CT 06457
(860) 638-2400
Ages 11-18

Skipping Stones
A Multicultural Children's Quarterly
P.O. Box 3939
Eugene, OR 97403
(503) 342-4956
All ages

Skylark
Purdue University Calumet
2200-169th Street
Hammond, IN 46323
All ages

Spring Tides
Savannah Country Day
Lower School
824 Stillwood Road
Savannah, GA 31419
(912) 925-8800
Ages 5-12

Stone Soup: The Magazine by Children
Children's Art Foundation
P.O. Box 83
Santa Cruz, CA 95063
(408) 426-555
Ages 6-13

Word Dance Magazine
435R Hartford Turnpike
Vernon, CT 06066
(860) 870-8614
Ages 5-14

The Writer's Slate
P.O. Box 734
Garden City, KS 67846
All ages

Young Author's Magazine
P.O. Box 81847
Lincoln, NE 68501-1847
All ages

Young Voices
P.O. Box 2321
Olympia, WA 98507
(206) 357-4683
All ages

Your Local Newspaper
Check with your local newspaper to see
if it hosts a kids' page.

Figure 72. Publishers of children's work (continued).

Potential Audiences for Type III Products

- Parents & Siblings
- Peers & Classmates
- Primary Classrooms
- Students During Lunch (in Cafeteria)
- Other Schools/Classes in the District
- Regular School Assemblies
- PTO & PTA Members
- The Principal
- Bulletin Boards & Display Cases
- Children in Daycare Centers
- On-line Sites
- Children in the Pediatric Wing of a Hospital
- Children in the State Facility for Disabled
- Magazines that Accept Children's Work
- Children's Page in Local Newspaper
- Radio Listeners
- Cable TV Viewers
- Local Agency Related to Topic
- City Council Members
- Rotary Club Members
- Senior Center
- Shopping Mall Patrons
- Town Hall
- Bank Lobby
- Local Business Related to the Topic
- Clubs, Societies, Organizations (Local, State or National)
- College Education Class
- Any Natural Outlet Related to a Student's Work

Figure 73. Potential audiences for type III products.

to contact one of the publishing companies and magazines that specialize in or are receptive to the contributions of young writers, artists and researchers.

The biggest single dilemma in implementing the SEM is helping students get started on Type III activities. Type III Enrichment represents qualitatively different learning experiences from Type I's or Type II's. It is important for teachers to realize that they themselves must engage in some activities that are different from the usual activities that define the traditional teacher's role. This point cannot be overemphasized! It is impossible to foster differential types of learning experiences through the use of ordinary teaching methods. If educators want students "to think, feel and do" like practicing professionals, then they, as enrichment specialists and teachers, must also learn how to raise a few of the questions that professionals ask about the nature and function of their own work. In other words, educators must go one step beyond the typical questions raised in problem focusing situations and move on to product focusing. There are two major purposes in raising these questions. The first is obviously to focus upon one or more products and target audiences. The second purpose is somewhat less direct, but equally crucial. Teachers must begin to help students think, feel and believe that they can be creative producers.

Almost everything that children do in school casts them in the role of lesson learners. Even when working on so called "research reports," the student nearly always perceives his or her purpose as that of "finding out about . . ." When teachers ask their students why they are working on a report, they often receive responses such as: *"I'm working on this report to find out about the eating habits of the gray squirrel; about the exports of Brazil; about the Battle of Gettysburg."*[3] There is nothing wrong with finding out about things—all student and adult inquirers do it. The big difference is that practicing professionals do it for a purpose beyond merely finding out about something for its own sake. (The possible exception may be trivia experts!) This purpose, which we might refer as a product purpose, is what Type III Enrichment is all about. Thus, the key to helping students feel like creative producers, rather than mere absorbers of knowledge, is to help them explore some of the questions that creative professionals raise about why they are investigating a particular topic or problem. In some cases it may be necessary for teachers to seek assistance from professional persons or resource materials, but by and large, their own present knowledge about the work of creative professionals will ordinarily enable them to ask more sophisticated types of questions.

Here is the key question in product focusing: "What do [ecologists, photographers, teachers, choreographers, short story writers, etc.] do with their creative products?" The answer to this question is almost always expressed in terms of a major concept— communication of results in appropriate form(s) with appropriate audience(s). Thus,

---

[3] Occasionally students in enrichment programs will respond to a why question by saying something like, "I'm developing my critical thinking skills." We suspect they have picked up a little of our jargon! (Did you ever hear a research scientist say he/she is looking up or collecting data to develop his/her critical thinking skills?) We are not against learning to develop these skills (Type II Enrichment), but such exercises are precisely what we do too much of in resource programs. In Type III Enrichment we want the youngster to apply his/her skills to a real-world situation. The purpose of Type III is different from the traditional "learning-about-something" purpose of most "research reports."

educators must ask students to think about the related questions: "How and with whom does the [ecologist, photographer, etc.] communicate?" Here are a few examples:

Ecology

Key Question: What do ecologists do with the results of their research?

Answer: They attempt to use the information to influence the general public and/or policy-making bodies regarding ways in which humans can preserve their environment and make better use of their natural resources.

Creative Writers, Puppeteers

Key Question: What do creative writers and puppeteers do with their stories, scripts and puppet shows?

Answer: They attempt to bring enjoyment into people's lives by evoking emotions (happiness, understanding of a social problem, humor, etc.) or making them better informed about a particular issue or topic.

The teacher's role in the above situations is threefold. First, they must help students do some brainstorming about potential outlets and audiences. Second, they must assist in the location of methodological resource materials such as a book on puppet making or presenting data in graphic or tabular forms. In this regard, the teacher is serving the student as a methodological resource person. The third role of the teacher is to open doors for communicating creative products with appropriate audiences. They must telephone the day care center and ask if the puppet show can be presented. They must call and perhaps meet with the manager of the shopping mall to ask if he or she will allow a display to be set up. They must arrange to transport students to the radio or television station. They must see to it that children are not discriminated against because they "missed" classes while pursuing a special activity. Such actions on the parts of teachers reflect their responsibility to be managerial resource persons rather than persons who continually disseminate knowledge, dispense materials, and orchestrate exercises. Unless teachers of advanced ability students are willing to assume these differential responsibilities there is little likelihood that special programs will ever be more than jazzed-up exercises.

Not All Ideas Are Type III's

A factor that should be kept in mind is that not every student interest or exploratory experience can or should be steered toward a Type III activity. This point is best illustrated by the following example.

A group of sixth grade students were exploring various career areas of their choice (Type I). The youngsters looked up information about educational requirements, salary range, working conditions, etc. and were in the process of preparing posters for display throughout the school.

A teacher chatted informally with three students. Charlie wanted to be a surgeon and Alice was interested in becoming a veterinarian. Although it was obvious that these two students could not become practicing professionals without several years of advanced training, Charlie responded favorably to a suggestion that he might learn more about dissection by working with a high school biology teacher. Alice was enthusiastic about a suggested possibility of serving a Saturday internship at a local animal hospital. These suggested follow-up activities are not bona fide Type III experiences, but they do reflect a concern for individual attention beyond the general career exploration exercise that all students were pursuing.

The third student in this group, however, presented a golden opportunity for Type III Enrichment. Ellen was interested in design and wanted to become an art teacher. When asked if she would like to develop some lessons and teach various aspects of design to small groups of second and third graders, she literally glowed with enthusiasm. A single question had opened the door to a possible Type III experience. With the appropriate methodological and managerial assistance, she could be "thinking, feeling and doing" like a practicing professional in a matter of weeks.

This example illustrates several points. First, not every area of interest can be converted into a Type III experience. Teachers can examine other types of advanced level follow-up activities by taking the time to explore possibilities and offer suggestions on an individual basis. Second, a Type III experience was identified for one student, and one out of three isn't bad! It may take several additional exploratory activities (or other experiences) before Charlie and Alice are launched into Type III involvements. The point is that teachers should not expect to achieve the goal of Type III Enrichment in every situation. Finally, all of the above was accomplished in approximately ten minutes by simply asking the right questions and caring about students as individuals.

There is one overriding goal to the development of learning opportunities based on the concept of Type III Enrichment. This goal is larger than the products students prepare or the methods they learn in pursuing their self-selected problems. The largest goal is that students begin to think, feel and act like creative producers. Our most potentially able young artists and scholars must develop the attitude that has reinforced the essence of creative people since the beginning of time: *I can do . . . I can be . . . I can create.*

Enrichment Clusters and Type III Experiences

Enrichment clusters provide yet another vehicle for action information in Type III investigations. As defined in Chapter 10, enrichment clusters (Renzulli, 1994) are non-graded groups of students who share common interests and come together during specially designed time blocks to pursue these interests. The *ultimate goal* of an enrichment cluster is to pursue a Type III investigation—to explore an interest using real-world methodology and deliver a product or service to an authentic audience. Certainly not all students who participate in enrichment clusters will want to become involved in a Type III investigation, and for these students, clusters will serve as valuable Type I or Type II experiences. Enrichment clusters are extremely fertile ground for encouraging and promoting interests that may develop into exciting Type III's. Since enrichment clusters are highly supportive of individual learning styles, this goal may be accomplished in a variety of ways. The primary difference between the initiation of Type III's we have been discussing thus far and those initiated through an enrichment cluster is that in enrichment clusters, the real-world problem is more often explored as a group process and there is a division of labor within the group. The group's common denominator is interest in the issue or topic, and while everyone in the group may not perform the same function, everyone may work toward a common product or service. For example, in a newspaper cluster, different students may explore specifics such as reporting, writing, cartooning, photojournalism, graphic design, or editing. The final group product may be a school newspaper, the focus of which reflects the interests and involvement of those who participate in the cluster. The background and implementation of enrichment clusters are discussed in depth in Chapter 10.

Examples of Type III Enrichment

For many years individuals starting SEM programs have asked us to provide them with examples of Type III investigations that could be shared with parents, teachers and students. We have found that one of the best ways to provide inservice about the SEM is by showing examples of each of the enrichment activities. Many enrichment specialists have told us that their Talent Pool students are unable to envision what a Type III project entails. Many parents have no idea how to help their children pursue a Type III investigation. In fact, many enrichment specialists using the SEM for the first time are unsure about what exactly is involved in a Type III investigation. We have included a representative sample of Type III investigations in this chapter. By explaining to students how these Type III ideas occurred and by sharing excellent examples of other student products, they may become inspired to escalate the quality of their own work. As students complete their independent investigations, it might be wise to photograph, copy, or videotape exemplary products for use with students and future program orientations.

The Type III examples included in this chapter reflect different grade levels, interests and final products. Portions of various Type III products (sample pages, pamphlets, time lines) are included so that they may be reproduced, handed out to students, or made into transparencies for parents, classroom teachers and students (see Figures 74-76). Many students get ideas for their own Type III investigations from the work of other students. In fact, many ideas for Type III's can be replicated. For example, an original historical walking tour was completed in Torrington, Connecticut. This tour was shared with many enrichment specialists and has been replicated in a wide variety of school districts.

Implementing Type III Enrichment

The Management Plan for Individual and Small Group Investigations

The *Management Plan for Individual and Small Group Investigations* is an educational "device" whose format is not very different from the procedures or "ways of thinking"

The Louisa May Alcott Cookbook

by Gretchen Anderson, Grade 5
Haynes School, Sudbury, Massachusetts

Description of Type III
Gretchen spent a year and a half working on a cookbook that combined vignettes of scenes from Little Women and Little Men with many authentic 19th century recipes for making the foods described in the novels. Cooking was Gretchen's hobby and she became fascinated with the foods mentioned in the novels and learned how to recreate them. Because Gretchen believed that other youngsters would also be interested in these foods, she sent her book to Little Brown Company. *The Louisa May Alcott Cookbook* was accepted and became the first book contracted by them with a child author.

Teacher's Role and Comments
Gretchen's teacher, Elizabeth D. Beloff, reported that Gretchen's enthusiasm for reading the books and researching the recipes could not sustain her through the writing of each scene and the incredible attention to detail necessary in creating the recipes.

Therefore, Ms. Beloff needed to complete the following steps to help Gretchen complete her project.

1. Vary the assignments (e.g., text writing/research/recipe writing).
2. Assign tasks that could be completed in one or two sessions.
3. Break large segments into small parts.
4. Use a system to record accomplishments (e.g., weekly or daily check sheet).

Gretchen's teacher also indicated that Gretchen was always able to envision the book, but had a problem getting organized. She was able to help her by suggesting ways of organizing information. Particularly useful was a file box to keep recipes and notecards that recorded steps to be taken.

Figure 74. Type III enrichment sample—Louisa May Alcott cookbook.

Christmas

It looked like a merry Christmas after all. Jo awoke on this special morning to find a lovely crimson book of the story of Christmas. But, when the girls went downstairs, their dear Marmee had gone. Hannah, the cook, informed them that she had gone to help a poor family. When Marmee returned, the Marches celebrated by giving the poor family their breakfasts.

> When the Marches arrived at the poor family's house
> how the big eyes stared and blue lips smiled.
>   'Ach, mein Gott! It is good angels come to us!'
> said the poor woman, crying for joy.
>   'Funny angels in hoods and mittens,'
> said Jo, and set them all laughing.
> > *Little Women, p. 26*

Anyone would be pleased to be served this lovely breakfast, even if it weren't Christmas.

BUCKWHEAT CAKES   Difficulty = ★★

Ingredients:
   1/3 cup of fine bread crumbs
   2 cups of very hot milk (scalded)
   1/2 tsp. of salt
   I tablespoon of molasses
   1/4 yeast cake
   1/2 cup of lukewarm water
Buckwheat flour

Materials:
   Measuring cup
   Measuring spoons
   Griddle or frying pan
   Ladle
   Spatula

Method:
   1. Pour the milk over the bread crumbs.
   2. Let them soak for thirty minutes.

Figure 74. Type III enrichment sample—Louisa May Alcott cookbook (continued).

An Illustrated History of Albertville, Alabama

by Beth Gurrard, Ashley Williams, Jana Rucks, and many others
Alabama Avenue Middle School, Albertville, Alabama

Description of Type III

This book originally began as an independent study project for a third grader. Because of the interest it generated, this study soon became a class project. After receiving a grant from the National Endowment for the Humanities, it later involved 120 students from the town. The project required three years to complete and the resource teacher, Jane Newman, found that each year, more students became interested in becoming involved. Each student or group of students selected a topic of interest for small group investigation and research. The senior high students served as editors and completed the photography and art work. Several area residents served as mentors including an amateur historian who had pursued individual research for fifteen years and a local resident who was a history professor and an associate director of a center for the study of southern history and culture.

Jane Newman, the project teacher, also had a teacher at each of the five schools in Albertville who coordinated the research completed by students. Jane found that because the project was so large, students had to be reminded often of the benefits of their contribution. She and the other project teachers also learned to divide the project into smaller segments so that students could experience some closure periodically.

The printed copies of the book were distributed to the Albertville Historical Society, newcomers to the community by the Chamber of Commerce, interested citizens of the Albertville area, and all third and fourth grade classes in Albertville for use in conjunction with their Social Studies book.

Figure 75. Type III enrichment sample—Illustrated history of Albertville, Alabama.

LOCATION

Albertville is located in the northeastern part of Alabama. It is the largest city in Marshall County and is called "the heart of Sand Mountain."

Sand Mountain is a foothill of the Appalachians. The Sand Mountain plateau covers an area about 25 miles wide by 75 miles long.

GENERAL HISTORY

Imagine you were walking through Albertville about 200 years ago. Instead of paved sidewalks, you would use Indian trails. Instead of brick buildings, you would see tall hickory, oak, and poplar trees.

You might stop to drink water from a cool stream where ferns and moss grow along the creek banks. You might also see more wild strawberries growing than you could count!

Black bears, cougars, deer, and many other kinds of wild animals would be roaming about. The Albertville area was also home to the Cherokees at this time. You may have been invited to spend a night at an Indian Village.

As a matter of fact, that's just what happened to Davy Crockett when he crossed Sand Mountain in 1812.

1

CONTENTS

ix

Figure 75. Type III enrichment sample—Illustrated history of Albertville, Alabama (continued).

$200,000 Bike Path System

by Sean Sweeney, Brenda Roos, Kim VanDell, Brian Mohr, Gary Gibb, Kevin Hatch,
Allison Duchow, Jill Havens, Chris Soberg (Grades 8 and 9)
Fowler Junior High School, Tigard, Oregon

Description of Type III
Because many of the city streets of Tigard, Oregon were barely wide enough for two cars to pass, this group of students worked with their teachers Bill Dolbeer and Jay Leet, to get a ballot measure passed that would provide bike paths for the city. The following chronology tells the story.

BIKE PATH PROJECT—TIME LINE, OCT. 1980-JULY 1981
October 1980
—Arrival at project idea.
—Visits from Raeldon Barker, City Administrator in Tigard and Frank Curry, Tigard Public Works Director.
—Wrote to Eugene, Oregon for their master plan—studied.
—Wrote to Beaverton, Oregon for their master plan—studied.
—Visit from Washington County Bikeway Planner.
—Visit from member of Tigard Park Board.

November 1980
—Discovered Tigard's 1974 "Comprehensive Plan for Bicycle/Pedestrian Pathways."
—One part of group focused in on Tiedeman Road, an extremely dangerous street adjoining our school.
—The other part decided to revise Tigard's 1974 plan and check community opinion about bike path needs.

December 1980
—Development of community survey.
—Measuring and photographing of Tiedeman Road.
—Testing and revising of survey.
—Distribution of surveys (about 2500).

January 1981
—Tallying and analysis of surveys.
—Preparation of presentation for Tigard Park Board.
—Presentation of findings to Tigard Park Board.

February 1981
—Development of a three-phase plan for bike paths.
—First presentation to Tigard City Council (Feb. 17).
—Presentation to Tigard Rotary.

Figure 76. Type III enrichment sample—$200,000 bike path system.

March 1981
—Revision of phased plan.
—Presentations to City Council.
—Presentation to Tigard Lions Club.
—Discussion of plan with individual City Council members.

April 1981
—City Council agrees to place $200,000 serial level on May 19th ballot.
—Writing of measure and filing with County Elections Department (we thought!).
—Presentations to parent groups at Fowler, Charles F. Tigard Elementary and Tigard High School.
—Preparation of flyer.

May 1981
—Bike-A-Rama at Fowler (May 16th) with prize giveaway and five mile ride on proposed streets.
—Mapping, producing and posting of lawn signs around Tigard.
—Printing and door-to-door distribution of flyer (about 6,000).
—May 19th—ELECTION DAY—OUR MEASURE IS NOT ON THE BALLOT!
—The county conducts an investigation. Findings—No one is at fault, all should share blame for lack of communication.
—The state conducts an investigation. Their findings to come out in June.
—In an emergency session May 22nd, Tigard City Council approves placing our measure on the ballot June 30th.
—We file the measure again in Hillsboro, May 26th.
—Channel 2 News does a story on our project.
—Down come the lawn signs.

June 1981
—The Secretary of State's report comes out, placing blame on the Washington County Elections Dept. (June 4th).
—Letter writing campaign to all the radio and TV stations in Portland to have public service announcements made.
—Redesigning of flyer.
—Printing, stuffing, mailing of new flyer (about 6,000).
—County elections responsibility shifted to county administrator (June 9th).
—Lawn signs repainted and up again.
—UH-OH! The state says our re-filed ballot measure may be invalid because of the ballot's wording (June 18th).
—At another emergency City Council meeting (June 19th), one sentence is added to our measure to satisfy state requirements.
—The County Election Coordinator is suspended for two weeks without pay.
—Channel 8 TV News (John) does a feature on our project.
—JUNE 30TH—ELECTION DAY. OUR MEASURE IS ON THE BALLOT.

July 1981
—Voter turnout is very light, but our measure passes by more than a 2/3 margin.
—Channel 8 TV does a follow-up story on our project.
—Down come the lawn signs. Summer vacation begins

Figure 76. Type III enrichment sample—$200,000 bike path system (continued).

Type III Enrichment: Individual and Small Group Investigations

TIGARD BIKEPATH PEDESTRIAN WALKWAY PLAN

THE LEVY

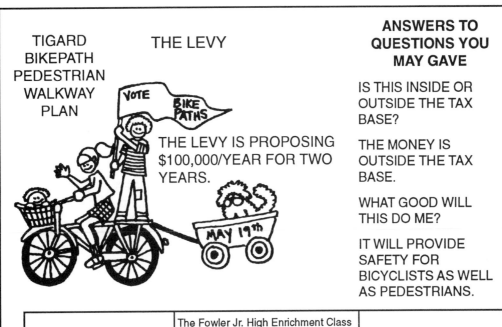

THE LEVY IS PROPOSING $100,000/YEAR FOR TWO YEARS.

ANSWERS TO QUESTIONS YOU MAY GAVE

IS THIS INSIDE OR OUTSIDE THE TAX BASE?

THE MONEY IS OUTSIDE THE TAX BASE.

WHAT GOOD WILL THIS DO ME?

IT WILL PROVIDE SAFETY FOR BICYCLISTS AS WELL AS PEDESTRIANS.

WHAT WILL THIS COST ME?

IT ALL DEPENDS ON HOW MUCH THE ASSESSED VALUE OF YOUR HOME IS. THE PRICE WILL BE 18¢/$1000 OF ASSESSED VALUATION. FOR A $140,000 HOME IT WILL COST $25.20 PER YEAR. THAT MEANS ABOUT THE PRICE OF A CANDY BAR, 50¢, PER WEEK.

The Fowler Jr. High Enrichment Class has been working on a plan to develop a bike path system that will benefit the people of Tigard.

Members of the class are 9th graders
Sean Sweeney
Brenda Roos
Kim VanDell
Brian Mohr
Gary Gibb
Kevin Hatch

and 8th graders
Allison Duchow
Jill Havens
Chris Soberg

Class instructors are Bill Dolbeer and Jay Leet.

We have proposed Phase I of a Bike Path Plan with the assistance of Public Works Director, Frank Currie. This plan will include streets most traveled by both pedestrians and bicyclists.

Our proposal was approved by the City Council and we wrote the ballot with the help of City Administrator Ray Barker and City Recorder Doris Hartig. We have watched our ideas grow to actualities and have learned much about city government in the process.

We urge each of you to vote May 19!

TIGARD BIKEPATH PEDESTRIAN WALKWAY PLAN

Figure 76. Type III enrichment sample—$200,000 bike path system (continued).

that are followed by the first-hand inquirer. The adult inquirer intuitively follows certain activities described on the *Management Plan.* For example, a sociologist working on an attitude survey may not actually list his or her intended audiences. However, the writer usually has a fairly good idea of the journals to which his or her results may be submitted and of the professional societies or organizations where such a research paper might be presented.

Information from the *Total Talent Portfolio* (discussed in Chapter 5) and the third column of the *Compactor* (discussed in Chapter 6) should always be the starting point for completing the *Management Plan.* After the student has identified a general area in which he or she would like to do advanced level work and has used appropriate problem focusing techniques (such as the one for historians described by Gottschalk), the student can begin to fill in the material requested in the box entitled "Specific Area of Study." A great deal of careful thought should be given to completing this section because all subsequent activities will reflect the degree of clarity with which the problem is focused and stated. The teacher and student(s) should attempt to answer the three questions listed by using a frame of reference that characterizes the actual thinking of a real investigator who is pursuing a particular problem in his or her field. A community resource person in that field or a methodology book may help.

At this point it may be helpful to examine a sample *Management Plan* (see Figure 77). We note in the example that the "Specific Areas of Study" has been completed by raising explicit questions and listing particular objectives. The model for completing this section should closely approximate the ways in which a researcher states a hypothesis or lists specific research questions. Although the form that this section will take may vary (e.g., declarative statements, questions, and/or lists of objectives), it is important to keep in mind that first-hand inquirers pursue a problem with more functional goals in mind than merely finding out the facts about a person, place or thing. In other words, the real inquirer investigates a topic in order to do something with the information acquired. It is an objective of almost all types of inquiry and artistic endeavor to communicate results gained to the appropriate audiences, and this general goal of investigative activity should always be kept in mind as one completes the "Specific Area of Study."

The "Intended Audiences" and "Intended Products and Outlets" are further designed to help "steer" the student toward thinking about the final form that his or her investigation will take and about the audiences potentially concerned with the results. These are based on the role and purpose of the first-hand inquirer discussed above.

The audiences and outlets are perhaps the key to differentiating between the orientation of normal student reportage and that of first-hand inquiry. It is neither necessary nor practical for teachers to have the names of all possible audiences and outlets at their fingertips. However, persons programming for advanced ability students ought to be capable of finding out about the existence of audience and outlets. Are there any historical societies or conservation groups in the community? Do they publish newsletters or have regularly scheduled meetings? Would they be receptive to including a student's

MANAGEMENT PLAN FOR INDIVIDUAL AND SMALL GROUP INVESTIGATIONS
(Actual Size: 11" x 17")

Prepared by: Joseph S. Renzulli
Linda H. Smith

NAME	Annemarie Maccalous	GRADE	Five
TEACHER	Mrs. Cellerino/Mrs. Freminos	SCHOOL	Harwinton

	Beginning Date	Estimated Ending Date
	Nov. 1	April 30
Progress Reports Due on Following Dates	Dec. 20 Feb. 1 March 3

GENERAL AREA(S) OF STUDY (Check all that apply)

√ Language Arts/Humanities   — Science   __ Personal and Social Development
√ Social Studies   √ Music   √ Other (Specify) Genealogy
— Mathematics   √ Art   √ Other (Specify) Drama

INTENDED AUDIENCES Which individuals or groups would be most interested in the findings? List the organized groups (clubs, societies, teams) at the local, regional, state, and national levels. What are the names and addresses of contact persons in these groups? When and where do they meet?

1. Channel 5 (T.V.)
2. TAG FAIR
3. Other Classes
4. School Visitors
5. TAG Room

INTENDED PRODUCT(S) AND OUTLETS What form(s) will the final product take? How, when, and where will you communicate the results of your investigation to an appropriate audience(s)? What outlet vehicle (journals, conferences, art shows, etc.) are typically used by professionals in this field?

1. Videotape entitled "A Living Genealogy."
2. Storyboard.
3. Scrapbook.

GETTING STARTED What are the first steps you should take to begin this investigation? What types of information or data will be needed to solve the problem? How can it be gathered, classified, and presented? If you plan to use already categorized information or data, where is it located and how can you obtain what you need?

1. Write questions for interviews with my grandparents and/or other people.
2. Begin writing script for my play.
3. Do research in the city library—use microfilm and old newspapers.

SPECIFY AREA OF STUDY Write a brief description of the problem that you plan to investigate. What are the objectives of your investigation? What do you hope to find out?

I intend to study my ancestry and collect pictures and other information for my videotape and scrapbook. I plan to write, direct, and produce a play entitled "A Living Genealogy." In this play I will portray all the different generations from myself to my great-grandparents.

METHODOLOGICAL RESOURCES AND ACTIVITIES List the names & addresses of persons who might provide assistance in attacking this problem. List the how-to-do-it books that are available in this area of study. List other resources (films, collections, exhibits, etc.) and special equipment (e.g., camera, tape recorder, questionnaire, etc.). Keep continuous record of all activities that are part of this investigation.

Books
Backyard History Book
    Weitzman, David
    Boston: Little, Brown & Co.
Sutor Saga
Beechers Saints or Sinners
Beecher Genealogy

Community Resources
Miss Calhoun, Torry
        Historical Society
Mr. Bentle, Raymond
        Harwinton Historical
        Society
Grandparents
Mother

A complete description of the model utilizing this form can be found in: *The Enrichment Triad Model: A Guide For Developing Defensible Programs For The Gifted And Talented.*
Creative Learning Press, Inc., P.O. Box 320, Mansfield Center, CT 06250.

Figure 77. Sample management plan for individual and small group investigations.

article in their newsletter or perhaps having a student present the results of his or her research at one of their meetings? Teachers may not know the answers to these questions, but the really crucial issue is whether or not they know how to take the necessary steps for finding out the answers. This is one of the most important ways that teachers can be a true resource to advanced ability students as they pursue Type III activities.

The sections "Getting Started" and "Methodological Resources and Activities" on the *Management Plan* are intended to provide a running account of the procedures and resources that are to be used throughout the duration of an investigative activity. Both of these sections should be completed cooperatively by the teacher and student and modifications should be made as new activities are followed through and as a greater variety of resources are brought to the student's attention. A "mushrooming effect" often takes place as teachers become more familiar with the resources in a given area of study and as the greater variety of resources enable them to advance the level of sophistication that is brought to bear upon a particular problem.

The completion of the "Getting Started" and "Methodological Resources" will often be a function of the teacher's familiarity with appropriate resource guides in given areas of study. For example, if a student is studying the attitudes of other students about an issue such as dress code regulations, an interviewer's manual and/or guidebook for constructing attitude questionnaires will be a key resource. In many cases these types of resources provide the step-by-step procedures that will assist students in completing these sections of their *Management Plan*.

In certain respects, "Getting Started" and "Methodological Resources" should parallel one another. "Getting Started" should list the early steps necessary for beginning an investigation and the types of information that will be needed to pursue the study, at least in the initial stages. Since early success is an important factor for continued motivation to complete the study, teachers should work very closely with students in helping them to complete this box. The information in the box can serve as a checklist for determining whether the student is heading in the right direction and setting target dates for progress reports. In certain instances, a student may want to layout the entire plan under "Getting Started" and in other cases the plan may begin here and continue under "Methodological Resources and Activities." In view of the wide variety of topics that students may choose to pursue and the many variations in methodology that characterize various areas of study, it is difficult to suggest a rigid prescription for completing these two sections of the *Management Plan*. In certain instances students may wish to design their studies through the use of a flow chart and record their activities in a log or notebook. If additional space is needed, the reverse side of the *Management Plan* or additional pages can be used.

Specification Form for Methodological Resource Books

The Specification Form for Methodological Resource Books (see Figure 78) could be the single most important device for introducing high levels of quality into students' Type III Enrichment activities. This form is designed to help record and analyze methodological resource books that contain information about how investigators go about carrying out authentic research activities within the various fields of knowledge.

Specification Form for Methodological Resource Books

General Field of Study _____

Title _____

Author _____ Publication Date _____

Publishers Address _____

_____

Cost_____ Location _____

Grade Level _____

1. Information About the Structure of the Field: Pages: Comments:	____ Yes	____ No	
2. Procedures for Problem Finding and Focusing: Pages: Comments:	____ Yes	____ No	
3. Description of Specific Methodological Skills: Pages: Comments:	____ Yes	____ No	
4. Suggestions for Format/Communication of Products:	____ Yes	____ No	
Pages: Comments:			
5. Suggestions for Studies/Investigations That Students Can Pursue: Pages: Comments:	____ Yes	____ No	

Figure 78. Specification form for methodological resource books.

It is these kinds of resource books that can help a student become a first-hand investigator through the use of appropriate methodology.

One of the goals of a program with Type III Enrichment should be to develop a diversified library of methodological resource books. In addition to providing a ready-made resource library for students who might develop interests in particular areas, these methodological resource books can also serve as the basis for Type II training or the facilitation of an enrichment cluster. The Specification Form for Methodological Resource Books is a guide that will help document, categorize and circulate information to staff members about the availability and nature of methodological resource books. The information at the top of the form provides basic bibliographic data and location of each book. The sections underneath provide five types of information about the book.

1. *Information About the Structure of the Field*
   Page references and information recorded in this box should provide students and teachers with basic information about the field of study, how a field of study is organized, and some of the goals and activities of persons who pursue this particular area of knowledge. Although information about the structure of the field is not the most important function of methodological resource books, one of our larger goals is to help students gain an appreciation for the broader world of knowledge and to view their own investigative activities within the larger perspective of a given field and the interrelationships among fields on the broader spectrum of knowledge.

2. *Procedures for Problem Finding and Focusing*
   The information in the procedural sections of methodological resource books is especially important for helping students identify potential areas of investigative activity and focus their problems in a more professional manner than is typically the case with persons who are "beginners" in real-world research activities and creative endeavors.

3. *Description of Specific Methodological Skills*
   This type of information represents the most important contribution that methodological resource books can make to students who are pursuing Type III investigations. It is the degree of specificity with which these skills are described that causes a book to be classified as a methodological resource guide. Information typically found in these sections consists of identifying variables, data sources, tools, equipment, instruments, and the step-by-step procedures for carrying out a study in a particular field of knowledge. Field guides and laboratory manuals are especially useful sources of methodological information because of their focus on specific procedures for gathering and preserving specimens or other types of data, recording observations, classifying information, and analyzing various types of data.

4. *Suggestions for Format/Communication of Products*
   Many methodological resource books, and especially those that are intended for beginners within various fields, contain examples and suggestions about how students might prepare their final products. Sample scientific articles, examples of formats that are used for various types of literary work, and outlines for research reports can often be found in methodological resource guides.

5. *Suggestions for Studies/Investigations That Students Can Pursue*
   Many of the methodological resource books that are intended for beginners frequently include specific suggestions for projects or investigative activity that can be carried out by young people. In many cases, the examples used to describe the application of various methodological techniques will serve as good suggestions for possible student activities.

It is a rare book indeed that will include information about all of the five categories described above. However, a combination of books coupled with advice by a specialist in that field will help ensure necessary coverage of a particular field. Since categories 2 and 3 are most important to the accomplishment of objectives for Type III Enrichment, teachers will want to concentrate their efforts on locating books that include information related to problem finding and focusing and descriptions of specific methodological skills within a given field of inquiry.

Although libraries should serve as major sources for locating methodological resource books, valuable suggestions can be obtained by experts in particular fields (university professors, graduate students, professional persons), subject area teachers who may have advanced knowledge about a particular field, and amateur groups or hobby clubs that have concentrated on action-oriented activities related to their particular areas of interest. Publishers catalogs, Books in Print, and reference computer databases in college and university libraries are also valuable sources of information about methodological resource books in a wide variety of fields.

As new acquisitions are obtained, a Specification Form should be completed and added to a loose-leaf "directory" for methodological resource books. New acquisitions can also be advertised through a program newsletter, staff meetings, and inservice training events. Whenever possible, a brief orientation or perhaps a detailed "walk through" of the books should be provided. These books will have limited value if they are not constantly brought to the attention of staff members and if their use is not encouraged at every opportunity.

Completing the Type III Mentor Matrix

The purpose of the Type III Mentor Matrix is to help recruit and categorize persons who will serve as mentors for individual students (or small groups) who decide to pursue a Type III study or even enrichment clusters. Although the broad areas have been indicated in Figure 79, teachers should feel free to enter whatever topics they would like in each column. At the secondary level teachers may wish to prepare an individual Matrix for each major subject matter area and enter subtopics within any given area in the various columns of the Matrix.

There are several sources of input for recruiting possible mentors for the Matrix. The first is responses to an adult interest survey, which should be completed by all staff members early in the school year. Response from this survey will highlight possible mentors within the school for specific topics. A second source of input is information that can be obtained through personal, informal contact with staff. Individual discussions are an excellent way to determine areas of specialized knowledge and help staff gain an

Type III Mentor Matrix

Grade	Language Arts	Math	Science	Social Studies	Arts	Other (specify)
K-3						
4-6						
7-9						
10-12						

Figure 79. Type III mentor matrix.

appreciation for the kinds of excitement that can result from this type of one-on-one interaction with individuals and small groups. A third source of mentors is parents. Teachers can send an informal survey home at the beginning of the year or request help with enrichment clusters (see Chapter 10). A final source of mentors is the community. Suggestions for community mentors can come from staff, parents, local agencies, or universities. A good network of community contacts and volunteers will take several years to build.

There are five major considerations that should be taken into account as teachers begin to complete the Type III Mentor Matrix:

1. Finding Time

A decision must be made regarding whether or not a given teacher will serve as a mentor to students within his or her classroom only or if mentorship services will be extended to students from other classrooms. The interests and expertise of any given teacher will obviously be extended to a larger target population if he or she is willing to meet students from other classrooms.

Certain organizational problems must be overcome and these problems relate mainly to identifying specified periods of time when students can meet with their mentors. If a school schedule has a built-in activity period and/or enrichment cluster period, certain portions of these or any other time blocks that are not devoted to regular instruction can be convenient for mentorship activities. Administrative support and cooperation are essential in helping to arrange schedules and identifying given time periods during which mentorship activities can take place. Each teacher who agrees to serve as a mentor should prepare a schedule indicating available time periods for individual meetings with students, and these times should be summarized on a master schedule to be distributed to other teachers and Talent Pool students. "Time" is an essential ingredient in the effective implementation of this approach. Therefore, it is imperative that teachers and administrators work cooperatively to develop a schedule that is both convenient and easily accessible.

2. Age/Grade Considerations

Many teachers get "locked-in" to certain age/grade levels and this arrangement frequently results in anxiety and reluctance to work with different ages. Many secondary teachers, for example, have expressed concerns about whether or not they would know how to deal with younger students. In our field test experiences, many teachers overcame their initial anxiety and developed highly successful mentorship relations with students. The same is true for primary and elementary level teachers who have worked with older students. Teachers should be encouraged to work with different ages.

3. Specificity of Topics

A major purpose of the Type III Mentor Matrix is to identify at least one person in each selected area who will assume mentorship responsibilities. Additional refinement can also be incorporated into this approach by asking teachers to indicate special topics within subject areas where they would prefer to give individual or small group assistance to students.

4. Expanding the Mentor Matrix Through Parent and Community Involvement

The Type III Mentor Matrix concept is primarily based on the involvement of teacher volunteers, but it is very important to extend this opportunity to parents and the community as well. This not only expands the number and diversity of available mentors and topics, but it also helps to build valuable community and parental ownership of and support for the enrichment program. In addition, parent and community involvement can generate motivation in students through the exposure to authentic methodologies of practicing professionals typically not available to classroom teachers.

5. Completion of the Matrix and the Management of Action Information Messages

A frequently raised question about the Type III Mentor Matrix is who should be responsible for preparing this form. In school districts that do not have enrichment specialists and/or program coordinators, the Enrichment Team in each building should be responsible for developing the Matrix and serving as a "clearinghouse" in directing the flow of *Action Information Messages* that might result in mentorship assignments. A conveniently located mailbox and a regular procedure for reviewing *Action Information Messages* will help to direct students to appropriate teachers. A more informal but effective approach is simply to have individual students (or their teachers) contact prospective mentors. When this approach is used, educators should guard against over-burdening any teacher who might be serving in a highly popular area or topic.

Regardless of which approach is used to direct the flow of *Action Information Messages*, it is important for all contacts and mentorship commitments to be recorded on the evaluation form provided for this aspect of a program. This information will be very useful in providing an overall analysis of the effectiveness of the approach. It can also provide a very powerful rationale for encouraging administrators to expand their support for staff involvement and perhaps even arranging for varying amounts of release time for those persons who provide extensive mentorship service. Documentation of all services will help administrators appreciate both the cooperative nature of faculty involvement in the special program and the ways in which integration is taking place between the special program and the faculty at large.

Suggestions for Conducting a Type III Fair

An excellent way to share the work of students who have completed (or are in the process of completing) a Type III investigation is the organization of a Type III Fair. The primary purpose for organizing a fair is not to provide an audience for students' findings, but to 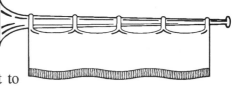 provide students from other schools (who may or may not be involved in the enrichment program) an opportunity to see and learn from the work of students who have completed Type III investigations. A real audience for a Type III investigation consists of the logical outlet for the type of work the student, as a first-hand inquirer, has produced.

Another major purpose for the organization of a Type III Fair is the sharing of excellent work with parents, community members, and other staff, including administrators, classroom teachers, specialists, and aides. The Type III Fair provides an opportunity for students who have worked for a long period of time to explain their work to interested observers. We consider the display of excellent work a way to cement the support of these decision makers for the continuation and expansion of the enrichment program.

We have seen different ways and methods for organizing a Type III Fair. Figure 80 contains a checklist that provides tips for preparing a successful Type III Fair. In some districts, each elementary or secondary school has its own Type III Fair. In one elementary SEM program in Connecticut, approximately 50 students are included in the Talent Pool each year. Generally, 40 to 50 percent of these students complete a Type III investigation each year. At the Type III Fair, each student who has completed his or her work spends approximately five minutes presenting the various stages of his/her work, displaying the final product and discussing the audience and benefits of the project. However, it would not be feasible for a very large number of Talent Pool students to make this type of presentation. One large school system that has implemented the SEM from grades one through twelve holds an annual Type III Fair at which 300 Type III products are displayed each year. The cafeteria of an elementary school is used to display written products and the library/media center is used to display products that require electrical outlets (slide shows, videotapes, filmstrips, computer programs, etc.). The gymnasium is used throughout the evening for performances that are written and produced by children as Type III investigations in the arts.

Students should be notified of the date of the Type III Fair early in the school year so they may set aside this evening. A special notification serves as a "gentle enforcer" to encourage students to work towards the completion of their products. Students should keep a file of their notes and rough drafts and logs of their activities. If students use any type of contract or *Management Plan*, those forms should also be kept intact for the evening of the Type III Fair.

Parents should be notified about this special event through newsletters and progress reports that are sent home regularly by the enrichment specialist. Personal invitations can also be sent to parents, as well as classroom teachers, principals, the superintendent of schools, and board of education members. Parents of students who have Type III products on display can be asked to provide refreshments.

The Type III Fair can be held at any time, but experience has shown that because of the high percentage of families in which both parents work, it is advisable to schedule some time for parents to view students' work in the evening as well as the afternoon. One large district in Connecticut reserves the afternoon (3:30-4:30 PM) and the evening (7:00-9:00 PM).

Students' Type III investigations are usually displayed on tables in a cafeteria or media center in attractive and professional ways. As was stated earlier, the major audience for the Type III investigation is usually not those who attend the fair. However, students are encouraged to provide care and attention to detail in the work that is displayed for parents and other guests. Students are asked to stand near their Type III product for either the first or second hour of the evening. This provides an opportunity for visitors to question students on their research inquiry, data gathering techniques, or other procedures. Many classroom teachers who do not have students in the Talent Pool but attend the Type III Fair are favorably impressed by the task commitment of a student

Checklist for Preparing Type III Fairs

Early in the year:

✓ *Establish the date.* Although the Type III Fair will usually occur in May or June, early planning will help avoid conflicts with other school and community events and help ensure attendance by teachers, board of education members, city officials, etc. Review the school system's master calendar and obtain approval from the superintendent.

✓ *Make arrangements for a building and clear the date with the building principal.* Determine the hours of the program and when students in the building will have an opportunity to visit the fair.

✓ Provide an orientation session for the students. This session will help students set a target date for their projects. Viewing a video and pictures of previous Type III Fairs will help students get a sense of the event and generate some creative ways to display their own materials.

Two to three months prior:

✓ *Make announcements and solicit help.* Send an initial "Save the Date" message home and post an announcement in your program newsletter. At this point, request volunteers for assistance with set up, refreshments, transport of students from various schools, scavenging of equipment, videotaping and pictures, program computer work, name tags, certificates, and clean up. A committee can be formed from parent responses.

Two to three weeks prior:

✓ *Develop a program with input from principals involved.* A brief written program should be provided for each visitor to the Type III Fair and contain a general statement about the purposes of Type III Enrichment, product display categories (scientific, literary, artistic, etc.), and times and locations of any special events (such as a dramatic presentation, parent participation activity, media presentation, etc.).

✓ *Meet with committee/parent volunteers.* Review the program and individual tasks with volunteers, locate any additional needed volunteers, and answer questions. Refreshments, name tags, and student certificates should all be underway.

✓ *Invite local officials.* Individual letters of invitation should be sent to the superintendent, principals, central office administrators, teachers, and all elected town officials. They may be written by students on school stationery, prepared as a formal announcement, or designed by students as a flyer. Educators may also choose to invite State Representatives, U.S. Representatives, and Senators if they reside locally.

Figure 80. Checklist for preparing type III fairs.

Checklist for Preparing Type III Fairs

✓ *Invite the media.* An invitation can be sent to all local newspapers, television and radio stations. It should include a brief description of the fair and the kinds of materials that will be on display. Follow-up calls or direct contact by students will help attract attention and ensure attendance.

✓ *Make final announcements.* Send announcements home to parents and alert the community through local bulletin boards, community newsletters, newspapers, and radio stations.

✓ *List required equipment.* A checklist should be prepared of necessary equipment, such as projectors, computers, tape recorders, extension cords, three-prong adapters, etc. A committee volunteer should be responsible for locating materials the day of the fair, checking function, and returning materials after the fair. All equipment should be labeled to ensure proper return.

✓ *Rehearse with students.* All students who are making presentations at the fair should have the opportunity to rehearse with other students. Appropriate dress, conduct and procedures should be reviewed.

✓ *Review videotape and photograph procedures with volunteers.* One or two persons (either students or adults) with good photography skills should be responsible for documenting the Type III Fair. Photos of individual displays should be taken before the fair begins to get a clear shot of the display, as well as during the fair to record the excitement of the moment. A special effort should also be made to photograph public officials, board of education members, parents, and other visitors. These photographs are valuable for subsequent year orientation sessions, as data for summary evaluations, or for a celebration bulletin board in the school.

Follow-up:

✓ *Thank all volunteers involved with the fair.* Individual "thank you" letters should be sent to anyone involved in planning or carrying out the fair, including parents, teachers, principals, and media people who covered the event. These letters can come from the program director or superintendent, as well as students.

✓ *Develop a file for subsequent years.* Keep track of the schedule, time line, volunteers, problems, and needed changes. Assess the fair and keep notes for improvements.

Figure 80. Checklist for preparing type III fairs (continued).

who can share five or six rough drafts of his or her work in ever escalating stages of quality.

For districts who have an "Arts" component to their SEM program, the Type III Fair can provide a beautiful integration of the academic and arts programs. One district sponsored a foreign folk dancing festival in the gymnasium by students who had been involved in dance throughout the year. Parents of students involved in both the academic and arts program wandered in throughout the evening, and at one point, 200 people were dancing around the gymnasium! As one district has modeled for us, works of art can be displayed in hallways and alongside academic products and music composed by musically talented students can be played throughout the evening.

Whenever possible, it is a good idea to use the Type III Fair as an occasion for a local "media event." Invitations to newspaper reporters and local television stations will help to stimulate community awareness about the program, as well as an opportunity for recognition of the hard work that has been carried out by students. The nature of Type III Enrichment provides teachers with numerous highly visible products of youngsters' ability, task commitment and creativity. It is these products that can be most effectively used to gain support for the human and financial resources devoted to special enrichment programs. We have found time and time again, that the very best form of "advocacy" is the program itself.

Establishing a "Research Foundation"

One of the ways that teachers can help students develop the attitude of a practicing professional is to establish a "Research Foundation" that will serve as a source of funding for projects that may require some financial support. This easy-to-implement procedure is modeled after the kinds of activities ordinarily pursued by real-life researchers in the adult world. In addition to serving an important motivational function, the Research Foundation is also designed to help students gain skills in proposal writing, budgeting and clarifying the specific objectives of projects that are undertaken in the Type III dimension of a program.

Procedures for Setting Up a Research Foundation

Guidelines should be drawn up specifying the maximum amount of money that can be sought for a funded project, information for the project proposal, a budget, and a budget justification. The maximum amount of funds will, of course, vary from district to district and year to year, depending upon the total amount of money available and the categories for which monies may be requested. Funds should be restricted to materials, equipment, and services ordinarily not available through regular school procedures. Financial support is usually awarded for books and materials that cannot be easily obtained through libraries or regular school supply channels, such as computer tapes, software, communication needs (photocopying, telephone expenses and postage), and other types of supplies such as film, film processing services, art supplies, scripts, etc. Guidelines should specify exactly what types of materials can be purchased through the use of Research Foundation funds and students should be encouraged to do some "comparison shopping" and "cost projecting" as they prepare their proposal and budget.

A sample application for a Research Foundation proposal is presented in Figure 81. Although most of the information requested is self-explanatory, teachers may want to devote a lesson or two to reviewing the procedures for applying to the Research Foundation. They can also review one or more sample proposals to highlight information that is ordinarily required for successful funding.

Sources of Funds for the Research Foundation

Many programs that use the SEM ordinarily set aside a certain amount of money each year for use by students involved in Type III Enrichment. The acceptance of the objectives for Type III Enrichment and approval of a Research Foundation should justify an item in the program budget devoted to this function. Additional the sources of funds might come from parent organizations, service clubs, and businesses in the community. Teachers can also establish a requirement in their guidelines for repayment of a certain proportion of "profits" that might be derived from student activities that were funded by the Research Foundation. For example, a comic book publishing company was developed by a group of students who subsequently returned some of their subscription monies to the School Research Foundation.

Whenever funds are obtained from sources outside the school, recognition of these contributions should be made in program newsletters, newspaper articles, and other announcements related to the program. Students should also be required to include a statement on their final products that indicates support from the Research Foundation. Statements such as, "This project was supported in part by a grant from the Elmwood Schools Research Foundation" will help to give recognition to the school's Research Foundation and provide students with an opportunity to experience the same types of acknowledgment and recognition that are typically found in the adult world.

Procedures for Reviewing Proposals for the Research Foundation

Since one of the roles of a Research Foundation is to provide incentive and encourage motivation, it is important to approve as many proposals as possible, even if at a very limited level of funding. This approach suggests that educators may not formally reject proposals, but rather work with students to modify and improve their proposals and perhaps even suggest lower levels of funding than originally requested. Thus, the proposal review process will actually serve an important educational function by providing students with feedback and technical assistance in the process of proposal development.

A Research Foundation also provides for another level of involvement on the parts of more experienced students. Educators might invite a small number of students to be members of a proposal review team that includes teachers, the program coordinator, parents, and administrators. A brief set of guidelines for reviewing proposals should be drawn up and each member of the team should be asked to review the proposals independently. Following independent review, the group should meet as a whole to discuss their individual suggestions and prepare a set of recommendations.

Grant Application for Type III Funds

Name: _____   School: _____

Grade: _____   Date: _____

Area of Proposed Study (Science, Math, etc.):

Specific Area of Study:
State the description of the problem or the questions that you are investigating.

Methodology:
How long have you been working on your project?

What steps have you already completed in your investigation?

What resources have you used or do you intend to use? (List books, magazines, phone calls, interviews, computer, etc.)

Product:
What is your intended product? (Please describe)

Audience:
Who will see your product? Who will benefit from the work you have completed? (Explain)

Figure 81. Grant application for type III funds.

Grant Application for Type III Funds

Evaluation:
Will you complete a self-evaluation of your work?

Budget—Estimated Costs:

Materials	$ _____
Equipment	$ _____
Instructional Supplies	$ _____
Books	$ _____
Communication, Printing	$ _____
Binding	$ _____
Transportation	$ _____
Travel	$ _____
Professional Services	$ _____
Technical Services	$ _____
Cleaning, Repairs, Maintenance	$ _____
Tuition	$ _____
Dues, Fees	$ _____
Subscriptions	$ _____
Rentals	$ _____
Other (specify)	$ _____
_____	$ _____
_____	$ _____
Total	$ _____

Written Statement:
Explain why you believe you should be awarded this grant for your project.

Please complete this form and give it to the enrichment specialist. It will be reviewed by a funding team and the decision will be sent to you approximately two weeks after submission.

Figure 81. Grant application for type III funds (continued).

Chapter 9

Procedures for Evaluating Type III Enrichment

The Student Product Assessment Form

The *Student Product Assessment Form* (*SPAF*) was the result of a comprehensive instrument development research project (Reis, 1981) that was directed toward establishing the reliability and validity of this instrument and assessing the quality of products that were produced by various groups of students participating in programs for advanced ability students (see Figure 82). The validity and reliability of *SPAF* were established through a year long series of studies, using a technique developed by Ebel (1951). Levels of agreement among raters on individual items of the scale ranged from 86.4 percent to 100 percent. By having a group of raters assess the same set of products on two occasions, with a period of time between ratings, we established a reliability coefficient of .96 for the instrument. Information about the reliability of this instrument should be brought to the attention of decision makers in order to establish the credibility of an educator's approach to the evaluation of student products. In other words, when questions about "hard data" and objectivity are raised, the fact that educators are using a research based instrument of proven value will help to overcome many of the concerns that traditionally are raised about the merits of various approaches to evaluation.

The instrument is composed of fifteen items designed to assess both individual aspects, as well as overall excellence of products. Each item reports a single characteristic on which raters should focus their attention. Items 1 through 8 are divided into three related parts:

1. *The Key Concept.* This concept is always presented first and is printed in large type. It should serve to focus the rater's attention on the main idea or characteristic being evaluated.
2. *The Item Description.* Following the Key Concept are one or more descriptive statements about how the characteristic might be reflected in the student's product.
3. *Examples.* In order to help clarify the meaning of the items, an actual example of a student's work is provided. These examples are intended to elaborate upon the meaning of both the Key Concept and the Item Description. The examples are presented after each item description.

Item 9 contains seven different components and details an overall assessment of the product. When completing the ratings for this assessment of a student's product, raters attempt to evaluate the product in terms of their own values and certain characteristics that indicate the quality, esthetics, utility, and function of the overall contribution. In other words, raters are encouraged to consider the product as a whole by using their own judgment and relying upon their own guided subjective opinions when completing this component.

The results of product assessment should be summarized in the main body of an evaluation report. When this approach is used it is important to make the readers aware that the individual assessment forms, *Management Plans*, and actual products are available for their review. It is not necessary to evaluate every product for a formal evaluation. A

Student Product Assessment Form (SPAF)

Joseph S. Renzulli
Sally M. Reis

Rationale Underlying This Assessment Form

The purpose of this form is to guide your judgment in the qualitative assessment of various types of products developed by students in enrichment programs. In using the instrument three major considerations should always be kept in mind. First, the evaluation of more complex and creative types of products is always a function of human judgment. We do not think in terms of percentiles or standard scores when we evaluate paintings, architectural designs or the usefulness of a labor-saving device. We must consider these products in terms of our own values and certain characteristics that indicate the quality, esthetics, utility, and function of the overall contribution. In other words, we must trust our own judgment and learn to rely upon our guided subjective opinions when making assessments about complex products.

A second consideration relates to the individual worth of the product as a function of the student's age/grade level and experiential background. For example, a research project that reflects an advanced level investigation and subsequent product by a first grader might not be considered an equally advanced level of involvement on the part of a sixth grader. Similarly, the work of a youngster from a disadvantaged background must be considered in light of the student's overall educational experiences, opportunities and availability of advanced level resource persons, materials and equipment.

The third consideration relates to the most important purpose of any evaluation—student growth and improvement. This assessment instrument should be used to guide students toward excellence and therefore we strongly believe that it should be shared and discussed with students before the product is started. In other words, we believe the instrument should be reviewed with students during the early planning stages of the product. Students should have the opportunity to know and fully understand on what basis their final products will be assessed.

Instructions for Using the Assessment Form

Although most of the items included in the form relate directly to characteristics of the final product, it will be helpful if you also have access to any planning devices that have been used in the development of the product. Such planning devices might consist of logs, contracts, management plans, proposals or any other record keeping system. A planning device can help you to determine if pre-stated objectives have been met by comparing statements of objectives from the planning device with the final product. If such a planning device has not been utilized or is unavailable, you may want to request that the student complete a form that will provide you with the necessary background information. It is recommended that some type of planning device accompany all products that are submitted for rating. If it can be arranged, you may also want to interview the student who completed the product.

Figure 82. Student product assessment form.

Student Product Assessment Form (SPAF)

In using the *Student Product Assessment Form* it will sometimes be necessary for you to do some detective work! For example, in determining the diversity of resources, you may need to examine footnotes, bibliographies or references and materials listed on the planning device. You may also want to have the student complete a self-evaluation form relating to the completed product. This form may help to assess task commitment and student interest.

The *Student Product Assessment Form* can be used in a variety of ways. Individual teachers, resource persons or subject matter specialists can evaluate products independently or collectively as members of a team. When two or more persons evaluate the same product independently, the average rating for each scale item can be calculated and entered on the Summary Form. When used in a research setting or formal evaluation situation, it is recommended that products be independently evaluated by three raters. One of these ratings should be completed by the teacher under whose direction the product was developed. A second form should be completed by a person who has familiarity with the subject matter area of the product. For example, a high school science teacher might be asked to rate the work of an elementary grade student who has completed a science-related product. The third rater might be someone who is independent of the school system or program in which the work was carried out.

Item Format

At first glance the items on the assessment form may seem to be long and complicated, but they are actually quite concise. Each item represents a single characteristic that is designed to focus your attention. The items are divided into the following three related parts:

1. **The Key Concept.** This concept is always present first and is printed in large type. It should serve to focus your attention on the main idea or characteristic being evaluated.
2. **The Item Description.** Following the Key Concept are one or more descriptive statements about how the characteristic might be reflected in the student's product. These statements are listed under the Key Concept.
3. **Examples.** In order to help clarify the meanings of the items, an actual example of students' work is provided. The examples are intended to elaborate upon the meaning of both the Key Concept and the Item Description. The examples are presented following each item description.

Important Note: The last item (No. 9) deals with an overall assessment of the product. In this case we have chosen a somewhat different format and examples have not been provided. When completing the ratings for Item No. 9 you should consider the product as a whole (globally) rather than evaluating its separate components in an analytic fashion.

Figure 82. Student product assessment form (continued).

Student Product Assessment Form (SPAF)

Some of the items may appear to be unusually long or "detailish" for a rating scale but our purpose here is to improve the clarity and thus inter-rater reliability for the respective items. After you have used the scales a few times, you will probably only need to read the Key Concepts and Item Descriptions in order to refresh your memory about the meaning of an item. Research has shown inter-rater reliability is improved when items are more descriptive and when brief examples are provided in order to help clarify any misunderstanding that may exist on the parts of different raters.

Non-Applicable Items

Because of the difficulty of developing a single instrument that will be universally applicable to all types of products, there will occasionally be instances when some of the items do not apply to specific products. For example, in a creative writing project (poem, play, story) either the Level of Resources (No. 3) or Diversity of Resources (No. 4) might not apply if the student is writing directly from his/her own experiences. It should be emphasized however, that the non-applicable category should be used very rarely in most rating situations.

How to Rate Student Products

1. Fill out the information requested at the top of the Summary Sheet that accompanies the *Student Product Assessment Form*. A separate Summary Sheet should be filled out for each product that is evaluated.
2. Review the nine items on the *Student Product Assessment Form*. This review will help to give you a "mind set" for the things you will be looking for as you examine each product.
3. Examine the product by first doing a "quick overview" of the entire piece of work. Then do a careful and detailed examination of the product. Check (√) pages or places that you might want to reexamine and jot down brief notes and comments about any strengths, weaknesses or questions that occur as you review the product.
4. Turn to the first item on the *Student Product Assessment Form*. Read the Key Concept, Item Description and Example. Enter the number that best represents your assessment in the "Rating" column on the Summary Sheet. Enter only whole numbers. In other words, do not enter ratings of 3 1/2 or 2 1/4. On those rare occasions when you feel an item does not apply, please check the N/A column on the Summary Sheet. Please note that we have only included an N/A response option for Item 9a on the Overall Assessment.
5. Turn to the second item and repeat the above process. If you feel you cannot render a judgment immediately, skip the item and return to it at a later time. Upon completion of the assessment process, you should have entered a number (or a check in the N/A column) for all items on the Summary Sheet.
6. Any comments you would like to make about the product can be entered at the bottom of the Summary Sheet.

Figure 82. Student product assessment form (continued).

Student Product Assessment Form
Summary Sheet

Name(s) _____ Date _____

District _____ School _____

Teacher _____ Grade _____ Sex _____

Product (Title and/or Brief Description) _____

_____

Number of weeks students worked on product _____

Factors	Rating*	Not Applicable
1. Early Statement of Purpose	_____	_____
2. Problem Focusing	_____	_____
3. Level of Resources	_____	_____
4. Diversity of Resources	_____	_____
5. Appropriateness of Resources	_____	_____
6. Logic, Sequence and Transition	_____	_____
7. Action Orientation	_____	_____
8. Audience	_____	_____
9. Overall Assessment	_____	_____
A. Originality of the Idea	_____	_____
B. Achieved Objectives Stated in the Plan	_____	_____
C. Advanced Familiarity with the Subject	_____	_____
D. Quality Beyond Age/Grade Level	_____	_____
E. Care, Attention to Detail, etc.	_____	_____
F. Time, Effort, Energy	_____	_____
G. Original Contribution	_____	_____

Comments:

Person completing this form: _____

*Rating Scales:

Factors 1-8:
5-To a great extent
3-Somewhat
1-To a limited extent

Factors 9A-9G:
5=Outstanding
4=Above average
3=Average
2=Below average
1=Poor

Figure 82. Student product assessment form (continued).

Student Product Assessment Form

Joseph S. Renzulli
Sally M. Reis

1. EARLY STATEMENT OF PURPOSE
   Is the purpose (theme, thesis, research question) readily apparent in the early stages of the student's product? In other words, did the student define the topic or problem in such a manner that a clear understanding about the nature of the product emerges shortly after a review of the material?

   For example, in a research project dealing with skunks of northwestern Connecticut completed by a first grade student, the overall purpose and scope of the product were readily apparent after reading the introductory paragraphs.

5	4	3	2	1	N/A
To a great extent		Somewhat		To a limited extent	

2. PROBLEM FOCUSING
   Did the student focus or clearly define the topic so that it represents a relatively specific problem within a larger area of study?

   For example, a study of "Drama in Elizabethan England" would be more focused than "A Study of Drama."

5	4	3	2	1	N/A
To a great extent		Somewhat		To a limited extent	

3. LEVEL OF RESOURCES
   Is there evidence that the student used resource materials or equipment that are more advanced, technical, or complex than materials ordinarily used by students at this age/grade level?

   For example, a sixth grade student utilized a nearby university library to locate information about the history of clowns in the twelfth through sixteenth century in the major European countries.

5	4	3	2	1	N/A
To a great extent		Somewhat		To a limited extent	

Figure 82. Student product assessment form (continued).

Student Product Assessment Form

4. DIVERSITY OF RESOURCES
Has the student made an effort to use several different types of resource materials in the development of the product? Has the student used any of the following information sources in addition to the standard use of encyclopedias: textbooks, record/statistic books, biographies, how-to books, periodicals, films and filmstrips, letters, phone calls, personal interviews, surveys or polls, catalogs and/or others?

For example, a fourth grade student interested in the weapons and vehicles used in World War II read several adult-level books on this subject which included biographies, autobiographies, periodicals, and record books. He also conducted oral history interviews with local veterans of World War II, previewed films and film strips about the period and collected letters from elderly citizens sent to them from their sons stationed overseas.

5	4	3	2	1	N/A
To a great extent		Somewhat		To a limited extent	

5. APPROPRIATENESS OF RESOURCES
Did the student select appropriate reference materials, resource persons, or equipment for the topic or area of study?

For example, a student who was interested in why so much food is thrown away in the school cafeteria had to contact state officials to learn about state requirements and regulations which govern what must and can be served in public school cafeterias. With the aid of her teacher, she also had to locate resource books on how to design, conduct and analyze a survey.

5	4	3	2	1	N/A
To a great extent		Somewhat		To a limited extent	

6. LOGIC, SEQUENCE, AND TRANSITION
Does the product reflect a logical sequence of steps or events that ordinarily would be followed when carrying out an investigation in this area of study? Are the ideas presented clearly and logically and is there a smooth transition from one idea or subtopic to another?

For example, a student decided to investigate whether or not a section of his city needs a new fire station with a salaried staff rather than the present volunteer staff. First the student needed to research different methods of investigative reporting such as appropriate interview skills. Next the student conducted interviews with both salaried and volunteer fire station staff. He then needed to learn about methods of survey design and reporting in order to analyze local resident opposition or support for the new fire station. After other logical steps in his research were completed, his accumulated findings led him to interviews with the Mayor and the Board of Safety in the city and then to several construction companies that specialized in bids on such buildings. His final product was an editorial in the local newspaper which reflected his research and conclusions.

5	4	3	2	1	N/A
To a great extent		Somewhat		To a limited extent	

Figure 82. Student product assessment form (continued).

Student Product Assessment Form

7. ACTION ORIENTATION

Is it clear that the major goal of this study was for purposes other than merely reporting on or reproducing existing information, ideas, or knowledge? In other words, the student's purpose is clearly directed toward some kind of action (e.g., teaching ways to improve bicycle safety, presenting a lecture on salt pond life); some type of literary or artistic product (e.g., poem, painting, costume design); a scientific device or research study (e.g., building a robot, measuring plant growth as a function of controlled heat, light and moisture); or some type of leadership or managerial endeavor (e.g., editing a newspaper, producing/directing a movie).

For example, a student decided to study the history of his city. After an extensive investigation, the student realized that other history books had been written about the city. He found, instead, that no one had ever isolated specific spots of historical significance in the city which were easily located and accessible. He began this task and decided to focus his research on producing an original historical walking tour of the city.

5	4	3	2	1	N/A
To a great extent		Somewhat		To a limited extent	

8. AUDIENCE

Is an appropriate audience specified or readily apparent in the product or *Management Plan*?

For example, the student who researched the history of his city to produce an original walking tour presented his tour to the city council and the mayor. They, in turn, adopted it as the official walking tour of the city. It was reproduced in the city newspaper and distributed by the local historical society, library and given out to registered guests in the city's hotels and motels.

5	4	3	2	1	N/A
To a great extent		Somewhat		To a limited extent	

9. OVERALL ASSESSMENT

Considering the product as a whole, provide a general rating for each of the following factors and mark the space provided to the right of the item:

SCALE

5 = Outstanding   4 = Above Average
3 = Average   2 = Below Average
1 = Poor

A. Originality of the idea. _____
B. Achieved objectives stated in plan. _____
C. Reflects advanced familiarity with the subject matter for a youngster of this age/grade level. _____
D. Reflects a level of quality beyond what is normally expected of a student of this age and grade. _____
E. Reflects care, attention to detail, and overall pride on the part of the student. _____
F. Reflects a commitment of time, effort and energy. _____
G. Reflects an original contribution for a youngster of this age/grade level. _____

Figure 82. Student product assessment form (continued).

stratified random sample (by grade level and various areas of student interest) can be used to provide a fair picture of the types of work that are being pursued in the special program. Whenever random samples are used, it is important to secure agreement (from boards or funding agencies) about sample sizes prior to deciding the actual number of products to be rated. It is also important to describe in detail exactly how a truly random and unbiased approach will be used to select products for rating.

Sharing the Student Product Assessment Form With Talent Pool Students

An almost universal characteristic of students of all ages is a desire to know how they will be evaluated or "graded." We would like to begin by saying that we strongly discourage the formal grading of Type III endeavors. No letter grade, number or percent can accurately reflect the comprehensive types of knowledge, creativity and task commitment that are developed within the context of a Type III Enrichment endeavor. At the same time, however, evaluation and feedback are an important part in any educational experience and students should be familiar with evaluation procedures from the outset.

The best way to help students gain an appreciation for the ways in which their work will be evaluated is to conduct a series of orientation sessions organized around *SPAF*. Two or three examples of completed student products that highlight varying levels of quality on the respective scales from the *SPAF* instrument will help students gain an appreciation for both the factors involved in the assessment, as well as examples of the manifestation of each factor. In many ways these sessions represent an excellent way to teach students about the nature of a Type III Enrichment project and the difference between a traditional "report" on one hand and a first-hand investigative activity on the other. Over a period of several years, it would be a good idea to collect various examples of student products that highlight outstanding levels of accomplishment on one or more of the *SPAF* scales.

"Data" From the Management Plan

There are several important types of evaluation information that can be derived directly from an analysis of several *Management Plans*. Each of these types of information is consistent with the objectives for Type III Enrichment set forth on the summary sheet of this chapter. For example, one objective calls attention to student involvement in various interdisciplinary studies. By simply tallying the numbers of check marks in the "General Areas of Study" section from several *Management Plans* teachers can provide some factual (and even statistical) information about the variety of disciplines that can be found in Type III Enrichment projects. Similarly, the same objective refers to advanced levels of knowledge and methodology used within particular disciplines. Information relating to this objective may be obtained by analyzing several *Management Plans* for books and/or resource persons that students ordinarily would not come into contact with in regular curricular activities or through the use of ordinary school textbooks or library materials. Categorical tallies of intended audiences, products and outlets will help to highlight the ways in which students are achieving the objectives set forth for Type III Enrichment. Even the objective related to task commitment can be documented by simply presenting data about the average length of time that students spend on their Type III projects. This information coupled with *Management Plans*, notes and rough drafts of student work, Student Product Assessment Forms, the products themselves, and perhaps examples of sophisticated resources such as college level books, esoteric scientific equipment, computer software, etc. will provide a comprehensive and impressive array of evaluation information.

Additional Procedures for Evaluating Type III Enrichment

On the pages that follow, we have included additional forms and procedures that have been used to evaluate Type III Enrichment and provide parents with feedback about student involvement in other types of enrichment (see Figures 83-86). The information on these forms may be modified or combined in whatever ways teachers feel will be most effective in analyzing the ways in which their own program implements the Type III dimension of the SEM. Teachers also might want to make use of one or a combination of the numerous evaluation instruments that are included in the appendices of *A Guidebook for Evaluation Programs for Gifted and Talented* (Renzulli, 1975). This guidebook includes more than thirty instruments that have been specifically designed to evaluate various aspects of programs for advanced ability students. Taken collectively, the instruments can serve as an excellent reservoir of items from which teachers can select evaluation procedures that are most relevant to the Type III Enrichment dimension of their program, as well as other aspects of their overall programming efforts. As is always the case with any evaluation effort, the most important consideration is the degree to which evaluation instruments and procedures reflect the extent and quality of services that are unique to any given program or dimension thereof. For this reason, we recommend that teachers begin developing evaluation procedures by exploring a wide variety of available instruments and making selections based on the individual needs and points of focus in their own program.

Teacher Training Activities

This section includes several activities that are designed to help teachers develop various skills necessary for the facilitation of Type III Enrichment. Some of the activities are specifically designed for those persons who are responsible for working directly with students on Type III Enrichment projects. Other activities will include general staff activities related to procedures such as identifying action information and exploring various types of outlets and audiences for student work. Although most programs that employ enrichment specialists for advanced ability students ordinarily place responsibility for the facilitation of Type III Enrichment with these persons, a long range objective of a program should be to encourage every teacher to feel competent and comfortable in the facilitation of Type III experiences.

Learning the Process Yourself

Our first teacher training activity is somewhat different from other teacher training experiences that have been recommended in this book. We believe that the best way to internalize the many obvious and subtle teaching methods that involve the facilitation

Type III Enrichment Teacher Evaluation Form

Student _____ Grade _____

Teacher _____ Date _____

A. Your child exhibits strengths in the areas checked below:

_____ Is eager to learn—possesses inner motivation
_____ Demonstrates task commitment
_____ Cooperates and shares with peers
_____ Uses flexible thinking skills
_____ Uses fluent thinking skills
_____ Demonstrates originality
_____ Uses critical thinking skills
_____ Assumes a leadership role
_____ Demonstrates creative problem solving skills
_____ Demonstrates an ability to plan logically

B. Your child has participated in these Type II activities:

C. Investigation of a Type III problem:

Parent Signature _____

Teacher's Signature _____

Figure 83. Type III enrichment teacher evaluation form.

Parent Evaluation of Student's Product

Name _____ Date _____

Student's Name _____

1. Has your child discussed his/her product with you at home?

2. Have you noticed any changes in your child's interests or use of free time since he/she began working on the product?

3. Please comment below on your child's task commitment, involvement and interest level while the independent study or group project was being developed.

4. Please assess the overall quality of your child's product below.

5. Please add any other comments about the enrichment program that you would like to offer.

Figure 84. Parent evaluation of student's product.

Student Product Self-Evaluation Form

Name _____ Grade _____

School _____ Date _____

1. Describe your feelings about working on your project. Did you enjoy working on it?

2. List some of the things you learned while working on your project.

3. Were you satisfied with your final project?

4. List some of the ways your enrichment teacher helped you on your project.

5. Do you think you might like to work on another product in the future? Do you have any ideas for this product?

Figure 85. Student product self-evaluation form.

Student Process and Product Evaluation Form

Name _____ Grade _____

School _____ Date _____

Type I Activities

Interest Centers _____

Speakers _____

Field Experiences _____

Media _____

Computer Work _____

COMMENTS: _____

_____

_____

Type II Activities

☐ Fluency   ☐ Evaluation   ☐ Values Clarification

☐ Flexibility   ☐ Observation   ☐ Hypothesizing

☐ Elaboration   ☐ Interpretation   ☐ Comparison

☐ Originality   ☐ Appreciation   ☐ Awareness

☐ Analysis   ☐ Commitment   ☐ Classification

☐ Synthesis

COMMENTS: _____

_____

_____

Type III Activities

Individual or Group Project _____

Topic of Study _____

Method of Inquiry _____

Product _____

Audience _____

COMMENTS: _____

_____

_____

Enrichment Clusters

_____

_____

Mentors

_____

_____

Figure 86. Student process and product evaluation form.

of Type III Enrichment can best be approached through the careful reading of a small book entitled, *A Student's Guide to Conducting Social Science Research* (Bunker, Pearlson and Schulz, 1975).[4] This inexpensive paperback was specifically designed for classroom teachers to help them guide students in developing and conducting authentic social science research investigations. This book is organized around the following nine major steps that are involved in first-hand investigative activity:

1. Deciding what to investigate.
2. Formulating hypotheses or exploratory questions.
3. Selecting a method.
4. Developing a research design.
5. Training in the selected method.
6. Collecting data.
7. Drawing conclusions from the data.
8. Writing up what has been done.
9. Planning further research.

This book is divided into three major sections. The first section deals with an overview of the methods by which social scientists conduct research. The second section provides a detailed description of two studies that typify the work of social scientists. The third section provides readers with the opportunity to engage in a series of "practice" research activities that represent the typical work of social scientists. References are provided for those individuals who might like to go beyond the information given and learn more about sophisticated methods and procedures of research methodology. This book contains a wealth of easy-to-understand methods and procedures, as well as numerous guides and worksheets for activities such as constructing questionnaires; gathering, tabulating and preparing data; constructing charts and graphs that represent data; and organizing research reports.

In addition to serving a teacher training function, this book can also be used as an excellent unit of study for students or an individual guide for independent study. After teachers have become thoroughly familiar with the book, they might want to organize a series of Type II lessons around the content of this excellent and very action-oriented guidebook. Although there are many other possible approaches to the development of teaching skills for the facilitation of Type III Enrichment, this neat little book encapsulates the essence of major teacher responsibilities under one cover. It is for this reason that we believe the small amount of time required to review this material will be economical in terms of both a teacher's own time and effort and the small expense of the book. Finally, we believe that the book will serve as an idea-generating experience for students when used as a Type II mini-course or part of any lessons that might be directed toward teaching various research skills. Some of the studies described could themselves be replicated or modified to provide a ready-made starting point for several Type III Enrichment projects in the social sciences.

---

[4] This book can be ordered from: Human Sciences Press, a division of Behavioral Publications, In., 72 Fifth Avenue, New York, NY 10011.

SIMSITS

On the pages that follow we have included three SIMSITS that can be used to train teachers in various aspects of the overall Type III process. Since the objectives and procedures are described in the Facilitators' Guide for each activity, we will only list the titles and general purpose at this point in the text.

1. **Turning on Your Own Light Bulb.** This activity is designed to help familiarize staff with the procedures involved in identifying student interests and transmitting *Action Information Messages.*

2. **The Intake Interview.** This activity is designed to help teachers gain experience in interviewing students and determining whether or not student interests reflect a "readiness" before revolving into Type III Enrichment. This activity also includes skills related to the beginning steps of problem focusing.

3. **Problem Focusing.** The two simulations included in this problem focusing activity are designed to provide practice in dealing with the process of transforming general interests into specific problems. In the first example, the student is highly motivated and already interested in a particular topic. In the second case, the interest is not as strong and the student's participation may well depend on building motivation, as well as focusing on a particular topic within the general subject matter area.

Chapter 9

SIMSIT 4
FACILITATOR'S GUIDE

Turning on Your Own Light Bulb
A Simulation on the Use of Action Information Messages

Teacher Training Objectives
- Major Objective: To become familiar with the concept and completion of *Action Information Messages*.
- To learn more about some of the interests of fellow staff members.
- To identify potential resource persons for Type I and Type III Enrichment.
- To help open up lines of communication among staff members, administrators and persons working in the enrichment program.

Number of People Involved
Unlimited, but we suggest that if the staff of a particular building is larger than 20 persons, the group should be divided so that group size remains no larger than 20.

Approximate Time
One-half hour

Materials and Equipment
Instructions for Participants, Blank Light Bulb, Example of a Completed Light Bulb, Chalkboard for Recording Responses

Directions
This activity is designed to help classroom teachers and administrators gain some initial familiarity with the concept of *Action Information Messages* by actually completing "Light Bulbs" on persons with whom they are very familiar—themselves. The activity is considered to be an "ice breaker" for both getting a feel for completing these forms and perhaps learning a little more about the interests of other staff members. It is important for both teachers and administrators to participate in this activity.

Pass out the directions, the sample Light Bulb and a blank Light Bulb to each person. If there are more than 20 persons in the room, divide the total group into subgroups so that the maximum size of any single subgroup is 20 or less. Appoint a facilitator for each subgroup. If staff from more than one school are present, try to keep people from each building together.

After everyone has read the directions, suggest that they take no more than ten minutes to complete their Light Bulb. Assure them that you are looking for past, present or potential interests rather than the innermost secrets of their personal life. Also remind the group of the major objective and assure them that this is not a "sneaky" way to carry out a human relations activity.

SIMSIT 4
Action Information Message (continued)

Before they begin to complete their Light Bulb, remind the group:

- To write about themselves in the third person, using the words "This Person" whenever they are making reference to themselves; and avoid revealing their identity by using his/her or he/she.
- To try to disguise or minimize well-known or extremely obvious interests that will allow for easy detection. Remind them that this is a guessing game, and although they must be truthful, they can help to heighten competition and excitement by avoiding salient interests that will be easily recognized by others. Suggest that they include potential interests as well as past and present interests.

After ten minutes have passed, collect the Light Bulbs, mix them up to avoid detection by seating arrangement and number them. Place the following matrix on the chalkboard and suggest that participants make a copy of the matrix on a blank sheet of paper. (You may want to prepare individual matrices for distribution prior to carrying out the activity.)

	First Choice (3 points)	Second Choice (2 Points)	Third Choice (1 point)
1.			
2.			
3.			
4.			
5.			
6.			

SIMSIT 4
Action Information Message (continued)

Read each Light Bulb aloud and ask participants to identify the person described in the Light Bulb by recording their choices on their individual matrix. After each person has written their responses, ask them to read their choices aloud and tally each response on the board. This approach will help to heighten interest and a spirit of mystery and competition. *Persons should randomly list the names of three other participants when their own Light Bulb is read aloud.*

After all the Light Bulbs have been read aloud, go back through them and ask the "Mystery Person" to identify him or herself. You may want to briefly review the Light Bulb while doing this so as to refresh the groups' memory. Circle the correct response on the chalkboard or write the name of the appropriate person if no one has made a correct guess. Ask participants to circle each correct response on their individual matrix and calculate their score by adding up the number of circled responses in each column and multiplying by the point value for the respective columns.

End the activity with a general discussion and encourage participants to share additional information about their interests. At a later date you may want to contact individuals in an effort to involve them in various aspects of the enrichment program. Depending upon the nature and degree of involvement within any particular interest area, you may be able to recruit persons for a Type I experience, Type II training activity, enrichment cluster, or Type III involvement as a mentor or advisor.

SIMSIT 4
Action Information Message (continued)

Instructions for Participants

This activity is designed to help teachers and administrators gain some initial familiarity with the concept of *Action Information Messages*. The activity has been developed in the form of a guessing game in which you are asked to fill out a Light Bulb about yourself. The rules of the game are very simple. Write out your own Light Bulb by describing some of your past, present or potential interests. Although you must be honest in describing your interests, you may want to avoid or disguise certain interests for which you are well known. This approach will help to prevent easy detection by persons who will be attempting to guess your identity. For example, if most people are aware that you actively participate in a community theater group, you may want to avoid mentioning this present involvement, but describe a related activity that might have taken place in the past or that might be one of your "secret" ambitions for the future. Thus, you might write, "This person won great critical acclaim when he/she starred in a backyard play at the age of six" or "This person's secret ambition is to be the villain in a television soap opera."

As you complete your Light Bulb, think back to some of your school age or college activities that may not be familiar to the persons with whom you presently work. Don't be afraid to interject a little humor or fantasy and keep in mind that the activity is designed to help give you a "feel" for *Action Information Messages* rather than to probe the deepest secrets of your personal life!

A sample Light Bulb from the field test of this activity is provided for orientation purposes. Please write your Light Bulb in the third person by referring to yourself as "this person." Avoid detection by gender through the use of his/her or he/she. In the competition that follows the completion of the Light Bulbs, each person's statement will be read aloud and all members of the group will be asked to guess the identity of the writer. Each participant earns points according to the accuracy of his or her choices and the person with the greatest number of points is the winner!

Important Note: When your own Light Bulb is read aloud simply record the names of three others persons from the group at random. This will give everyone the same number of points for their own Light Bulbs and avoid self-identification when responses are recorded on the chalkboard.

Chapter 9

SIMSIT 4
Action Information Message (continued)

ACTION INFORMATION MESSAGE

GENERAL
CURRICULUM AREA _____

ACTIVITY OR TOPIC_____

IN THE SPACE BELOW, PROVIDE A BRIEF DESCRIPTION OF THE INCIDENT OR SITUATION IN WHICH YOU OBSERVED HIGH LEVELS OF INTEREST, TASK COMMITMENT OR CREATIVITY ON THE PART OF A STUDENT OR SMALL GROUP OF STUDENTS. INDICATE ANY IDEAS YOU MAY HAVE FOR ADVANCED LEVEL FOLLOW-UP ACTIVITIES, SUGGESTED RESOURCES OR WAYS TO FOCUS THE INTEREST INTO A FIRST-HAND INVESTIGATIVE EXPERIENCE.

* This person would like to learn how to build a log cabin and incorporate solar design into it.

* This person would like to live off the land. He/she would like to trap animals, gather and prepare food.

* This person would like to learn darkroom techniques so he/she can take and develop photos.

* This person would like to study the role of female athletics in our society.

TO:

FROM:

DATE:

☐ PLEASE CONTACT ME

☐ I WILL CONTACT YOU TO ARRANGE A MEETING

J. S. R. '81

SIMSIT 5
FACILITATOR'S GUIDE

The Intake Interview
A Simulation on Determining Student Readiness for Type III Enrichment

Teacher Training Objectives
- Major Objective. To gain experience in interviewing students who may or may not be ready to revolve into the resource room to begin a Type III investigation.
- To learn how to determine whether or not a student's interest in a topic is sincere and whether or not the student shows signs of possessing or developing the task commitment necessary to complete a Type III investigation.
- To develop skills in the beginning stages of problem focusing through helping students begin their research.

Number of People Involved
Three teams of two persons per team

Approximate Time
One-half hour

Materials and Equipment
Directions for the Enrichment Specialist, Directions for the Student, Tape Recorder or Camcorder (optional)

Directions
Select two persons to serve as enrichment specialists and two others to play the role of the student. Provide each of the four with the appropriate set of directions and ask them to leave the room for a few minutes to practice their respective roles. Ask the participants not to communicate with one another or share their separate sets of directions with persons playing the role opposite theirs.

While the participants are practicing their roles, review both sets of directions with the remainder of the group (who will serve as observers) and ask them to make notes about particularly good strategies or techniques that they observe during the simulations. Invite the first team (one enrichment specialist and one student) to return to the room and arrange two chairs side-by-side in the front of the room. Ask the enrichment specialist to begin the simulation by asking "Bobby" about the Light Bulb that was sent by his/her classroom teacher.

If the interview is progressing positively at the end of five minutes, allow it to continue and reach a natural ending, but do not let any interview last more than 10 minutes. Recording the interview for possible replay and analysis during the subsequent discussion period is optional. Repeat the process with the second team.

SIMSIT 5
The Intake Interview (continued)

The follow-up discussion should focus on the observers' perceptions of how the interview was handled by the enrichment specialist. Observers should try to assess if the teacher determined if the student's interest in the topic was genuine, if the task commitment to proceed with the Type III investigation seemed to be present, if the student really seemed to want to become involved in the Type III, and if the student understood the nature and amount of work that might be involved. The goal of the enrichment specialist here, of course, is not to "scare off" the student, but to assess whether or not a strong interest and motivation does exist. The individuals playing the parts of the students can individually determine whether or not they may or may not want to "revolve in" so the situation may totally change from one team to another. Follow-up discussion may also focus on whether or not the enrichment specialist was able to begin the process of "problem focusing." The facilitator should allow a free exchange of ideas and encourage the group to draw up some general guidelines for conducting an intake interview. The facilitator may want to review Chapter 9 before beginning this simulation.

SIMSIT 5
The Intake Interview (continued)

Directions for the Enrichment Specialist

You are an enrichment specialist in an SEM program. You recently received an *Action Information Message* (Light Bulb) from a sixth grade classroom teacher which stated the following about a Talent Pool student in her classroom:

> Bobby has recently indicated an interest in learning about whaling. He seems to have become interested in why certain species of whales are becoming extinct. I have no idea where this topic will lead Bobby, but wanted to let you know about the expressed interest.

You know that you should now schedule an interview to assess Bobby's interest and determine his task commitment to proceed with this investigation. Additionally, you have to start the difficult process of "problem focusing," helping Bobby to scale down his interests to a manageable investigation. The interview should be the beginning steps of this process if the interest is genuine and the commitment sincere.

SIMSIT 5
The Intake Interview (continued)

Directions for the Student

You are a sixth grade student who recently watched a television special about the whaling industry and the extinction of several species of whales. Since then you have read two or three articles about this subject and want to learn more. You know all about the "revolving in" process, but you have no idea what your final project or product might be. You're looking forward to discussing your interest with the enrichment specialist, but at the same time you're a little apprehensive because you've heard from other students how hard the work can be once you've "revolved in.

SIMSIT 6
FACILITATOR'S GUIDE

From General to Specific
A Simulation on Problem Focusing

Teacher Training Objectives
- Major Objective. To train teachers in the process of problem focusing, a necessary strategy in the development of students' Type III investigations.
- To sensitize teachers to the types of frustration that may result when students are attempting to "tackle too much" or when they are not able to identify a solvable problem or specific interest within a broader area.

Number of Persons Involved
Team A: Enrichment specialist and "Donny" (a student)
Team B: Enrichment specialist and "Chris" (a student)

Approximate Time
45 minutes to one hour

Materials and Equipment
Directions for Enrichment Specialist (A and B), Directions for Students (Chris and Donny), Action Information Message (Chris), Tape Recorder or Camcorder (optional)

Directions
Select two persons to serve as the enrichment specialist A and student A (Donny) and two persons to serve as enrichment specialist B and student B (Chris). Provide each participant with the appropriate set of directions and ask them to leave the room for a few minutes to practice their respective roles. Ask them not to communicate with one another or share their separate sets of directions with persons playing the role opposite theirs.

While the participants are practicing their roles, review both sets of directions with the remainder of the group (who will serve as observers). Ask the observers to watch carefully for particularly good techniques in problem focusing on the parts of the enrichment specialists. The goal may even be to come up with a list of "how to" strategies for problem focusing. After these directions have been reviewed, invite the first team [enrichment specialist A and Student A (Donny)] back into the room. In this simulation, Donny has already completed a great deal of work and really displayed his interest and task commitment.

SIMSIT 6
Problem Focusing (continued)

The important part of this SIMSIT activity is for participants (and observers) to examine the variety of ways in which a problem might be focused. Different teachers will use varying techniques. However, it is essential that all strategies be observed and discussed because there is no "right" way to guide a student from a general area of interest to a specific problem within the general area. We have found that even students who have a definite interest in a topic beforehand (e.g., Donny), will often flounder in the development of a Type III if their teacher cannot help them focus their investigation into a more researchable question or particular type of creative endeavor. Our experience in guiding students through Type III investigations has shown us that once students have brainstormed several questions they might want to answer through their research, it becomes relatively easy to use these questions as the basis for choosing one or two questions that will become the major focus of the investigation.

Activity B is concerned with a student who has a strong interest in astronomy but is somewhat overwhelmed with various options for further investigative activity. She became interested in astronomy because of an outstanding Type I experience that was arranged by the enrichment specialist. Her classroom teacher submitted the Light Bulb to the enrichment specialist, but what is significant in this example is that neither teacher has sufficient background in astronomy to engage in advanced-level problem focusing.

This example should highlight the need to obtain assistance from outside resource persons or from advanced-level books that may need to be obtained from libraries that are more sophisticated than those that are at hand. The resource persons might be secondary science teachers, college and university personnel, or amateur astronomers in your community. The important point is that advanced-level problem focusing may require expertise that is beyond that of the persons participating in the simulation. If the participants do not arrive upon the use of outside resource persons or materials as a course of action, you might provide some helpful hints in this regard. It is, of course, entirely possible that the enrichment specialist will be able to take some direction from the student himself or herself by reviewing the notes the student has already accumulated and the books that have been used to gain some initial information about astronomy. The teacher's general orientation about problem focusing and the meaning of a Type III experience may be sufficient if outside resources and materials are not available.

SIMSIT 6
Problem Focusing (continued)

Directions for Enrichment Specialist A

You are an enrichment specialist in an SEM program. You've been working with a second grade student named Donny for a month and you're extremely impressed with his task commitment. Donny is a very bright boy who loves sports. He came into the enrichment room because he wanted to write a children's book about baseball. In the month that he's been working with you, he's taken over twenty pages of notes on baseball, drawn diagrams of the baseball diamond, pictures of the kinds of equipment the players wear and the types of bats and balls used. He's also taken notes on the ways the game has changed and the number of teams that currently are involved in the leagues. He has also read extensively on the history of the sport, how it's changed over the years and has used several different sources to do this research including seven children's books from the school library.

This is the problem: Donny now knows that many children's books have been written about baseball and he's interested in doing something new. He is also interested in so many different areas that he's getting overwhelmed. He comes to you with a simple question: What do I do now?

SIMSIT 6
Problem Focusing (continued)

Directions for Student A (Donny)

You are a second grade student in an SEM program. You've been really excited about revolving into the enrichment room to work on your favorite topic, sports. You wanted to write a children's book on baseball. However, you've quickly learned that many other children's books have already been written. You've taken loads of notes and found out some really interesting things—especially about the history of baseball. Nobody knows how the game really started.

You don't know what to do next, so you decide to ask your teacher.

SIMSIT 6
Problem Focusing (continued)

Directions for Enrichment Specialist B

You are the enrichment specialist in an SEM program. You've been watching a sixth grader named Chris for about fifteen minutes and you know that she needs help. Chris is somewhat of a dilemma to you. She's been in your Talent Pool for three years and completed a Type III during the first year. Last year she had two ideas for Type III projects but she never really followed through on anything. When her teacher submitted the attached *Action Information Message* to you, you were thrilled because Chris is an extremely bright girl and really has a creative mind. You helped her find two or three books and you've recently located a slide/tape presentation on the planets that you have for her today.

Chris has been wandering about the room for fifteen of the twenty minutes she's been with you. You know that she's bored with taking notes and you suspect that it's because she's trying to do too much. You know that you have to try to help her to focus her problem and narrow the topic so she can begin to work more productively. You also know that Chris needs some encouragement and needs to have a definite product in mind. You suspect that if you can't help Chris define and focus her study, she'll give up in frustration. You decide to call her over and talk to her about her Type III study.

SIMSIT 6
Problem Focusing (continued)

Directions for Student B (Chris)

You are a sixth grade student in the Talent Pool of your school. This is your third year in the Talent Pool. During your first year you participated in the completion of a group Type III about aerial mapping and photography. You had a couple of ideas last year that you started on, but you never really got going on anything. Since then, you have not revolved in to complete a Type III investigation. About two months ago, you attended a Type I that was arranged by the enrichment specialist on astronomy. The Type I was called COSMOS and you really got excited about it. You told your classroom teacher about it and she submitted a "Light Bulb" to the enrichment specialist. You revolved in a week later and have now been involved in reading about astronomy for three weeks. You're getting a little worried because you're not quite sure what to do next. Astronomy is such a broad topic and so much has been written on it. Your Type III ideas are completely "up in the air."

SIMSIT 6
Problem Focusing (continued)

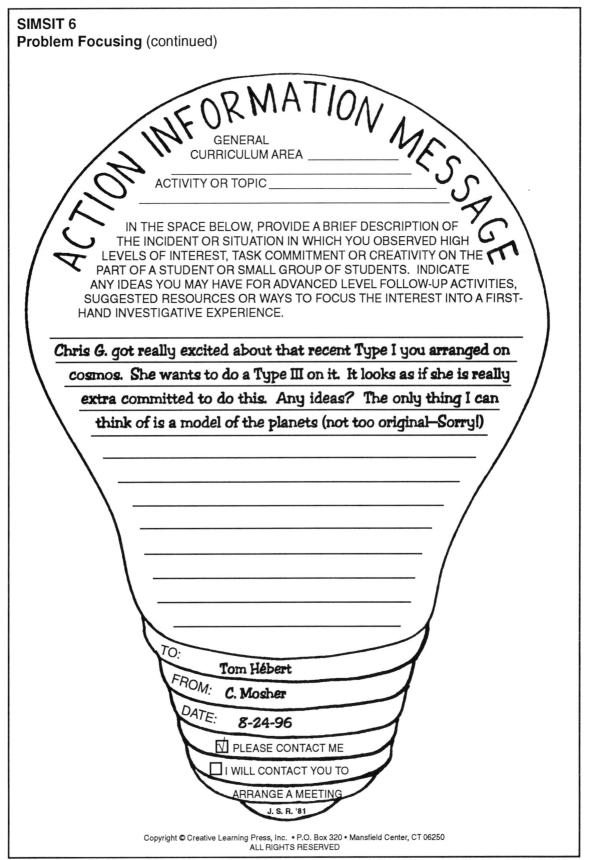

ACTION INFORMATION MESSAGE

GENERAL
CURRICULUM AREA _____

ACTIVITY OR TOPIC _____

IN THE SPACE BELOW, PROVIDE A BRIEF DESCRIPTION OF
THE INCIDENT OR SITUATION IN WHICH YOU OBSERVED HIGH
LEVELS OF INTEREST, TASK COMMITMENT OR CREATIVITY ON THE
PART OF A STUDENT OR SMALL GROUP OF STUDENTS. INDICATE
ANY IDEAS YOU MAY HAVE FOR ADVANCED LEVEL FOLLOW-UP ACTIVITIES,
SUGGESTED RESOURCES OR WAYS TO FOCUS THE INTEREST INTO A FIRST-
HAND INVESTIGATIVE EXPERIENCE.

Chris G. got really excited about that recent Type I you arranged on
cosmos. She wants to do a Type III on it. It looks as if she is really
extra committed to do this. Any ideas? The only thing I can
think of is a model of the planets (not too original—Sorry!)

TO: Tom Hébert

FROM: C. Mosher

DATE: 8-24-96

☑ PLEASE CONTACT ME

☐ I WILL CONTACT YOU TO

ARRANGE A MEETING

J. S. R. '81

Chapter 10

Enrichment Teaching and Learning:
Enrichment Clusters

An enrichment cluster program is one of the easiest and most visible components of the Schoolwide Enrichment Model (SEM). It provides a valuable opportunity for all students to develop their interests, strengths, and talents. This chapter summarizes information presented in the manual, *Enrichment Clusters: Using High End Learning to Develop Talents in All Students* (Renzulli, Reis, Gentry, Moran, & Warren, 1995), and offers a practical method for implementing a successful enrichment cluster program. The following pages include an outline of the steps for organizing clusters, examples of clusters, and assessment and evaluation options. For more in-depth data about enrichment clusters (background information and results from recent research studies), refer to the above manual and a videotape available from The National Research Center on Gifted and Talented—Phone: (860) 486-4676 and Fax: (860) 486-2900.

Enrichment Clusters: What Are They?

Enrichment clusters (Renzulli, 1994) are non-graded groups of students who share common interests and come together during specially designed time blocks to pursue these interests. Like extra-curricular activities and programs such as 4–H and Junior Achievement, the main rationale for participation in one or more clusters is that *students and teachers want to be there*. All teachers (including Music, Art, Physical Education, etc.) are involved in organizing clusters. Numerous schools also involve parents and other community resource persons in the implementation of a cluster program.

As discussed in Chapter 2, enrichment clusters are a component of the SEM (Renzulli & Reis, 1985; Renzulli, 1994). The major purpose of a cluster is for students to work with adults to produce or deliver an authentic product or service to a real-world audience. Everything students do in a cluster is directed toward this goal. This rule provides opportunities for students to learn relevant content and use authentic processes within the context of student-selected product or service development activities. The clusters place a premium on the development of higher order thinking skills and the creative and productive *application* of these skills to real-world situations.

Enrichment clusters are similar to extra-curricular activities and programs such as sports, yearbooks, and other clubs. The clusters meet at designated times, are open to a variety of ages, and membership is based on choice and interests. Common goals make real cooperativeness a necessity and "divisions of labor" within the clusters allow for differentiated levels of expertise and involvement, varying levels of challenge, and opportunities for different types of leadership to emerge on the part of students. For example, a student in a newspaper cluster can explore positions such as editor, artist, reporter, feature writer, sports writer, advertising manager, cartoonist, etc. This type of learning environment is highly supportive of individual differences and promotes the development of self-concept, self-efficacy, cooperativeness, and positive feelings that result from being a member of a goal-oriented team. To put it another way: *Every child is special if educators create conditions in which that child can be a specialist within a specialized group* (Renzulli, 1994).

Enrichment clusters revolve around major disciplines, interdisciplinary themes, or cross-disciplinary topics. A theatrical/television production group, for example, might include actors, writers, technical specialists, and costume designers. Clearly, the clusters deal with how-to knowledge, thinking skills, and interpersonal relations that apply in the real world. Instead of lesson plans or unit plans, three key questions guide learning:

- *What do people with an interest in this area do?*
- *What knowledge, materials, and other resources do individuals need to authentically do activities in this area?*
- *In what ways can individuals use the product or service to affect the intended audience?*

Because enrichment clusters focus on real-world issues, student exploration in any given cluster topic may continue indefinitely, unlike a typical classroom unit of study. Clusters are offered for an extended time block, usually from one hour to one-half day per week

---

Major Features of Enrichment Clusters

1. The **Golden Rule** of Enrichment Clusters: All activity is directed toward the production of a product or service.

2. Students *and* teachers select the clusters in which they will participate. *All* students and teachers are involved.

3. Students are grouped across grade levels by interest areas.

4. There are no predetermined lessons or unit plans.

5. The authentic methods of professional investigators are used to pursue product and service development.

6. Divisions of labor are used to guarantee that all students are not doing the same thing.

7. Specially designated time blocks are set aside for clusters.

8. The **Silver Rule** of Enrichment Clusters: The rules of regular schooling are suspended!

and they sometimes continue over several semesters (or even years) if interest remains high and there is a continuous escalation of student engagement and product quality. Students enter a cluster based on interests and other information gleaned from another key component of the SEM, the *Total Talent Portfolio* (Renzulli, 1994). Some students who develop high levels of expertise in a particular area may be asked to serve as an assistant or a facilitator of their own cluster (usually provided for younger students), thereby continuing the exploration of that topic.

Background of Enrichment Clusters

The model for learning used with enrichment clusters is based on an inductive approach to the pursuit of real-world problems rather than traditional, didactic modes of teaching. This approach, entitled enrichment learning and teaching, is purposefully designed to create a learning environment that places a premium on the development of higher order thinking skills and the authentic application of these skills in creative and productive situations. The theory underlying this approach (Renzulli, 1994) incorporates the work of theorists such as Jean Piaget (1975), Jerome Bruner (1960, 1966), and John Dewey (1913, 1916), and the applications of constructivist theory to classroom practice. Enrichment clusters promote cooperativeness within the context of real-world problem solving and provide superlative opportunities for promoting self-concept. The federal report *National Excellence: A Case for Developing America's Talent* (U.S. Department of Education, 1993) included the following goals: provide more challenging opportunities to learn, increase learning opportunities for disadvantaged and minority children with outstanding talents, broaden the definition of gifted, and emphasize teacher development. This report emphasized the role gifted education programs could have on general education and further called for the improvement of education for *all* of America's students, stating that schools must:

- *Expand effective education programs and incorporate more advanced materials into the regular school program.*
- *Provide all students with opportunities to solve problems, analyze materials and situations, and learn form real-life experiences.*
- *Serve students identified as having outstanding talent in many places—the regular classroom, a special class, the community, at a university or museum, in front of a computer, or anywhere the opportunity meets the need.*
- *Create flexible schools that enable all students, including the most able, to be grouped and regrouped according to their needs and interests.*

Enrichment clusters meet these challenges because they are designed to offer all students an opportunity for challenging, self-selected, real-world learning experiences. Within clusters, students are grouped by interests and focused toward the production of real-world products or services.

Six Steps to Implementing Enrichment Clusters

In two years of field testing enrichment clusters (Reis, Gentry, & Park, 1995), the following steps emerged as an economical set of strategies for implementing enrichment clusters into school programs. Before initiating these implementation steps, a decision must be made regarding the person or persons who will organize and/or coordinate the enrichment clusters. Successful programs have been coordinated by parent volunteers, enrichment specialists, or Schoolwide Enrichment Teams. As discussed in Chapter 3, it is imperative that any school involved in implementing the SEM first develop an Enrichment Team of teachers, administration, staff, parents, and even students. The purpose of such a team is to develop and offer enrichment opportunities for students, while planning and supporting the entire SEM. The Schoolwide Enrichment Team helps build ownership, and as a result, becomes a key component of a successful schoolwide program.

Step 1: Assess the Interests of Students and Staff

Many teachers try to extend a degree of choice to students, but it is usually within the limits of a curriculum which may seem overwhelming and confining. Enrichment clusters offer an opportunity to regularly explore interests and develop talents in a way that differs substantially from the activities of a classroom environment. Unlike a regular class, interests become a primary focus when facilitating a cluster program—not age, grade, or achievement level. Not only do staff members choose the topic they want to share and explore with students, but students select the cluster in which they want to participate. A common interest brings the group together to work toward a shared product or service. Our research indicates that grouping by interest may be more effective than traditional grouping patterns in producing or delivering meaningful products or services. Choice and a division of labor also exist within the cluster, depending on students' strengths, styles, and preferences. Everyone in a puppeteer cluster, for example, may work on the production of a puppet show, but students may select different roles within the cluster, such as scriptwriter, puppet designer, set designer, or music director.

Since common interest is the basis of enrichment cluster grouping, it is essential to first assess the interests and talents of students and staff when developing an enrichment cluster program. This will not only provide information about student interests, but will also encourage staff to consider their own individual strengths and talents. Often, adults may not realize that their specific hobby or interest can translate into a meaningful experience for interested students. Teachers are usually thrilled to have the opportunity to facilitate a cluster that lets them share their favorite hobby or interest with students who have the same interest.

Present or potential student interests can be identified using a variety of interest assessment instruments, such as *If I Ran the School* (Burns, 1992a). This instrument consists of general fields or families of interest and specific areas within a field (see Figure 87). Students are asked to select ten topics which they might like to explore from the general areas of Science, Social Studies and History, Mathematics, Art, and Language Arts.

We recommend that this survey be completed at home with the hope that students will make thoughtful selections. Our research has indicated that responses generated in class are subject to peer influence and stereotyped responses. We believe that surveys completed at home may more accurately represent student interests. A note on the

If I ran *the school*

AN INTEREST INVENTORY
developed by
Deborah E. Burns
designed by Del Siegle

Name _____

Grade _____   Teacher _____

> If I ran the school, I would choose to learn about these ten things. I have thought about my answers very carefully and I have circled my best ideas for right now.

I am really interested in:

Science
1. The Stars and Planets
2. Birds
3. Dinosaurs and Fossils
4. Life in the Ocean
5. Trees, Plants and Flowers
6. The Human Body
7. Monsters and Mysteries
8. Animals and Their Homes
9. Outer Space, Astronauts, and Rockets
10. The Weather
11. Electricity, Light, and Energy
12. Volcanoes and Earthquakes
13. Insects
14. Reptiles
15. Rocks and Minerals
16. Machines and Engines
17. Diseases and Medicine
18. Chemistry and Experiments

Social Study
1. Families
2. The Future
3. Our Presidents
4. The United States
5. Other Countries
6. History and Long Ago Times
7. Famous Men and Women
8. Problems We Have in Our Town
9. Holidays
10. Native Americans, Asian Americans, Hispanics and African Americans
11. Explorers
12. People Who Live and Work in Our Town
13. Travel and Transportation

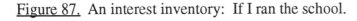

Figure 87. An interest inventory: If I ran the school.

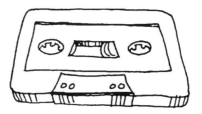

Math
1. Math Games and Puzzlers
2. Measuring Lines, Liquids, Weight
3. Shapes and Sizes
4. Buying and Money
5. Calculators and Computers
6. Building
7. Counting and Numbering
8. Calendars and Time
9. Math Stories and Problems

Language Arts
1. Writing a Book
2. Writing Poems
3. Writing Plays and Skits
4. Writing Newspapers
5. Making Speeches
6. Sign Language
7. Making a Book
8. Comic and Cartoon Strips
9. Letter Writing
10. Spanish and French
11. Talking and Listening to Stories
12. Making a New Game or Puzzle

Arts
1. Cartoons
2. Art Projects
3. Painting
4. Clay
5. Acting
6. Dancing
7. Drawing
8. Writing Music
9. Photography
10. Movies
11. Puppets
12. Radio and Television
13. Famous Artists and Their Work
14. Making New Toys
15. Magic
16. Mime

Careers
1. Doctors
2. Lawyers
3. Police Work
4. Fire Fighters
5. Scientists
6. Builders
7. Reporters
8. Store Workers
9. Sports Stars
10. Actors
11. Veterinarians
12. Farmers
13. Writers
14. Engineers
15. Artists
16. Inventors

You forgot to list some of my very special interests. They are: _____

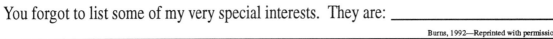

Burns, 1992—Reprinted with permission

Figure 87. An interest inventory: If I ran the school (continued).

philosophy of the program sent home with the survey may help reduce parental influence. If time is an issue, students can complete the surveys in class.

If I Ran the School is most appropriate for upper elementary grades (3rd and up). Younger students have not yet been exposed to a broad variety of topics and their interests may still be developing. Most of these children (K-2) seem to express an interest in everything and have trouble limiting their choices. *My Book of Things and Stuff* (McGreevy, 1982) is a very effective interest assessment for primary students. Other interest assessment instruments include both elementary and secondary versions of the *Interest-A-Lyzer* (Hébert & Sorensen, 1997; Renzulli, 1977b, 1997; Renzulli & Rizza, 1997).

An adult interest survey, *Inspiration: Targeting My Ideal Teaching Situation* (Gentry & Renzulli, 1995) was developed especially for persons who might be interested in facilitating clusters (see Figure 88). In this survey, adults are asked to consider their interests and talents by listing hobbies, affiliations, professional and personal experiences, and other personal choice options. It may be completed at a faculty meeting in less than 15 minutes or may be taken home to provide faculty time for more reflective responses. All faculty and staff members and members of the community who might facilitate a cluster should compete and return *Inspiration* to the persons coordinating the enrichment cluster program.

Once responses from *Inspiration* and *If I Ran the School* (or other interest assessments) are tabulated, the major interests of students and staff can help determine popular enrichment cluster topics. In our pilot programs, we first identified the top 20 interest areas of the students and then tried to match those student interests with staff, parent, and community talents (see Figure 89). Many of the most prevalent student interests can be predicted (dinosaurs, magic, and computers), but others may be surprising.

If clusters are organized around student and adult interests, excitement will be generated from both students and staff. When interests and strengths are the focus, student and staff motivation and confidence increase because interests enhance learning and frequently reveal hidden talents that might not emerge in traditional structured learning situations.

Step 2: Create a Schedule

Before beginning an enrichment cluster program, it is crucial that a specific time is identified for cluster activities. If possible, cluster scheduling should be done prior to the school year when school schedules are determined, so the program does not displace existing programs. To be successful and valued, clusters should have a "place" within the school week and not compete for time with pull-out programs, specials, or teacher planning time. In order to keep the focus on talent development, *all* students should be involved in enrichment clusters and not excluded from pursuing their interests, because of conflicts with Physical Education, Remedial Reading, Band, Chorus, or other special programs. As we have discussed, the activities that take place within clusters are different from other activities in the school and should be defined in a distinct time block. This time should not be used as a "catch-all" for school photos, standardized tests, etc. If this occurs, students and staff will learn that enrichment activities are not valued by the school.

INSPIRATION: TARGETING MY IDEAL TEACHING AND LEARNING SITUATION

Marcia Gentry
Joseph S. Renzulli
University of Connecticut

Background

The ideal teaching and learning situation occurs when students and teachers with common interests come together for the purpose of developing an authentic product or service that is an application of their common interest. Teachers are a rich resource for students when they examine their own interests in ways that reach far beyond their content expertise and general classroom experience. However, when asked what special talents and interests they have, many teachers fail to recognize their own interests as a valuable resource or they recognize only those interests that relate to their current teaching assignment. This questionnaire is designed to help teachers explore their professional *and* personal interests and talents.

Directions: Part A

The purpose of this survey is to help you explore your interests, experiences, and talents with an eye toward developing an ideal teaching and learning situation. The questionnaire is not a test and there are no right or wrong answers. Past, present, and future interests and experiences can serve as the basis for a rich, authentic educational experience for both you and your students. In short: *If you could share anything with a group of interested students, what would it be?*

Read through the questionnaire and give your answers careful consideration. Answer honestly and completely. When you've completed the survey, review your answers with the following question in mind: *If I could share one of my interests in a learning situation, what would it be?*

Figure 88. An adult interest inventory: Inspiration.

Professional Experiences:

1. What is your favorite subject to teach?

2. List any special units you've developed for your classroom.

3. What is your favorite area of knowledge? List any areas of knowledge such as astronomy, photography, geology, geography, archaeology, or any other "ologies" or "ographies" in which you have an interest.

4. Name one thing you have always wanted to teach but never had the opportunity to teach.

5. List any special courses or programs that you have taught or would like to teach.

Figure 88. An adult interest inventory: Inspiration (continued).

6. Pretend that you have received a federal grant to develop some innovative curricular materials. The only stipulations are that: (1) the materials should span 2 to 3 grade levels, (2) the materials must focus on activities that are not ordinarily included in regular textbooks or curricular guides, and (3) you must state the general and specific areas and the topical focus of the materials.

<u>Grade levels</u>

___ Preschool
___ Primary (1-3)
___ Elementary (4-6)
___ Junior High (7-9)
___ High School (10-12)
___ College
___ Special Populations (specify)
_____
___ Other

<u>General Curricular Area(s) Specified</u>

___ Mathematics
___ Science
___ Humanities
___ Social Sciences
___ Language Arts
___ Music
___ Drama
___ Art
___ Other

Briefly describe the topical focus of the materials and innovative approaches you would develop.

7. Pretend that you can invite four persons (living or dead; famous or not) to give a series of lectures (or workshops) in your classroom related to some aspect of your interests or course content. Whom would you invite?

1. _____   3. _____

2. _____   4. _____

From your choices listed above, place a star next to your very first choice. Why is this person your first choice?

8. Briefly describe the one thing that you feel has been your most creative contribution to teaching.

<u>Figure 88.</u> An adult interest inventory: Inspiration (continued).

9. Describe something that you have done to help a single child (or small group of children) develop personally, creatively, and/or academically, but that did not involve instructing or directly teaching something to the child.

Personal Experiences

10. List the clubs, organizations and extra-curricular activities in which you have been involved during each of the following stages of your life (include hobbies and services):

Elementary School: _____

_____

Secondary School: _____

_____

College: _____

_____

Adult: _____

_____

11. List any work you've published.

12. Where have you traveled?

13. Which place was most special and why?

Figure 88. An adult interest inventory: Inspiration (continued).

14. What do you do in your spare time? If there were no limitations, what would you do in your spare time?

15. Have you ever done any creative things "on your own?" List some of the things you have done (beginning as far back as you can remember) that were not related to school assignments, extra-curricular activities, or activities organized by clubs. Such things might include writing poetry, composing music, organizing political action, starting an organization, business, etc.

16. What "cause" would you take up if you had the time?

Figure 88. An adult interest inventory: Inspiration (continued).

DEVELOPING MY IDEAL TEACHING AND LEARNING SITUATION

Imagine having the time to work with students in an area that is truly an interest of yours. Imagine that these students share your interest and passion for this area. Picture the time to work with these students scheduled into the school day. Next, think of examples of authentic products and services that you and these students could develop within this area. This type of enrichment learning and teaching closely defines the ideal teaching situation.

Directions: Part B

After reviewing your responses to **Part A** of this questionnaire, consider which of your interests you would enjoy sharing with students. Answer the following questions and use your answers as a basis for developing a vision about what might take place in your own ideal teaching and learning situation.

If I could share one of my interests in a learning situation, what would it be?
_____

A. What do people with an interest in this area do? List as many different ideas as you can.

B. What materials and resources are needed to address this interest area? Place a star by those things which you already have. Make notes by those you can obtain.

C. What products or services might be produced or offered by people with an interest in this area? List as many varied ideas as you can. Circle those that you think might be adapted to use with students.

Figure 88. An adult interest inventory: Inspiration (continued).

If an enrichment cluster program is to be implemented after the school year has begun, it is important to procure staff input at every step, since the schedule affects everyone. Staff and faculty support can be obtained at a staff meeting or through an Enrichment Team, composed of representative staff members. Staff participation in the planning process will help to earn support from the entire staff and ensure the success of the program. The faculty and staff should determine several things including:

- *The length of the cluster series.*
- *The number of series per year.*
- *The day(s) of week when the clusters will be held.*
- *The time of day & length of each session.*
- *Specific dates.*

The length of the cluster series can vary, from a 3-4 week pilot to a weekly cluster time which occurs all year long. In our field tests, the clusters started with a short schedule or "pilot" series. Accordingly, students and staff had the opportunity to familiarize themselves with the cluster philosophy and routine. A pilot 4-week series in the fall provides a chance to evaluate the success of the program, resolve any conflicts, and plan a longer series for the spring. Eventually, faculty and parents may decide to continue clusters on a weekly basis throughout the year, as they did in our field test sites.

Some schools have planned their cluster series to take advantage of special events of the season. For example, an elementary school in Mansfield, Connecticut planned several clusters around a common theme—a fall holiday concert. A dance cluster, set design cluster, and a drama cluster all culminated in a schoolwide performance. In this way, clusters were integrated into schoolwide functions and provided consistent times in the schedule which may have been otherwise unavailable to work toward a schoolwide

Top Twenty Student Interests

1. Dinosaurs
2. Calculators and Computers
3. Cartoons
4. Art Projects
5. Volcanoes and Earthquakes
6. Monsters and Mysteries
7. Math Games and Puzzles
8. Life in the Ocean
9. Animals and Their Homes
10. Magic
11. Holidays
12. Spanish and French
13. Drawing
14. Rocks and Minerals
15. Making New Toys
16. Stars and Planets
17. Outer Space, Astronauts, and Rockets
18. Reptiles
19. Chemistry and Experiments
20. Clay

Figure 89. Top twenty student interests as determined by a schoolwide interest assessment.

goal. A similar schedule can be organized for the spring, with a culmination planned to celebrate a spring concert.

The day(s) of the week and frequency of cluster activities depends upon school needs and preferences. Some schools have scheduled clusters on Fridays as a culmination to the week, others prefer to "break up" the week with cluster activities midweek. Based on our field tests, we recommend that clusters meet at least once a week for continuity. If children have to wait two weeks between projects, interest and recall may wane. The time of day and length of each session also varies by school. In our field tests we found that a variety of schedules were successful. In one program, clusters met for an hour each week in the afternoon. (Teachers found that an hour per session is the minimum time needed—anything less was rushed and did not provide adequate time to accomplish a successful hands-on exploration and product development.) In another pilot site, clusters met for two hours each week. Teachers in another site did not want clusters to meet at the end of the day, because they found that time was needed at the end of each cluster activity to enable students to share what happened in the clusters with their classmates in their regular classes.

In middle school or high school, creating a schedule for enrichment clusters is completed by building a set time into a weekly schedule. This enables secondary schools an opportunity to schedule, activities that often take place after school. When activities are extra-curricular and offered after school, participation may be limited due to transportation and time conflicts. By scheduling a time within the school day, the enrichment clusters can truly be schoolwide and involve all students. Activities that involve the school newspaper, yearbook, and drama can have a place within the school day and a number of others clusters can be created to meet student and staff interests.

Scheduling is an individual decision at each school and should be done with staff input. Preferences and local issues must be considered and a schedule should be developed that accommodates school needs.

Step 3: Locate People and Staff to Facilitate Clusters

Once interests are compiled and a schedule created, facilitators within popular interest areas should be identified. Locating volunteers to facilitate enrichment clusters can be as involved as a school wants to make it. Some schools rely primarily on teachers and staff to facilitate successful clusters, while others include parents, community people, local businesses, and public agencies. Bringing in outside people requires extra effort, but we have found it well worth the work. Figure 90 summarizes sources of potential talent for cluster facilitators.

Teachers

The first and obvious place to find persons to facilitate clusters is in school. The adult interest survey discussed earlier, *Inspiration: Targeting My Ideal Teaching and Learning Situation,* may reveal the hidden talents, interests, and/or hobbies of staff that might not be recognized (even by the interested adult!). At one of our pilot schools, a teacher who completed the survey indicated that she really enjoyed playing in a handbell choir at her church, but did not feel competent to organize a handbell cluster. With some encouragement, she eventually teamed up with the school nurse and the choir director to facilitate "The Windham Chimers Handbell Choir Cluster" and created an extremely successful and enriching experience for both the adults and students.

At first, teachers may believe they have to offer a cluster topic that is "educational" or related to the curriculum. While they may do this, it is also important to stress that they may choose a topic of personal interest to them and something they will enjoy sharing and exploring with students. The cluster may revolve around a topic that the teacher does not consider a talent, but something they may wish to explore and learn together

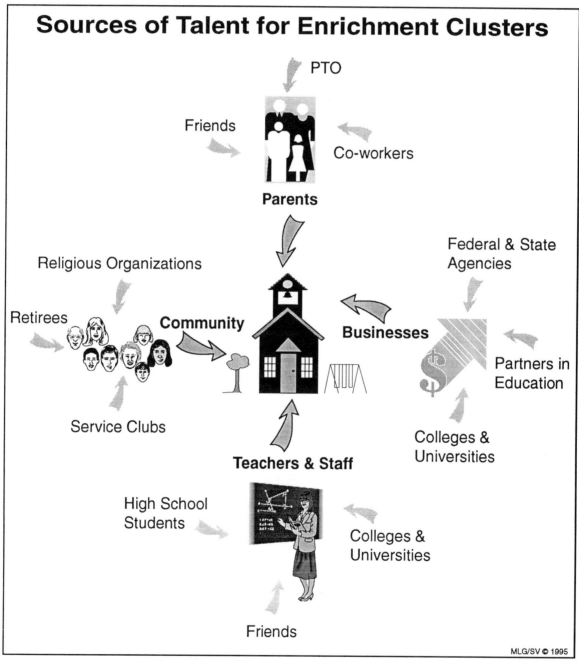

Figure 90. Sources of talent for enrichment clusters.

with students. We distributed the tabulation of top student interests at a staff meeting and several teachers organized their cluster based on these student interests. We encouraged teachers to "team up" with a community person or staff member, providing the opportunity to work with a friend, share new ideas, and have fun in the process.

Support Staff

In addition to teachers, support staff can provide a wealth of resources for the clusters. Successful clusters involve *everyone* in the school and we have found exceptional cluster activities happen with instructional assistants, student teachers, secretaries, custodians, specials teachers, principals, and even superintendents! All staff should be encouraged to become involved in clusters. Since all of these people may not be reached through a staff meeting, it is best to approach them individually at first, until everyone becomes familiar with the program. For these individuals, clusters offer an opportunity to do something outside the normal routine of the school schedule.

Many examples serve as success stories. An instructional assistant at one of our pilot schools had a flair for baking and organized "The Culinary Institute." Students explored the science of baking and experimented with measuring, variations in ingredients, and developing their own recipes. The group then compiled the recipes into a booklet that was then shared with the school. Another cluster was organized by a custodian, who worked with students on exploring building operations. These students in turn provided a service to interested classes by sharing a newly developed diagram that explained how the school worked from the inside out. Another cluster facilitated by a secretary addressed the real-life situation of office management and running a school. These students developed a plan for more efficient and consistent behaviors in the office that were designed to improve the school's image, including a written protocol for answering the phone and a standardized format for morning announcements. They also developed trivia for the morning announcements to help capture other students' attention.

Parents

Often there is a good deal of overlap between staff and student interests, but there will always be student interests that are not covered by school staff interests. These are areas that may be best suited to outside facilitators. Parents and community volunteers can provide resources, materials, and authenticity within a specific profession or topic that can be extremely exciting and motivating to students (and adults as well!).

Parents should be sent home a letter that invites them to facilitate a cluster (see Figure 91). Parents can also be approached through a teacher, at PTO meetings, by sending a flyer home, or through a phone call. They may be reluctant at first, but may be more inclined to become involved if they are given a list of ideas from which to choose. One parent expressed that she didn't have any specific talents to share with students. However, when she was provided with a list of possible cluster descriptions, "Math Games and Puzzles Guild" appealed to her because of her love for puzzles and math. She decided to develop a cluster on her own in which groups of students explored different types of games and puzzles. With the help of this parent, students developed their own board games to share with family and friends.

Memo

TO: All Interested Parents, Teachers and Board Members
FROM: Staff and PTO of Windham Center School
RE: Invitation to Organize an Enrichment Cluster

As you may know, the Enrichment Team at Windham Center School is organizing a series of enrichment clusters for all students in the school. Enrichment clusters are organized as multi-aged groups of students who share a common interest with the person organizing the cluster. We will begin with a pilot series scheduled to run during the afternoons of November 11, November 18, December 2 and December 9. We hope you will be interested in submitting an idea based upon a personal interest or talent.

The main rationale for participation in a cluster is that students and presenters want to be there. Based on an interest, students will select one cluster which they will attend beginning with the four-session pilot series. After the pilot, a longer series of enrichment clusters will be organized to begin in January.

Enrichment clusters are organized around major disciplines, interdisciplinary themes, or cross-disciplinary topics (e.g., a theatrical production group that includes actors, writers, technical specialists, costume designers, etc.). Enrichment clusters will be connected in various ways to the regular curriculum already offered. You don't have to be the "expert" in the topic you select. You and your students can explore a topic together.

Descriptions of sample enrichment clusters are listed following this letter to help give you some ideas for different types of clusters that can be organized. Your own description may be very different from the samples. Feel free to "team up" with a friend. If you would like to assist with a cluster, that is another option.

If you are interested in organizing or helping with an enrichment cluster, please complete the attached form by November 1. We hope you'll join us in this exciting opportunity for students! Thanks!

Figure 91. Enrichment cluster invitation to parents and school personnel.

Parents:

EnrichmenT
CLUSTERS
Need Your Help!

We have tabulated your child's interest surveys. These are the top interests of the school:

1. Dinosaurs & Fossils
2. Calculators & Computers
3. Cartoons
4. Art Projects
5. Volcanos & Earthquakes
6. Math Games & Puzzles
7. Magic
8. Holidays
9. Life in the Ocean
10. Monsters & Mysteries
11. Spanish
12. Animals & Their Homes

Do you have a special interest in any of these topics?
Do you know of anyone in the community who might?
Do you have yet another interest to share with students?

In order to help students pursue their interests, we need help in locating people who could come in to offer a cluster. If you or someone you know is interested in pursuing any of these topics with a small group of students, please contact Carol Moran before Christmas vacation.
Thank you!

The next two series of clusters will meet Tuesdays from 1:30 - 2:30 PM for two 5-week sessions: **Feb. 7, 14, 28, March 7, 14; and March 21, 28, April 4, 18, 25.**

Figure 91. Enrichment cluster invitation to parents and school personnel (continued).

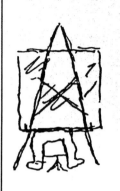

EnrichmenT

CLUSTERS

– Response Form –

Name _____

Address _____

Daytime Phone _____ Evening Phone _____

Name of Proposed Cluster _____

Description of Proposed Enrichment Cluster (2-4 sentences)

_____

_____

_____

_____

_____

_____

_____

_____

_____

_____

Brief biography of Enrichment Cluster Teacher for Inclusion in Brochure (1–2 sentences)

_____

_____

_____

_____

Age Level of Students Preferred for Enrichment Cluster _____

Minimum Number of Students Needed in the Enrichment Cluster _____

Maximum Number of Students Needed in the Enrichment Cluster _____

Figure 91. Enrichment cluster invitation to parents and school personnel (continued).

Another way to involve parents is to ask if they would be willing to assist with a cluster. Once parents assist and become familiar with the program, they may feel less intimidated. Those parents who have seen the clusters in action might be more inclined to facilitate a cluster in the future. Some parents may not be aware of their skills or talents or may not feel competent to teach. It should be stressed that the enrichment clusters do not involve traditional lesson plans, but rather operate in a flexible framework that enables the students' interests to direct the cluster.

Many parents who work and cannot commit to helping with a full series of clusters can become involved in a variety of other ways. These parents may be willing to help for a week or two, serve as a Type I guest speaker, assist with phone calls, help with computer activities, act as a "back up" in case of illness, or provide transportation to cluster field trips. One popular cluster in a Mansfield, Connecticut school focused on careers and invited a different parent to share his or her career with students each week. Cluster organizers should make it clear to parents that they are welcome at any time and that any input is valuable and appreciated.

Community Volunteers

A huge untapped resource of options for cluster volunteers can be found outside the school environment. Obviously, these resources are unique to each community and depend upon the individuals and businesses within the community. A good place to begin is to ask staff and parents for suggestions. Community volunteers are generally willing and eager to spend time "for a good cause" in a mentor role, but if they cannot, they may be able to suggest someone who can. See Chapter 7 for suggestions on how to locate community contacts and build a network of names.

If a specific profession based on student interests is needed, the phone book can serve as a comprehensive resource. Public agencies are another great place to explore. Parks, youth services, police departments, and fire departments are generally willing and able to spend time with students and have had past experience working with groups of children. Volunteering to facilitate a cluster is often a win-win situation. In one of our pilot sites, a local park provided a biologist to facilitate a cluster on forest and wildlife biology. The students gained the benefit of first-hand experience with a wildlife biologist and the resources and materials that he brought, while the park benefited from the chance to set up some youth programs of their own based on their experience with the cluster.

We suggest following these steps when procuring volunteers not affiliated with the school:

1. *Create a "network."* Ask teachers, staff, parents, and others for suggestions and check local businesses, retirement communities, agencies, public organizations, leagues, and clubs. From these sources a good list of possibilities can be developed. Program coordinators can also circulate invitation letters around the community to share program needs and goals with prospective volunteers (see Figure 92).
2. *Call prospective volunteers.* Describe the program briefly. If someone seems interested, but does not want to commit to a full series, look for ways to accommodate their needs, such as being a guest speaker or a field trip host. Some of these leads may become helpful contacts for finding other cluster facilitators.

Community Members: Share Your Talent With Local Students

- **Work with small groups of children**
- **Choose a personal interest or skill to share**
- **Team up with a friend**
- **Gain community exposure**

What: Enrichment Cluster Program
Who: Small Groups, Grades K-5
When: 1 1/2 Hour/Week, January through March '95
Where: Elm Middle School

We are interested in providing authentic enrichment experiences for local students. This program is one component of the Schoolwide Enrichment Model. We are looking for community members who are interested in sharing their interests and talents with K-5 students.

Topics Most Needed:

- Inventions/Technology
- Dinosaurs & Fossils
- Animal Behavior
- Astrology
- Mineralogy
- Art Projects
- Cartoons
- Dance/Music
- Magic
- Math Games
- Chemistry
- Toy Construction
- Holidays

Deadline: Dec. 21st

Questions?
Need an Idea?
Interested in Signing Up?

For more information:
Call Carol Moran to sign up to facilitate your own Enrichment Cluster.

Figure 92. Enrichment cluster invitation to community members.

3. *Meet with interested volunteers.* Discuss cluster philosophy in greater detail, provide literature on the program, discuss school procedures, and answer questions. For volunteers outside the school, a personal contact is very important. Not only do the volunteer's abilities need to be assessed, but the volunteer will feel more comfortable after seeing the school, meeting the coordinator, and discussing the program. For obvious reasons, the importance of timeliness and dependability also needs to be stressed when orientation is provided for new cluster facilitators.

4. *Once a volunteer has started a cluster, maintain communication.* A folder in the school office for each cluster facilitator can host as a "mailbox" and contain information such as student list changes, questions or concerns, helpful ideas, etc. The person or persons responsible for running the cluster program may not always be available and this type of system will help allay any problems.

Any outside facilitator should be paired with a school staff member to help with questions, assist with cluster activities and discipline, and in the event of illness or absence, facilitate the cluster. Some staff members will have chosen to assist with a cluster instead of facilitating one on their own and these people should be paired with community volunteers. Every effort should be made to allow staff to choose the cluster with which they assist.

Student Teachers, Interns, and Older Students

Student teachers and interns can also be an excellent resource for organizing clusters. These students are usually eager to gain experience working with small groups of children and have some background knowledge and interest in education. Students who may attend nearby colleges or universities are another valuable resource, as they often need to fulfill a community service requirement for graduation. If they are in the field of education, they need to spend time in classroom settings. Enrichment programs provide valuable opportunities for these students to share their skills and talents with younger students, while gaining experience for their own careers.

Older students, either locally or within the school, can also facilitate clusters. Local high school enrichment teachers, honors class teachers, or guidance counselors may be able to provide referrals. Even within an elementary or middle school, older students can work with younger students under the guidance of an adult supervisor. As was the case with community volunteers, it is essential that these students be paired with a staff person.

Locating people to facilitate clusters may seem like a lot of work, but it can be as simple or involved as needed for each school situation. Many schools use only staff and a few parent volunteers to facilitate clusters and it works wonderfully. We have presented a comprehensive list of possibilities from which selections may be made, depending on individual school needs, time, and resources. The ways in which the community can be involved will depend on the amount of help available for implementing the program from people such as student interns, enrichment specialists, staff members, or Enrichment Team members. The more involved everyone is in making decisions and implementing the program, the greater the ownership and the better the chance of success.

Chapter 10

Step 4: Provide a Facilitator Orientation

Once cluster facilitators have been located, it is critical to review the goals and philosophy of enrichment clusters with them, so they do not become mini-courses, theme units, or traditional teacher-directed experiences. Remembering their own experiences from school, volunteers may feel they need to follow a directive approach and "teach" a subject using a lecture format, ditto sheets, or drills. Teachers may initially want to continue the type of teaching that occurs in their classrooms. However, student-directed experiences, hands-on activities, and student exploration are essential ingredients for successful, productive clusters.

Ideally, clusters involve Type III independent explorations that include: interest, advanced content, advanced methodology, authentic audience, and authentic evaluation (Renzulli, 1994). The development of a product or service should be within these constructs. Clusters also offer students the opportunity for Type I and Type II Enrichment that can evolve into authentic Type III experiences. These points all need to be emphasized with cluster facilitators.

One way to do this is to explain that the focus of the clusters should be on how a practicing professional works—moving from knowledge *about* a topic to first-hand investigation or knowledge *how*. Cluster facilitators will need to address problems and products within a real-world methodology and direct learners to a real audience. Questions such as the following can be used by cluster facilitators with students:

- *What product or service do people in this field produce?*
- *How do they produce it?*
- *What resources and methodologies do they need?*
- *How and to whom do they communicate the results?*

Accordingly, successful cluster facilitators help students:

- *Discover what people in a particular field of knowledge know and do.*
- *Use skills and activities related to the field.*
- *Develop a real-world product or service which they can present to an authentic audience.*

As clusters become an integral part of the school, the philosophy of enrichment clusters will become clearer and the implementation will become easier. Overview and orientation may need to be done with new facilitators. The SIMSIT offered at the end of this chapter provides several effective activities for orientation with prospective facilitators.

It is important to stress that cluster facilitators assume the roles of mentors or coaches, rather than those of traditional teachers. People who have been involved with extra-curricular activities such as athletics, 4-H clubs, scouting, yearbook, etc. are already familiar with the type of role a facilitator can play within the enrichment clusters. The focus of enrichment clusters is to have the students pursue their interests and become self-sufficient in obtaining their goals. The facilitator's role is to guide them through this process. Facilitators can modify the information and activities addressed within the cluster based upon student strengths and learning styles. Program coordinators should send cluster facilitators a general letter that addresses concerns about cluster organization and implementation (see Figure 93).

Step 5: Register Students by Placing Them Into Clusters That Interest Them

Registration is key to cluster success. By placing student in clusters with others who share their interest, an exciting synergy is created. If time permits, cluster descriptions and the registration form should be sent home so students can discuss choices with their parents or guardians, though registration can be done effectively in class. If registration is done in class, it is still advisable to keep parents informed by sending home information about the cluster descriptions. Below we describe two options that can be used for cluster registration (both have been used successfully):

1. Students complete forms at home and return them to school. As the forms are returned, students are placed in one of their cluster choices. This method uses a first-come, first-serve approach. When a cluster "fills," it is closed.
2. The students examine forms at home and complete them later in class. This method can be more efficient and is advisable if time is an issue. Students are placed in one of their choices, but may need to be shuffled in order to address possible size and age limitations.

Several points should be considered when registering students:

- *Cluster size. Ideally, a cluster should involve no more than 15 students (as space and personnel permit), though the maximum and minimum number of students will vary depending on the content. For example, a theater cluster may need at least 15 or 20 students and may be able to accommodate 30 students because of the many diverse roles in such a cluster. On the other hand, an on-line computer cluster may be limited to 10 students due to space and equipment considerations.*
- *Students should select three clusters of similar importance to them. Since some clusters will be more popular than others, it will be easier to fulfill requests if students are asked to make three choices, rather than three ranked choices (1st, 2nd, 3rd). If there is a cluster choice that a student absolutely must have, he/she can indicate that as a first choice on the form, using circles, stars, red ink, etc.*
- *Students should be registered at least one week before the clusters begin. This will give facilitators advance notice of student numbers. Occasionally one or two clusters receive too few registrations and must be canceled. When this happens, facilitators can be reassigned to help with other clusters. One elementary school offered a puppetry cluster designed for fifteen students. Forty students indicated this as a top choice, while several other clusters had no student interest and were canceled. Facilitators from these clusters agreed to help out in the puppetry cluster, which was expanded to include the additional students in two adjoining classrooms. The original facilitator provided instruction and moved between classrooms, as the other adults helped individual students.*

March, 1995

Dear Cluster Facilitator,

Thank you for your interest in organizing an enrichment cluster this spring. It is an exciting opportunity for the students and we are thrilled that you are interested in volunteering some time.

The clusters will meet March 21, 28, April 4, 18, and 25 from 1:00 - 2:30 PM. We suggest that you arrive early for each cluster session. Please stop at the office before each session to sign in and pick up your folder with the class list and room assignment. If you know you are going to be absent for any of the clusters, please let me know as soon as possible.

If you need to purchase materials, there is a small fund of $25 per cluster. Turn in your receipts to me and I will refund your purchase. If you need to spend more than $25, let me know and we will work on a solution.

Plan on having 10 - 15 students in your cluster. I will try and team you up with a staff member who will assist you with your cluster.

During the enrichment clusters, remember to have fun! If you are feeling nervous or unsure about this experience, please relax. Although lesson plans are not needed, a planned, flexible framework for the cluster will allow the students' interests to direct the cluster. You should be able to modify the information and activities presented in the cluster to suit your students' interests and learning styles. Students have selected your cluster because they are interested in the topic. Think of yourself as a mentor or coach rather than a teacher. You can provide information as the need arises.

Successful cluster coaches should help students to: (1) discover what people involved in the cluster topic know and do, (2) use skills and do activities related to the cluster topic, and (3) develop a real-world product or service which they can present to an audience.

If you have any questions, please do not hesitate to call me at the school or at my home. Thank you in advance for your assistance.

Sincerely,

Carol Moran
Enrichment Specialist

Figure 93. Letter to cluster facilitator.

- *Cluster descriptions should include all possible roles that students may assume within the cluster.* For example, in a theater cluster there are a variety of different things that students with varying talents and interests might choose to do, such as direct, write, design, act, develop stage sets, and many more. By providing a list of possible roles, various students may be attracted to the cluster. Without the roles listed, it might be assumed that the only role within a theater group would be acting.

- *Each cluster should include an appropriate representation of ages, gender, and abilities.* A cluster with 15 first graders and one fifth grader might need to be reconsidered. Also, it is a good idea with primary students to include at least two children from the same class so that they feel comfortable. Although facilitators decide age ranges within the clusters, flexibility should be maintained for placement of exceptional younger students into intense areas of interest.

- *The student/adult ratio should be satisfactory.* Program coordinators should consider the number of special needs students, the age of students, the topic/activity, and the experience level of adults when organizing clusters. Community or parent facilitators should always be paired with a staff member.

- *Extra adult supervision may be needed for some clusters.* Younger students and particular activities or field trips may require additional help.

- *Students' choices should be appropriate for their interests and abilities.* In one of our sites, some special needs students had specific needs which could not be met in some clusters, so their selections were monitored with input from their special education teachers to assure appropriate placement.

- *Lists should remain flexible.* Since students select their clusters based on interests, it is rare that they will be unhappy with their assigned cluster; but it can and does occur. When this happens, the student can be reassigned to another cluster, join a scheduled Type I Enrichment experience (such as a speaker, film, or a supervised enrichment center), or remain in the cluster until the end of the series.

Registration can be completed efficiently by members of the Enrichment Team, parent volunteers, or instructional assistants. A computer database of students in the school will provide a quick and easy format for developing lists of students by class and by cluster. These lists should then be distributed to homeroom teachers and cluster facilitators.

Step 6: Celebrate Your Success

Celebration of clusters can take many forms, depending on the nature of the cluster (see Figure 94). The product or service from a drama cluster will be very different from the product or service of a horticulture cluster. Because of their popularity, clusters are easy to celebrate. Celebration of clusters is significant for two reasons: (1) it provides an important avenue for the sharing of student products and services with an authentic audience and (2) it helps build support for a program by spreading awareness to administrators, board of education members, parents, and the community.

Whenever appropriate, schools should invite newspaper reporters, community members, parents, and board of education members to come and view the unique products and services that emerge from clusters. By "going public" with the efforts of the cluster program, schools can generate community excitement and involvement which lends itself to school pride and sense of accomplishment.

Some schools host an awards ceremony and present certificates of achievement to students for cluster involvement (see Figure 95). Copies of these certificates can be included in the students' *Total Talent Portfolio*. By recognizing a student's accomplishments, schools can build upon the student's enthusiasm and transfer his/her excitement into the regular classroom. Cluster sharing can also provide Type I experiences for other students.

It is also equally important to thank all cluster facilitators and volunteers. This can be done individually by sending thank you notes or certificates, making special presentations at a schoolwide assembly or appreciation tea, highlighting efforts in the school newspaper, or offering a combination of events.

Sample Clusters

The following pages list some examples of actual clusters that cover various disciplines. Note the emphasis on products and services in each description, the diversity of possible student roles within the cluster, and the real-world nature of the cluster. Distributing a copy of this list can be extremely helpful in guiding and motivating reluctant facilitators (staff members, parents, community members). Enrichment specialist can develop their own list of descriptions or copy ideas developed during a SIMSIT. The possibilities are virtually endless!

Ideas for Celebrating Enrichment Clusters

Award Ceremony
Banner Behind Airplane
Banquet
Billboard
Book
Breakfast or Lunch Celebration
Brochure
Chamber of Commerce Display
Displays at Malls
Home Page on the Internet
Invite a School Board Member
Local or National Television
Multimedia Presentation
Newsletters
Newspaper Article
Open House
Parade of Products

Performances Outside of School
Photo Album
Portfolio Certificates
Product Fair
Product Rap for Radio or TV
PTA Meetings
Puppet Show
Reception
School Assembly
School Display Cases
School Television
Service Vendor Fair
Skit or Play
Slide Show or Video
Student Presentation in Community
Talent Fair

Figure 94. Ideas for celebrating enrichment clusters.

ENRICHMENT CLUSTER PROGRAM

Certificate of Recognition

This is to certify that

_____

has completed the 1995-1996
enrichment cluster Program
in the following clusters:

_____

_____

Principal

Cluster Enrichment Specialist

Figure 95. Enrichment cluster portfolio certificate.

Chapter 10

Storytelling Club

Facilitated by Pat Elliot, Fourth Grade Teacher

Do you have the gift of gab? Do you enjoy telling and listening to tall tales? In this cluster, we'll take a look at folktales, myths and legends that are used in storytelling. We'll watch some storytellers and practice their techniques. Join first grade teacher Pat Elliot as we produce our own storytelling video to be shared with other classrooms or perform some live storytelling!

Forest & Wildlife Biologists Society

Facilitated by Kevin O'Shea, Graduate Student

Explore the world of the wildlife biologist! With natural resources student Kevin O'Shea, you might build a bird sanctuary, create a nature path behind the school, search for bones in a pellet coughed up by an owl, examine real skulls and skins, or search for clues of wildlife. Background material for this cluster will come from James Goodwin State Forest.

Culinary Institute

Facilitated by Edna Horan, Paraprofessional

What makes a cake rise? Learn about the science of baking with expert chef Mrs. Horan. Learn about how a chef prepares a favorite dish, what happens when a key ingredient is left out, why some flavors taste good together, and discover how a new recipe is developed. Experiment with how a recipe can be altered to suit different tastes or feed more people. Create your own unique treats and group recipe book to share with the school!

Young Sculptors, Inc.

Facilitated by Richard Jaworowski, Local Artist

How does a sculptor work? How is a piece of "rock" transformed into a work of art? What happens to the finished piece? Explore the process of creating your own three-dimensional work of art using authentic tools and plaster. You may discover that creating your piece is as much fun as enjoying the finished product! View some works in marble and learn about one artist's perspective. Richard Jaworowski is a local sculptor who has been carving for over 20 years. Wear old clothes or bring a smock.

Young Entrepreneurs

Facilitated by Cheryl Smith, Teacher

How does a business operate and make money? Do *you* have the savvy? What product or service might you "sell?" To whom would you market it? How and where would you advertise it? Practice business skills with the school store or invent your own business. Who knows, we may even make the Fortune 500!

In House Ad Agency, Inc.

Facilitated by Mary Rizza, Graduate Student

"New! Free! Improved!" We are bombarded daily with advertising messages, but how truthful are the ads we see? How strong are the claims? How do ads affect the decisions we make? We'll examine some ads and look for bias, exaggeration, and facts. We'll also learn how to create effective ads for real businesses and test our persuasive abilities.

Gamers Institute

Facilitated by Lynn Weeks, Parent

Explore the world of math games and puzzles with parent Lynn Weeks. Investigate visual games and optical illusions, dice games and probability, origami, and games of logic and problem solving. Learn how a game company might develop their popular games. Develop your own board game or puzzle and share it with the group in a game "meet."

Invention Convention

Facilitated by Robert Erikson, Physics Professor; Max Nam, Physics Student; and Sandra Rijs, Third Grade Teacher

Are you an inventive thinker? Would you like to be? Brainstorm a problem, try to identify many solutions, and design an invention to solve the problem. Create your invention individually or with a partner under the guidance of Bob Erikson and Max Nam. You may share your final product at the Young Inventors' Fair, a statewide day-long celebration of creativity.

Computer League

Facilitated by Paula McNally, Art Teacher and Computer Enthusiast

This cluster offers an introduction to the new classroom version of Prodigy. We will explore the advantages of working on-line and discover the almost infinite ways to use the "information superhighway." Learn and play some of the games and communicate with students in another school. Become an "on-line expert" and help others in your school learn how to access the information superhighway!

Windham Chimers Handbell Choir

Facilitated by Angela Riccardo Salcedo, Music Director and Organist, St. Andrews Church; Marsha Creese, Reading Specialist; and Mari Shooks, School Nurse

This cluster is for those who enjoy music! Travel to St. Joseph's church to learn how to create beautiful music with handbells. Students will get the opportunity to participate in a group choir and learn how to operate handbells for a group performance at school.

Police Academy

Facilitated by Detective Lee Griffin, Police Officer

In this cluster, you will learn how to investigate a crime. What are the first steps you must take? How will you go about solving the mystery? Work with others in the cluster to develop an original product as a result of being involved in this school "police force." Learn about the realities of detective work and the service that police officers provide with professional police officer Lee Griffin.

Young Artists Guild

Facilitated by Mary Taylor, Art Teacher

Learn about how real artists work and explore different creative experiences. In this cluster you will be able to choose an area of interest such as calligraphy, drawing, or sculpture and learn how to perfect your skills in that area. You will have the opportunity to share your work with others in an art show.

History of the Motion Picture

Facilitated by Richard Larson, Teacher and Film Enthusiast

Explore the world of movies and film makers. You will be introduced to the first motion picture, *The Great Train Robbery*, silent pictures and the great influences of the era. You can also pursue an in-depth study of specific film genres, such as Horror, Comedy or Sci-Fi. Richard Larson, a fourth grade teacher, is fascinated with the Golden Age of Hollywood. Students in this cluster will work on film reviews for the student body and be encouraged to create their own film posters.

Young Authors, Inc.

Facilitated by Ann Doros, Language Arts Consultant

Let your imagination be your guide in this cluster offered by Ann Doros, Language Arts consultant. Become a genuine author by writing creatively in a variety of genres such as poetry, fiction, drama, and short story. You can enter finished pieces in contests and/ or send them to various children's magazines for publication consideration.

School Newspaper—Hot Off the Press!

Facilitated by Dave Geary, Parent and Editor

Have you ever wanted to work on a newspaper? Come be a reporter, photographer, editor, or layout artist as we spread the news of the school with our own newspaper! Investigate a story, write a comic strip, report on a school issue, interview a teacher, or create advertisements.

The Amazing You (Blood & Guts: A Working Guide to Your Insides)

Facilitated by Dr. Michael Gerich and Kelli MacFarlane, Physical Education Teachers

Come try activities designed to enhance your total body awareness. You will discover how to use your mind to become more skillful, fit, and knowledgeable about your physical abilities. Our personal trainers, physical education teachers Dr. Michael Gerich and Kelli MacFarlane will guide us as we learn about our bodies and design personalized fitness programs for ourselves or members of our family.

Endangered Animals Society, Inc.

Facilitated by Carole Norrish, Parent

Bengal Tigers, Sea Turtles, Manatees, Orangutans . . . spread awareness of these endangered animals through your participation in this group! Research an endangered animal that interests you, explore habitat destruction and ways that we can help save these animals, develop posters to post in town, make squares for an endangered animals quilt, create a book, write to a national organization for more information, or adopt an animal. Come with your ideas!

Preschool Teachers, Inc.

Facilitated by Candice Strick, Preschool Teacher

Do you wonder what teachers do in their spare time and how they come up with ideas for lessons? Would you enjoy sharing your experience and knowledge with some three to five year olds? In this cluster you will learn strategies teachers use to prepare and teach lessons. You will experience the thrill of working with real students and practice developing a lesson plan and teaching it to a preschooler, under the guidance of preschool teacher Candice Strick.

Young Aviators

Facilitated by Paul Varga, Flight Instructor

Explore the dynamics of flight. Learn about and explore forces that cause changes in air pressure, lift, thrust, drag, and gravity. A field trip to the local airport will provide a close-up view of some smaller planes.

Dairy Farmers

Facilitated by Janet Smith, Math Teacher and Bill Haddad, Principal

Have you ever wondered how it feels to milk a cow? What happens to the milk? Come learn about dairy farming, how to care for cows, and the many uses of milk (besides drinking!). We'll take a field trip to a dairy farm.

WEE Deliver Postal Service

Facilitated by Debbie Anderson, Parent

Do you like sending and receiving mail? Do you know what happens to a letter once it is mailed? Come to this cluster and learn about the U.S. Postal System and how it works. We will set up and run our own "post office" right here in the school! Materials for the WEE Deliver program are provided by the U.S. Postal Service.

Young Lawyers

Facilitated by John McGrath, Parent and Lawyer

How does the law affect children? What are some legal issues that face children today? What happens in a courtroom? We'll explore law from your point of view, visit a courtroom, and experience a mock trial with John McGrath, a local lawyer and parent.

Lights, Camera, Action!

Facilitated by Catina Caban-Owen, Social Worker

Learn what is involved in video production and the various techniques used by professionals, then decide how you would like to participate. Do you prefer script writing, acting, directing, or operating the camera? Catina is a social worker at the school who will be guiding this cluster. Two thumbs up!

Puppeteers Workshop

Facilitated by Yusomil Bonet, Teacher

Learn about the world of puppets in this cluster! Experiment with creating several different types of puppets, such as finger puppets, marionettes, and hand puppets. Develop your own character to use in a performance. Help write or star in a puppet show and bring your puppet to life!

Builders, Inc.

Facilitated by Mrs. Macchi and Mrs. Sellman, First Grade Teachers

Come join us for a hands-on experience in the world of construction. Students will become architects and builders as they decide on the size of their project, materials to use, and the process they need to follow to reach completion. This group will explore issues of safety in construction, the importance of the planning process, and talk with a real builder about the process of building. Students will become the general contractors under the guidance of Mrs. Macchi and Mrs. Sellman.

Bravo! Children's Theater

Facilitated by Chris Lamb, Teacher

All the world's a stage as we explore the joy of theatrical performance. In preparation, we will choose a performance, design and create costumes and sets, collect props, learn to apply stage make-up, and practice our acting abilities. Kindergarten teacher Fran Foley will be our stage manager as we experience the smell of greasepaint and the roar of the crowd.

Kitchen Scientists

Facilitated by Anne Joseph, Paraprofessional

Bubble, bubble, toil and trouble. What common ingredients in your kitchen can be used to create science experiments? What makes a cake rise? Does the weather affect baking? What are some different types of sugars? Does salted water boil faster than unsalted water? We'll test some of these questions and come up with some of our own.

Mr. Frank's School Improvement

Facilitated by Frank Albano, School Janitor

How does a building work? What needs maintenance or fixing? Would you like to identify potential problems and help solve them? Come explore the world of pipes and bricks with Frank Albano, the school's Mr. Fixit to discover secrets of the school.

Assessment and Evaluation

To assure successful enrichment clusters, a formative evaluation is strongly suggested. We recommend beginning with a short pilot series lasting from three to four weeks, which can be used as the basis for adjustments and refinements to a longer, more permanent schedule of clusters. Staff input and assistance in planning and development of both the pilot series and the permanent series will help assure a successful program.

Several instruments (Reis, Gentry, & Park, 1995) have been developed to assist with assessment and evaluation components of the enrichment clusters.

Parental Attitudes About Enrichment Opportunities (Gentry & Reis, 1995). This instrument is useful for schools wishing to measure changes in parent perception and satisfaction as they implement enrichment cluster programs. It was developed during the pilot study of enrichment clusters because a suitable instrument did not exist for evaluating parents' attitudes about enrichment within their school. Appropriate content validity, construct validity and reliability information were obtained for the instrument. The final instrument contains an operational definition of enrichment and demographic items including name, relationship to the child, and child's grade. This is followed by ten statements which use a 5-point Likert scale as a response format. These ten statements represent two reliable factors with items one through seven measuring parents' perception of enrichment (alpha reliability = .87), and items eight through ten measuring parents' satisfaction with enrichment (alpha reliability = .77). The final section includes three open-ended questions to which parents may respond in writing (see Figure 96).

Student Survey About Enrichment Clusters (Gentry & Maxfield, 1995). This instrument is useful for assessing how enrichment clusters provide for interest/ enjoyment, challenge, meaning, and choice as seen by the students in the clusters. It was developed to assess students' attitudes towards enrichment clusters with respect to the dimensions of *interest/enjoyment, challenge, meaning,* and *choice*. Appropriate content validity, construct validity and reliability information were obtained for the instrument. The final instrument is student-friendly and contains 27 items which measure the above-mentioned dimensions with alpha reliabilities of .91, .79, .79, and .81 respectively. Students respond to the items by checking a box that corresponds to a 5-point Likert scale (see Figure 97).

The Student Product Assessment Form (SPAF) (Reis, 1981). This instrument is useful with enrichment clusters because it provides a valid and reliable basis for assessing product quality as a measure of achievement. *SPAF* includes two components. The first is related to the process of product development and includes eight items which have a 5-point Likert scale and a "Not Applicable" category. Each of these items is comprised of three parts: the key concept, a description of that item, and examples to help provide clarity. The second component of *SPAF* is related to the overall quality of the products. It includes 7 items which have a 4-point Likert scale. This instrument has a high inter-rater reliability ($\partial = .961$) for the total of all items, if more than one rater is evaluating the product. Content validity was established through analysis and critical evaluations of subject matter experts and specialists in educational research (Reis, 1981). Copies of the summary sheet of the *SPAF* can be added to students' talent portfolios as a means of documenting their products. A copy of the *SPAF* is included in Chapter 9.

Portfolio Certificates. We suggest providing portfolio certificates to students to help document their involvement in the enrichment clusters. These certificates can become a part of each student's *Total Talent Portfolio*. A sample certificate was provided earlier (see Figure 95).

Parental Attitudes About Enrichment Opportunities

Parent's Name: _____   Child's grade: _____

I am the child's: ____Mother   ____Father   ____Guardian

Following are ten statements. Please respond to them by circling the number that best represents your answer, using this scale:

> For the purposes of this questionnaire, **enrichment** is defined as planned experiences beyond regular classroom work designed to enrich your child's education. Examples include speakers, videos and interest-based activities that extend learning.

1	Always
2	Often
3	Sometimes
4	Seldom
5	Never

1. My child has opportunities for enrichment experiences in school.   1 2 3 4 5

2. During school my child is encouraged to develop and pursue his/her talents.   1 2 3 4 5

3. My child develops projects in the classroom that reflect his/her interests.   1 2 3 4 5

4. My child has opportunities to work with other students in his/her classroom who share common interests.   1 2 3 4 5

5. My child's school offers enrichment opportunities for all students.   1 2 3 4 5

6. My child enjoys the enrichment opportunities in his/her school or classroom.   1 2 3 4 5

7. My child is happy about attending school.   1 2 3 4 5

8. I am informed about the educational enrichment activities for my child at school.   1 2 3 4 5

9. I have the opportunity to become involved with enrichment opportunities in school.   1 2 3 4 5

10. I am satisfied with enrichment opportunities/experiences my child receives at school.   1 2 3 4 5

Please comment briefly on the following items: (Use the back of the page if needed)

1. What do you like most about your child's school experience?

2. What changes would you like to see made regarding your child's school or classroom experiences?

3. Please provide other comments that will help us understand your attitude toward school and satisfaction with your child's experience in his/her classroom or school.

Figure 96. Parental attitudes about enrichment opportunities instrument.

Name: _____

Grade: **3   4   5   6** (circle one)

Teacher: _____

Gender: **Girl   Boy** (circle one)

Cluster: _____

Student Survey About . . .

Enrichment Clusters

Marcia Gentry & Lori R. Maxfield
University of Connecticut

We would like to know how you feel about enrichment clusters. Read each sentence and indicate how much you agree with it by **putting an X** in the box. There are no right or wrong answers. Your answers will be kept secret. Remember to mark an X for each sentence. In the example below, the person **agreed** with the sentence.

	Strongly Disagree	Disagree	Undecided	Agree	Strongly Agree
Example: My cluster is enjoyable.				X	
1. I like what I do in my cluster.					
2. What I do in my cluster fits my interests.					
3. What I do in my cluster is interesting.					
4. The activities I do in my cluster are enjoyable.					
5. I have an opportunity to work on things in my cluster that interest me.					
6. I look forward to my cluster.					
7. What I learn in my cluster is interesting to me.					

Figure 97. Student survey about enrichment clusters.

	Strongly Disagree	Disagree	Undecided	Agree	Strongly Agree
8. I like working in a cluster.					
9. I have to think to solve problems in my cluster.					
10. My projects offer useful solutions to problems.					
11. I use challenging materials and books in my cluster.					
12. The cluster leader encourages me to solve challenging problems.					
13. I study problems that affect my life.					
14. I like the projects I work on in my cluster.					
15. My projects are important to others.					
16. My projects are important to me.					
17. My cluster leader challenges me to do my best.					
18. My work can make a difference.					
19. When we work together, I can choose my partners.					
20. I can choose to work in a group.					
21. I can choose my own projects.					
22. I can choose to work alone.					
23. I can choose materials to work with in the cluster.					
24. When there are many jobs, I can choose the ones that suit me.					
25. I can choose an audience for my product.					

Thank you.
Please make sure that you have indicated an answer for each sentence.

Figure 72. Student survey about enrichment clusters (continued).

Enrichment Cluster Facilitator Evaluation Form. This form solicits feedback from persons who facilitate enrichment clusters. This evaluation form deals with cluster content, scheduling, successes, and suggestions and can be used to improve the overall cluster program. This form can be adapted as needed (see Figure 98).

Enrichment Clusters Student Evaluation Forms. As with the facilitator feedback form, these forms were developed to assess student satisfaction with their cluster experiences. Two forms were developed, one for primary and another for upper elementary students. Both are short, easy to complete, and provide insight into student experiences in their clusters. These forms can also be adapted as needed (see Figures 99 and 100).

These instruments can be used both informally and formally to provide insight into the effectiveness and quality of an enrichment cluster program. It is important to document student successes and product development and maintain examples of student progress in their *Total Talent Portfolios.*

Conclusion

Enrichment clusters are designed to build involvement and ownership of the enrichment program by all, since the program includes all staff and students and encourages participation by parents and community members. Since clusters use multi-grade groupings, they naturally strengthen school cohesiveness. Because groupings are based on student choice, clusters actively promote student interests and provide effective opportunities for Type I, Type II, and particularly Type III explorations. Enrichment clusters also provide opportunities for teachers to explore their own interests and "try out" new topics. Since the whole school is involved in an enrichment cluster program, gifted education pedagogy is extended to *all* students.

Enrichment Clusters
Facilitator Evaluation Form

Name (Optional) _____

Your feedback and input are essential to the success of the enrichment cluster program. By taking a few minutes to complete the evaluation questions below, you will be assisting us in improving and further developing enrichment clusters for students.

1. What did you enjoy most about facilitating your cluster?

   _____
   _____
   _____
   _____

2. Were the clusters well organized? How can the program be changed or improved?

   _____
   _____
   _____
   _____

3. What were the students' reactions to your cluster?

   _____
   _____
   _____
   _____

4. What types of advanced content did you present in your cluster?

   _____
   _____
   _____
   _____

5. What products (if any) were produced by students in your cluster?

   _____
   _____
   _____
   _____

(Over)

Figure 98. Enrichment clusters facilitator evaluation form.

6. Are you interested in facilitating another cluster?   Yes _____   No _____

   If yes, what topic? _____

   _____

   _____

   _____

7. Can you recommend other potential facilitators and possible topics for the next session?

   _____

   _____

   _____

   _____

   _____

8. What recommendations would you make for scheduling the clusters (i.e., how many sessions, length of sessions)?

   _____

   _____

   _____

   _____

   _____

   _____

   _____

   _____

   _____

9. Other comments:

   _____

   _____

   _____

   _____

   _____

   _____

   _____

   _____

   _____

Thank You!

Figure 98. Enrichment clusters facilitator evaluation form (continued).

Enrichment Clusters
Student Evaluation Form (Grades K-2)

Grade: _____ Cluster Name: _____

We would like to know how you feel about your experience in your enrichment cluster. Please read each statement carefully and circle the face that shows how you feel about each statement. A happy face means that you agree with the statement. A face that is neither happy nor sad means that you are not sure how you feel about the statement. A sad face means that you disagree with the statement.

1. I liked my cluster.

   Agree   Disagree

----

2. I learned new things in my cluster.

   Agree   Disagree

----

3. My cluster teacher was interesting.

   Agree   Disagree

----

4. I would like to be in an enrichment
   cluster again.

   Agree   Disagree

(Over)

Figure 99. Enrichment clusters student evaluation form (grades K-2).

Please answer the following questions:

5. I think an enrichment cluster should be offered on the following topic(s):

_____

_____

_____

_____

_____

_____

6. One thing I learned in my enrichment cluster was:

_____

_____

_____

_____

_____

7. The thing I liked best about my enrichment cluster was:

_____

_____

_____

_____

_____

_____

8. One change I would make to improve my enrichment cluster is:

_____

_____

_____

_____

_____

_____

Thank You!

Figure 99. Enrichment clusters student evaluation form (grades K-2) (continued).

Enrichment Clusters
Student Evaluation Form (Grades 3-6)

Grade: _____ Cluster Name: _____

We would like to know how you feel about your experience in your enrichment cluster. Please read each statement carefully and circle the number that shows how you feel about each statement. A number 1 means that you agree with the statement. A number 2 means that you are not sure how you feel about the statement. A number 3 means that you disagree with the statement.

	1 Agree	**2**	**3** Disagree
1. I enjoyed my cluster.			
2. I learned new information/skills in my cluster.	**1** Agree	**2**	**3** Disagree
3. My cluster teacher was interesting.	**1** Agree	**2**	**3** Disagree
4. I am interested in participating in more enrichment clusters.	**1** Agree	**2**	**3** Disagree

(Over)

Figure 100. Enrichment clusters student evaluation form (grades 3-6).

Please answer the following questions:

5. I think an enrichment cluster should be offered on the following topic(s):

_____

_____

_____

_____

_____

_____

6. One thing I learned in my enrichment cluster was:

_____

_____

_____

_____

_____

_____

7. The thing I liked best about my enrichment cluster was:

_____

_____

_____

_____

_____

_____

8. One change I would make to improve my enrichment cluster is:

_____

_____

_____

_____

_____

_____

Thank You!

Figure 100. Enrichment clusters student evaluation form (grades 3-6) (continued).

SIMSIT 7
FACILITATOR'S GUIDE

Developing Enrichment Clusters
A Simulated Planning Activity

Teacher Training Objectives
- To orient teachers and volunteers to the goals, philosophy, and focus of an enrichment cluster program.
- To prepare teachers and volunteers for enrichment cluster facilitation.

Number of People Involved
All involved in enrichment cluster facilitation

Approximate Time
45 minutes to 1 hour

Materials and Equipment
VCR, Chart Paper, Markers

Directions
Initially, it is important to discuss the goals, philosophy, and focus of enrichment clusters with new facilitators, so that clusters do become student-directed experiences that accommodate different interests and learning styles within advanced content and methodology. It should be stressed with facilitators that clusters can provide the opportunity for Type I, Type II, and Type III investigations. The focus of clusters should be on how a practicing professional works—moving from knowledge *about* a topic to firsthand investigation or knowledge of *how* to work in an area. It is important to stress that cluster facilitators should assume the role of mentors or coaches, in order to help students pursue their interests and practice becoming self-sufficient learners. The following questions provide an ideal beginning point for any cluster:

- What product or service do people in this field produce? How do they produce it?
- What resources and methodologies do they need?
- How and to whom do they communicate the results?

SIMSIT 7
Developing Enrichment Clusters (continued)

The following activities are designed to provide an orientation for facilitators.

1. Give a quiz as a preassessment and awareness tool, to be reviewed at the end of the session. It can include 10 - 15 true/false items such as: *Clusters require a lesson plan, clusters require curricular needs*, and *enrichment facilitators must be teachers*. Review the quiz to check for understanding of clusters.

2. Show the video *Enrichment Clusters: Using High-End Learning to Develop Talents in all Students* and discuss it. This video package is available from The National Research Center on the Gifted and Talented, 362 Fairfield Road, U-7, Storrs, CT 09269-2007. Cost: $85.

3. Discuss the nature of clusters and advanced content. Refer to sample titles and descriptions (included earlier in the chapter); highlight those clusters that seem particularly interesting or inspiring.

4. Administer the adult interest survey, *Inspiration: Targeting My Ideal Teaching and Learning Situation.* Based on the results from the survey, have adults develop ideas for "mock clusters" and break into "cluster groups." Pose the following questions to encourage each interest group to find the direction and focus of their cluster:

   - What will be the name of this cluster?
   - What will be the product or service?
   - What roles might cluster participants assume?
   - What resources and methodologies are needed?
   - Who will be the authentic audience for the product or service?

   You may choose to model an example first before asking groups to develop their answers. During group discussions, have participants record their answers on chart paper for discussion.

   After the groups have developed ideas for their clusters, have them share their responses with the whole group to help reinforce the nature and philosophy of enrichment clusters. Encouraging discussion about different possible directions the clusters might take helps emphasize the fact that student interests really should drive the cluster activities.

5. Address overall comments and questions about clusters. Common issues may involve scheduling, logistics, field trips, expenses, and space.

Conclusion

Developing a Five Year Plan

Needs Assessment

One of the first steps for the development of a new Schoolwide Enrichment Model (SEM) program is to conduct some type of needs assessment in order to decide where to start program planning. A needs assessment can be a formal process completed by sending a two or three-page instrument to each faculty member. The results from this assessment can be tallied and reviewed by the new enrichment specialist and an advisory committee which might consist of the original planning committee or representatives from Enrichment Teams in each building. The trends that are apparent from the needs assessment can be the beginnings of the first stage of enrichment specialist planning. In some ways a formal needs assessment can be an extremely positive way to start planning a program. Unfortunately, needs assessment instruments sometimes cause negative feelings to be expressed by faculty members *before* they even have any interaction with the enrichment program.

An alternate approach is for the Enrichment Team, enrichment specialist or program enrichment specialist (if one is available) to conduct an informal needs assessment. This informal needs assessment can help to make decisions about initial program planning activities. For example, in one district the new enrichment specialist learned that her position had been created because five elementary students had been accelerated beyond eighth grade Math and Language Arts material in fourth grade. No one in the district had any idea what to do next! Obviously, serving these youngsters became a major priority for the new enrichment specialist. Individual programs were developed and the regular curriculum was totally modified to meet their needs. In this instance, the first task of the enrichment specialist was apparent. It was, in fact, the reason for the creation of her job. In other cases, the decision about first steps is not quite as obvious.

We suggest that after being hired for the position, the enrichment specialist should make an appointment with each principal with whom he/she will be directly working. Some key questions that might be asked during this meeting include:

- *Do you have faculty members who might be willing to serve on an Enrichment Team?*
- *Do you anticipate any particular issues with your general staff regarding curriculum compacting?*
- *What types of instructional grouping are currently used by teachers in this building?*

- *What kinds of inservice do you think your staff will need to implement the program?*
- *What are your thoughts and concerns about the implementation (or expansion/ change) of this program in your building?*

Responses to these questions may give the enrichment specialist some important information about what needs to be done first and may help identify potential problems that may be eliminated before they occur.

Steps in Developing a Five Year Plan

Based upon the information gathered from interviews, discussions with teachers and administrators, and program documents (handouts, handbooks, identification forms, nomination forms, parent correspondence), decisions should be made about goals for the first five years of the program. We recommend that a tentative five year plan be drafted for a variety of reasons. Quite often, enrichment specialists become overwhelmed with the task at hand and have no idea where to start. When one looks at what is involved in a fully organized program, it's easy to lose track of what has been accomplished and instead, concentrate only on what remains to be done! By conducting a needs assessment, the enrichment specialist can organize a list of priorities and make decisions about what should be done first, second and third. This decision should be made with the planning committee. The first step in making decisions about what the objectives should be for each year is the tabulation of all of the suggestions provided by principals, teachers and other interest groups. Additionally, the enrichment specialist should take into account what has already occurred in the district. For example, if extensive inservice has already been conducted, formal inservice sessions might not become a first year goal. In a SEM program the list might be similar to the one below:

Possible First Year Goals for a SEM Program

Conduct orientation sessions for parents and students.

Organize Enrichment Teams in each school.

Provide professional development for teachers and administrators.

Select pilot schools or grades to implement the program.

Implement Type I, II, III activities.

Develop a handbook for teachers with information about definition, identification, programming model, etc.

Develop a brief program booklet for parents.

Plan a reasonable budget.

Evaluate the program.

Organize a Type III Fair.

This partial list is a compilation of the most logical choices for the first year objectives of a SEM program. However, for a number of reasons, other priorities may have to be put ahead of one or more of these objectives. For example, the group of fourth grade students, who have been accelerated through eighth grade Math and now have no Math program for grade five, will have to take precedence over some of the objectives listed above.

We recommend using a form such as the one presented in Figure 101 when mapping out objectives for a SEM program. As stated earlier, the section of objectives should be based on two factors: (1) what has already been accomplished in the program and (2) what the informal or formal needs assessment suggest needs to be done.

The program objectives listed in Figure 102 reflect the implementation of a new enrichment program in a district where a program had not previously existed. In the planning year, an enrichment committee should be organized to make certain decisions about the program and select an enrichment specialist who can then help implement the program. We strongly recommend that the superintendent ask each principal to provide his or her staff with information about the new program and invite interested individuals to volunteer and serve on the committee.

In our experience, the best programs are those that start small. If resources are limited in a school district, the best way to start a program is with a pilot school. If a district only has one enrichment specialist and there are four elementary schools, two middle schools and a senior high school all waiting for services, the best starting point may be the establishment of one pilot "model program" in which energies can be concentrated while the enrichment specialist also tries to start Enrichment Teams in all of the other schools. We strongly suggest that this option be considered rather than having one resource teacher attempt to spend a half day in each school and end the year accomplishing very little.

The establishment of an outstanding pilot program can serve as a model for the rest of the district. Other principals will begin to say, "When do I get a program like that?" and parents will begin to urge the board of education to expand this excellent program. If it is not reasonable to begin a pilot program in all schools, we suggest selecting a school where the program has the best chance of success due to faculty and administrative support.

During the first year, decisions about what should be accomplished will stem from what has been completed in the pilot year. If a school accomplishes all of the objectives listed in the planning year, then the program objectives for the first two years will resemble those shown Figures 103 and 104. As the years progress, it will become easier to identify new objectives and make decisions about program expansion. The program objectives listed in Figure 105 might be considered for the years immediately following the beginning of a new SEM program.

As the program develops and becomes an accepted part of the school system, the enrichment specialist may begin to have the luxury of selecting more specific target goals. This may be accomplished only after the program is firmly in place. We have found that with careful advance planning, the program can become accepted and firmly established in the first or second year of implementation. When this occurs, the enrichment specialist can become more involved in other important tasks.

In Figure 106, we have organized a wide range of possible SEM program activities. Some of these activities have been identified as major objectives for early years of a SEM program. Other entries from this list can be considered for beginning programs if a school or district's needs warrant such a decision. The remaining items can be viewed as suggested objectives for later years of a program.

Enrichment Specialist's Checklist

Selecting Objectives

Year 1:
      1.

      2.

      3.

      4.

Year 2:
      1.

      2.

      3.

      4.

Year 3:
      1.

      2.

      3.

      4.

Year 4:
      1.

      2.

      3.

      4.

Year 5:
      1.

      2.

      3.

      4.

Figure 101. Enrichment specialist's checklist.

Objectives for a New SEM Program

Planning Year

1. Organize a districtwide committee with representation from each school (or district in a countywide area).

2. Meet regularly with the planning team to discuss options and faculty preferences and subdivide responsibilities for the implementation of the program.

3. Organize the planning committee to read, visit other programs in the area, look into different identification and programming options, and report to the board of education and the superintendent.

4. After reporting to the board and the superintendent on the preference for definition, programming model and program design, encourage the board to hire a program enrichment specialist/resource teacher (depending on the size of the district).

5. With the enrichment specialist, select a definition, identification system, programming model and reasonable starting point—a pilot school or certain grade levels to be served by the program.

Figure 102. Objectives for a new SEM program (planning year).

Objectives for a New SEM Program

Year 1:

1. Provide inservice and literature on the program for all administrators in the district.

2. Provide inservice for all instructional staff on the definition, identification system, programming model, and their responsibilities in the program.

3. Organize Enrichment Teams in each building (perhaps use members of the planning committee to 'chair' the teams).

4. Begin the process of identifying Talent Pool members at the appropriate grade levels and start providing services to students on a regular basis at the pilot school(s) and/or grade level(s).

5. Start a pilot enrichment cluster program during the second half of the school year.

6. Evaluate what has occurred and present the evaluation, a slide show of highlights, and a budget to the board of education at the end of the year.

Figure 103. Objectives for a new SEM program (year 1).

Objectives for a New SEM Program

Year 2:

1. Continue preceding year's activities, including ongoing identification of Talent Pool members, inservice and staff development, services to Talent Pool students (Type I and II Enrichment on a regular basis, compacting and ability to "revolve into" Type III Enrichment), services to non-Talent Pool students through the Enrichment Team, and program evaluation.

2. Consider when and how to expand program depending on available staff and resources. Work to expand the enrichment cluster program in each school.

3. Develop a community/faculty resource pool and plan a beginning scope and sequence for Type II Enrichment.

4. Develop a handbook/booklet/flyer about the program that can be sent to teachers, administrators, and parents.

5. Organize a *Type III Fair*.

Figure 104. Objectives for a new SEM program (year 2).

Objectives for a New SEM Program

Years 3-5:

1. The expansion of Type I opportunities by:

   Scheduling bi-monthly buildingwide Type I's.
   Organizing a districtwide system for arranging Type I speakers, Type II mini-courses and Type III mentors.
   Encouraging classroom teachers to make and share interest development centers, etc.

2. The diffusion of Type II techniques into the regular classroom by:

   Model teaching of Type II skills.
   Encouraging classroom teachers to team teach Type II's.
   Organizing inservice for classroom teachers in the major objectives of Type II Enrichment.
   Regularly scheduling enrichment clusters in each school.

3. The expansion of the program into:

   The primary grades.
   The secondary level.
   The Art program.

4. The establishment of communication vehicles by:

   Creating schoolwide newsletters.
   Starting a district newsletter.
   Sending home parent progress reports.

5. Continue working on the expansion of curricular modification and differentiation strategies through curriculum compacting and replacement activities.

Figure 105. Objectives for a new SEM program (years 3-5).

Possible SEM Program Activities

Inservice

Conduct orientation session for administrators and classroom teachers.

Conduct orientation session for parents and interested community members.

Conduct periodic meetings to discuss progress, explain program and share achievements and problems.

Arrange for one or more classroom teachers or administrators to attend a conference on enrichment and/ or differentiation.

Planning

Establish file of community resources for enrichment clusters or Types I and II Enrichment.

Schedule initial set of Type I presentations.

Prepare basic process development lessons (Type II).

Prepare orientation session for teachers, parents and students.

Develop ideas for program newsletter.

Develop charts/bulletin boards on Triad, CPS, independent study, product alternatives, fields of study, etc.

Select or develop interest assessment device/tool.

Communication

Advertise upcoming speakers and enrichment clusters and provide written post-presentation summaries to teachers.

Respond quickly to teachers'/students' requests for information or input regarding project ideas.

Share results of students' interest inventories, investigations and progress through informal teacher conferences.

Share Type II training materials with classroom teachers.

Conduct periodic meetings to discuss progress of program, explain the program and share achievements and problems.

Distribute a periodic teacher/parent newsletter describing current activities within the gifted program.

Figure 106. Possible SEM program activities.

Possible SEM Program Activities

Public Relations/Community Awareness

Develop or update program handbook or brochure.

Develop Triad bulletin board for the office, library or main corridor of the school.

Prepare a "slide show" that explains major components of the program.

Develop (in your slide show) one or more "flow through" examples showing how Type I and Type II Enrichment results in Type III Enrichment.

Present the progress of the program to the board of education.

Invite school board members to visit the program.

Distribute the enrichment cluster brochure to all schools and PTA/PTO groups in the district.

Invite your state representative or senator to visit the program.

Arrange for one or more Type III's to be displayed in community buildings (banks, state senate office, library, etc.).

Schedule a fair to display completed Type III projects.

Photograph Type I and Type II speakers, demonstrations, performances, and other activities.

Involve non-program students in Type I and Type II Enrichment.

Teach Type I and Type II lessons in the regular classroom at teacher's request.

Arrange for classroom teachers to do Type I or Type II training with program participants.

Arrange for displays, presentations or publications of students' Type III's within the school.

Photograph all (or almost all) Type III projects.

Arrange for articles about your program in a local newspaper or magazine.

Distribute a periodic teacher/parent newsletter describing current activities within the enrichment program.

Type I Enrichment

Establish a schoolwide Enrichment Team in one or more buildings.

Review local or county filmstrip and audio/videocassette catalogs for possible Type I's.

Review materials catalogs, newspaper listings, equipment listings, and new library acquisitions for possible Type I's.

Arrange community speakers' presentations around the interests of program participants.

Advertise the coming of these speakers and provide written post-presentation summaries to teachers.

"Debrief" students after a speaker's session to suggest possible follow-up activities (i.e., Type II or Type III).

Figure 106. Possible SEM program activities (continued).

Possible SEM Program Activities

Type I Enrichment *(continued)*

Construct Type I interest centers for use in the resource room or regular classroom.

Teach Type I mini-courses as interest dictates.

Arrange for classroom teachers to provide Type I experiences for all students.

Aid in locating appropriate enrichment speakers for classroom teachers.

Encourage students to develop Type I centers or presentations based on past or current interests.

Type II Enrichment

Review commercial catalogs for potential Type II materials.

Plan basic sequence of Type II skill development.

Teach Type II skills on a regular basis.

Share Type II training materials with classroom teachers.

Arrange for classroom teachers to do Type II training with program participants.

Type III Enrichment

Start a radio or television production company or other performance-oriented outlet vehicle.

Start a student newspaper, magazine or other written/visual outlet vehicle.

Work with individual or small groups of students on a regular basis as they complete Type III investigations.

Obtain advanced level materials for particular students (or group) from sources outside the school.

Arrange for faculty members to serve as mentors for students' Type III projects.

Arrange for community persons to serve as mentors for students' Type III projects.

Arrange for displays, presentations or publications of students' Type III projects within the school.

Develop a library of how-to books, topical dictionaries, etc.

Develop Type III idea file.

Figure 106. Possible SEM program activities (continued).

Some Final Thoughts About Getting Started

In summary, the responsibilities of an enrichment specialist are many and varied. Accepting the position can be a great challenge because it can result in the creation of a comprehensive schoolwide enrichment program. This goal, however, cannot be established without a considerable effort on the part of many people including principals, classroom teachers, and resource room teachers. In this final part of the conclusion, we attempt to answer some of the most frequently asked questions about planning an enrichment program.

This section describes the difficult task of accepting and learning to work with different styles and personalities, budget concerns, and program expansions. A chronological list of steps for implementing a SEM program is provided in Figure 107. The steps listed in this time line are practical and have been field tested in schools across the country. It is important to remember that this model is flexible and should be modified to fit the needs of individual schools and districts.

Accepting Different Styles and Personalities

An enrichment specialist will often be placed in the position of working on a daily basis with many different types of people. If several enrichment specialists are employed by a district or county, it is quite possible that they will each run their enrichment programs and resource rooms in a slightly different way. We believe that it is essential that enrichment specialists have the flexibility to be able to let their own personalities emerge. As long as it is clear that the philosophy used in the district or county is based on the SEM, individual styles should be encouraged to emerge in a natural way. Teachers should feel free to come up with their own innovations. This will, in turn, allow their own creativity to be a positive role model to their students.

When we visit different schools and resource rooms within a district, we are always impressed by the variety and innovations within each resource room. For example, one SEM program enrichment specialist spent time locating mentors within a large senior citizen complex within her city. At the end of the year she had located and trained sixteen outstanding community members who all became Type III mentors in subsequent years.

An enrichment specialist must also be able to accept different administrative and classroom styles and personalities. One beginning enrichment specialist admitted that she must assume a different role in each building in her district. Some principals will readily accept an enrichment program and insist that it is exactly the type of program they have been advocating for years. Others will dislike it *if* it interrupts their schedule. If a schoolwide Type I is to be scheduled, some administrators will be extremely flexible and say that any time, any day is fine, while others insist that the only good time is from 8:06-8:42 on Wednesday mornings. Enrichment specialists must learn to be able to work with many different kinds of people and realize that the enrichment program will survive and flourish in direct proportion to the support it has from classroom teachers and administrators.

It has been our experience that the first few years of an enrichment program are critical. Most administrators and classroom teachers who tend to be slightly flexible about the

Chronological Steps for Implementing a SEM Program

Time (Approximate)	Task	Notes
Spring of the year before the program is started.	Inservice for administrators, classroom teachers and parents.	Topics: 1) Three-Ring Conception of Giftedness.* 2) Triad Model, Enrichment Clusters. 3) Talent Pool Identification. 4) Curriculum Compacting. *Preliminary inservice sessions should be brief and should provide overviews of these topics.
Spring of the year before the program is started.	Make decisions about forming the Talent Pool.	1) Identify and/or develop tools to be used for gathering the "two basic criteria" (i.e., testing data and teacher nomination). 2) Establish cut-off scores on achievement tests for initial placement in the Talent Pool. 3) Determine which alternate pathways will be used by the district.
Spring of the year before the program is started.	Form the Talent Pool.	For Example: 1) Gather the names of all students in grades the program will serve who score in the 85th percentile or above (total local battery). 2) Send preliminary Talent Pool list (based on achievement test scores) to teachers along with blank nomination forms. Have teachers complete forms for any students (not already on the list) whom they would like to include in the Talent Pool. 3) Gather alternate pathway data and/or nominations. 4) Collect additional information on students nominated by an alternate pathway. 5) Have case conferences on all alternate pathways and nominations. 6) Send out revised Talent Pool list that includes students admitted via testing data, teacher nominations and alternate pathways.

Figure 107. Chronological steps for implementing a SEM program.

Chronological Steps for Implementing a SEM Program

(continued)

Time (Approximate)	Task	Notes
		Include a special nomination letter that will serve as a "safety valve." Additional students can be nominated at this time. 7) Completed lists of Talent Pool students should go to individuals responsible for setting up grouping for Reading and Math. This may help to facilitate the compacting process.
Spring of the year before the program is started. (May also be done in the fall.)	Form Type I Committee of interested classroom teachers, parents, and/or students.	Team will be responsible for planning enrichment activities, including a pilot Enrichment cluster program.
Spring of the year before the program is started. (May also be done in the fall.)	Meet with parents of students who were in the traditional gifted program, if one existed in the school.	1) Explain the SEM program and how it differs from the traditional program. Stress the three-ring conception of giftedness and the "fairness" of the model. 2) Ask parents to volunteer for Type I committee and to facilitate clusters.
Fall of school year in which SEM is implemented.	First week of school activities.	1) Review records of students who are new to the district for possible inclusion in Talent Pool. 2) Distribute Talent Pool list to teachers. Check again for omissions and special nominations.
As early as possible in the school year.	Schedule brief inservice or request time at faculty meeting.	1) Review procedures for implementing the various program components. 2) Hand out *Action Information Messages*.

Figure 107. Chronological steps for implementing a SEM program (continued).

Chronological Steps for Implementing a SEM Program

(continued)

Time (Approximate)	Task	Notes
Immediately following final formation of Talent Pool list.	Schedule parent meeting after sending out letter informing parents that their son/daughter is in the Talent Pool.* *A separate meeting may have already been held for parents whose children have been in the program previously.	1) Explain briefly the Triad Model, three-ring conception of giftedness, curriculum compacting, and enrichment clusters. 2) Distribute blank *Action Information Messages* (or indicate where they can be obtained in the school) for parents to complete if an interest is observed. 3) Distribute form entitled "Things My Child Likes To Do." 4) Distribute "Community Resource File Forms" requesting volunteers for Type I, Type II presentations, and Type III mentorships.
Early in September.	Schedule orientation meeting for Talent Pool students (can be by grade level or a combination of grades: K-1, 2-3, 4-6). It may take more than one session to cover the orientation.	1) Explain what services students will be receiving. 2) Explain Triad Model briefly to students not familiar with it. 3) Show slides or actual examples of Type III's whenever possible. 4) Explain terminology. 5) Discuss curriculum compacting briefly. 6) Hand out *Action Information Messages* for students to complete if an idea for a Type III develops.
Early in the school year.	Schedule Talent Pool students into Type I and Type II Enrichment on a weekly basis.	1) Check schedule with classroom teachers—45 minutes to an hour weekly (this may change as year progresses). 2) Begin process of curriculum compacting for these Talent Pool students. 3) Plan schedule of Type II training activities. 4) Have Talent Pool students complete the Interest-A-Lyzer during the first few weeks of scheduled training time.

Figure 107. Chronological steps for implementing a SEM program (continued).

Chronological Steps for Implementing a SEM Program (continued)		
Time (Approximate)	**Task**	**Notes**
Early in the school year.	Reconvene and/or establish the Type I Enrichment committee. Meet with faculty members and administrators to choose a weekly time slot for Type I activities.	Type I Enrichment activities should be scheduled through general enrichment and enrichment clusters to: 1) The entire school. 2) Entire grade levels (e.g., all fourth graders). 3) Groups of interested students (e.g., all 4th, 5th, & 6th graders studying magnets). 4) Interested Talent Pool students.
Throughout the year.	Receive *Action Information Messages*.	Steps to follow: 1) Contact the classroom teacher & arrange an intake interview with the student. 2) Accept and revolve student into Type III Enrichment or recommend alternate action.
Throughout the year.	Help students to complete Type III investigations.	Steps to follow: 1) Begin procedures for curriculum compacting and schedule student from curriculum strength area into additional Type III hours whenever possible. 2) Send periodic progress reports to parents and classroom teachers. 3) Assist student in filling out *Management Plan*. 4) Review *Student Product Assessment Form* with student.
Throughout the year.	Organize enrichment cluster program.	Follow Steps outlined in Chapter 10.

Figure 107. Chronological steps for implementing a SEM program (continued).

Chronological Steps for Implementing a SEM Program
(continued)

Time (Approximate)	Task	Notes
Early in the school year.	Discuss methods of communicating Type I events planned in the school with Enrichment committee. Plan for a regularly scheduled Type I Newsletter (or Type I section in a general school newsletter).	Teachers who are planning Type I activities in their classroom should be encouraged to share this information with Type I Enrichment committee. (This information should be relayed to the Type I Enrichment committee at their regularly scheduled monthly meeting and through the newsletter.)
Early in the school year.	Arrange (with the assistance of the Type I committee) some beginning of the year Type I Enrichment experiences.	After each Type I activity, discuss with participating Talent Pool students possible follow-up opportunities (i.e., Type II, Type III, clusters.)
Early in the school year.	Send out first teacher newsletter.	Include: 1) Scheduled Type I events and enrichment cluster plans for the year. 2) Type II suggestions for use in the regular classroom. 3) Type III investigations that are actually taking place. 4) Calls for help (assistance for Type III's). 5) Suggestions and scheduled mini-courses. 6) Mentor searches.
Throughout the year.	Scheduling.	Revise schedule as more Type III studies are begun.
Throughout the year.	Evaluation.	Meet with your administrators to develop some form of evaluation plan by discussing program goals. Consider evaluation forms discussed in this book.

Figure 107. Chronological steps for implementing a SEM program (continued).

Conclusion

program come to accept and in the majority of cases, support most aspects of it in time. As benefits to students and staff become more obvious, more support is generated. Therefore, enrichment specialists should remember that it is essential that they respect the individual differences and styles of administrators and classroom teachers while simultaneously trying to effect change in a school.

From our experience, we have also found that a quality SEM program requires four to five years to develop. Persons interested in an enrichment specialist's position should be aware of this and decide whether or not they are willing to commit this amount of time for the development of such a program. A change of personnel in the early years of a program can have a very negative impact and make it difficult to achieve the many objectives set forth in this book.

Budgeting

Another responsibility of a district or countywide enrichment specialist is preparing a budget for the enrichment program. Many enrichment specialists who work in SEM programs budget according to the different types of enrichment experiences offered to students. For example, a certain amount of money is set aside for Enrichment Teams to use for Type I experiences. Although the majority of Type I activities can be arranged at no cost, some honorarium, travel expense or even film rental costs may be incurred. It is a good idea to have a certain amount of funds allocated for this purpose so that students can experience certain Type I's that might have been out of the range of the program.

As we explained earlier, there are two kinds of Type II training involved in SEM programs. One kind of Type II training is planned in advance and involves teaching Talent Pool and non-Talent Pool students process training skills such as: critical and creative thinking, problem solving, advanced research skills, and others. The way this can be accomplished was explained earlier and involves creating a "scope and sequence" of Type II training skills, both within the classroom and in the resource room. We are often asked how much money should be set aside to order the materials needed for process training. The answer to that question depends upon many factors including: the amount of resources already in the school or district, the sharing that can be developed between the classroom teacher and the resource teacher, and the *careful* perusal of materials that should take place before materials are ordered.

Some enrichment specialists are able to fully organize materials for Type II training in an elementary school, both within the resource room and classrooms, for two or three hundred dollars. Most SEM programs set aside a specific amount of funds to initially outfit a K-6 or 7-12 resource room with Type II training activities. Regardless of the dollar amount, some funds should be reserved for ordering Type II materials. Whenever possible, the resource teacher who will be using the materials should decide what should be purchased. The enrichment specialist should, however, have some input into what is to be used by all of the enrichment specialists (at certain grade levels) to guarantee that the districtwide scope and sequence is being followed and that certain Type II skills are being introduced to students and reinforced in subsequent years.

The second kind of Type II training cannot be budgeted in advance, for it usually results from the interests of students and can be carried out either in classrooms or in enrichment clusters. If a Type I has been arranged featuring a speaker who is an expert on solar energy and a group of students become interested in learning more about solar energy, some Type II training in the area should be arranged. For example, a mini-course on solar energy might be scheduled by a volunteer (or by a paid resource person from a nearby science center). The resource teacher may be able to do the follow-up but needs to purchase materials such as solar cells. Most experienced SEM enrichment specialists leave a certain amount of money in a line item entitled Type II mini-courses and/or materials which enables them to draw upon those funds as the year progresses and interests emerge.

One of the most important aspects of a budget for a SEM program is the flexibility needed to be able to hold in reserve funds for Type III's or enrichment clusters held during the academic year. SEM enrichment specialists generally write these funds into their budget for the entire year. For example, most school budgets are completed the winter or spring before school starts. If some funds can be held in reserve for Type III needs or enrichment cluster supplies, purchase orders can be used to draw upon those funds for Type III expenses. It is essential that some funds be available to the enrichment specialist to enable him/her to purchase the materials necessary for students to complete Type III investigations. In most communities, PTO or PTA funds have been used to fund the enrichment cluster program. In some higher socioeconomic communities, parents often offer to help the program by buying the batteries, solar cells, robot parts, or whatever is necessary to complete the study their youngster is undertaking. However, parents should never be *required* to purchase the materials needed for Type III projects. If they are, few youngsters from economically disadvantaged families will ever be able to participate in Type III Enrichment.

We have found that the amount necessary for each kind of enrichment is often based upon the funds available! However, most SEM enrichment specialists with several years of experience indicate that their budget has increased slightly each year. We know of excellent programs with very small budgets and we know of programs with large budgets where students are never encouraged to revolve into Type III Enrichment. By taking into account the suggestions offered in this section, some funds for each kind of enrichment can be budgeted.

Continuation, Expansion, and Improvement

Once the program is in operation it becomes the responsibility of the enrichment specialist to maintain what has already been developed, as well as expanding services into other areas and continuing to improve what is being offered. For example, if Enrichment Teams are organized in each school, the enrichment specialist should plan to meet with each team on a periodic basis and provide encouragement and feedback. Ideas about enrichment clusters from other schools should be shared and distributed, as well as ideas about scheduling and organization. Names of resource persons used by other teams and titles of excellent films, videotapes and slideshows should be forwarded by the enrichment specialist from one Enrichment Team to another. The enrichment specialist should try to establish a district resource list that can be sent to each Enrichment Team. When the enrichment specialist attends an Enrichment Team meeting, he or she should listen carefully to the feedback of the team and attempt to resolve any concerns or problems. If an administrator is not being flexible about time for regularly scheduled enrichment experiences, the enrichment specialist may then make an appointment to talk to the administrator about this and try to seek a resolution. However, the enrichment specialist should never let any Enrichment Team meeting turn into a complaint session. If they listen to all of the reasons they can't accomplish something, they may never take the first steps to accomplish anything.

The steps outlined in Figure 107 can be used to gain ideas for how and when certain components of the program can be started, but they should only serve as a guide. Each school and district should modify the SEM to meet the unique needs of its students, teachers and administrators. We hope the task of developing these programs will be pleasurable and that the enjoyment of student success will help encourage teachers to continue their efforts.

References

Adler, M. J. (Ed.). (1990). *The syntopicon: An index to the great ideas.* Chicago: Encyclopedia Britannica.

Albert, R. S. (1975). Toward a behavioral definition of genius. *American Psychologist, 30,* 140-151.

Barron, F. (1969). *Creative person and creative process.* New York: Holt, Rinehart & Winston.

Barth, R. S. (1990). *Improving schools from within.* San Francisco: Jossey-Bass.

Betts, G. T. (1986). The autonomous learner model for the gifted and talented. In J. S. Renzulli (Ed.), *Systems and models for developing programs for the gifted and talented* (pp. 27-55). Mansfield Center, CT: Creative Learning Press.

Bloom, B. S. (1956). *Taxonomy of educational objectives handbook I: Cognitive domain.* New York: David McKay.

Bloom, B. S. (Ed.). (1985). *Developing talent in young people.* New York: Ballantine Books.

Bloom, B. S., & Sosniak, L. A. (1981). Talent development vs. schooling. *Educational Leadership, 38,* 86-94.

Bruner, J. S. (1960). *The process of education.* Cambridge, MA: Harvard University Press.

Bruner, J. S. (1966). *Toward a theory of instruction.* Cambridge, MA: Harvard University Press.

Bunker, B. B., Pearlson, H. B., & Schulz, J. W. (1975). *A student's guide to conducting social science research.* New York: Human Sciences Press.

Burns, D. E. (1990). *Pathways to investigative skills.* Mansfield Center, CT: Creative Learning Press.

Burns, D. E. (1992a). *If I ran the school.* Storrs, CT: University of Connecticut, The National Research Center on the Gifted and Talented.

Burns, D. E. (1992b). *SEM network directory.* Storrs, CT: University of Connecticut, Teaching The Talented Program.

References

Clifford, J. A., Runions, T., & Smith, E. (1986). The learning enrichment service (LES): A participatory model for gifted adolescents. In J. S. Renzulli (Ed.), *Systems and models for developing programs for the gifted and talented* (pp. 92-124). Mansfield Center, CT: Creative Learning Press.

Dellas, M., & Gaier, E. L. (1970). Identification of creativity: The individual. *Psychological Bulletin, 73,* 55-73.

Dewey, J. (1913). *Interest and effort in education.* New York: Houghton Mifflin.

Dewey, J. (1916). *Democracy and education.* New York: Houghton Mifflin.

Dunn, R., & Dunn, K. (1992). *Teaching elementary students through their individual learning styles: Practical approaches for grades 3-6.* Boston: Allyn & Bacon.

Dunn, R., & Dunn, K. (1993). *Teaching secondary students through their individual learning styles: Practical approaches for grades 7-12.* Boston: Allyn & Bacon.

Ebel, R. L. (1951). Estimation of the reliability of ratings. *Psychometrika, 16,* 407-424.

Feldhusen, J., & Kolloff, P. B. (1986). The purdue three-stage enrichment model for gifted education at the elementary level. In J. S. Renzulli (Ed.), *Systems and models for developing programs for the gifted and talented* (pp. 126-152). Mansfield Center, CT: Creative Learning Press.

Freeman, F. S. (1962). *Theory and practice of psychological testing.* New York: Holt, Rinehart & Winston.

Gardner, H. (1983). *Frames of mind.* New York: Basic Books.

Gentry, M. L. (1996). *Ability grouping: An investigation of student achievement, identification, and classroom practices.* Unpublished doctoral dissertation, University of Connecticut, Storrs.

Gentry, M. L., & Maxfield, L. R. (1995). *Student survey about enrichment clusters.* Storrs, CT: University of Connecticut, The National Research Center on the Gifted and Talented.

Gentry, M. L., & Reis, S. M. (1995). *Parent attitudes about enrichment opportunities.* Storrs, CT: University of Connecticut, The National Research Center on the Gifted and Talented.

Gentry, M. L., Reis, S. M., Renzulli, J. S., Moran, C., & Warren, L. (1995). *Enrichment clusters: Using high-end learning to develop talents in all students* (V955). Storrs, CT: University of Connecticut, The National Research Center on the Gifted and Talented.

Gentry, M. L., & Renzulli, J. S. (1995). *Inspiration: Targeting my ideal teaching and learning situation.* Storrs, CT: University of Connecticut, The National Research Center on the Gifted and Talented.

George, P. (1993). Tracking and ability grouping in the middle school: Ten tentative truths. *Middle School Journal, 24*(4), 17-24.

Gottschalk, L. (1969). *Understanding history: A primer of historical method* (2nd. ed.). New York: Alfred A. Knopf.

Guilford, J. P. (1967). *The nature of human intelligence.* New York: McGraw-Hill.

Guilford, J. P. (1977). *Way beyond the IQ.* Buffalo, NY: Bearly.

Hébert, T. P., & Sorensen, M. F. (1997). *The secondary interest-a-lyzer.* Mansfield Center, CT: Creative Learning Press.

Hoover, S., Sayler, M., & Feldhusen, J. F. (1993). Cluster grouping of elementary students at the elementary level. *Roeper Review, 16,* 13-15.

Imbeau, M. B. (1991). *Teachers' attitudes toward curriculum compacting: A comparison of different inservice strategies.* Unpublished doctoral dissertation, University of Connecticut, Storrs.

Jaeger, R. M. (1992). *"World class" standards, choice, and privatization: Weak measurement serving presumptive policy.* Paper presented at the Annual Meeting of the American Educational Research Association, San Francisco, CA.

Kirschenbaum, R. J. (1983). Let's cut out the cut-off score in the identification of the gifted. *Roeper Review, 5,* 6-10.

Kirschenbaum, R. J., & Siegle, D. (1993). *Predicting creative performance in an enrichment program.* Paper presented at the Association for the Education of Gifted Underachieving Students 6th Annual Conference, Portland, OR.

Kulik, J. A., & Kulik, C.-L. C. (1992). Meta-analytic findings on grouping programs. *Gifted Child Quarterly, 36,* 73-77.

LaRose, B. (1986). The lighthouse program: A longitudinal research project. *Journal for the Education of the Gifted, 9,* 224-32.

Madaus, G. F. (1992). *The influence of testing on teaching math and science in grades 4-12.* Boston: Center for the Study of Testing, Evaluation and Educational Policy, Boston College.

McGreevy, A. (1982). *My book of things and stuff: An interest questionnaire for young children.* Mansfield Center, CT: Creative Learning Press.

McInerney, C. F. (1983). *Cluster grouping for the gifted, the bottom line: Research-based classroom strategies.* St. Paul, MN: LINE.

References

McLaughlin, M. W., & Talbert, J. E. (1993). *Contexts that matter for teaching and learning.* Stanford, CA: Center for Research on the Context of Secondary School Teaching.

Nicholls, J. C. (1972). Creativity in the person who will never produce anything original and useful: The concept of creativity as a normally distributed trait. *American Psychologist, 27,* 717-727.

Oakes, J. (1985). *Keeping track: How schools structure inequality.* New Haven, CT: Yale University Press.

Olenchak, F. R. (1988). The schoolwide enrichment model in the elementary schools: A study of implementation stages and effects on educational excellence. In J. S. Renzulli (Ed.), *Technical report on research studies relating to the Revolving Door Identification Model* (2nd ed., pp. 201-247). Storrs, CT: University of Connecticut, Bureau of Educational Research.

Olenchak, F. R., & Renzulli, J. S. (1989). The effectiveness of the schoolwide enrichment model on selected aspects of elementary school change. *Gifted Child Quarterly, 32,* 44-57.

Olson, L. (1992). Fed up with tinkering, reformers now touting 'systemic' approach. *Education Week, 12*(1), 30.

Phenix, P. (1964). *Realms of meaning.* New York: McGraw-Hill.

Piaget, J. (1975). *The development of thought: Equilibration of cognitive structures.* New York: Viking.

Purcell, J. H. (1993). The effects of elimination of gifted and talented programs on participating students and their parents. *Gifted Child Quarterly, 37*(4), 177-187.

Reis, S. M. (1981). *An analysis of the productivity of gifted students participating in programs using the revolving door identification model.* Unpublished doctoral dissertation, University of Connecticut, Storrs.

Reis, S. M., Burns, D. E., & Renzulli, J. S. (1992). *Curriculum compacting: The complete guide to modifying the regular curriculum for high ability students.* Mansfield Center, CT: Creative Learning Press.

Reis, S. M., Gentry, M. L., & Park, S. (1995). *Extending the pedagogy of gifted education to all students: The enrichment cluster study* (Research Monograph 95118). Storrs, CT: University of Connecticut, The National Research Center on the Gifted and Talented.

Reis, S. M., & Renzulli, J. S. (1982). A research report on the revolving door identification model: A case for the broadened conception of giftedness. *Phi Delta Kappan, 63,* 619-620.

Reis, S. M., & Renzulli, J. S. (1992). Using curriculum compacting to challenge the above-average. *Educational Leadership, 50*(2), 51-57.

Reis, S. M., Westberg, K. L., Kulikowich, J., Caillard, F., Hébert, T. P., Plucker, J. A., Purcell, J. H., Rogers, J., & Smidst, J. (1993). *Why not let high ability students start school in January? The curriculum compacting study* (Research Monograph 93106). Storrs, CT: University of Connecticut, The National Research Center on the Gifted and Talented.

Renzulli, J. S. (1975). *A guidebook for evaluating programs for the gifted and talented.* Mansfield Center, CT: Creative Learning Press.

Renzulli, J. S. (1976). The enrichment triad model: A guide for developing defensible programs for the gifted and talented. *Gifted Child Quarterly, 20,* 303-326.

Renzulli, J. S. (1977a). *The enrichment triad model: A guide for developing defensible programs for the gifted.* Mansfield Center, CT: Creative Learning Press.

Renzulli, J. S. (1977b). *Interest-a-lyzer.* Mansfield Center, CT: Creative Learning Press.

Renzulli, J. S. (1978). What makes giftedness? Re-examining a definition. *Phi Delta Kappan, 60,* 180-184, 261.

Renzulli, J. S. (1981). *Action information message.* Mansfield Center, CT: Creative Learning Press.

Renzulli, J. S. (1986). The three-ring conception of giftedness: A developmental model for creative productivity. In R. J. Sternberg & J. E. Davidson (Eds.), *Conceptions of giftedness* (pp. 332-357). New York: Cambridge University Press.

Renzulli, J. S. (Ed.). (1988). *Technical report of research studies related to the enrichment triad/revolving door model* (3rd ed.). Storrs, CT: University of Connecticut, Teaching The Talented Program.

Renzulli, J. S. (1992). A general theory for the development of creative productivity through the pursuit of ideal acts of learning. *Gifted Child Quarterly, 36,* 170-182.

Renzulli, J. S. (1994). *Schools for talent development: A comprehensive plan for total school improvement.* Mansfield Center, CT: Creative Learning Press.

Renzulli, J. S. (1997). *Interest-a-lyzer* (Revised Edition). Mansfield Center, CT: Creative Learning Press.

Renzulli, J. S., & Reis, S. M. (1985). *The schoolwide enrichment model: A comprehensive plan for educational excellence.* Mansfield Center, CT: Creative Learning Press.

Renzulli J. S., & Reis, S. M. (1987). *The schoolwide enrichment model videotape training program for teachers and administrators* [Film]. Mansfield Center, CT: Creative Learning Press.

Renzulli, J. S., & Reis, S. M. (1994). Research related to the schoolwide enrichment model. *Gifted Child Quarterly, 38,* 2-14.

References

Renzulli, J. S., Reis, S. M., Gentry, M. L., Moran, C., & Warren, L. (1995). *Enrichment clusters: Using high-end learning to develop talents in all students.* Storrs, CT: University of Connecticut, The National Research Center on the Gifted and Talented.

Renzulli, J. S., Reis, S. M., & Smith, L. H. (1981). *The revolving door identification model.* Mansfield Center, CT: Creative Learning Press.

Renzulli, J. S., & Rizza, M. (1997). *The primary interest-a-lyzer.* Mansfield Center, CT: Creative Learning Press.

Renzulli, J. S., & Smith, L. H. (1977). *Management plan for individual and small group investigations of real problems.* Mansfield Center, CT: Creative Learning Press.

Renzulli, J. S., & Smith, L. H. (1978a). *Compactor.* Mansfield Center, CT: Creative Learning Press.

Renzulli, J. S., & Smith, L. H. (1978b). *Learning styles inventory: A measure of student preference for instructional techniques.* Mansfield Center, CT: Creative Learning Press.

Renzulli, J. S., Smith, L. H., White, A. J., Callahan, C. M., & Hartman, R. K. (1976). *Scales for rating the behavioral characteristics of superior students.* Mansfield Center, CT: Creative Learning Press.

Renzulli, J. S., Smith, L. H., & Reis, S. M. (1982). Curriculum compacting: An essential strategy for working with gifted students. *The Elementary School Journal, 82,* 185-194.

Rogers, K. B. (1991). *The relationship of grouping practices to the education of the gifted and talented learner* (RBDM 9102). Storrs, CT: University of Connecticut, The National Research Center on the Gifted and Talented.

Shapiro, R. J. (1968). Creative research scientists. *Psychologia Africana*, Supplement No. 4.

Singal, D. J. (1991). The other crisis in American education. *The Atlantic Monthly, 268*(5), 59-74.

Slavin, R. E. (1987). Ability grouping: A best-evidence synthesis. *Review of Educational Research, 57,* 293-336.

Steele, J. (1982). *The class activities questionnaire.* Mansfield Center, CT: Creative Learning Press.

Sternberg, R. J. (1985). *Beyond IQ: A triarchic theory of intelligence.* New York: Cambridge University Press.

Sternberg, R. J. (1986). A triarchic theory of intellectual giftedness. In R. J. Sternberg & J. E. Davidson (Eds.), *Conceptions of giftedness* (pp. 223-243). New York: Cambridge University Press.

Sternberg, R. J. (1988). A three-faceted model of creativity. In R. J. Sternberg (Ed.), *The nature of creativity* (pp. 125-147). New York: Cambridge University Press.

Torrance, E. P. (1962). *Guiding creative talent.* Englewood Cliffs, NJ: Prentice-Hall.

Torrance, E. P. (1969). Prediction of adult creative achievement among high school seniors. *Gifted Child Quarterly, 13,* 223-229.

Torrance, E. P. (1979). *The search for satori and creativity.* Buffalo, NY: Bearly.

Treffinger, D. J. (1982). Demythologizing gifted education: An editorial essay. *Gifted Child Quarterly, 26*(1) 3-8.

Treffinger, D. J. (1986). Fostering effective, independent learning through individualized programming. In J. S. Renzulli (Ed.), *Systems and models for developing programs for the gifted and talented* (pp. 429-460). Mansfield Center, CT: Creative Learning Press.

United States Department of Education, Office of Educational Research and Improvement. (1993). *National excellence: A case for developing America's talent.* Washington, DC: U.S. Government Printing Office.

Wallach, M. A. (1976). Tests tell us little about talent. *American Scientist, 64,* 57-63.

Weiner, P. P. (Ed.). (1973). *Dictionary of the history of ideas.* New York: Scribner's Sons.

Wheelock, A. (1992). *Crossing the tracks: How untracking can save America's schools.* New York: New Press.

Winebrenner, S., & Devlin, B. (1994). *Cluster grouping fact sheet: How to provide full-time services for gifted students on existing budgets.* Lombard, IL: Phantom Press.

Zuckerman, H. (1979). The scientific elite: Nobel laureates' mutual influences. In R. S. Albert (Ed.), *Genius and Eminence* (pp. 241-252). New York: Pergamon Press.

Further **R**eading

Evolution of the Schoolwide Enrichment Model

1. The Enrichment Triad Model

Books and Research Monographs:

Beecher, M. (1995). *Developing the gifts and talents of all students in the regular classroom: An innovative curricular design based on the enrichment triad model.* Mansfield Center, CT: Creative Learning Press.

Gubbins, E. J. (Ed.). (1995). *Research related to the enrichment triad model* (RM95212). Storrs, CT: University of Connecticut, The National Research Center on the Gifted and Talented.

Reis, S. M., & Renzulli, J. S. (1985). *The secondary triad model: A practical plan for implementing gifted programs at the junior and senior high school levels.* Mansfield Center, CT: Creative Learning Press.

Renzulli, J. S. (1975). *A guidebook for evaluating programs for the gifted and talented.* Mansfield Center, CT: Creative Learning Press.

Renzulli, J. S. (1977). *The enrichment triad model: A guide for developing defensible programs for the gifted.* Mansfield Center, CT: Creative Learning Press.

Renzulli, J. S., & Reis, S. M. (Eds.). (1986). *The triad reader.* Mansfield Center, CT: Creative Learning Press.

Renzulli, J. S., & Reis, S. M. (1991). *Complete triad trainers inservice manual.* Mansfield Center, CT: Creative Learning Press.

Renzulli, J. S., & Smith, L. H. (1979). *A guidebook for developing individual educational programs for gifted and talented students.* Mansfield Center, CT: Creative Learning Press.

Articles, Book Chapters and Papers:

Reis, S. M., & Renzulli, J. S. (1984). Key features of successful programs for the gifted and talented. *Educational Leadership, 41,* 28-34.

Reis, S. M., & Renzulli, J. S. (1985). The secondary enrichment triad model: A practical plan for excellence without elitism. *NASSP Bulletin, 69*(482), 31-38.

Reis S. M., & Renzulli, J .S. (1986). The secondary triad model. In J. S. Renzulli (Ed.), *Systems and models for developing programs for the gifted and talented* (pp. 267-305). Mansfield Center, CT: Creative Learning Press.

Renzulli, J. S. (1970). Identifying key features in programs for the gifted (Reprint). In J. E. Rabenstein (Ed.), *Exceptional children: An overview* (pp. 65-69). New London, CT: MSS Educational Publishing.

Renzulli, J. S. (1976). The enrichment triad model: A guide for developing defensible programs for the gifted and talented. *Gifted Child Quarterly, 20,* 303-326.

Renzulli, J. S. (1977). Developing defensible programs for the gifted and talented (Reprint). *Realizing Their Potential* (pp. 38-47). Norfolk, VA: Virginia Council for Gifted and Talented Children.

Renzulli, J. S. (1977). The enrichment triad model: A guide for developing defensible programs for the gifted and talented, Part II. *Gifted Child Quarterly, 21,* 237-243.

Renzulli, J. S. (1978). Developing defensible programs for the gifted and talented. *Journal of Creative Behavior, 12,* 21-30.

Renzulli, J. S. (1978). A system for identifying gifted and talented students. *Realizing their potential* (pp. 78-87). Norfolk, VA: Virginia Council for Gifted and Talented Children.

Renzulli, J. S. (1978). What makes giftedness? Re-examining a definition. *Phi Delta Kappan, 60,* 180-184.

Renzulli, J. S. (1980). A practical model for designing individual education programs for gifted and talented children. *Gifted Child Today, 11,* 3-8.

Renzulli, J. S. (1980). An alternative approach to identifying and programming for gifted and talented students. *Gifted Child Today, 15,* 4-11.

Renzulli, J. S. (1983). Rating the behavioral characteristics of superior students. *G/C/T, 19,* 30-35.

Renzulli, J. S., & Hartman, R. K. (1971). Scales for rating the behavioral characteristics of superior students (SRBCSS). *Exceptional Children, 38,* 211-214.

Renzulli, J. S., Hartman, R. K., & Callahan, C. M. (1971). Teacher identification of superior students. *Exceptional Children, 38,* 211-214.

Renzulli, J. S., & Reis S. M. (1986). The enrichment triad/revolving door model: A schoolwide plan for the development of creative productivity. In J. S. Renzulli (Ed.), *Systems and models for developing programs for the gifted and talented* (pp. 216-266). Mansfield Center, CT: Creative Learning Press.

Renzulli, J. S., & Reis S. M. (1993). Developing creative productivity through the enrichment triad model. In S. Isaksen, M. Murdock, R. Firestein, & D. Treffinger (Eds.), *Nurturing and developing creativity: The emergence of a discipline* (pp. 70-99). Norwood, NJ: Ablex.

Renzulli, J. S., & Smith, L. H. (1977). Two approaches to the identification of gifted students. *Exceptional Children, 43,* 512-519.

Renzulli, J. S., & Smith, L. H. (1984). Learning style preferences: A practical approach for classroom teachers. *Theory Into Practice, 18,* 44-50.

Renzulli, J. S., Smith, L. H., & Reis S. M. (1983). Curriculum compacting: An essential strategy for working with gifted students (Reprint). *Gifted Education International, 1,* 97-102.

2. The Revolving Door Identification Model

Books and Research Monographs:

Renzulli, J. S. (Ed.). (1988). *Technical report of research studies related to the enrichment triad/revolving door model.* Storrs, CT: University of Connecticut, Teaching The Talented Program.

Renzulli, J. S., & Reis S. M. (Eds.). (1986). *The triad reader.* Mansfield Center, CT: Creative Learning Press.

Renzulli, J. S., Reis, S. M., & Smith, L. H. (1981). *The revolving door identification model.* Mansfield Center, CT: Creative Learning Press.

Articles, Book Chapters and Papers:

Delisle, J., Reis, S. M., & Gubbins, E. J. (1981). The revolving door identification and programming model: Some preliminary findings. *Exceptional Children* 48(2), 152-156.

Reis, S. M. (1981). *An analysis of the productivity of gifted students participating in programs using the revolving door identification model.* Unpublished doctoral dissertation, University of Connecticut, Storrs.

Reis, S. M. ,& O'Shea, A. A. (1984). An innovative enrichment program: The enrichment triad/revolving door model. *Special Education in Canada, 58*(4), 135-139.

Renzulli, J. S. (1980). Revolving door: A truer turn for the gifted. *Learning, 8,* 91-93.

Renzulli, J. S. (1983). Guiding the gifted in pursuit of real problems: The transformed role of the teacher. *Journal of Creative Behavior, 17,* 49-59.

Renzulli, J. S. (1983). The revolving door identification model: A new approach to some persisting problems in identifying and programming for gifted and talented students. *Proceedings of the Seventh Annual Blumberg Conference, 7,* 45-70.

Renzulli, J. S. (1984). The triad/revolving door system: A research based approach to identification and programming for the gifted and talented. *Gifted Child Quarterly, 28,* 163-171.

Renzulli, J. S., & Delisle, J. R. (1982). The revolving door model of identification and programming for the academically gifted: Correlates of creative production. *Gifted Child Quarterly, 25,* 89-95.

Renzulli, J. S., & Owen, S. V. (1983). The revolving door identification model: If it ain't busted don't fix it, if you don't understand it don't nix it. *Roeper Review, 6,* 39, 40.

Renzulli, J. S., & Reis, S. M. (1983). Inservice training techniques for the implementation of triad/revolving door programs. *National Association for Gifted Children Convention Abstracts, 13,* 98.

Renzulli, J. S., & Reis, S. M. (1984). The revolving door identification model: A non-elitist approach to serving the gifted and talented. *The School Administrator, 41,* 15-16.

Renzulli, J. S., Reis, S. M., & Smith, L. H. (1981). The revolving door: A new way of identifying the gifted. *Phi Delta Kappan, 62,* 648.

Stoddard, E. P., & Renzulli, J. S. (1983). Improving the writing skills of talent pool students. *Gifted Child Quarterly, 27,* 21-27.

3. The Schoolwide Enrichment Model

Books and Research Monographs:

Burns, D. E. (1990). *Pathways to investigative skills: Instructional lessons for guiding students from problem finding to final product.* Mansfield Center, CT: Creative Learning Press.

Burns, D. E. (1995). *A student handbook about our classroom's new enrichment program.* Storrs, CT: University of Connecticut, The National Research Center on the Gifted and Talented.

Hilliard, S., & Sattler, J. (1987). *Nuts & bolts: A practical guide for implementing a junior high middle school enrichment program.* Mansfield Center, CT: Creative Learning Press.

Purcell, J. H., & Renzulli, J. S. (in press). *Total talent portfolio: A guidebook for teachers as talent developers.* Mansfield Center, CT: Creative Learning Press.

Reis, S. M., Westberg, K. L., Kulikowich, J., Caillard, F., Hébert, T. P., Plucker, J. A., Purcell, J. H., Rogers, J. B., & Smidst, J. M. (1993). *Why not let high ability students start school in January? The curriculum compacting study* (Research Monograph 93106). Storrs, CT: University of Connecticut, The National Research Center on the Gifted and Talented.

Reis, S. M., Burns, D. E., & Renzulli, J. S. (1992). *Curriculum compacting: A guide for teachers.* Storrs, CT: University of Connecticut, The National Research Center on the Gifted and Talented.

Reis, S. M., Burns, D. E., & Renzulli, J. S. (1992). *Facilitators guide to help teachers compact curriculum.* Storrs, CT: University of Connecticut, The National Research Center on the Gifted and Talented.

Reis, S. M., Gentry, M. L., Park, S., Moran, C., & Warren, L. (1995). *Extending the pedagogy of gifted education to all students: The enrichment cluster study* (Research Monograph 95118). Storrs, CT: University of Connecticut, The National Research Center on the Gifted and Talented.

Renzulli, J. S. (1994). *Schools for talent development: A practical plan for total school improvement.* Mansfield Center, CT: Creative Learning Press.

Renzulli, J. S. (1995). *Building a bridge between gifted education and total school improvement* (RBDM 9502). Storrs, CT: University of Connecticut, The National Research Center on the Gifted and Talented.

Renzulli, J. S. (1997). *The interest-a-lyzer family of instruments teacher's manual.* Mansfield Center, CT: Creative Learning Press.

Renzulli, J. S., & Reis, S. M. (1985). *The schoolwide enrichment model: A comprehensive plan for educational excellence.* Mansfield Center, CT: Creative Learning Press.

Renzulli, J. S., & Reis, S. M. (1991). *Complete triad trainers inservice manual.* Mansfield Center, CT: Creative Learning Press.

Renzulli, J. S., & Smith, L. H. (1979). *A guidebook for developing individualized educational programs for gifted and talented students.* Mansfield Center, CT: Creative Learning Press.

Starko, A. (1986). *It's about time: Inservice strategies for curriculum compacting.* Mansfield Center, CT: Creative Learning Press.

Further Reading

Articles, Book Chapters and Papers:

Chislett, L. M. (1994). Integrating the CPS and schoolwide enrichment models to enhance creative productivity. *Roeper Review, 17*(1), 4-7.

Gavin, M. K. (1995). Curriculum compacting in mathematics. *CAG Communicator, 26*(2), 11-12, 33-34

Hébert, T. P. (1995). Curriculum compacting: An appropriate intervention for gifted underachievers. *CAG Communicator, 26*(2), 14, 35-36.

Imbeau, M. B. (1995). Implementing curriculum compacting: Suggestions for assisting teachers. *CAG Communicator, 26*(2), 9-11.

Olenchak, F. R., & Renzulli, J. S. (1989). The effectiveness of the schoolwide enrichment model on selected aspects of elementary school change. *Gifted Child Quarterly, 33,* 36-46.

Reis, S. M. (1990). Curriculum compacting. *Advocate of Connecticut Association for the Gifted, 8*(4), 3, 14-15.

Reis, S. M. (1995). What gifted education can offer the reform movement: Talent development. In J. Genshaft, M. Bireley, & C. L. Hollinger (Eds.), *Serving gifted and talented students: A resource for school personnel* (pp. 371-387). Austin, TX: Pro-Ed.

Reis, S. M. (1996). Curriculum compacting: Modifying the curriculum for above-average students. *CAG Communicator, 26*(2), 1, 27-32.

Reis, S. M., & Burns, D. E. (1987). A schoolwide enrichment team: Methods for promoting community and faculty involvement in a gifted program. *Gifted Child Today, 10*(2), 27-32.

Reis, S. M., & Purcell, J. H. (1993). An analysis of content elimination and strategies used by elementary classroom teachers in the curriculum compacting process. *Journal for the Education of the Gifted, 16*(2), 147-170.

Reis S. M., & Renzulli, J. S. (1985). The secondary level enrichment triad model: A practical plan for excellence without elitism. *Secondary School Journal, 38,* 31-38.

Reis, S. M., & Renzulli, J. S. (1988). Developing challenging programs for gifted readers. *The Reading Instruction Journal, 32,* 44-57.

Reis, S. M., & Renzulli, J. S. (1988). The role and responsibilities of the gifted program coordinator. *Roeper Review, 11,* 66-72.

Reis, S. M., & Renzulli, J. S. (1989). Providing challenging programs for gifted readers. *Roeper Review, 12,* 92-97.

Reis, S. M., & Renzulli, J. S. (1989). The secondary triad model. *Journal for the Education of the Gifted, 13,* 55-77.

Reis, S. M., & Renzulli, J. S. (1992). The library media specialist's role in teaching independent study skills to high ability students. *Library Media Quarterly, 21,* 27-35.

Reis, S. M., & Renzulli, J. S. (1992). Using curriculum compacting to challenge the above-average. *Educational Leadership, 50*(2), 51-57.

Reis, S. M., & Renzulli, J. S. (1994). Research related to the schoolwide enrichment triad model. *Gifted Child Quarterly, 38*(1), 7-20.

Reis, S. M., & Schack, G. D. (1993). Differentiating products for the gifted and talented: The encouragement of independent learning. In C. J. Maker (Ed.), *Critical issues in gifted education: Programs for the gifted in regular classrooms* (Vol. III, pp. 160-186). Austin, TX: Pro-Ed.

Reis, S. M., & Westberg, K. L. (1994). The impact of staff development on teachers' ability to modify curriculum for gifted and talented students. *Gifted Child Quarterly, 38*(3), 127-135.

Renzulli, J. S. (1988). The search for excellence: A modest proposal for scholastic change. *Roeper Review, 10,* 200-204.

Renzulli, J. S. (1990). A practical system for identifying gifted and talented students. *Early Childhood Development, 63,* 9-18.

Renzulli, J. S. (1993). Schools are places for talent development: New directions for the schoolwide enrichment model. *CAG Communicator, 24*(7), 4-13.

Renzulli, J. S. (1994). New directions for the schoolwide enrichment model. *Gifted Education International, 10,* 33-36.

Renzulli, J. S. (1994). Teachers as talent scouts. *Educational Leadership, 52*(4), 75-81.

Renzulli, J. S. (1996). Schools for talent development: A practical plan for total school improvement. *The School Administrator, 53*(1), 20-22.

Renzulli, J. S., & Purcell, J. H. (1995). Restructuring: From student strengths to total school improvement. *NASSP Bulletin, 79*(574), 46-57.

Renzulli, J. S., & Purcell, J. H. (1995). Total school improvement. *Our Children, 1*(1), 30-31.

Renzulli, J. S., & Purcell, J. H. (1996). Gifted education: A look around and a look ahead. *Roeper Review, 18*(3), 173-178.

Renzulli, J. S., & Reis, S. M. (1985). A scope and sequence approach to process development. *Gifted Child Today, 21,* 2-5.

Renzulli, J. S., & Reis, S. M. (1988). Gifted programs as vehicles for schoolwide change. *Challenge Update, 4,* 10-11.

Renzulli, J. S., & Reis, S. M. (1990). Gifted programs as vehicles for schoolwide change. *The Journal of the California Association for the Gifted, 20,* 29-30.

Renzulli, J. S., & Reis, S. M. (1991). Building advocacy through program design, student productivity and public relations. *Gifted Child Quarterly, 35,* 182-187.

Renzulli, J. S., & Reis, S. M. (1991). The reform movement and the quiet crisis in gifted education. *Gifted Child Quarterly, 35,* 26-35.

Renzulli, J. S., & Reis, S. M. (1991). The schoolwide enrichment model: A comprehensive plan for the development of creative productivity. In N. Colangelo, & G. A. Davis, (Eds.), *Handbook of Gifted Education* (pp. 111-114). Boston: Allyn & Bacon.

Renzulli, J. S., & Reis, S. M. (1993). Using the schoolwide enrichment triad model to provide programs for underserved gifted and talented students. In B. Wallace & H. B. Adams, (Eds.), *Worldwide perspectives on the gifted disadvantaged* (pp. 216-236). Bicester, England: A. B. Academic Publishers.

Renzulli, J. S., Smith, L. H., & Reis, S. M. (1987). Update of individual educational programs for gifted and talented students. *Gifted Child Today, 11,* 34-40.

Schlichter, C. L., & Olenchak, F. R. (1992). Identification of inservice needs among schoolwide enrichment schools. *Roeper Review, 14*(3), 159-162.

Smith, D. (1991). Lessons learned from coordinating a schoolwide enrichment program. *Gifted Child Today, 14*(4), 12-14.

Westberg, K. L. (1995). Successful curriculum compacting. *CAG Communicator, 26*(2), 19-20,43.

Videos:

The National Research Center on the Gifted and Talented. (1995). *Curricular options for "high-end" learning* (V943). Storrs, CT: University of Connecticut.

Reis, S. M. (1993). *Curriculum compacting: A process for modifying curriculum for high ability students* (V921). Storrs, CT: University of Connecticut, The National Research Center on the Gifted and Talented.

Reis, S. M. (1993). *Where has all the challenge gone? Meeting the needs of gifted students in the regular classroom.* Storrs, CT: The Schoolwide Enrichment Model Network.

Gentry, M. L., Reis, S. M., Renzulli, J. S., Moran, C., & Warren, L. (1995). *Enrichment clusters: Using high-end learning to develop talent in all students* (V955). Storrs, CT: University of Connecticut, The National Research Center on the Gifted and Talented.

Renzulli, J. S. (1993). *Schools for talent development: A practical plan for total school improvement using the schoolwide enrichment model.* Storrs, CT: The Schoolwide Enrichment Model Network.

Renzulli, J. S. (1995). *Resources for high-end learning and total school improvement.* Storrs, CT: The Schoolwide Enrichment Model Network.

Renzulli J. S., & Reis, S. M. (1987). *The schoolwide enrichment model videotape training program for teachers and administrators.* Mansfield Center, CT: Creative Learning Press.

Appendix A

Action Forms

Action Forms are planning guides that are designed to help educators find effective ways to organize, implement, maintain, and evaluate different aspects of the Schoolwide Enrichment Model program. These "roadmaps" provide direction for the decision-making process by offering a list of alternative resources and/or activities from which specific selections can be made. These visual displays allow educators an opportunity to review all possible courses of action at a single glace and locate any omissions, duplications or conflicting activities. In addition to helping teachers "enforce" the implementation and maintenance of key program components, these forms also serve as vehicles for the documentation of program activities and provide a ready-made set of data for program evaluation.

The Class Survey Sheet
Talent Development Action Record
The Compactor
Type I Planning and Documentation Form
Resource Directory Form
Type I Resources by Subject Area
Planning Matrix for Organizing and Teaching Type II Skills With Commercial Enrichment
    Materials
Materials and Activities Selection Worksheet for Planning Type II Enrichment
Enrichment Materials Specification Form
Action Information Message (Elementary Version)
Action Information Message (Secondary Version)
The Management Plan for Individual and Small Group Investigations
Specification Form for Methodological Resource Books
Type III Mentor Matrix

Class Survey Sheet

School _____ Grade _____ Teacher _____ Date _____

Check (√) if placed in Talent Pool	Name or Student Identification Numbers	BASIC CRITERIA							ALTERNATIVE PATHWAYS OF ENTRANCE TO THE TALENT POOL						COMMENTS
		Ability Test Scores		Teacher Nomination					Parent Nomination	Peer Nomination	Self-Nomination	Tests of Special Aptitude	Product Ratings	Other	If special reason for placement in Talent Pool. If further explanation of supplemental information (i.e., other categories are needed, etc.)
		(1)	(2)	Learning	Motivation	Creativity	Leadership	Other							

Talent Development Action Record
for:

_____

Date	Grade	Teacher	Clusters	Curriculum Compacting	Exploratory Activities (Type I's)	Skill-Related Activities (Type II's)	Self-Selected Independent Investigations (Type III's)

INDIVIDUAL EDUCATIONAL PROGRAMMING GUIDE
The Compactor

Prepared by: Joseph S. Renzulli
Linda M. Smith

NAME _____ AGE _____ TEACHER(S) _____ Individual Conference Dates And Persons

SCHOOL _____ GRADE _____ PARENT(S) _____ Participating in Planning Of IEP

CURRICULUM AREAS TO BE CONSIDERED FOR COMPACTING Provide a brief description of basic material to be covered during this marking period and the assessment information or evidence that suggests the need for compacting.	PROCEDURES FOR COMPACTING BASIC MATERIAL Describe activities that will be used to guarantee proficiency in basic curricular areas.	ACCELERATION AND/OR ENRICHMENT ACTIVITIES Describe activities that will be used to provide advanced level learning experiences in each area of the regular curriculum.

☐ Check here if additional information is recorded on the reverse side.

Type I Planning and Documentation Form

Check all that apply:	Content Areas				
____ General Matrix _____ ____ Grade Level _____ ____ Subject Area _____ Methods of Delivery					TOTAL
I. Resource Persons					
Speakers					
Enrichment Clusters					
Demonstrations					
Artistic Performances					
Panel Discussion/Debate					
E-Mail					
Other _____					
II. Media					
Films					
Filmstrips					
Slides					
Audio Tapes/CDs					
Videotapes					
Television Programs					
Newspaper/Magazine Articles					
Computer Programs					
Other _____					
III. Other Resources					
Interest Development Centers					
Displays					
Field Trips					
Museum Programs					
Learning Centers					
Internet					
Other _____					
TOTAL					

Resource Directory Form

Name:

Topic:

Address:

Phone:

Materials Available: ☐ Film ☐ Video
☐ Display ☐ Samples
☐ Other _____

Mode of Delivery: ☐ Mentor ☐ Field Trip
☐ Presentation ☐ Enrichment Cluster
☐ Other _____

Cost:

Contacts Made:

Type I Resources by Subject Area

TOPIC	AGENCY & CONTACT PERSON	PHONE	MATERIALS	MODE OF DELIVERY	NOTES

Planning Matrix for Organizing and Teaching Type II Skills With Commercial Enrichment Materials

I. Cognitive Training

	K-3	4-8	9-12
A. Creative Thinking Skills			
B. Creative Problem Solving and Decision Making			

Planning Matrix for Organizing and Teaching Type II Skills With Commercial Enrichment Materials

I. Cognitive Training (continued)

	K-3	4-8	9-12
C. Critical and Logical Thinking			

II. Affective Training

A. Affective Skills			

Planning Matrix for Organizing and Teaching Type II Skills With Commercial Enrichment Materials

III. Learning How-To-Learn Skills

	K-3	4-8	9-12
A. Listening, Observing, and Perceiving			

Planning Matrix for Organizing and Teaching Type II Skills With Commercial Enrichment Materials

III. Learning How-To-Learn Skills (continued)

	K-3	4-8	9-12
B. Reading, Notetaking, and Outlining			

Planning Matrix for Organizing and Teaching Type II Skills With Commercial Enrichment Materials

III. Learning How-To-Learn Skills (continued)

	K-3	4-8	9-12
C. Interviewing and Surveying			

Appendix A

Planning Matrix for Organizing and Teaching Type II Skills With Commercial Enrichment Materials

III. Learning How-To-Learn Skills (continued)

	K-3	4-8	9-12
D. Analyzing and Organizing Data			

Planning Matrix for Organizing and Teaching Type II Skills With Commercial Enrichment Materials

IV. Using Advanced Research Skills and Reference Materials

	K-3	4-8	9-12
A. Preparing for Type III Investigations			

Planning Matrix for Organizing and Teaching Type II Skills With Commercial Enrichment Materials

IV. Using Advanced Research Skills & Reference Materials (continued)

	K-3	4-8	9-12
B. Library Skills			
C. Community Resources			

Planning Matrix for Organizing and Teaching Type II Skills With Commercial Enrichment Materials

V. Written, Oral, and Visual Communication Skills

	K-3	4-8	9-12
A. Written Communication			

Planning Matrix for Organizing and Teaching Type II Skills With Commercial Enrichment Materials

V. Written, Oral, and Visual Communication Skills (continued)

	K-3	4-8	9-12
B. Oral Communication			

Planning Matrix for Organizing and Teaching Type II Skills With Commercial Enrichment Materials

V. Written, Oral, and Visual Communication Skills (continued)

	K-3	4-8	9-12
C. Visual Communication			

Materials and Activities Selection Worksheet
for Planning Type II Enrichment

Grade: _____

Subject(s): _____

I. Cognitive Training

	Enrichment Room	Regular Classroom	
		Group Activities	Self-Selected Activities
A. Creative Thinking Skills			
B. Creative Problem Solving and Decision Making			
C. Critical and Logical Thinking			

II. Affective Training

A. Affective Skills		

Materials and Activities Selection Worksheet for Planning Type II Enrichment

III. Learning How-To-Learn Skills

Grade: _____

Subject(s): _____

	Enrichment Room	Regular Classroom	
		Group Activities	Self-Selected Activities
A. Listening, Observing and Perceiving			
B. Reading, Notetaking and Outlining			
C. Interviewing and Surveying			
D. Analyzing and Organizing Data			

Materials and Activities Selection Worksheet
for Planning Type II Enrichment

IV. Using Advanced Research Skills & Reference Materials

Grade: _____

Subject(s): _____

	Enrichment Room	Regular Classroom	
		Group Activities	Self-Selected Activities
A. Preparing for Type III Investigations			
B. Library Skills			
C. Community Resources			

Materials and Activities Selection Worksheet
for Planning Type II Enrichment

V. Written, Oral, and Visual Communication Skills

Grade: _____

Subject(s): _____

	Enrichment Room	Regular Classroom	
		Group Activities	Self-Selected Activities
A. Visual Communication			
B. Oral Communication			
C. Written Communication			

Enrichment Materials Specification Form

_____ Major Process Area(s) _____

_____ Major Content Area(s) _____

Planning Matrix Classification _____

Title:_____

_____

Cost: _____

Order No.: _____

Grade/Age Level(s):_____

Author:_____

Publisher (Address): _____

_____

Brief Description:

(For a more complete description see):

Format (Workbook, Flash Cards, Video, etc.):

Topics or Units of Study in the Regular Curriculum Related to These Materials:

Thinking and/or Feeling Processes Developed:

Local Resource Person(s) Familiar With Materials (Please check the names of persons who are willing to conduct workshops or demonstration lessons):

Comments:

Action Information Message
(Elementary Version)

ACTION INFORMATION MESSAGE

GENERAL
CURRICULUM AREA _____
_____

ACTIVITY OR TOPIC _____
_____

IN THE SPACE BELOW, PROVIDE A BRIEF DESCRIPTION OF
THE INCIDENT OR SITUATION IN WHICH YOU OBSERVED HIGH
LEVELS OF INTEREST, TASK COMMITMENT OR CREATIVITY ON THE
PART OF A STUDENT OR SMALL GROUP OF STUDENTS. INDICATE
ANY IDEAS YOU MAY HAVE FOR ADVANCED LEVEL FOLLOW-UP ACTIVITIES,
SUGGESTED RESOURCES OR WAYS TO FOCUS THE INTEREST INTO A FIRST-
HAND INVESTIGATIVE EXPERIENCE.

TO:

FROM:

DATE:

☐ PLEASE CONTACT ME

☐ I WILL CONTACT YOU TO

ARRANGE A MEETING

J. S. R. '81

Date Received _____

Date of Interview
with Child _____

Date When
Services Were
Implemented _____

These forms are prepared on 3-part NCR paper and can be purchased in sets of 100 from Creative Learning Press.
Actual size 81/2" x 11".

Action Information Message
(Secondary Version)

TO: _____ Talent Pool Class Teacher
_____ Program Coordinator
_____ Other

FROM: Student (print name) _____

Teacher (print name) _____

Other _____

General Curriculum Area: _____

_____

Idea for Investigation of Study: _____

_____

_____

ACTION
INFORMATION
MESSAGE

MEMO

In the space below, provide a brief description of evidence of high levels of task commitment or creativity on the part of a student or small group of students. Indicate any ideas you may have for advanced level follow-up activities, suggested resources or ways to focus the interest into a first-hand investigative experience.

Date Received _____

Date of Interview _____

Mentor Located _____ Yes _____ No

Name of person who will be responsible for facilitating this Type III

These forms are prepared on 3-part NCR paper and can be purchased in sets of 100 from Creative Learning Press. Actual size 81/2" x 11".

MANAGEMENT PLAN FOR INDIVIDUAL AND SMALL GROUP INVESTIGATIONS

(Actual Size: 11" x 17")

Prepared by: Joseph S. Renzulli
Linda H. Smith

NAME _____ GRADE _____

TEACHER _____ SCHOOL _____

Beginning Date _____
Estimated Ending Date _____

Progress Reports
Due on Following Dates _____

GENERAL AREA(S) OF STUDY (Check all that apply)

___ Language Arts/Humanities   ___ Science   ___ Personal and Social Development
___ Social Studies   ___ Music   ___ Other (Specify)
___ Mathematics   ___ Art   ___ Other (Specify)

SPECIFY AREA OF STUDY
Write a brief description of the problem that you plan to investigate. What are the objectives of your investigation? What do you hope to find out?

INTENDED AUDIENCES
Which individuals or groups would be most interested in the findings?. List the organized groups (clubs, societies, teams) at the local, regional, state, and national levels. What are the names and addresses of contact persons in these groups? When and where do they meet?

1. _____
2. _____
3. _____
4. _____
5. _____

INTENDED PRODUCT(S) AND OUTLETS
What form(s) will the final product take? How, when, and where will you communicate the results of your investigation to an appropriate audience(s)? What outlet vehicle (journals, conferences, art shows, etc.) are typically used by professionals in this field?

METHODOLOGICAL RESOURCES AND ACTIVITIES
List the names & addresses of persons who might provide assistance in attacking this problem. List the how-to-do-it books that are available in this area of study. List other resources (films, collections, exhibits, etc.) and special equipment (e.g., camera, tape recorder, questionnaire, etc.). Keep continuous record of all activities that are part of this investigation.

GETTING STARTED
What are the first steps you should take to begin this investigation? What types of information or data will be needed to solve the problem? If "raw data," how can it be gathered, classified, and presented? If you plan to use already categorized information or data, where is it located and how can you obtain what you need?

Specification Form for Methodological Resource Books

General Field of Study _____

Title _____

Author _____ Publication Date _____

Publishers Address _____

_____

Cost_____ Location _____

Grade Level _____

---

1. Information About the Structure of the Field: _____ Yes _____ No
   Pages:
   Comments:

---

2. Procedures for Problem Finding and Focusing: _____ Yes _____ No
   Pages:
   Comments:

---

3. Description of Specific Methodological Skills: _____ Yes _____ No
   Pages:
   Comments:

---

4. Suggestions for Format/Communication of Products: _____ Yes _____ No
   Pages:
   Comments:

---

5. Suggestions for Studies/Investigations That Students
     Can Pursue: _____ Yes _____ No
   Pages:
   Comments:

Type III Mentor Matrix

Grade	Language Arts	Math	Science	Social Studies	Arts	Other (specify)
K-3						
4-6						
7-9						
10-12						

Appendix B

Sample Total Talent Portfolio

Total **T**alent PORTFOLIO

for

_____

Elementary

Record of Use

Reviewer	Date reviewed	Date material added

Total Talent Portfolio

Status Information

K 1 2 3 4 5 | K 1 2 3 4 5

Abilities
Grades (areas of greatest strength):

Reading
Language Arts
Mathematics
Social Studies
Science
Art
Music
PE
Other:

Standardized Tests:

Interests:
General Areas:

Performing Arts
Creative Writing & Journalism
Mathematics
Business/Management
Athletics
History
Social Action
Fine Arts & Crafts
Science
Technology
Other:

Specific Interests:

Style Preferences
Instructional Style Preferences:

Discussion
Lecture
Learning Games
Interactive Electronic Learning
Simulations
Independent Study
Peer Tutoring
Learning Centers
Mentorship
Other:

Learning Environment Preferences:

Self-oriented
Peer-oriented
Adult-oriented
Combination
Other:

Thinking Style Preferences:

Legislative (Creating)
Executive (Facilitating)
Judicial (Evaluating)
Other:

Expression Style Preferences:

Written
Oral/Discussion
Manipulative
Artistic
Display/Performance
Dramatization
Service/Leadership
Multi-media
Other:

Talent Development Action Record

for:

_____

Date	Grade	Teacher	Clusters	Curriculum Compacting	Exploratory Activities (Type I's)	Skill-Related Activities (Type II's)	Self-Selected Independent Investigations (Type III's)

Talent Development Recommendations

Kindergarten: _____
_____
_____
_____
_____

Grade 1: _____
_____
_____
_____
_____

Grade 2: _____
_____
_____
_____
_____

Grade 3: _____
_____
_____
_____
_____

Grade 4: _____
_____
_____
_____

Grade 5: _____
_____
_____
_____
_____

Total Talent Portfolio

Action Information

_____

_____

_____

_____

_____

_____

_____

_____

_____

_____

_____

_____

_____

_____

Student's Goals

_____

_____

_____

_____

_____

_____

_____

_____

_____

_____

Co-Curricular Activities and Lessons

_____

_____

_____

_____

_____

_____

_____

_____

The Total Talent Portfolio
J. Renzulli, J. Purcell, B. Berube, L. Brenneman, K. Dolan, K. Kwaitkowski,
D. Novak, S. Park, A. Pecora, & K. Schultz

Name Index

Subject **I**ndex

Dear Parent,

Teachers know and experts agree that the only way for children to master sight words—those high-frequency, often nondecodable words essential to reading fluency—is through practice. With *100 Words for Kids to Read in Kindergarten*, we are pleased to offer a tool to help your child practice essential sight words in an engaging, effective format.

We created the book with the guidance of literacy experts and classroom teachers. Broken down into manageable groups, words are introduced in context and reinforced through inviting activities, puzzles, and games. Each sequence of activities is carefully designed to touch on reading, writing, and usage—taking children beyond mere visual recognition of sight words to genuine mastery. At the end of the book, you'll find a certificate of completion to celebrate your child's accomplishments.

The journey through these skill-building pages will help your child make the successful transition from learning to read to reading to learn. We hope you and your child enjoy the trip!

The Editors

Contents

GROUP 1

Find the Word

Read the story. Then follow the directions below.

Lilly has a cat.

The cat is little.

The cat goes to Lilly.

goes

has

The

goes

go

1. Put a (circle) around the word **a**.

2. <u>Underline</u> the word **is**.

3. Put a box around the word **The**. (two times)

4. Put a ✔ above the word **little**.

5. Put a △ above the word **goes**.

Word Math

➤ **Make new words by adding letters to the letter a.**
We did the first one for you.

1. a + t = ___at___

2. a + n = ___AN___

3. a + s = ___AS___

Now circle the new words you made in the sentences below.

1. The girl is at home.

2. The boy has an apple.

3. The dog is as big as the girl.

Copy & Circle

➡️ **Read each word below. Copy it. Then circle the word in the sentence.**

Read.	**Copy.**	**Circle.**
1. he	*he*	Will he swim?
2. is	*is*	Her coat is blue.
3. the	*the*	I liked the movie.
4. has	*has*	She has a dog.
5. it	*it*	I will eat it later.

Find and circle the words from the word list in the letter below.

Dear Mom and Dad,

Camp is the best! I made a new friend. His name is John. He is from California. John has a turtle. He says it likes to snack on lettuce.

See you in a few weeks!

Love,
Kahlil

is
the
He
has
it

Match It!

Draw a line from each sentence to the picture it matches.
We did the first one for you.

1. He is a boy.

2. A girl has a little dog.

3. She is by the tree.

4. He goes to school.

5. It is an apple.

What's Missing?

➡️ **Fill in the boxes below to make words from the word list.**

1. W a s ✓

2. S h e ✓

3. b o y ✓

4. i s ✓

5. t o

to
was
boy
is
she

Use words from the word list to complete the sentences.

1. I _was_ home yesterday.

2. My cat _is_ fluffy.

3. Mark is a smart _boy_.

4. Where did _she_ go?

5. I go _to_ bed at 8:00 PM.

© Scholastic Inc.

Word Shapes

Write words from the word list in the boxes below.
The boxes show the shape of the letters.

1. A T

2. G i R L

3. B o y

4. h a s

5. a N n

an
has
boy
at
girl

One Letter at a Time

➡ Fill in the letters one at a time to build a word pyramid.
We did the first one for you.

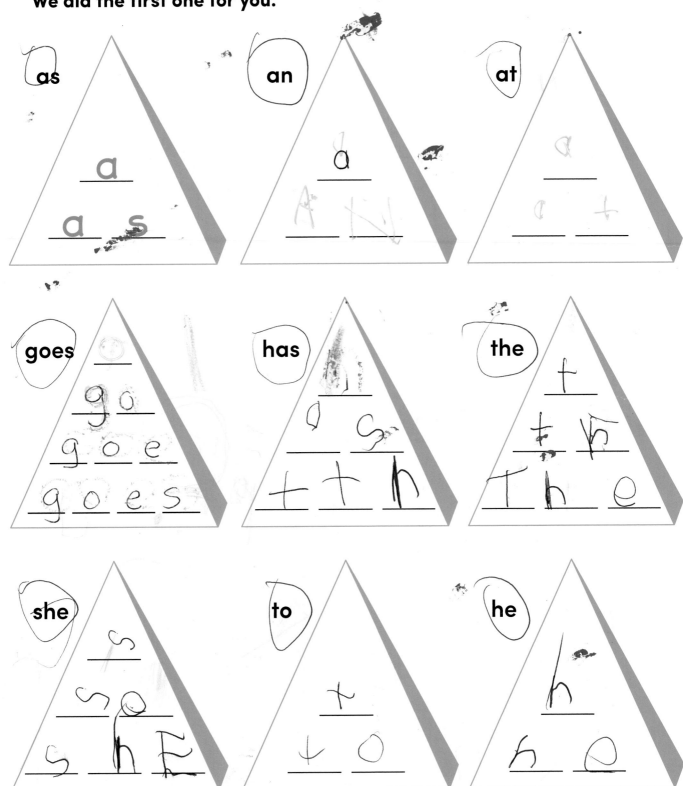

GROUP 2

down

have

in

jump

am

fast

I

me

off

out

on

my

play

ran

up

run

Who Am I?

➡️ **Read about Samantha. Then answer the questions about you.**

My name is Samantha.

I am six years old.

I have brown hair.

This is a picture of me.

Now it is your turn.

My name is _____Samantha_____.

Circle one:

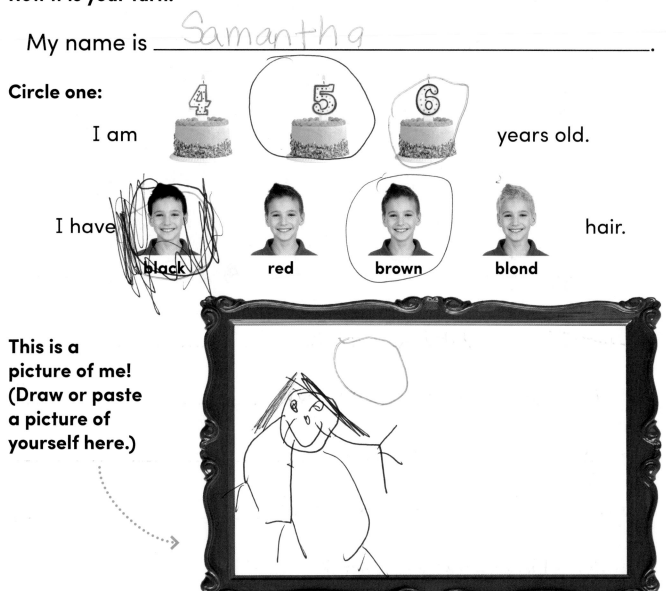

I am   4   ⑤   6   years old.

I have   **black**   **red**   **brown**   **blond**   hair.

This is a picture of me! (Draw or paste a picture of yourself here.)

Which Word?

Read the story. Then answer each question with a blue word from the story. We did the first one for you.

My dog Pete can play.

He can jump.

He can run fast.

I ran with Pete.

1. Which blue word rhymes with **last**? _fast_

2. Which blue word rhymes with **man**? CAN

3. Which blue word starts with **p**? ~~Pete~~ PIay

4. Which blue word rhymes with **fun**? FAST

5. Which blue word starts with **j**? JUMP

15

Copy & Circle

➡️ Read each word below. Copy it. Then circle the word in the sentence.

Read.   **Copy.**   **Circle.**

1. run   RY    I like to run.

2. jump   jump   A horse can jump high.

3. play   _____   Puppies like to play.

4. have   _____   I have juice every morning.

5. down   _____   Janelle sat down.

Find and circle the words from the word list in the to-do list below.

After-School To-Do List

Monday – Have dinner with Grandma.

Tuesday – Walk down to the lake.

Wednesday – Jump rope with Kathy.

Thursday – Run with my dog.

Friday – Play checkers with Zoe.

Which Way Is Up?

➡ **Look at each picture. Then circle the correct word for each sentence. Write the word on the line.**

1.

The cat is ___On___
on   off
the box.

2.

The cat jumps ___down___.
up   down

3.

The cat is ___in___
on   in
the box.

4.

The cat gets ___out___
in   out
of the box.

17

What's Missing?

➡️ **Fill in the boxes below to make words from the word list.**

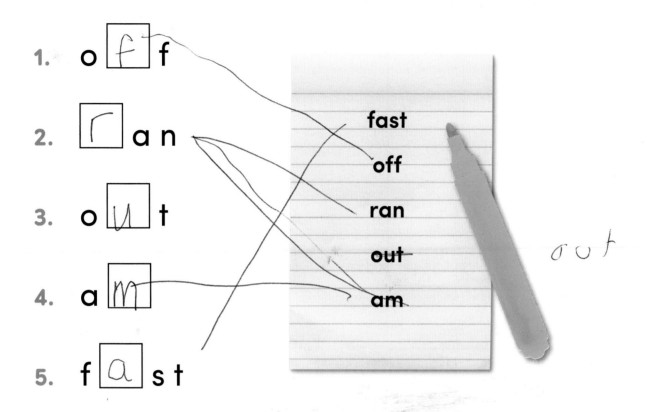

1. o | f | f
2. | r | a n
3. o | u | t
4. a | m |
5. f | a | s t

Word list (on notepad):
fast
off
ran
out
am

out

Use words from the word list to complete the sentences.

1. David went _____ to play.

2. Take _____ your hat.   off

3. Mary Ann __RAN__ to catch the bus.

4. I _____ sick.

5. That horse is __FAST__!

Word Shapes

Write words from the word list in the boxes below.
The boxes show the shape of the letters.

1. JUMP

2. I

3. fast

4. IN

5. out

Word list in thought bubble:
I
in
jump
fast
out

Mystery Letter

➡ In each set of words, the same letter is missing. Can you find the mystery letter in each set? The letters you need are in the Letter Box. We did the first one for you.

Letter Box

u p ~~m~~ ~~o~~ n

1. __m__e

___m___y

ju__m__p

The mystery letter is __m__.

4. _____p

r_____n

o_____t

The mystery letter is _____.

2. d_____wn

_____ff

_____n

The mystery letter is _____.

5. ra_____

i_____

o_____

The mystery letter is _____.

3. u_____

_____lay

jum_____

The mystery letter is _____.

GROUP 3

father

are

did

don't

friend

yes

good

you

and

not

no

mother

do

they

had

were

we

Read and Spell

➡ **Read the story, then put a ✓ next to the correct word that completes each sentence. Write the word on the line. We did the first one for you.**

Fred's father went to the park. Fred and his mother were there. Fred played with his mother and father. They had a good time at the park.

1. Fred was at the park with his __mother__ .

   ☐ muther   ☐ mohter   ✓ mother

2. Fred saw his _____ at the park.

   ☐ father   ☐ fahter   ☐ fother

3. Fred was with his mother _____ father.

   ☐ an   ☐ nad   ☐ and

4. They _____ all at the park.

   ☐ ware   ☐ wir   ☐ were

5. _____ played.

   ☐ Thay   ☐ They   ☐ Thew

Yes or No?

➡ **Read the story. Then answer the questions. Circle your answers. Write your answers on the lines.**

Jen is a girl. Jen is six.

Jen does not like bugs.

Jen likes mud. Are you

like Jen?

1. Are you a girl?

_____ , I _____ a girl.
   Yes   **No**   **am**   **am not**

2. Are you six?

_____ , I _____ six.
   Yes   **No**   **am**   **am not**

3. Do you like bugs?

_____ , I _____ like bugs.
   Yes   **No**   **do**   **don't**

4. Do you like mud?

_____ , I _____ like mud.
   Yes   **No**   **do**   **don't**

Copy & Circle

➡️ **Read each word below. Copy it. Then circle the word in the sentence.**

Read. **Copy.** **Circle.**

1. friend _____ My friend lives near me.

2. father _____ My father is a chef.

3. we _____ Where will we go for dinner?

4. mother _____ My mother is a doctor.

5. are _____ Where are you going?

Find and circle the words from the word list in the story below.

Our Community

We live in a great town. My mother and father know just about everyone in town. My best friend lives next door. All the people here are so nice. I don't ever want to leave.

father
We
mother
are
friend

My Good Friend

➡ **Use the words from the word list to write a story about your friend.**

good

are

friend

We

I have a _____. We like to play.

_____ have fun. We _____

_____ friends. Who is your good friend?

_____ **is my good friend!**
(Write your friend's name here.)

**This is a picture of my friend.
(Draw or paste a picture of
your friend here.)**

What's Missing?

 **Fill in the boxes below to make words from the word list.**

1. ☐ e

2. N ☐

3. d o n ' ☐

4. a n ☐

5. Y ☐ s

We

No

don't

Yes

and

Use words from the word list to complete the sentences.

1. Jill _____ Sara are best friends.

2. I _____ like to be late.

3. _____ are on the soccer team.

4. _____, I see the dolphins!

5. _____, I don't want to go.

Match It!

➡ **Look at the pictures. Then read the sentences.**
Draw a line from each picture to the sentence that matches it.

1. A mother and father
have a little boy.

2. Lisa, Myra, and Amy
are good friends.

3. A boy and girl play.

Now try this!

Draw a picture that matches this sentence:

My friend and I play.

One Letter at a Time

➡ Fill in the letters one at a time to build a word pyramid.
We did the first one for you.

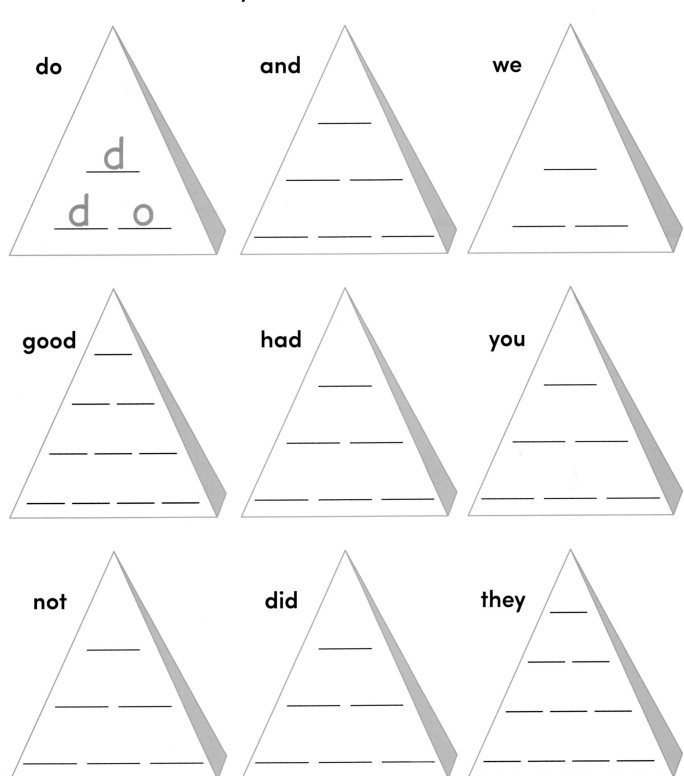

GROUP 4

ate

day

be

from

for

rain

eat

night

look

sit

of

if

stop

sat

went

with

will

Which Word?

Read the story. Then answer each question with a blue word from the story. We did the first one for you.

A cookie is on the bed. Will Kyle sit on it? Kyle sat on the cookie. Will he eat the cookie? No, but Kyle's piglet will be happy to eat the cookie. Kyle's piglet ate the cookie.

1. Which blue word ends with the letter l? _____Will_____

2. Which two blue words begin with the letter s?

   _____ _____

3. Which blue word rhymes with **Kate**? _____

4. Which blue word rhymes with **tree**? _____

5. Which blue word rhymes with **seat**? _____

6. Which three blue words end with the letter **t**?

   _____ _____ _____

Match It!

➡ Read the poem. Then choose a blue word from the poem to match each picture below. We did the first one for you.

It rains all night, it rains all day.
The rain won't stop. We cannot play.
Look! See the sun. The day is new.
Now I want to play with you!

1. __night__

2. _____

3. _____

4. _____

5. _____

Copy & Circle

➡️ **Read each word below. Copy it. Then circle the word in the sentence.**

Read.	Copy.	Circle.
1. from	_____	Pilar is from Mexico.
2. if	_____	I wonder if he's home.
3. went	_____	We went to the museum.
4. stop	_____	A red light means "stop."
5. will	_____	I will go to the library later.

Find and circle the words from the word list in the story below.

My Vacation

Last summer, our family went to California for vacation. We drove from Phoenix, Arizona. We visited Yosemite National Park. If we go again next year, Mom says we will tour the studios in Hollywood.

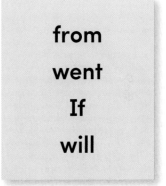

from

went

If

will

Friends Share

➡ Use the words from the word box to complete the story.

Jake _____ to the zoo

_____ Kevin and Noah.

for	from	with
of	If	went

At the zoo, Jake had a box _____

popcorn. The popcorn was _____

Kevin, Noah, and Jake. Kevin had popcorn

_____ Jake's box. _____

Noah wants popcorn, he can have some, too.

What do you share with your friends?

Now try this!
Draw a picture of something you share with your friends.

© Scholastic Inc.

What's Missing?

➡️ **Fill in the boxes below to make words from the word list.**

1. n i ☐ h t

2. s i ☐

3. r ☐ i n

4. ☐ o r

5. d ☐ y

sit

day

for

rain

night

Use words from the word list to complete the sentences.

1. Please _____ in the front of the classroom.

2. Most bats eat at _____.

3. This cookie is _____ Sam.

4. I walk my dog every _____.

5. I felt a drop of _____.

Rhyming Pear Tree

➡️ **Find a word that rhymes with each pear on the tree. Use words from the word box. Write the word on the line. We did the first one for you.**

night	day	stop
will	ate	look
be	went	sat

1. play

day

2. light

_____

3. book

_____

4. late

_____

5. fill

_____

6. mop

_____

7. me

_____

8. cat

_____

9. bent

_____

35

Build It Up!

➡️ **Trace each sight word. Then copy it in the building block next to the word.**

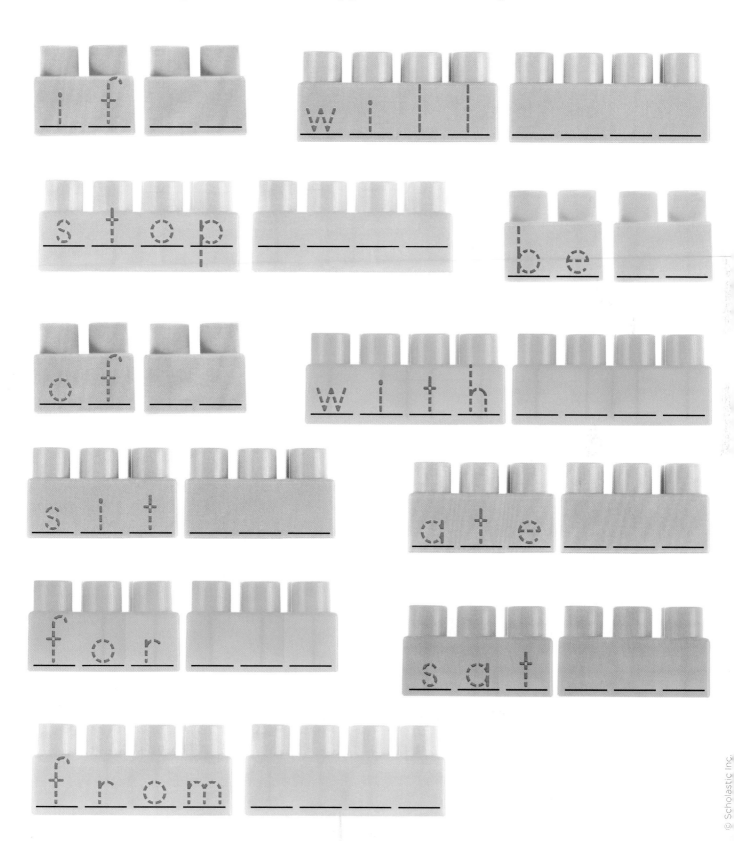

GROUP 5

black

blue

can

green

go

this

book

that

want

new

old

orange

saw

red

yellow

see

car

Go, Car, Go!

➡ **Read the story. Then circle the word that best completes each sentence. Write the words on the lines.**

Dorian's father has a

red car. The red car is old.

It cannot _____ fast. Dorian
              go   goes

_____ his father in the red car. It did
   see   saw

not go. Dorian's father _____ a new car.
                           want   wants

Dorian's father has a new car! The new car

is blue. Dorian _____ with his father
                  can   can go

in the blue car. It _____ fast.
                       go   goes

Dorian goes in the fast, blue car with his father.

Now try this!
Write a sentence about a car.

_____

_____

This or That?

This   new
that   old
~~book~~

→ Use the words from the word box to fill in the blanks in the sentences below. Use the pictures to help you. We did the first one for you.

 **THIS**  **THAT**

1.  This book is yellow, but that _____book_____ is red.

2.  This book is green, but _____ book is blue.

3.  This car is new, but that car is _____.

4.  This bag is old, but that bag is _____.

5.  _____ hat is blue, but that hat is red.

39

© Scholastic Inc.

Copy & Circle

➡️ **Read each word below. Copy it. Then circle the word in the sentence.**

Read.   **Copy.**   **Circle.**

1. see   _____   Do you see the bird?

2. book   _____   I read one book a week.

3. yellow   _____   My rain boots are yellow.

4. old   _____   How old are you?

5. go   _____   I go to Florida every spring.

Find and circle the words from the word list in the clue below.

Treasure Hunt

Follow the road until you see a yellow stone. Turn right and walk to the blue house at the end of the road. In the mailbox, you will find an old book. Go to page 5 and follow the directions there.

yellow

Go

old

book

see

What Am I?

➡ Color each word in the picture with its color name. What do you see?

BLUE

ORANGE

RED

BLACK

GREEN

YELLOW

blue blue blue
blue blue blue blue
blue orange blue blue
orange yellow orange blue
orange yellow yellow orange blue
orange yellow orange blue
orange orange blue
blue red
blue green blue red black red
green green red black blue
green green red black red
blue green blue blue red blue
blue blue blue green green
blue blue blue blue green
blue blue green

Now write and circle the correct answer.

I see two _____.

flowers   birds

What's Missing?

➡️ **Fill in the boxes below to make words from the word list.**

1. t h ☐ t

2. ☐ e e

3. w a n ☐

4. c ☐ r

5. b l a ☐ k

black

car

that

see

want

Use words from the word list to complete the sentences.

1. Do you _____ some milk and cookies?

2. I _____ Andy walking down the block.

3. How much is _____ hat?

4. I like the _____ chair.

5. My mother has a blue _____.

Sort It Out!

➡ Put each word from the word box in the circle where it belongs. We did the first one for you.

blue	book	orange
go	green	red
saw	see	car

THINGS

_____

_____

_____

_____

ACTIONS

_____

_____

_____

_____

COLORS

blue _____

_____

_____

_____

One Letter at a Time

Fill in the letters one at a time to build a word pyramid.
We did the first one for you.

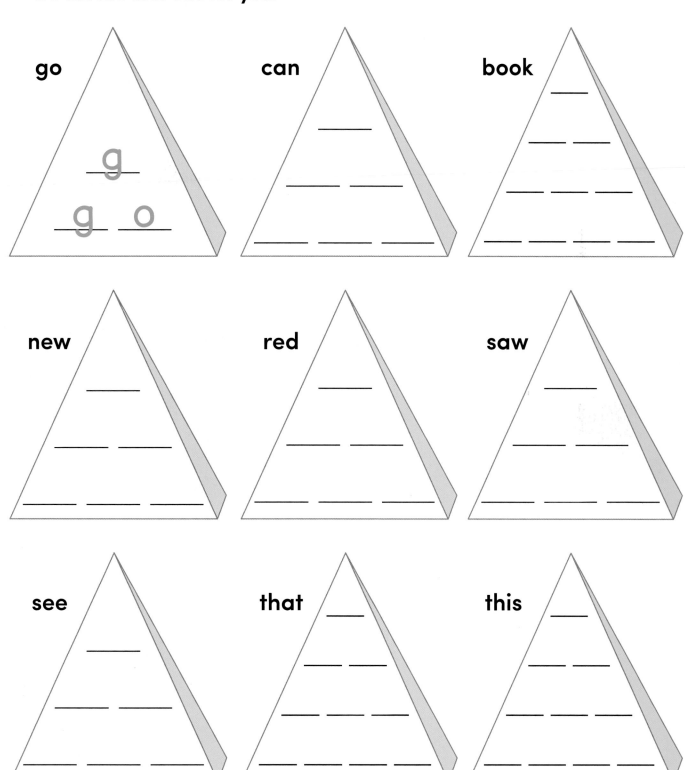

go

can

book

new

red

saw

see

that

this

44

GROUP 6

five

come

eight

came

give

gave

get

four

one

got

nine

seven

six

ten

three

two

Letter Detective

➡️ Read the story. Then use the letters from the Letter Box to complete the words in the sentences below. You will use some letters more than once.

It is Jan's birthday. She wants her friends to come to her party. She will give balloons to her friends. She will get presents from her friends.

Fay and Ernesto came to Jan's party. They gave presents to Jan. They got balloons from Jan. They had fun at the party.

1. Did Fay c_____me to Jan's party?

   Yes, she c_____me to Jan's party.

2. Did Fay g_____ve a present to Jan?

   Yes, she g_____ve a present to Jan.

3. Did Fay g_____t a balloon from Jan?

   Yes, she g_____t a balloon from Jan.

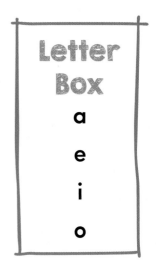

Letter Box

a

e

i

o

How Many?

➡️ **What can you find in Jake's messy room? Look at the picture. Then answer the questions below. Choose words from the word box.**

five	one
eight	two
ten	seven
three	six
four	nine

1. How many teddy bears are in Jake's room?

   _____

2. How many footballs do you see? _____

3. How many rubber duckies do you see? _____

4. How many soccer balls are in Jake's room?

   _____

Copy & Circle

➡️ **Read each word below. Copy it. Then circle the word in the sentence.**

Read.	**Copy.**	**Circle.**
1. came	_____	She came with me to the store.
2. give	_____	Please give me the book.
3. one	_____	Which one will you take?
4. come	_____	What time will you come over?
5. eight	_____	Our dog had eight puppies.

Find and circle the words from the word list in the journal entry below.

eight	give
came	one

Sara's Journal

Sunday, November 30

WOW! My eight closest friends

came with me to the Museum of Natural History for my

birthday. There was also one parent for every three

kids in our group. We had a sleepover at the museum!

It was the best present anyone could ever give me.

Sparky and Lisa's Day

➡️ **Read each question. Then look at the clock. Use the number words from the word box to write the correct time on the line.**

one	two	three	four	five
six	seven	eight	nine	ten

1. What time does Sparky take his morning walk?

 _____ o'clock

2. What time does Lisa give Sparky his bath?

 _____ o'clock

3. What time does Sparky meet Lisa after school?

 _____ o'clock

4. What time does Sparky wake Lisa up in the morning?

 _____ o'clock

What's Missing?

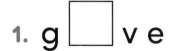 **Fill in the boxes below to make words from the word list.**

1. g ☐ v e

2. ☐ i v e

3. t h r ☐ e

4. f o ☐ r

5. c o m ☐

four

three

gave

come

five

Use words from the word list to complete the sentences.

1. I have _____ fingers on each hand.

2. There are _____ seasons.

3. Why don't you _____ over tonight?

4. I _____ my old bike to my younger sister.

5. My neighbor has _____ dogs.

Word Shapes

Write words from the word list in the boxes below.
The boxes show the shape of the letters.

1.

2.

3.

4.

5.

four

gave

get

one

eight

Scrambled Words

➡️ **Unscramble the letters below to make words from the word list.**

1. A E C M ☐☐☐☐
   1

2. I F V E ☐☐☐☐

3. O G T ☐☐☐
   2

4. R H T E E ☐☐☐☐☐
   5

5. W O T ☐☐☐
   4

6. N E V S E ☐☐☐☐☐
   3

two

got

seven

five

three

came

Copy the letters in the numbered cells to answer the question.

What begins with "t," is filled with "t," and ends with "t"?

___ ___ ___ ___ **P** ___ ___
 1   2   3   1   4   5

What Am I?

➡️ What kind of animal is hidden in this picture?
Follow the directions to find out.

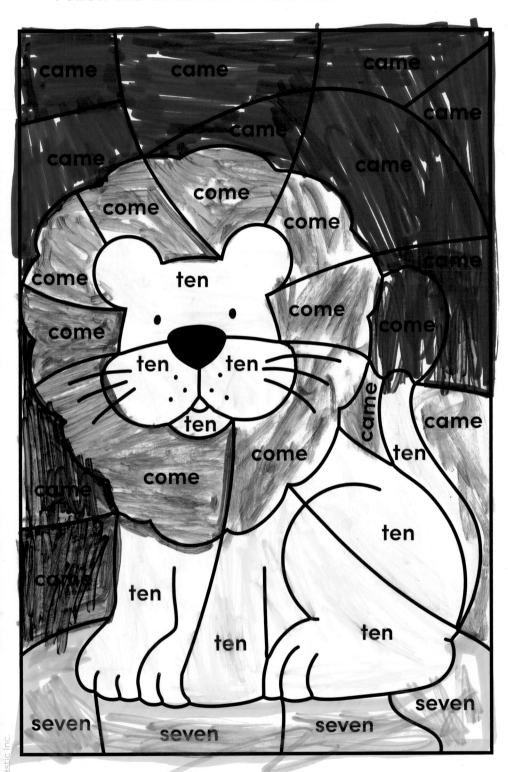

If the word is **come**, color the space

ORANGE

If the word is **ten**, color the space

YELLOW

If the word is **seven**, color the space

GREEN

If the word is **came**, color the space

BLUE

53

My 100 Words

Group 1

a	girl	little
an	goes	she
as	has	the
at	he	to
boy	is	was
by	it	

Group 2

am	jump	play
down	me	ran
fast	my	run
have	off	up
I	on	
in	out	

Group 3

and	friend	they
are	good	we
did	had	were
do	mother	yes
don't	no	you
father	not	

Group 4

ate	if	sit
be	look	stop
day	night	went
eat	of	will
for	rain	with
from	sat	

Group 5

black	green	see
blue	new	that
book	old	this
can	orange	want
car	red	yellow
go	saw	

Group 6

came	get	six
come	give	ten
eight	got	three
five	nine	two
four	one	
gave	seven	

NAME THAT ✳WORD!✳

Name That Word! Board Game

(See page 58 for directions on how to play.)

Start

boy

Pick a card.

Say the number that comes before five but after three.

stop

Go ahead one space.

sat

Spell the word that sounds the same as *two.*

Pick a card.

Spell a word that sounds the same as *ate* but is a number.

see

Say a word that is the opposite of *day.*

Pick a card.

Say a word that means the opposite of *big.*

for

Go back one space.

blue

goes

Pick a card.

Say a word that rhymes with *last* and means the opposite of *slow.*

ran

Pick a card.

Say a word that rhymes with *flew* and means the opposite of *old.*

my

Go ahead one space.

red

Say a word that rhymes with *chain* and means "water that falls in drops from the sky."

come

Go back one space.

Say a word that rhymes with *are* and names something people use to travel.

I

Say a word that rhymes with *cold* and means the opposite of *young*.

Pick a card.

Say a word that means the opposite of *bad*.

did

Pick a card.

Say a word that rhymes with *look* and is something you read from.

Say a word that means the opposite of *take*.

Pick a card.

be

Say a word that rhymes with *bend* and describes someone you like.

got

Pick a card.

ten

Say a word that means the opposite of *on*.

Say a word that starts with *o* that is a color and also the name of a fruit.

it

Pick a card.

jump

Say a word that rhymes with *when* and is a number.

Say a word that rhymes with *neat* and tells what people do at dinner.

Finish

Name That Word!

BOARD GAME

What You Need to Play

- The game board on pages 56–57

- Word Cards (cut from pages 59–62)

- Two players

- A game piece, such as a coin or a button, for each player

- One die

How to Play

- Place all the Word Cards facedown in a pile.

- Roll the die. Move your piece the number of dots on the die.

- If you land on a pink circle, say a word that rhymes with the word in the circle.

- If you land on "Pick a Card," your partner picks a Word Card and reads the word on the card out loud. You have to spell it. If you spell the word correctly, move ahead one space. After you follow the directions on that space, it is your partner's turn.

- If you land on any other circle, follow the directions.

- The first person to reach *Finish* wins!

girl	play	came	father
don't	down	was	green
black	sit	mother	have

Name
That
Word!

Name
That
Word!

Name
That
Word!

Name
That
Word!

Name
That
Word!

Name
That
Word!

Name
That
Word!

Name
That
Word!

Name
That
Word!

Name
That
Word!

Name
That
Word!

Name
That
Word!

has	were	they
yellow	saw	out
from	went	will
gave	seven	three

Name That Word!

Name That Word!

Name That Word!

Name That Word!

Name That Word!

Name That Word!

Name That Word!

Name That Word!

Name That Word!

Name That Word!

Name That Word!

Name That Word!

FOR OUTSTANDING ACHIEVEMENT

CONGRATULATIONS!

This certificate is awarded to

I'm proud of you!